Co-operative Enterprise in Comparative Perspective

Co-operative Enterprise in Comparative Perspective

Exceptionally Un-American?

Jason S. Spicer

OXFORD
UNIVERSITY PRESS

Oxford University Press is a department of the University of Oxford. It furthers
the University's objective of excellence in research, scholarship, and education
by publishing worldwide. Oxford is a registered trade mark of Oxford University
Press in the UK and certain other countries.

Published in the United States of America by Oxford University Press
198 Madison Avenue, New York, NY 10016, United States of America.

© Oxford University Press 2024

All rights reserved. No part of this publication may be reproduced, stored in
a retrieval system, or transmitted, in any form or by any means, without the
prior permission in writing of Oxford University Press, or as expressly permitted
by law, by license, or under terms agreed with the appropriate reproduction
rights organization. Inquiries concerning reproduction outside the scope of the
above should be sent to the Rights Department, Oxford University Press, at the
address above.

You must not circulate this work in any other form
and you must impose this same condition on any acquirer.

CIP data is on file at the Library of Congress
ISBN 978–0–19–766507–7

DOI: 10.1093/oso/9780197665077.001.0001

Printed by Integrated Books International, United States of America

In memory of Janice Stanton

Contents

List of Figures and Tables ix
Acknowledgments xi

1. **Introduction: Co-operative Enterprise, Exceptionally Un-American?** 1
   American Co-operative Development through a Comparative Lens 3
   The Argument in Brief 7
   Plan and Outline of the Book 12

2. **Conceptualizing the Comparative Development of Co-operative Enterprise** 17
   Co-operatives 101: A Primer 18
   Case Selection and Overviews 35
   Comparing Institutionalisms: Historical Institutionalism versus Field Theory 39

3. **Finland, the Co-operative Commonwealth?** 50
   Co-operatives as an Offensive Strategy in Finnish Nation-Building, 1800s–1945 56
   Co-operatives as Defense: Finlandization, the Cold War, and a Tale of Two Co-operative Movements, 1946–1995 68
   Co-operatives as Globalization Insurance: Liberalization, European Integration, and the Return of Russia, 1995–Present 73
   Finland's Co-operatives, Geography, and the Evolution of Fields 79

4. **Co-operatives as the Heart of France's Social and Solidarity Economy** 82
   The French Evolution? Co-operatives' Slow Emergence in Modern France, 1780s–1860s 88
   A Field in Full: From "the Co-operative Republic" to Les Trente Glorieuses, 1870s–1960s 102
   The Rise of the Social and Solidarity Economy, 1970s/80s–Present 112
   Co-operative Development: A French Evolution 125

5. **Liberalism and Co-operatives: New Zealand's Strange Bedfellows** 127
   New Zealand as a "Utopian Capitalist" Experiment Gone Awry: 1840–1870 133
   Field Settlement: Alternative Ownership in the Making of Modern New Zealand, 1870–1970 138
   Field Rupture: Co-operatives Adapt to the Liberalization of New Zealand, 1984–Present 147

6. American Cooperation in the 19th Century: A Field Denied   155
    A Field in Formation? Four Strands of Antebellum American Cooperation,
      1790–1860   158
    The Role of Slavery in Constraining Antebellum Cooperation   171
    Postbellum American Cooperation: "Wage Slavery" and the Knights of
      Labor, 1865–1880s   179
    American Cooperation in the 19th Century: A Field Denied   194

7. American Cooperation since 1900: An Incomplete and Partially Organized Field   198
    Partial Field Successes: Populist Farmers, Progressive Credit Unions,
      New Deal Utilities   200
    Cooperation Lost: Consumers' Retail Goods and Mutually Owned
      Financial Enterprises   216
    Worker and Multi-Stakeholder Co-operatives: A Dream Deferred?   230
    American Cooperation: An Incomplete Field   242

8. Conclusions of a Chrononaut   244
    Co-operatives as Exceptionally Un-American   246
    From Factors to Fields: The Value of a Field Theory Approach   247
    From Theory to Practice: Conclusions for the American
      Co-operative Movement   262

Appendix   *269*
References   *273*
Index   *301*

List of Figures and Tables

Figures

1.1	Co-operatives and Crisis.	3
1.2	Co-operative prevalence at scale ($75MM+).	6
1.3	American co-operatives: field environment, mid-1800s.	9
2.1	The seven co-operative principles.	20
2.2	The birthplace of the co-operative.	21
2.3	Connecting ownership to sustainability.	28
2.4	The "vicious cycle" for U.S. co-operatives.	30
3.1	Helsinki's consumer co-operatives.	52
3.2	Finnish co-operatives—field environment, 1900.	55
3.3	OP Bank headquarters, Helsinki.	63
3.4	The Red and White co-operatives' rapid growth.	67
3.5	Finland's EU integration and co-operatives: partial field displacement.	75
4.1	The French Revolution, 1790s→Second Revolution/Empire, mid-1800s field architecture.	85
4.2	Scarabée Biocoop.	119
4.3	France's "creative class" co-operatives.	121
4.4	The ESS in regional action: Paris.	123
5.1	Co-operative businesses keep New Zealand's wealth local. co-operative	128
5.2	New Zealand's frequent omission from world maps reflects its persistent remoteness.	129
5.3	Field shift: New Zealand co-operatives and 1980s liberalization.	132
5.4	Wellington offices of Loomio.	153
6.1	American co-operatives: field architecture, 19th century.	157
6.2	Co-operative communities and slavery.	171
6.3	Former Co-operative Wholesale Society headquarters, East London (Whitechapel).	191
7.1	U.S. Tax War on Co-operatives.	225
7.2	Gompers vs. Hillquit, congressional testimony on co-operatives, labor, and socialism, 1916.	233
8.1	Cards from the classic version of Chrononauts.	245

x   List of Figures and Tables

Tables

2.1	The Seven Co-operative Principles of the International Co-operative Alliance	19
2.2	Major Types of Co-operative Enterprises and Related "Alternative Enterprise" Forms	23
2.3	Comparative Co-operative Policy Features Today	38
2.4	Translating Conceptual Vocabularies: Historical Institutionalism and Strategic Action Field Theory	44
8.1	Comparing and Evaluating the Utility of Historical Institutionalism and Field Theory to Co-operative Development	249
8.2	Factors Shaping Development of the Co-operative Field (and Its Field Environment), by Case	252
A.1	Libraries, Special Collections, Archives, and Museums Consulted	269
A.2	Select/Representative List of Organizations Interviewed	271

Acknowledgments

Writing a book is a lot of work, and not just for the author or the editor (who, in this case, was the amazing James Cook at Oxford University Press: thank you, James, for all your support). There are, accordingly, endless individuals to acknowledge and thank.

The first, of course, are the participants in the American co-operative movement, as well as those in the global co-operative movement and in the comparative case countries. Literally hundreds of individuals opened doors and made their time, knowledge, connections, and resources available to me, embodying the spirit of mutual aid and solidarity that the co-operative business model attempts to animate. One person in particular, however, must be mentioned by name for all that she did to open doors around the world for me: Hanan El-Youssef. Without her indefatigable efforts, none of this would have been possible.

Beyond the co-operative movement, there are four sets of academic communities that played a role in my bringing this book to fruition. In chronological order, they stem from my time studying at Johns Hopkins, at UC Berkeley, in Cambridge at MIT and Harvard, and from my involvement with the Society for the Advancement of Socio-Economics (SASE).

As an undergraduate at Johns Hopkins, I first encountered the extraordinary historical works on American labor and populist movements written by Lawrence Goodwyn and Leon Fink, in a freshman history class on American radicalism taught by Ron Walters and aided by his teaching assistant Jon Boyd. Those books, which are substantively referenced in this one, never left my mind, even after many decades away from them, in part because of how well they were taught. At Johns Hopkins, I also encountered the power of comparative-historical sociology in the many graduate courses I had the privilege of taking as an undergraduate, thanks to the outstanding mentorship of my adviser, Beverly Silver, who imparted to me an understanding of the power of the social sciences for asking and answering difficult, important questions. Thank you, Beverly, for your continued encouragement over many decades.

Though I dropped out of a PhD at UC Berkeley, during my time there Neil Fligstein helped me begin to understand the power of institutions in ways which left a lasting impact on my thinking, and in ways which—I hope—show up in this book. From my time in Cambridge countless faculty members and staff at both MIT and Harvard invested in me and my work and helped make this book a reality. My doctoral adviser, Phil Thompson, and committee members, Kathleen Thelen and James DeFilippis (Rutgers), provided me with exceptional scholarly examples of how to approach the task of this book, through their own outstanding monographs. The MIT Center for International Studies, MIT Community Innovators Lab (CoLab), and Hugh Hampton Young Fellowship provided valuable funding for the fieldwork for this project. Peter Hall, Suzanne Berger, and Paul Pierson each left marks through their teaching in various ways. Most important, my longtime friend and scholarly collaborator Tamara Kay provided constant encouragement while we were both in Cambridge and in the years since. Her belief in my ability to get this done has perhaps made the difference in my seeing it through.

An enormous thank you to my SASE crew and fellow Network A co-organizers (Joyce, Katherine, Victor, Marc, Philipp, Paola). This organization, its journal (*Socio-Economic Review*), and its annual conference have all become an intellectual home for me, one where the ideas and phenomena examined in this book are not seen as marginal or strange, as they are in so many other venues, but are welcomed and valued.

To two scholarly collaborators and friends, Evan Casper-Futterman and Christa Lee-Chuvala, thank you for helping me in my related academic work to further develop the ideas in this book in unexpected directions and dimensions, and to laugh at the absurdity of academia along the way. Special thanks to my research assistants at the University of Toronto, most notably Tash Cheong and Keisha St. Louis-McBurnie, for assistance in various parts of this manuscript, as well as my CUNY Baruch College Research Assistant, Megan Teehan.

A few personal thanks: though the Rev. Sandhya Rani Jha drives me to madness sometimes, without their pastoral care and fellowship I would not have become a person who would write a book like this. To members of my chosen family not yet mentioned—the Rabinovich-Buchalter family, Carin, Lawrence, Kate, and Danny—thank you for your love and encouragement. You're the best. Last, but not least: thanks, Mom.

1
Introduction

Co-operative Enterprise, Exceptionally Un-American?

> I looked back at these moments of extraordinary politics, when the dream of a real alternative emerges, a . . . third way between totalitarian communism and savage capitalism. Looking back at those junctures, the dream that has come up again and again is this idea of co-operatives. This idea of co-operatives did not fail—it was never tried.
> —Naomi Klein, interview with Oscar Reyes (2007)

> We've got to upend the lie we've been told for decades, the one that says: This is how the system works. This is how globalization works. This is how capitalism works. This is how employers and employees will always relate to each other.
> —U.S. Senator Bernie Sanders with John Nichols (2023)

Co-operative enterprises are democratically owned and governed, typically by their workers, customers, or suppliers. They have long appealed, as Naomi Klein suggests, as a third-way alternative to systems based on either profit-maximizing, investor-owned firms (IOFs) or state-owned enterprises. But how do co-operative businesses achieve lasting, durable scale in different contexts, particularly in rich democracies like the United States? That is the central question I ask in this book.

When viewed from a period of societal crisis, the prospects for lasting co-operation at scale might seem bright. Indeed, in the long, tumultuous decade after the global financial crisis in the late 2000s[1] through the COVID-19-related economic disruptions of the early 2020s, interest in co-operatives

---

[1] Scholars and popular writers have described the 2010–2020s as a period of multiple crises in the West/Global North, relating to climate change, populism/political democracy, racism, and economic inequality, among others, all of which were exacerbated and brought into starker relief by the COVID-19 pandemic of 2020–21.

Co-operative Enterprise in Comparative Perspective. Jason S. Spicer, Oxford University Press. © Oxford University Press 2024.
DOI: 10.1093/oso/9780197665077.003.0001

rose in the United States and globally (Spicer 2020; Webster et al. 2016). During the COVID-19 pandemic, mutual aid networks formed to address a range of challenges, from food insecurity to social care (Lofton et al. 2022; Bell 2021; Howard 2020), and displaced employees went into business for themselves via worker co-operatives or high-tech, app-based platform co-operatives, as they had in response to the previous decade's financial crisis. In 2020, The Drivers Co-operative, a platform co-operative owned by over 2,500 taxi drivers, formed in New York City and became the largest U.S. worker-owned co-operative seemingly overnight. As a Boston-based co-operative enterprise developer said to me later that year, "Our phone is ringing off the hook.... People always turn to co-ops in a crisis." In 2022, as the pandemic's initial economic disruptions gave way to more systemic concerns about the sustainability of globalized supply chains, a New York City co-operative developer told me the most recent crisis had only served to "accentuate a decade of heightened ... crisis-fueled interest in the co-op model, at least here in the U.S."

Co-operatives, however, are not just temporary tools for small-scale use during a period of crisis. The International Co-operative Alliance (ICA), the global apex body or "meta-organization" for the co-operative movement and co-operative enterprises, estimates co-operatives' total gross revenue at over $3 trillion, of which the largest 300 account for over $2 trillion (ICA 2021). They offer a clear, proven, scalable alternative to the IOF and its associated "cutthroat" form of footloose global capitalism, as Senator Bernie Sanders has often stated.

Worker-, producer-, and consumer-owned co-operative businesses—enterprises designed to serve the "use-value" needs of their member-owners—exist for a different purpose and logic than IOFs, as repeatedly affirmed by social scientists, and accordingly yield a host of socioeconomic benefits (Rothschild 1979; Rothschild and Whitt 1986; Schneiberg King, and Smith 2008; Dahl 1985; Wright 2010; Wright 2013; Michie 2017; Meyers 2022; Harcourt 2023). They offer a possible long-term economic path forward, one which is potentially more sustainable and equitable and which may not yield the socioeconomic problems generated by the model of neoliberal globalization that has been primarily achieved through IOFs. Given this promise and potential, how do co-operatives come to achieve a lasting, durable scale in different national contexts?

American Co-operative Development through a Comparative Lens

Amid the nation's recent flurry of co-operative activity, one might think that America today is a hotbed of co-operative entrepreneurship. Indeed, in the wake of the global financial crisis, which was the worst economic downturn in 80 years and which birthed the Occupy movement and a new wave of activism targeting economic inequality, the American co-operative movement achieved a string of successes. Over the subsequent decade, in at least a dozen states and 20 cities, U.S. local governments undertook actions to remove barriers, incentivize development, and provide direct support to co-operative entrepreneurs, reflecting not only increased interest in society in these models but also heightened sophistication on the part of co-operative entrepreneurs and advocates (Spicer 2020; Sutton 2019; see Figure 1.1). Their efforts culminated in the first non-tax-related piece of U.S. national legislation in several decades, the 2018 Main Street Employee Ownership Act, followed by the 2022 Worker Ownership, Readiness, and Knowledge (WORK) Act of 2022, with more such legislation proposed. Alongside these actions, the

Figure 1.1 Co-operatives and Crisis. The New Economy Coalition highlights the scaling and development of co-operatives and related ownership forms as a solution to today's socioeconomic problems. They are one of many U.S. advocacy organizations promoting such an approach.

number of U.S. worker co-operatives nearly doubled between 2010 and 2018 (Harvey 2018), and U.S. credit unions' assets also more than doubled (Board of Governors of the Federal Reserve System [1943] 2021). As noted above, in 2020, a new start-up, The Drivers' Co-operative, quickly became the largest worker co-operative in the United States, with over 2,500 member-owner drivers; as of mid-2023, it was in the process of expanding to 9,000 drivers, according to its 2023 annual report.

Such concentrated interest in co-operatives, however, is not new. Co-operative formation has never been "randomly distributed in time, but appeared in distinct waves" (Rothschild and Ollilainen 1999, 586; cf. Rothschild and Whitt 1986; Meyers 2022), typically during periods of crisis.[2] In fact, crisis-induced interest in the co-operative business model in the United States and elsewhere goes back to the very founding of the co-operative movement in the mid-1800s in the United Kingdom (Wilson, Webster, and Vorberg-Rugh 2014). Co-operatives were then a new economic innovation and a new organizational technology, created and institutionalized in response to the upheavals of the twinned 19th-century phenomena of industrialization and urbanization.

Why are alternatives like the co-operative linked to crisis? During periods of upheaval, as the legitimacy of the status quo cracks and public confidence in the dominant institutional structures and arrangements which constitute a society's "steering system" declines and is questioned, individuals may give greater consideration to new or existing alternatives to that steering system. In parallel, a range of state, market, and civil society actors may work to systematically organize these alternatives. This well-known phenomenon, variably called conjunctural or legitimation crises by social theorists (Habermas 1973; Fraser 1997; Gramsci 1926), explains why co-operatives always seem to come into view during crises, particularly such as those being experienced in the rich democracies today, where the status quo is one forged by liberal capitalism and the globalizing IOF. Accordingly, as prominent social scientists have pondered how or if liberal capitalism might end, they have speculated on the role alternatives like co-operatives might play longer term (Harcourt 2023; Henderson 2021; Tirole 2017; Streeck 2016; Streeck et al. 2016; Collier 2018; Davis 2016a, 2016b; Piketty 2014; Fourcade 2012).

This flurry of crisis-related cooperation does not necessarily mean, however, that the United States is fertile ground for co-operatives to endure at

---

[2] Though the cited sources are typically referring to waves in U.S. co-operative formation, such waves also characterize co-operative development elsewhere, as Antoni (1980) notes in his authoritative account of French worker co-operative development.

scale: prior crisis-linked waves of co-operative development have not always produced lasting results. The waves which occurred in the United States during the Great Depression and after the tumult of the 1960s' civil rights and countercultural movements both faded dramatically when these crises subsided (Upright 2020; Jackall and Levin 1984; Parker 1956; Kerr 1939). Naomi Klein's claim that co-operatives are a dream that have never been tried is thus not quite accurate. The co-operative model has been tried, again and again, but in certain places—like the United States—these efforts have not gotten as far as they have elsewhere, particularly at the scale needed to substantively affect the overall economy in the long run. As Shirom (1972, 533) observed a half-century ago, industrial and worker co-operatives "have not shown any ability to endure in the United States." Over a century ago, Cross (1906, 45), in his study of U.S. consumer co-operatives, pondered whether their comparative rarity and "failure" was because "the co-operative movement in the United States has never been satisfactorily organized." Other research (Spicer 2022) has not only statistically affirmed that large co-operative businesses are comparatively less common in the United States today, but they are also comparatively constrained by American public policy. (See Figure 1.2 and Table 2.3 for more detail).[3] Though there are a few domains where co-operatives have achieved significant scale in the United States (e.g., agriculture/farming), large American co-operatives are limited in number when compared to other rich democracies. In Finland, for example, large co-operatives are nine times more common than in the United States. Given repeated crisis-related waves of interest in co-operative entrepreneurship in the United States, how and why did it come to be a comparative laggard with respect to large-scale cooperation? And more important, what does the answer imply for the prospects of co-operative development in the United States?

If one studies American co-operative development efforts closely—as I have, since listening to calls for economic democracy by Occupy Wall Street participants in Zuccotti Park in 2011, when the idea for this project began—the question of "American exceptionalism," as referenced in the subtitle of this book, looms large. Is a co-operative economic vision achievable in the context of the grand "American experiment"? During fieldwork for this study, I was repeatedly told by scholars of the American economy, and by American

---

[3] Figure 1.2 shows two different measures of large co-operatives' extensiveness; see Spicer (2022) for more details. I developed one data set working from the OneSource business database, and the other utilizes the data behind the ICA's global co-operative monitoring project (jointly developed with EURICSE, the European Research Institute on Co-operatives and Social Enterprises). Both show the United States as quite low in co-operative prevalence, which is why it is in the lower left-hand corner of the figure. The OneSource data graphed in Figure 1.2 shows the percentage of all large firms that are co-operatives per country. The ICA data represented on the graph is total large co-operative revenue divided by country GDP.

6 Co-operative Enterprise

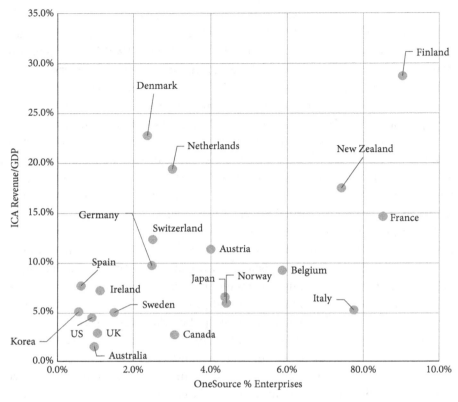

Figure 1.2 Co-operative prevalence at scale ($75MM+).
Source: Spicer 2022.

economic reformers and activists both outside and within the co-operative movement, that some Americans have an ingrained belief that co-operatives "simply don't work here" and are a "waste of time." They are, in essence, un-American. Why?

The most common refrain was that the United States is "too individualistic." Energy would therefore be better spent on "proven U.S. approaches" like collective bargaining via unions or living/fair wage laws. And yet these other approaches have required social solidarity and collective organizing to achieve their goals, their successes in the United States indicative of the American capacity to transcend individualism. In fact, U.S. social movements have often overcome the challenges of individualism to achieve social and economic change, and Americans have figured prominently in developing the modern "repertoire of contention" that social movements so often deploy (McAdam, Tarrow, and Tilly 2001). Further, as part of such movement-based efforts, the

United States has incubated and produced an extraordinary number of innovative, "collectivist-democratic" organizations (Chen and Chen 2021; Chen 2009; Rothschild 1979). Could an American co-operative movement thus not overcome individualism, just as so many other solidaristic movements have in the United States? Perhaps co-operatives' widespread and sustained, large-scale development just requires certain circumstances and conditions, which have simply not yet occurred in the United States?

American co-operative developers, meanwhile, are not naïve with respect to the challenges they face. They acknowledge the U.S. context can be difficult. During my research, they repeatedly articulated that it is a struggle to build a coherent co-operative framework, or what they increasingly call a "co-operative ecosystem" (Tanner 2013; Hoover and Abell 2016; Spicer and Zhong 2022), mirroring the language of the traditional mainstream economic concept of business ecosystems (Moore 1993, 1996), in which related enterprises form an interlinked economic world unto themselves.

Nonetheless, my earlier-referenced conversations and interviews with Boston and New York City co-operative developers in the early 2020s were more energized than they might have been just a few years before then. Why? American society had experienced what social movement and public policy scholars refer to as a triggering event: the Minneapolis police's murder of George Floyd. For reasons now being parsed by researchers, a series of conditions had converged in which movements for racial justice—including the Movement for Black Lives—seemed to break through in the national consciousness, as they had in the 1960s, with action linked to broader calls for a "Third Reconstruction" in America (Barber and Wilson-Hartgrove 2016). What does racial justice, or race, for that matter, have to do with co-operative enterprise? This book uses the United States as a central case to examine the larger question of how and why co-operative enterprise more generally comes to succeed or fail at durable scale in rich democracies. In the U.S. case, a central part of the answer to that question turns out to involve race.

The Argument in Brief

When I began this project, I did not necessarily expect to find that race would play such a central role in the story of co-operatives in America. Perhaps this reflects my own positionality as a White man. I had what I thought was a good list of what we social scientists call "working priors," that is, factors suspected of being responsible for the more limited success of U.S. co-operatives. Race, and social heterogeneity in general, was one such factor.

My initial suspicion, however, was that the rarity of co-operatives in America was mostly a function of "American exceptionalism," an argument used for nearly two centuries, since Tocqueville (1835), to cast America as a fundamentally different and distinct nation, with a unique history and founding built on individualism and liberalism, and that this explains its lack of support for socialism, universal healthcare, a labor party, and other social/public goods (Lipset 1996; Sombart 1906). Scholars have, of course, long argued for a central role for race in American exceptionalism (Hooks and McQueen 2010; Tyrrell 1991), with race historically implicated in U.S. class formation (Halpern and Morris 1997; Russell 2009; Omi and Winant 2014), an argument which has received renewed popular attention through efforts like Hannah-Jones's (2021) 1619 Project.

But factors other than economic liberalism and race also loomed large in explaining an exceptionally unco-operative America. Such factors include federalism, industry mix, and geography. Initially, after interrogating each of these other factors statistically, I found that the economic individualism/liberalism embedded in the American exceptionalism argument seemed a probable cause of the weaker American outcome (Spicer 2022). The conventional wisdom of co-operative advocates and other economic reformers I interviewed—that U.S. economic individualism was to blame—seemed plausible. Indeed, as that initial statistical analysis showed, a proxy variable for the systemic institutional arrangements associated with economic individualism (the liberal variety of capitalism in the Varieties of Capitalism framework; Hall and Soskice 2001) is strongly negatively correlated with the presence of large-scale co-operatives today across the rich democracies, even after controlling for other statistically significant factors like industry mix, geographic remoteness, and social heterogeneity (including race). A statistical snapshot in time, while useful, however, tells us only which factors are associated with the outcome. It tells us little about how and to what degree these various factors causally affected the historical development of co-operatives in the United States or elsewhere over time.

Using two competing schools of institutionalist theory (which I review in the next chapter) to compare the historical development of American co-operatives to the more successful French, Finnish, and New Zealand cases, this book identifies economic liberalism and systemic racism as the joint underlying causes of the co-operative movement's comparative initial failure in the United States, where a distinctly anti-co-operative variant of capitalism developed. These two factors have continued to jointly manifest over time, contributing to subsequent shortfalls in co-operative organizing efforts and producing an institutional incongruency between co-operatives and America's particular strain of liberal capitalism.

The sketch of the argument is this: only in the United States was the co-operative movement's initial development hampered by two exceptionally well-entrenched competing ownership models, which left the co-operative without a sufficient opening in the institutional or field environment to leverage and successfully construct a new field in the economy. These two field incumbents, which took the form of investor ownership via the IOF and race-based ownership of people via the system of chattel slavery, occupied a key space in the economy's field environment during the American co-operative movement's early development (Figure 1.3). Actors associated with these two competing models actively deprived the American co-operative movement of the resources it needed to construct a nationally robust field of action and to get on the political agenda.

Further, these challenges have not fully receded in subsequent rounds of organizing efforts. IOFs have become seemingly ever more entrenched in the U.S. economy, and systemic, economic racial injustice has persisted. Though slavery ended, successor Jim Crow institutions continued to structure the economy in ways which explicitly affected co-operatives for another century. Legacies of Jim Crow remain today in America's system of "racial capitalism" (Robinson 1983), marked by still-weak co-operative presence in the U.S. South.

Alone among the rich democracies, the U.S. co-operative movement today thus also lacks a comprehensive national enabling policy framework, making it comparatively more difficult for co-operative enterprises to organize and

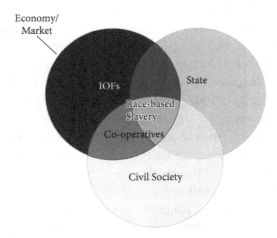

Figure 1.3 American co-operatives: field environment, mid-1800s.

coordinate their activities to scale. This has been a problem from the very first cycles of interest in co-operatives in the 1800s, when the movement's first political and organizational champions, first the communitarians and subsequently the Knights of Labor, fell short in efforts to organize and develop a "co-operative commonwealth" based on a well-coordinated co-operative enterprise system, in part due to the effects of race-based slavery (Gourevitch 2015).

Slavery is, unfortunately, everywhere in the legacy of the larger American story. How did it *specifically* matter for co-operatives? Slavery and its successor Jim Crow institutions, which restricted the economic lives and freedoms of Black Americans, initially deprived the American co-operative movement of a key part of its potential base of adherents. Enslaved persons were not free, as industrialization began, to form or participate in formal co-operatives.

But slavery *also* inhibited free White participation well into the postbellum era. Specifically, slavery directly shaped the co-operative field's framing and construction, impinging on the solidarity mechanisms at the heart of the co-operative model in the process. The Knights of Labor, like the communitarians before them, had called to end the "wage slavery" of rising industrial capitalism for all workers by using co-operatives which also included former Black slaves as member-owners. In so doing, their framing activated White fears of what we would today call a "great replacement": the replacement of White ownership of Black laborers, with multiracial collective ownership via the co-operative model. Their explicit connection of race-based slavery to wage slavery resulted in a deadly and violent backlash to stop co-operative development in the American South (DeSantis 2016).

American co-operators subsequently tried, with limited success, to remedy this initial failure. Agents and actors who advanced the interests of economic liberalism and systemic racism—from Northern business owners to Southern former slave owners, and the politicians who represented them—further splintered the force of the American co-operative movement, producing separate White and Black co-operative movements (Gordon Nembhard 2014; Carreiro 2015; Du Bois 1907; Cross 1906). These forces also animated an anti-co-operative bias in the United States, manifest in robust antitrust laws, Red Scares, and a corporate tax war waged in the U.S. Congress (Lauck 2000; McCabe 1945), all of which specifically targeted co-operatives in the 20th century and further reinforced the dominance of the institutional arrangements of racialized economic liberalism.

But this is more than an American story. Analyses of three other rich democracies where the co-operative model has been comparatively more successful at scale—Finland, France, and New Zealand—not only affirm and inform the approach used to understand the U.S. case but produce a more generalizable and comparative understanding of co-operative enterprise development. The cases reveal there are multiple pathways, engendered and enabled by different constellations of forces, in the successful development of a strong co-operative enterprise sector, or "co-operative ecosystem," which in turn supports and sustains the development of large-scale co-operatives. In the language of social science, diverse paths in national co-operative successes show a degree of equifinality: many different roads lead to Rome. While Finland's co-operatives, stoked by crisis, emerged as a revolutionary economic powerhouse seemingly overnight, development in both France and New Zealand was more gradual and evolutionary, leveraging different types of political and economic opportunities and "institutional voids" (Mair and Marti 2009), overcoming different obstacles in the process.

Yet there is also a common thread across the cases, which not only affirms the diagnosis of the underlying problem in the United States but also explains how and why co-operatives have been comparatively more successful elsewhere. In all three cases, co-operative advocates, most often via meta-organizations such as a co-operative apex body, were able to organize to take advantage of institutional voids or field openings in the economy that did not exist in the United States. They activated varying bases for solidarity to effectively organize and politically champion their cause to enact robust enabling policies, which then allowed them to adapt and compete. In the United States, the institutions and organizational models associated with economic liberalism and systemic racism have long occupied these voids, frustrating co-operative development efforts and limiting their entrenchment.

The comparative cases also suggest, however, that the co-operative movement's limits to date in the United States do not mean the model is forever doomed there. The potential for a more co-operative-rich America is not entirely lost. In periods of crisis, even in the United States, existing incumbent fields can be destabilized, yielding openings and opportunities which skilled social actors who are associated with challenger fields can leverage to improve their standing vis-à-vis dominant models. Might the American reawakening to the ongoing realities of racial injustice, sparked by George Floyd's murder, mean that the United States will more systematically redress the ongoing legacies of slavery and racism? In so doing, might it also pave the way for the development of a more robust co-operative economy? At this writing, the answer is unclear, but if the diagnosis of the underlying cause of co-operatives' comparative U.S. weakness is correct, the outlook is stronger than at any point in a half-century, particularly given renewed efforts by U.S. co-operatives to address racism today.

Beyond addressing the prospects for cooperation at scale, this book holds lesson for social scientists more broadly interested in long-term institutional change. To explain the case outcomes, I deploy two competing theoretical frameworks—strategic action field (SAF) theory and historical institutionalism (HI) —which seek to explain institutional structure and change over time. Specifically, the analysis affirms what proponents of SAF theory have previously claimed: that their more flexible, generalizable framework can encompass HI, while going beyond it in powerful ways. In the case of co-operatives, SAF theory enables us not just to understand how the co-operative model has evolved in different national contexts but also to diagnose how and why it failed to fully form in the United States.

Plan and Outline of the Book

In the next chapter, I review existing relevant research on co-operatives, including the ways in which American co-operatives today are comparatively constrained by a weak policy and business operating environment, which leaves them caught in a "vicious cycle" of institutional development rather than a "virtuous circle" (Acemoglu and Robinson 2012). I then build on emergent research (Scoville and Fligstein 2020; Kluttz and Fligstein 2016) which suggests field theory offers a more flexible, generalizable approach to understanding institutional emergence and evolution than HI. I introduce a thesaurus to translate across HI and field theory for use across the cases. I also further explain the method being deployed in this book, field tracing (Spicer, Kay, and Ganz 2019), as a subvariant of process tracing, which is common in comparative-historical work in political science and sociology.

Chapter 3 examines the Finnish case, the world's most co-operative-dense, high-income democracy, and one which possesses none of the features suspected of inhibiting co-operative development in places like the United States. Co-operatives in Finland developed at the same time as its late-breaking industrialization and its revolution for political independence at the dawn of the 20th century, taking advantage of institutional voids/field openings to produce a co-operative "big bang." Co-operatives were politically championed by the Finnish national independence movement and by Pellervo, a co-operative meta-organization. Their efforts resulted in the legal enabling of co-operatives by the nation's first independent government, as a solidarity-based means by which to achieve national political and economic independence from Russia. A robust, comprehensive co-operative policy and organizing framework was established in this juncture, one which has continued to evolve to meet changing conditions. Co-operatives served as part of a defensive economic strategy throughout the era of "Finlandization" to secure its continued independence against the geopolitical threat of Soviet annexation, and then evolved to serve as "globalization insurance" through the nation's integration into a neoliberal, global economy and the European Union. Reflecting how the co-operative has evolved through changing conditions, today Finland's banking, insurance, agricultural, retail/wholesale, and natural resource industries are dominated by the co-operative model. The Finnish case, however, cannot be understood without the insight that, in offering a middle way between American liberal capitalism and Soviet/Eastern bloc state-led economic collectivism, co-operatives have long enabled Finland to balance its geopolitical position between East and West.

In Chapter 4, I examine the French case, where co-operatives have become the heart of a coherently organized, legally defined "social and solidarity economy" sector. The chapter traces how co-operatives initially developed in the institutional void or field opening left by the French Revolution, which abolished not only corporations but almost all other economic organizations that came between the people and the state. Adding to the favorable context in France, where feudal corporations had held sway for longer than elsewhere, the nation also industrialized later and was marked by smaller-scale production until much later than the United States or United Kingdom, well into the 19th century. Initially operating in a legal twilight in the revolutionary shadow of the state, over the next two centuries through subsequent revolutions, empires, and republics, and often achieving prominence after crises, the co-operative movement slowly but consistently secured gradual, national legal recognition through an evolutionary process of layering, as more legal forms and policies were developed to accommodate four distinct co-operative movements, each with its own organizational structure and collectively well supported by multiple political parties. By the end of the 20th century, co-operatives had evolved into the linchpin subsector of a legally defined social and solidarity economy, which joins together all social purpose enterprises through an interlocking organizational structure. Ultimately, the French state repeatedly granted sanction and legitimacy to co-operatives in a way which respects their "prosocial" logic, through enabling legislation, special public economic development tools, and access to financing programs. Reflecting the long-lasting legacy of the French Revolution, however, the government subjects these enterprises to regulation in exchange for granting legitimacy to them as an allowable intermediary between the people and the state.

Chapter 5 examines the New Zealand case, which exposes the uneasy relationship between co-operatives and economic liberalism. As a liberal market economy (LME) like the United States, New Zealand is a critical case, one which shows that liberalism alone cannot explain why co-operatives have failed to achieve lasting prominence in the U.S. economy. This chapter traces how and why New Zealand, alone among LMEs, came to have so many co-operatives. Here, co-operatives and a strong state enterprise sector sprang up together in a different type of institutional void, one largely driven by the nation's geographic distance and remoteness, which contributed to the failure of initial efforts to create a capitalist utopian colony. Unlike in the United States, here the Knights of Labor were successful in creating a strong welfare state and a system of state-led socialism, which prevailed until the 1980s, when New Zealand became an LME in a late-breaking, left-led liberalization. New Zealand's co-operatives then evolved to survive an initially hostile liberalization by organizing to leverage a political backlash to continue to play a key role in connecting the remote nation to distant markets. As in the Finnish case, New Zealand's co-operatives also serve a geopolitical role, in that they root economic ownership and control domestically and reduce the threat of acquisition by their larger neighbors, Australia and China. The case further affirms the shortcomings of static institutionalist categories, like the LME designation, which fail to account for such evolutions over time.

In Chapter 6, I trace the origins of the American co-operative movement. After reviewing its development as an outgrowth of U.K. and European utopian socialist thought and practice via the American communitarian movement, I show how, in their initial phase of development, co-operatives took root everywhere but the American South, where slavery not only kept co-operatives' most-likely participants from creating such formal enterprises but inhibited White participation as well, presaging dynamics which would persist after the Civil War. The chapter also examines how the postbellum remnants of slavery, via Jim Crow institutional arrangements, interacted with an emergent anti–"wage slavery" framing of co-operatives by labor republicanists to produce exceptional resistance to the model, undermining the solidarity-based mechanisms co-operatives utilize to diffuse and scale. This was particularly the case in the American South, where attempts to spread the model after the Civil War faced violence and contributed to the downfall of the U.S. co-operative movement's postbellum political champion, the Knights of Labor, a point historically underdeveloped in existing accounts of this key labor organization. By the late 19th century, as the Second Industrial Revolution was in full swing, the United States lacked a comprehensive national co-operative development policy framework. Both IOFs, as well as the Jim Crow successor arrangements to the slavery-ownership plantation system, remained largely unchallenged by the co-operative movement, which splintered after the Knights' collapse.

Chapter 7 continues this American story, examining subsequent efforts to build a robust, national co-operative movement. Through the mid-20th century, the American co-operative movement operated on a fragmented basis through distinct subfields, splintered by race, industry, and co-operative subtype. Efforts to develop a cohesive, overarching organizational strategy and associated enabling policies were, at best, only partially successful. Another such period of resurgence, in the wake of the upheavals of the 1960s, ended in the 1980s, with limited lasting organizational or policy results. Today, another round of co-operative organizing efforts is again occurring. But as comparisons will reveal, in terms of its nationally scaled institutionalization into a coherent field, the U.S. co-operative organizing framework still remains fragmented and incomplete. Of note, and consistent with the historical, path-dependent argument advanced by this book, co-operatives continue to be particularly limited in the U.S. South. New Southern co-operative initiatives, however, as well as explicit national co-operative messaging and organizing around race, are today readily observable, as Chapter 7 notes.

Chapter 8 offers two sets of conclusions, one oriented to academic readers, and the other to practitioners. For social scientists interested in understanding comparative institutional variation in the economy, I revisit the theories introduced in Chapter 2 to synthesize what the co-operative case teaches us about how field theory can be deployed as a more flexible and generalizable framework for answering compelling research questions, one which can accommodate other institutionalist approaches while also going beyond them to generate new insights. Specifically, the co-operative case affirms three limits of HI which field theory remedies, enabling better explanation across a wider range of phenomena. A field theory treatment of co-operatives' development trajectories also suggests that firm-type mix is a key underconsidered explanation for capitalist variety around the world, as different firm types generate distinct fields and subfields, which variably compete in different contexts, producing different "organizational ecologies" (Schneiberg 2010) in different times and places. The co-operative case also shows how and why both geography and race conditioned the organizational development trajectory not just of co-operatives but of the broader economy as well, and shows how to incorporate both of these factors into institutional and field-level analysis.

Finally, Chapter 8 also reviews analytical implications of this book for actors in the co-operative movement today who may seek to shift the co-operative development path in America and beyond. The key point for such actors: forces which have limited U.S. co-operative development to date are contingent. What does that mean? It means that development paths can, through carefully timed and coordinated action at key moments, be substantively influenced. Another economy is thus still possible. Co-operative entrepreneurs, however, likely need to frame, message, and organize around co-operative policy change in a way which directly speaks to the underlying structural problems, as identified in this book, that yielded their challenges to begin with. In the U.S. context, that means explicit messaging around the historically dividing role that race and racism have played within the co-operative movement itself, and incorporating these considerations into economic organizing, coalition-building, and policy reform. But it also likely means organizing beyond the co-operative movement to ally with broader racial justice coalitions, to attack the underlying society-wide racism which has for so long plagued American co-operatives' ability to more broadly activate the solidarity-based mechanisms at the co-operative model's heart. Efforts along these lines are increasingly evident in the U.S. co-operative movement, as new generations center the truth uttered by Emma Lazarus in the 19th century, Martin Luther King Jr. and Fannie Lou Hamer in the 20th, and Janelle Monáe in the 21st: no one is free until we all are.

2
Conceptualizing the Comparative Development of Co-operative Enterprise

> National and state government agencies... don't even know we exist. It's unbelievably frustrating. In other countries, co-operatives have a seat at the table ... here, we ... fight for table scraps. We are running up the down escalator, with our hand behind our back ... pick your cliché.... America claims it's the land of equal opportunity ... a level playing field. That only applies to certain types of businesses.... [S]ometimes I feel like we don't stand a chance.
> —U.S. co-operative developer, 2018

As reviewed in the prior chapter, we know that large-scale co-operative enterprises are comparatively rarer in the United States than in most other rich democracies today. We also have a good sense of the policy and operating constraints that American co-operative entrepreneurs face in trying to establish and scale a business today, as I will review in this chapter, and the statistical factors that correlate with and explain these current constraints. U.S. co-operators live in a comparatively different environment than many of their counterparts elsewhere, leaving them feeling as if "they are running up the down escalator," as one interviewee suggested. How and why did this come to be?

To answer that question, this book offers a comparative-historical analysis on the development of the co-operative model at scale in the United States, which I treat as a central case of comparative and relative failure, as contrasted to three relative success cases: Finland, France, and New Zealand. In conducting the comparative-historical analysis, I deploy two competing theoretical frameworks commonly applied to understand and explain institutional variation, stability, and change: historical institutionalism and field theory. While both are useful for my research question, the latter is more comprehensive in explaining outcomes across the cases, as this book will show.

Before introducing these two frameworks later in this chapter, however, I first review what we know about co-operatives and how they achieve scale. I then review the cases and what we know about the comparative and relative constraints American co-operatives face today vis-à-vis their counterparts in the other countries, before detailing the book's conceptual and methodological approach.

Co-operatives 101: A Primer

Readers who are already familiar with co-operatives may wish to skip much of this section, which offers a focused overview of co-operative enterprise. Co-operatives are member-owned and controlled enterprises, typically using democratic, "one person, one vote" governance structures. The ICA, which is the global apex or "meta-organizing" body for co-operatives, defines them as adhering to seven principles (Table 2.1 and Figure 2.1). Through these principles, the co-operative contrasts with the "default" ownership model of today's economy: the investor-owned, joint-stock corporation, in which arm's-length or third-party investors, instead of members, control and own the firm, with control apportioned based on the ownership stake's size, and not on a democratic basis. I refer to this model throughout the book as the IOF (investor-owned firm).

Who qualifies as a co-operative member, and how is membership different from being a "member-owner" of a traditional IOF? Is not an investor just a specific type of member? This was the argument of Hansmann (1996), who viewed all firms as a form of co-operative. In a narrow sense, this is technically accurate. But in an entity formally organized as a co-operative, there is a difference: a member typically must have a substantive relationship or interest in the enterprise and its purpose, as reflected in co-operative principles 3 and 4. Members of a co-operative thus most commonly fall into one or more of the following categories: consumer, producer, or worker member-owners (Figure 2.2).

Members are typically customers who buy the enterprise's goods and services, producers who supply these items to the enterprise, or workers who manufacture or create the products or services of the enterprise. Some hybrid combination of these is also possible: multi-stakeholder co-operative forms in countries such as France (see Chapter 4) and the United Kingdom (Yeoman 2017) have also arisen. Today's high-tech platform co-operatives (Schneider and Scholz 2016) are often hybrid, multi-stakeholder co-operatives. Occasionally, co-operative or other social/mission-oriented investors who are

Table 2.1 The Seven Co-operative Principles of the International Co-operative Alliance

Principle	Detailed Definition
1. Voluntary and Open Membership	Co-operatives are voluntary organizations, open to all persons able to use their services and willing to accept the responsibilities of membership, without gender, social, racial, political, or religious discrimination.
2. Democratic Member Control	Co-operatives are democratic organizations controlled by their members, who actively participate in setting their policies and making decisions. Men and women serving as elected representatives are accountable to the membership. In primary co-operatives members have equal voting rights (one member, one vote) and co-operatives at other levels are also organized in a democratic manner.
3. Member Economic Participation	Members contribute equitably to, and democratically control, the capital of their co-operative. At least part of that capital is usually the common property of the co-operative. Members usually receive limited compensation, if any, on capital subscribed as a condition of membership. Members allocate surpluses for any or all of the following purposes: developing their co-operative, possibly by setting up reserves, part of which at least would be indivisible; benefiting members in proportion to their transactions with the co-operative; and supporting other activities approved by the membership.
4. Autonomy and Independence	Co-operatives are autonomous, self-help organizations controlled by their members. If they enter into agreements with other organizations, including governments, or raise capital from external sources, they do so on terms that ensure democratic control by their members and maintain their co-operative autonomy.
5. Education, Training, and Information	Co-operatives provide education and training for their members, elected representatives, managers, and employees so they can contribute effectively to the development of their co-operatives. They inform the general public—particularly young people and opinion leaders—about the nature and benefits of cooperation.
6. Cooperation among Co-operatives	Co-operatives serve their members most effectively and strengthen the co-operative movement by working together through local, national, regional, and international structures.
7. Concern for Community	Co-operatives work for the sustainable development of their communities through policies approved by their members.

Source: ICA 1995

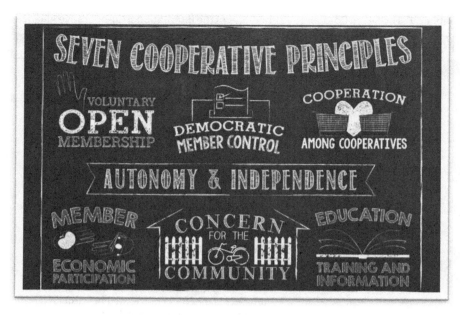

Figure 2.1 The seven co-operative principles (as displayed in various U.S. grocery store co-operatives).
Source: Used with permission from Willy Street Co-op, Madison, WI.

not consumers, workers, or producers of the co-operative's input or output may be co-operative member-owners, but they typically also have a nonfinancial relationship with or interest in the enterprise, rooted in the co-operative movement or related social movements.

Though there are obvious differences among these various types of co-operatives, all ultimately trace their organizational development back to the underlying co-operative enterprise movement (Wilson, Webster, and Vorberg-Rugh 2014) and typically explicitly identify with the co-operative label, as promulgated by the co-operative movement. Sometimes, in specific moments, other movements have also incubated co-operatives in new, innovative ways. In the United States (see Chapters 6 and 7), such overlaps have occurred between the co-operative movement and the farmer, labor, environmental, and civil rights movements, among others (Schneiberg, King, and Smith 2008; Schneiberg 2011; Upright 2020; Gordon Nembhard 2014). Co-operative enterprise models nonetheless are typically and primarily incubated to become recognizable "organizational archetypes" (Greenwood and Hinings 1988, 1993) by the overall co-operative movement, and are its byproduct. Such a process, whereby movements form, develop, and spread an organizational archetype to accomplish their goals, is consistent with broader literature on how movements construct new

Figure 2.2 The birthplace of the co-operative. The modern co-operative model was born just outside of Manchester in the early 1840s, in Rochdale, United Kingdom. The original location is now a museum (pictured) but was once visited by politicians, academics, and social actors from around the world, including Friederich Engels (signature pictured in visitor's book, bottom right), aiding the global diffusion of the model. Co-operatives UK, the nation's apex organization, is located nearby. Learning from failures of immediately prior waves of co-operatives created by King and Owen (Wilson, Webster, and Vorberg-Rugh 2014), the Rochdalians developed co-operative principles to enable stable development of each enterprise and created an approach to coordinating across co-operatives as well. By the 1860s, the Rochdalians had organized an interlocking co-operative system, led by a meta-organizing apex body, which had secured an enabling policy. Its central enterprise, the Co-operative Wholesale Society, became one of the first modern global enterprises (Chandler and Hikino 1990). Photos by the author.

organizational fields (Soule 2012; Fligstein and McAdam 2019), a point I will return to later in the chapter and throughout the book.

Reflecting co-operatives' distinct nature, in most rich democracies they also typically have their own incorporation statutes and/or tax status (Henry 2013). Other closely related legal forms, like credit unions, which are a form of consumer co-operative, and mutual benefit corporations and mutual society ownership models, which are somewhat common in insurance and banking in the United States and elsewhere, also typically identify as co-operatives, legally and/or organizationally.[1]

Alongside these formal co-operative ownership forms are several similar and related models (see Table 2.2). Though these other, similar forms are not the primary subject or focus of this book, some of them appear in the analysis because they are directly relevant to the co-operative development trajectories of the cases. Some are so similar that they may, in either law or practice, be functionally grouped with co-operatives. For example, consumer and community trust-owned enterprises, rare in the U.S. economy but significant in New Zealand (see Chapter 5), are a closely related form: these are enterprises held in trust for a designated consumer or community group, which may exert democratic control of ownership. U.K. law enables community interest company structures, as do multiple Canadian provinces; these are sometimes treated as a "close cousin" to the co-operative, as one informant stated. In select instances, some of these forms may partially share legislative frameworks and advocacy networks with co-operatives, as in France's social and solidarity economy (see Chapter 4). As decentralized autonomous organizations emerge, some co-operative movement participants are seeking to develop a unique co-operative structure for these entities.

Beyond these closely related forms are other, more distant relatives, which, though not co-operatives, can still be conceptualized as part of a universe of "alternative enterprises," in that they offer an IOF alternative (Parker, Van Alstyne, and Choudary 2016; Davis 2016b; Schneiberg 2017; Spicer and Lee-Chuvala 2021). Firms that are majority-owned and controlled through employee stock ownership plans (ESOPs), particularly those that operate with co-operative bylaws, now being called "esoperatives" in the United States (Spicer 2020), can sometimes operate similarly to worker co-operatives. But most ESOPs lack co-operative bylaws, and due to their lack of worker control,

---

[1] The United States also has limited equity co-operative apartments and mutual housing associations, which both effectively meet the definition of a co-operative. Due to a lack of comparable economy-of-scale drivers at the enterprise level and their general lack of employees, however, passive housing and landholding structures are generally not analyzed as a "business enterprise," are often treated separately by scholars, and are not centrally examined in this book, which focuses on co-operative *enterprise*.

Table 2.2 Major Types of Co-operative Enterprises and Related "Alternative Enterprise" Forms

Consumer co-operatives: owned by consumers
- Retail store co-operatives
- Energy co-operatives
- Credit unions
- Co-operative banks
- Popular banks (Europe, Canada)
- Mutual banks/insurers

Producer co-operatives: owned by businesses/entities
- Agricultural/farmer co-operatives
- Marketing/wholesale co-operatives
- Co-operatives of co-operatives

Worker co-operatives: owned by workers/employees
- Worker co-operatives
- ESOPeratives/democratic ESOP
- Francophone worker production societies, employment co-operatives

Multi-stakeholder co-operatives: owned by mix of stakeholders
- "Next Gen"/LLC investor co-operatives (U.S.), "Minnesota co-operatives," Limited Co-operative Association (U.S.), co-operative holding companies (U.S.)
- Collective interest co-operatives (France)
- Publicservice mutuals (U.K.)

Related forms: community/beneficial ownership
- Community interest company (U.K., CA); community benefit societies (U.K.); community contribution company (CA); community investment trusts (U.S.)
- Community/consumer trusts (New Zealand)
- Perpetual purpose trusts (U.S.)
- ESOP trusts (U.S.), employee ownership trusts (U.K., U.S.)
- Social and solidarity enterprises (Europe)
- Mutual and public benefit corporations (U.S.)
- B-corps (U.S.)
- Nonprofit industrial foundation ownership (various)

are not a type of co-operative. Relatedly, employee ownership trusts and perpetual purpose trusts, which are new models in the United States and United Kingdom, may wind up offering some of these benefits, but their policy frameworks are still emergent at this writing. Public benefit corporations and/or associations, long enabled in many U.S. states, may share some characteristics with co-operatives, in that their explicit goal is to serve the needs of the community members or the public rather than advance merely instrumental goals such as profit maximization. Another "B-corp" model, the benefit corporation, rapidly diffused in the 2010s to 33 states via enabling legislation (Berrey 2018). It is like the co-operative in that it incorporates social objectives other than profit maximization into its legally defined goals. There is also, separately, a voluntary "B-corp" designation, which firms not necessarily incorporated as B-corps can attain. Some U.S. co-operatives have additionally pursued this voluntary B-corp designation. But the public benefit corporation and the legal B-corp are not co-operatives, as they lack the same governance, control, and ownership mechanisms. The industrial foundation ownership model is common in Germany and Denmark (Hansmann and Thomsen 2013; Thomsen et al. 2018) but rare in the United States from the late 1960s through 2018 due to court decisions and tax legislation which inhibited them (Hansmann and Thomsen 2021). This model involves firms "virtually" or indirectly owned by a nonprofit foundation for a specific broad socioeconomic group; it also shares some ownership characteristics with co-operatives but is not typically analyzed as being comparable to them. The rich democracies' most common co-operative and related alternative enterprise structures are detailed in Table 2.2.

Where, when, and why does one find co-operatives?

According to the ICA, co-operatives can be found in virtually any country that allows them to form; 109 countries have organizations that are ICA members. In the United States, some of the largest and most successful co-operatives are well-known businesses. Outdoor retailer REI is the largest consumer-owned co-operative in the United States, with over 6 million member-owners, $3B in revenues, and over 150 locations, with 70% of its profits returned to members as a dividend rebate in a recent year. Most U.S. rural areas' electricity is supplied by customer-owned co-operatives, some of which can cover large areas. Florida's Natural Orange Juice and Ocean Spray are growers' or producers' co-operatives, and Organic Valley is an organic farmers' producer co-operative. All these brands are household names. What was up until recently the largest U.S. worker co-operative,[2] Co-operative Home Care Associates (CHCA), is majority-owned and controlled by women and people of color (Spicer, 2020). New York–based CHCA employs over 2,000 healthcare worker-owners, such as nurses and home healthcare aides, who own and control the business; they are also a voluntary designated B-corp and unionized (via Service Employees

---

[2] In 2020 they were overtaken in size by a taxi driver–owned co-operative in New York, now the largest in the United States.

International Union). A number of U.S. worker co-operatives are unionized, often utilizing an innovative labor-management council in a unionized co-op structure (Hanson-Schlachter 2017). Buying co-operatives and shared-service co-operatives (Clamp, Amendah, and Coren 2019) are two other types of co-operative and can be owned by one or more types of stakeholders (i.e., consumers or producers).

While co-operatives of many forms can be found across industries in the United States and around the world, they are more common in certain industries than others: banking/insurance, retail/wholesale, and agriculture are among the most prevalent in the United States and globally (Spicer 2022). There is a well-known reason for this. As established by Hansmann (1990, 1996) the transaction costs associated with co-operatives' democratic governance model are lower when the good (an input or an output) being co-operativized or mutualized is homogeneous, as this supports the development of shared economic interests between and among co-operatives' members. Assuming comparable production standards, there is little difference between one gallon or liter of milk and another, reflecting the homogeneity of the good. This makes it easier for dairy farmers, for example, who have a shared economic interest in finding a way to pool and process their milk to efficiently get it to buyers, to agree to the shared governance model of a milk-processing co-operative.

On a related front, other scholarship (Rothschild and Whitt 1986) has suggested that social homogeneity (and homophily) among members plays a similar role: shared bonds of solidarity rooted in a social identity can also form the basis for effective, low-cost co-operative decision-making. Notably, this work has generally examined such solidarity among socially marginalized groups, including African Americans, Finnish Americans, Mormons, and Jews in various societies, including America (Du Bois 1907; Cross 1906; Kercher, Kebker, and Leland 1941; Chambers 1962; Alanen 1975; Gordon Nembhard 2014; Rodgers, Petersen, and Sanderson 2016). Those whose economic needs are not met by other institutions thus may turn to co-operatives to self-meet these needs. Assumedly, however, the scale of enterprises serving such populations may be constrained not just by the resources within such groups but by their size, prevalence, and durability. Certain immigrant groups, for example, which are small in number or which are quickly integrated in a manner which diminishes their identity as a basis for economic solidarity, may form co-operatives, but they may not last at scale. It may also be difficult to organize at scale across such different groups.

The original British co-operative movement was generated by a group whose solidarity was both social and economic in nature. The Rochdale consumer co-operatives, just outside Manchester, were formed by weavers displaced from their work by mechanization. Thus their shared occupation-based social identity formed the basis for their cooperating to self-supply four basic, and fairly economically homogeneous, consumer goods they needed: butter, sugar, flour, and oatmeal (Figure 2.2). It has also been suggested (Salustri, Mosca, and Vigano 2015) that another basis for the member solidarity which fuels co-operatives can be geographic. Places which are marginalized in the global economy due to their small size or remoteness experience higher transaction costs and lower external trade volumes. They may be less attractive to globalizing IOFs due to their lower potential for large profits, leading them to be prone to market failures, creating an opportunity for local communities to self-organize through the co-operative model in response (Spicer 2022).

Despite the fact that co-operatives can be found all over of the world in different industries, the co-operative model *at scale* is actually quite rare throughout the rich democracies, and is especially rare in the United States. Fewer than 1% of American enterprises with annual revenues in excess of $75MM today are co-operatives or mutuals (Spicer 2022), a lower figure than in most rich democracies, and in fact one-10th the highest prevalence rate among rich democracies (Finland; see Figure 1.2). Why is this the case?

How co-operatives are different: distinct logic and specific coordination mechanism to scale

The general rarity of large co-operatives in rich capitalist democracies is in part a function of their distinct logic. As member-owned and controlled enterprises, co-operatives' appeal as an IOF alternative is driven by their wholly different rationality or "operating logic" and distinct "essence" (Guzman and Santos 2020; Staber 1989; Rothschild 1979), one which enables them to operate with the hybrid traits of both a business and a social movement (Upright 2020).

In capitalist contexts, this difference in logic acts as a double-edged sword: it drives interest in the model, but also means it can struggle to compete against the IOF under the weight of its different logic, driven by social purpose and substantive values. For some readers, this difference may be obvious. But for others, it may require greater explanation, through application of concepts which have informed the development of field theory, which will be centrally deployed across the cases to understand their trajectories.

Specifically, we can deploy two conceptual distinctions drawn from Karl Marx and Max Weber: first, the distinction between exchange, use, and labor theories of value, and second, between types of rationality. Marx, in developing his theory of capitalism, built on Ricardo and other classical political economists' labor theories of value. These theories included distinctions between the value of a good for its use, the value of a good for exchange (assumed to be established through exchange in a market of some kind), and the value of a good based on the labor required to make it. This labor value was in turn a function of the cost laborers required to "reproduce" themselves (Ricardo 1817; Marx 1867). Today, one might phrase this as the cost workers need to sustain themselves. Weber (cf. Kalberg 1980), meanwhile, theorized there were four ideal types of social action, two of which were *zweckrational*, or instrumental "means-end" rationality, and *wertrational*, or substantive rationality. This latter distinction between types of rationalities and logics has been well developed by scholars of organizations to understand co-operatives as a type of "hybrid enterprise" which combine both commercial and social purpose logics (Friedland and Alford 1991; Battilana and Dorado 2010).

Taken together, these two points about theories of value and types of rationality help conceptualize co-operatives' alterity vis-à-vis the IOF. In a typical IOF, owners' primary or sole relationship with the firm is a financial one, as an investor. Their chief goal is thus generally profit maximization, which is typically achieved two ways: by maximizing ongoing income return through retention and distribution of generated profits and dividends, and through capital return, via the sale of their equity ownership to another investor, typically valued as a multiple of the annual income expectation. The IOF thus typically exists to maximize exchange value, specifically focusing on maximizing the exchange value of the firm entity ("enterprise value") itself, through its ownership shares, leading to the dominance of instrumental rationality in the IOF. Indeed, in modern business, this is enshrined through the principle of maximizing shareholder value (Lazonick 2014; Lazonick and O'Sullivan 2000). Some have argued that IOFs are not legally required to maximize shareholder value by maximizing profits (Stout 2012, 2015), but such matters remain unsettled in U.S. case law. Beyond the United States, treatment of this issue varies, depending on how legal jurisdictions define and interpret corporate statutes. Nonetheless, in principle, the U.S. IOF is today understood to exist primarily to maximize shareholders' financial value.

In a co-operative, however, the member-owners' and co-operative's primary goal is typically *not* profit maximization; this is not why the co-operative exists. *It exists to meet the members' needs and for their specified use, at their control and direction.* The co-operative, as an institutional form, thus embodies an organizational focus on *use value* and displays a different *substantive rationality* to that end (Spicer and Lee-Chuvala 2021), one which is often collectivist-democratic (Rothschild 1979) in nature. An enterprise focused on uses can flexibly accomplish different goals for its owner-members, providing them with needed goods, services, or employment. If the enterprise is financially viable, covering its costs and, if needed or desirable, yielding an appropriate financial return for reinvestment or member distribution, it need not focus on profit maximization in the same way as an IOF.

A co-operative thus enables incorporation of other types of values beyond instrumental ones. In focusing on members' use-value needs, co-operatives can incorporate members' substantive values, whatever they may be, into the production process. One substantive value, particularly with worker-owned co-operatives, might be to pay workers a wage which reflects the full value of the labor they have spent to make the product, that is, a socially sustainable wage. Another value might be environmentally sustainable production and consumption, as often seen in U.S. grocery co-operatives (Upright 2020). These concerns are not just possible in the co-operative model, but in fact are an explicit part of co-operatives' seven identity principles, particularly principle 3 (see Figure 2.1). This is why, in the language of economics, co-operatives are able to achieve "prosocial" goals, that is, those that benefit society, in their operation, and have been widely studied for such benefits.

This distinct logic, one driven by use value and one which provides space for application of substantive value rationality, is evident in co-operatives' appeal to the current wave of actors interested in their promotion. Co-operatives can enable environmentally sustainable economic production by embedding sustainability costs at their source (see Figure 2.3); for example, member-owners can choose to patronize a co-operative (of any sort) which reduces or eliminates

Figure 2.3 Connecting ownership to sustainability. Groups like Fifty by Fifty explicitly make the connection that sustainability may require different ownership models, like worker co-operatives.
Source: Fifty by Fifty, www.fiftybyfifty.org.

carbon emissions and other environmentally negative aspects in its production process. This may mean that the product costs more, but if the co-operative can sell the product to its members at a price they are willing to pay and can cover costs, maximizing profit is not an issue. Similarly, individuals can choose to patronize a co-operative which pays workers the amount they need to socially sustain themselves. Rather than requiring that individuals and/or interest groups organize to make the state enforce such considerations upon all enterprises, co-operatives allow individuals to voluntarily embed these non-exchange-value, nonfinancial considerations into their economic lives and choices. This is a key point of differentiation between co-operatives and IOFs, which typically are presumed to seek to externalize all such costs wherever possible, and suggests why, in a capitalist world, co-operatives at scale are comparatively rare: when a firm type voluntarily chooses a higher cost structure, how can it compete against other firm types like the IOF, which do not bear such costs?

Finally, because of this different logic, co-operatives commonly also achieve economic scale differently (Spicer 2022). Co-operatives are not just a hybrid enterprise, with distinct internal traits that combine civil society–based and market-based logics, but are in fact a hybrid *field*, with relational modes of action between firms which differ from those of the IOF. This includes how they coordinate between firms to achieve scale. Rather than engage in hostile mergers and acquisitions, as is common with the IOF, co-operatives more often deploy some variation or part of what was historically called the "co-operative commonwealth strategy" (Gourevitch 2015), which today, as noted earlier, is increasingly called the "co-operative ecosystem" approach (Spicer and Zhong 2022). This is also a variation of what Kornai (1990) historically called "associative coordination."

In the co-operative commonwealth approach, which is how the U.K. co-operative movement originally achieved scale and is sometimes referred to as the Rochdale model of co-operative development (Wilson, Webster, and Vorberg-Rugh 2014), different types of co-operatives *cooperate*: they federate with one another horizontally in the same industry, while also federating to coordinate vertically, up and down the supply chain, create interlocking networks of co-operative businesses, complete with co-operative finance/banking and insurance to supply capital and enable expansion, as well as with an apex advocacy body which seeks accommodative policy and appropriate enabling legislation (see Figure 2.4). In coordinating this way, co-operatives reduce their contracting with firms which operate with a different logic and purpose (e.g., IOFs; cf. Wilson, Webster, and Vorberg-Rugh 2013). In the U.K. model, the central apex or meta-organizing body, originally called the Co-operative Central Board and later the Co-operative Union before becoming Co-operatives U.K., was critical to this coordination. But so, too, was

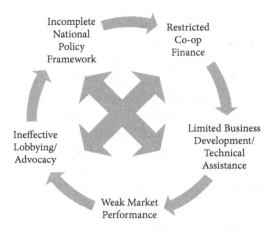

Figure 2.4 The "vicious cycle" for U.S. co-operatives.

a central Co-operative Wholesale Society, which coordinated trade and collaboration across the network of co-operatives, which by the late 19th century was one of the first modern global corporations (Chandler and Hikino 1990) and which subsequently inspired other co-operatives regarding the potential of achieving a different type of globalization through the co-operative model. Indeed, cooperation among co-operatives is one of the seven operating principles detailed by their global apex body, the ICA. But coordinating across co-operatives in this way is particularly problematic in some capitalist contexts, as the next subsection will detail.

Co-operative prevalence at scale? The puzzle

Literature on co-operatives' benefits could fill many bookshelves. Co-operatives, particularly worker co-operatives, are associated with improved employee morale, more meaningful work, reduced turnover, greater gender equality, less wage inequality, and a host of other positive traits (Meyers 2022; Spicer and Kay 2022; Chen and Chen 2021; Yeoman 2017; Carberry 2011; Zeuli and Radel 2005; Rothschild and Whitt 1986; Bernstein 1976). With their "one person, one vote" structure, they arguably best embody economic democracy and are also posited to be better aligned with political democracy, engendering better civic participation (Kaswan 2014; Dahl 1985; Pateman 1970, 2012).

Of particular importance, even though co-operatives are not particularly common at scale in any of the rich democracies today—accounting for at most just under 10% of large businesses even in comparatively co-operative-rich Finland—they can produce broader benefits for society even when they have a limited market share or presence, by acting as a "countervailing power" against capital, provided they have achieved "a certain minimum opportunity and capacity for organization," as articulated by John Kenneth Galbraith (1952, 13). Historically, this argument was advanced through the case of consumer co-operatives in Sweden (Hilson 2013, 2018; Roy 1969; Childs 1936), which showed that a large co-operative can reform capitalist IOFs' behavior across an industry, precisely by acting as a "countervailing power," as the threat of a large, member-owned enterprise offering better products or services for lower cost reformed and conditioned competing IOFs' actions.

So if co-operatives offer so many benefits, why are they so rare at scale, particularly in the United States? What do we know, from empirical social science, about how and why co-operatives come to achieve the lasting operational economies of scale needed to have a meaningfully widespread level of impact on the economy? It is first worth briefly explaining why scale matters at all. Simply put, economic phenomena are still dominated by scalar dynamics, as they have been for centuries. Economies of scale for inputs such as labor and capital are central to explaining individual firms' efficiency and viability; average and marginal unit costs decline as production levels rise from initially low levels, as upfront fixed costs become spread over a larger base of activity. This is a key reason why larger firms have higher survival rates than smaller ones (Esteve-Pérez and Mañez-Castillejo 2008). As a result, firms are subject to a well-known power law, or 80-20 rule, first observed by Pareto (1896): a few large units of observation (20%) account for most (80%) economic activity (Gabaix 2016). Large enterprises thus play an outsized role in driving macroeconomic outcomes and fluctuations (Gabaix 2016).

It is true that some large firms have recently been experiencing dislocation at the hands of smaller challengers, as traditional vertically integrated IOFs "fissure" (Weil 2014) in the wake of outsourcing and the rise of platform/web-based firms (Parker, Van Alstyne, and Choudary 2016; Davis 2016b). Yet despite expectations that such technologies would finally allow the realization of a long-anticipated "second industrial divide" toward flexible and, by implication, networked production by smaller firms (Piore and Sabel 1984), large firms have actually become *increasingly dominant* over the past three decades across most industries in high-income capitalist democracies (Autor et al. 2020), further affirming the power law Paretian distribution referenced above. This is not to say that individually small, specialist firms (Carroll 1985) and/or networked firms cannot carve out a market niche, nor that they can never coordinate to collectively account for more than a modest share of output. Rather, they do so in the shadow of increasingly dominant large firms which drive the overall economy, as empirics have affirmed (Autor et al. 2020). Indeed, the economic importance of large firms appears only to have been strengthened by technology, as high-tech platforms' (Galloway 2017) market shares grow. These firms may not employ as many individuals as leading legacy industry firms once did, such as the Big Three automakers (Davis 2016a, 2016b), but they nonetheless dominate their industry. In fact, as technology reduces marginal unit costs for some inputs, economies of scale are argued to grow more pronounced for platform firms and other enterprises transitioning into the digital era (Evans, Hagiu, and Schmalensee 2008; Evans and Schmalensee 2016). Though the structure of productive economies of scale may thus change under platform capitalism, economies of scale remain critical in explaining why large firms play a dominant role in the economy, and accordingly matter to our understanding of the institutional outcomes and structures of the economy.

Economies of scale *also* apply to co-operatives. Though there is no known global data set on the population of every single co-operative, studies of subtypes of co-operative enterprises in different countries confirm the dominance of larger co-operative enterprises. Recent censuses of the several hundred U.S. worker co-operatives in existence, for example, found that the largest worker co-operative alone accounted for more than half of all economic activity by such U.S. enterprises (Hoover and Abell 2016), consistent with similar country-specific analyses examining the size and firm population of different co-operative subtypes (Pérotin 2012; Battilani and Schroter 2011; Battilani and Schroter 2012). Though scale may come with drawbacks for co-operatives—the potential for reduced member voice and participation is a well-known issue at larger co-operative firms (Cornforth 1995)—co-operative enterprise participants today are nonetheless explicitly aware that achieving scale matters for their continued success, as stated and affirmed by co-operative movement participants themselves (Lingane 2015). This is due in part to how scale affects their economic viability (i.e., operation with an efficient cost structure) and survival (Cornforth 1995), as with IOFs.

To have more than a marginal impact in a world where economies of scale persist, co-operatives must not only form but subsequently survive and scale. How can they do this? Leading economists have highlighted the importance of this question. Piketty (2020, 510–13) has presumed co-operatives are rare under capitalism due to individual property rights, but offers limited evidence, or detail on the mechanisms, in support. The 2016 Nobel Economics laureate Bengt Holmstrom (1999, 404) noted that "peculiarly little attention has been spent on understanding the role of co-operatives and other non-corporate forms of organization. It has simply been assumed that most firms are business corporations." The 2014 Nobel laureate economist Jean Tirole (2017, 174, 177) asked, "Why is investor ownership and control so widespread throughout the world? Under what circumstances can modes of organization other than the capitalist enterprise—co-operatives or employee-managed firms, for instance—emerge and prosper? . . . Is there a failure of competition among possible forms . . . if so, is it up to the state to intervene?" Indeed, as sociologist Mayer Zald (1988, 17) stated a generation ago, "Enterprise forms are legally embedded. State action is required and we must study the political process involved in creating and sustaining enterprise forms." Further to both Tirole's and Zald's points, Mair and Rathert (2019) suggested that various alternative forms of market-based organizing, including co-operatives, may exhibit institutional incongruencies with different capitalist "families," suggesting that certain macro contexts may be more or less hospitable to these organizational forms. Empirically, this has been demonstrated to be the case (Spicer 2022), showing that even when statistically controlling for other relevant factors, co-operatives struggle in the policy and business operating environments of the liberal capitalist family, what Hall and Soskice's (2001) Varieties of Capitalism (VofC) call liberal market economies, operating with what Esping-Andersen (1990) called a residual welfare state.

Why is this? Co-operatives are a different type of business, one with a different logic with respect to costs and one which deploys different strategies than the IOF to achieve scale, as reviewed above. Both these features of co-operatives (their different logic and their natively preferred scaling mechanism) are incongruent with the arrangements of an LME with a residual welfare state, for two reasons. First, co-operatives struggle to compete in environments where other firms operating with a different, profit-maximizing logic (namely, IOFs) are not required by policy to internally embed the same social welfare and/or environmental costs that co-operatives often voluntarily do. LMEs with residual welfare states, like the United States, are marked by such a policy environment, as my research has shown (Spicer 2022). Conversely, co-operatives more readily survive to scale in countries where their choice to voluntarily embed additional costs is less of a comparative drag on cost competitiveness, that is, countries where "high floor" or "beneficial constraint" labor policies (Streeck 1997) are imposed on employers. These countries operate with stronger welfare regimes, another type of "comparative capitalism" framework as conceptualized by Esping-Andersen (1990, 1999). In such regimes, labor is less commodified than in the liberal, residual welfare regime of Anglo-American countries like the United States.

The second reason co-operatives struggle in these contexts is that their preferred, interfirm, field-level coordination strategy to achieve scale, reviewed in the preceding subsection, runs afoul of the dominant operating logic of firms in LMEs. VofC posits two main ideal-type families of economies among the rich democracies, distinguished by how firms are coordinated. In LMEs like the United States, firms are coordinated in a manner which is institutionally complementary (Mair and Rathert 2019) with the IOF. In LMEs, firms co-ordinate atomistically or individually, reflecting the dominance of a liberal logic: they operate at arm's length through formal market contracts, with lower degrees of cross-shareholding and less voluntary or informal interfirm cooperation, all as enforced through strong, well-developed antitrust laws. Employee education and training costs are also externalized, as a matter of both firm practice and public policy. This is institutionally incongruous with the co-operative model of coordinating to scale. Coordinated market economies (CMEs), conversely, have a coordination model which is institutionally complementary with the co-operative approach (Spicer 2022).

This is one reason why large-scale co-operatives are less common in LMEs today. LMEs, however, did not always exist, but rather recently emerged through a contested historical process. Furthermore, the liberal comparative capitalist family designations (LME, residual welfare state) are not the only factors to explain variation in large-scale cross-national co-operative prevalence today. While statistical analyses of cooperation at scale today still find an effect of these capitalist families after controlling for the other known factors, other control factors are *also* statistically significant (Spicer 2022). A pronounced history of liberalism is thus neither necessary nor sufficient to fully explain whether a country has many or few large co-operatives today; New Zealand, for example, ranks among the leading countries with respect to the prevalence of large-scale co-operatives. New Zealand is an LME with a residual welfare state.

Beyond liberalism, the other factors known to matter to co-operative prevalence at scale are not surprising ones. They are clearly implied by the existing micro- and meso-scaled literature on co-operatives/mutuals, as reviewed earlier in this chapter. Co-operative enterprises seem to fare better when there is strong solidarity between members, due to either common social solidarity-generating traits and characteristics (such as a shared religion or race) or a common economic interest rooted in product homogeneity in certain industries (as with dairy farmers). Co-operatives also seem to spring up as a response to state or market failure, particularly in places that are small and remote, that is, distant, and therefore difficult for states and global markets to penetrate.[3]

---

[3] The evidence for federalism, statistically, is unclear, but conceptually there is good reason to suspect it plays a role: co-operatives struggle to scale across borders with unharmonized co-operative laws (Henry 2005, 2013), and in some federal countries, depending on how federalism is constructed, subnational jurisdictions may have distinctly different enterprise laws. Unlike with the IOF, where the profit motive serves to induce harmonization across states (Gomory and Sylla 2013), the co-operative does not benefit from such incentive. As examined in other research (Spicer 2022), U.S. co-operative lawyers and developers relayed countless instances of how this lack of harmonization harms their efforts, resulting in increased search and transaction costs for would-be co-operative entrepreneurs.

Thus we know certain factors—industry mix, social homogeneity, geographical remoteness, and comparative capitalist families—statistically correlate with current cross-national co-operative prevalence because of how they condition co-operatives' ability to survive and scale. And the net result of these factors, collectively, is a hostile operating environment for co-operatives in the United States today (Spicer 2022). What we do not know is *how, why, or how much* these factors have variably and causally mattered *over time* to affect co-operatives. Ideally, if one had time series for all enterprise types over two centuries, panel data models could be used to estimate these effects. But such data do not exist. Further, analyses from such nonexperimental, observational data are unlikely to definitively establish causality, as a raft of social science research has argued over the past two decades. What one can do, however, is interrogate these factors using a comparative-historical approach and examine how and why the co-operative movement and its organizational forms relationally developed to become either complementary or incongruent with institutional and policy environments in different contexts.

Case Selection and Overviews

To determine both how and why the United States came to have fewer large co-operatives than other rich democracies, and to build toward a more generalizable understanding of the conditions for sustained co-operative scale over time, I selected three cases of comparative national success to contrast to the United States: Finland, France, and New Zealand. This "central case with comparisons" approach,[4] not uncommon in small-n comparative case study research in sociology and political science, features a central case which is given a lengthier analytical treatment than the comparative cases (McDonnell 2020; Barkey 2008; Steinmetz 2005; Jensen and Malesky 2018; Thelen 2004; Hartz 1955, 1969).

Case justifications. Why these cases? To contrast to the United States, a relative "low activity" country where large co-operative enterprises are comparatively rarer, I chose three "high co-operative activity" countries, where large-scale co-operatives are relatively more common (though still rare). I therefore selected cases to compare to the United States on the dependent

---

[4] This term is borrowed from Thelen (written personal correspondence, 2021).

variable (density of large-scale co-operatives),[5] choosing "high" outcome cases from among the rich democracies, focusing on cases which are both "representative" and "anomalous" (Gerring and Cojocaru 2016; Gerring 2016). The cases are anomalous because they have achieved comparatively high levels of co-operative activity. But they have also traveled along different institutional pathways to that outcome, reflecting the variable presence of different causal traits.

Among the larger set of rich democracies, just three (Finland, France, and New Zealand) appear "high" across various descriptive measures of large co-operatives' extensiveness (Spicer 2022). These countries also exhibit variation across socioeconomic and political factors statistically demonstrated to have an association with the current variation in large-scale co-operative prevalence, making them ideal for the research question (Spicer 2022): their "capitalist family," that is, their dominant variety of capitalism and welfare regime (e.g., liberal vs. non-/less liberal); industry mix/economic homogeneity; social homogeneity/homophily; and geographic features such as remoteness and size. Finland is a CME with a social democratic welfare state; is small, far from global markets; and is comparatively socially homogeneous. Economically homogeneous, "basic needs" industries, such as agriculture, have long been overweight in its economy. In many ways, it is nearly a mirror image of the United States, presenting with different features across nearly all germane characteristics. New Zealand and France, however, are mixed cases in terms of their features. New Zealand, like the United States, is an LME with a residual welfare state. It is also an Anglo-American country, which, as another former British colony, shares additional similarities with the United States in its cultural, political, and economic institutions. But it is also small, fairly homogeneous, and distant from markets, with a high degree of global economic marginality stemming from its remoteness. France, like the United States, is one of the world's most diverse economies, with

---

[5] Such a research design might, on first glance, appear to violate the conventional wisdom that one should never select cases, particularly in "small N" qualitative studies examining an "extreme" outcome, on the dependent variable (Geddes 1990; King, Keohane, and Verba 1994). But the research questions asked in this study include a focus on an outlier outcome in one particular case: why the dependent variable (large-scale co-operative frequency) is so comparatively low in the United States. Dependent variable selection bias would be a potential problem if one selected other low-activity countries (e.g., United Kingdom, Australia) for comparison. This would not allow me to isolate variation across the posited causal dimensions. In this instance, proper application of the rule against dependent variable selection warrants selection of comparison cases high in the dependent variable but are otherwise similar (i.e., rich democracies), except across the various posited causal dimensions. This is precisely the approach I have taken.

advanced, multi-industry manufacturing and services sectors. It is not remote, occupying a central position in the global economy. It is socially, religiously, and racially diverse, like the United States. But France is a CME with a conservative welfare state. Notably, all these countries boast strong agricultural/natural resources sectors, and co-operatives are strong across them, as in the United States. Yet unlike the United States, co-operatives are strong in *other* key industries, demonstrating how industry effects, or any other single factor alone, do not explain co-operative strength (Spicer 2022). New Zealand and France, with their mixed features and high concentrations of large co-operatives, further affirm there is no single "smoking gun" cause.[6] Rather, it is the combined effect of causal characteristics which are likely explanatory. Of note, the United Kingdom is sometimes referenced throughout the book as a fifth "shadow" case (Soifer 2021) due to its high degree of similarity to the United States across several traits and due to its historic and historical role as a field progenitor: it was the birthplace of the modern co-operative movement, as well as many of its byproduct organizational forms and its native and preferred scaling strategy, as noted earlier.

Case dynamics today. Reflecting the various bases of structural difference reviewed above, the policy environment for co-operatives today in each country is also markedly different, as I have analyzed elsewhere (Spicer 2022). To summarize these dynamics (Table 2.3, based on Spicer 2022), though co-operatives in all four countries today have national meta-organizing "apex bodies" (effectively a national version of the global ICA) to advocate for them, co-operatives in the United States are comparatively constrained and restricted across all aspects of the business development and coordination process, from their ability to access debt and equity to accessing government procurement contracts and economic development loan and grant programs,

---

[6] Federalism, it must be noted, has been statistically tested as a correlate of co-operative prevalence at scale (Spicer 2022) and has yielded mixed results; it is also highly correlated with the LME category, making it difficult to statistically isolate its effects given the small-n problem when analyzing the rich democracies; there are also different varieties of federalism (Stepan 2001). No federal country ranks high across measures of large co-operatives' extensiveness, though Germany ranks as a "middling" case. Given significant changes to Germany's borders, and given unique effects of two world wars on its political economy, Germany introduces other factors which eliminate it as a strong case. Germany's federalism is also manifestly different from that of the United States, with regions often effectively playing a major role in national policy. We do know that inasmuch as federalism produces varying rules across jurisdictions, this creates costs for co-operative scale (Henry 2013). Furthermore, unlike with the IOF, there is no profit incentive to induce harmonization across jurisdictions of regulations which affect firms. Nonetheless, the case outcomes do not allow for selection of a "success" case which is federal, limiting my ability to test this as a causal factor over time. Where relevant and possible, however, I do note federal dynamics, particularly in the U.S. federal case, when they emerge as germane in co-operative historical development.

38   Co-operative Enterprise

Table 2.3 Comparative Co-operative Policy Features Today

Factor	United States National	United States State/Local	New Zealand	France	Finland
Comprehensive co-operative enabling statute		Limited	Yes	Yes	Yes
Pro-demutualization laws/policies	Yes	Yes	Partial		
Significant state action to mutualize assets/firms			Yes	Yes	Yes
Finance: easy access to nonmarket equity/external investment (e.g., from other co-operatives)			Yes	Yes	Yes
Finance: plentiful access to public and co-operative actor debt			Partial	Yes	Yes
Procurement: Co-operatives included in social clauses for government contracts		Limited		Yes	Partial
Co-operative-like restrictions imposed on IOFs				Yes	Yes

and associated administrative and technical support. Co-operatives in the United States are subject to state and national legislation which restricts the scale and scope of their activities, rather than enabling it, and have also been constrained by the development of antitrust legislation which has long limited co-operatives' preferred interfirm coordination strategy to achieve scale. Many subtypes of co-operatives also lack standardized enabling legislation across the states, with some states not offering much enabling legislation at all, thereby yielding transaction costs (including additional legal fees and model search costs) associated with the adoption of the model, undermining its diffusion and uptake. When U.S. co-operatives manage to be successful despite these constraints, they then must navigate policies which not only fail to restrict demutualization and conversion to the IOF form, as in some other countries, but which outright encourage such conversion via favorable tax treatment.

The net result of these restrictions and constraints is what institutional economists would call a "vicious cycle" rather than a "virtuous circle" for American cooperators (Figure 2.4). Having established these current dynamics in other research, the question now at hand is: How—and why and when—did this come to be?

Comparing Institutionalisms: Historical Institutionalism versus Field Theory

In developing a framework to analyze how the hypothesized causal factors manifested over time to yield such comparative cross-case differences today, traditions from two different "new institutionalist" (Hall and Taylor 1996) paradigms loom large: historical institutionalism, and strategic action field theory.

Historical institutionalism. This subvariant of new institutionalism (Thelen 1999)[7] has been used to examine temporal evolutions and trajectories among comparative capitalist and welfare regime families (Hall and Thelen 2009; Thelen 2014) and to trace the comparative development trajectories of different economic institutions more generally in different countries, with a focus on the role of the state (e.g., Thelen 2004, 2009; Hacker 2004; Martin and Swank 2012, Béland 2007; Emmenegger 2015; Van Der Heijden and Kuhlmann 2017). Given that part of what we wish to understand is how a particular type of institution—the co-operative enterprise model—came to be developed with varying degrees of state legitimation and support, HI would seem a promising framework to apply.

HI has created a vocabulary, developed through inductive application to actual cases, to describe how institutions comparatively evolve over time in different settings. HI emerged in part to critique the "punctuated equilibrium" model of institutional continuity and change, then dominant in political science and allied fields such as sociology, economics, and business/management scholarship, which presumed that "unsettled" and "abrupt" periods, or "critical junctures," were the primary driver of institutional change (Streeck and Thelen 2005; cf. Swidler 1986; Collier and Collier 1991). To state it crudely, the idea was that revolutions are, indeed, quite revolutionary, and are the principal way in which dramatic institutional change occurs. HI arose to counter this idea. Its creators showed that the comparative development of different institutions was driven by incremental, evolutionary changes rather than by abrupt shocks. These evolutionary shifts, which unfold across long periods of seeming stability, can cumulatively result in marked change, both in a single case over time and across institutional developmental paths and trajectories between cases. Further, these incremental changes are not causally independent from one another, but are linked: events along the path depend on the prior trajectory, or are "path dependent" (Arthur 1989), and can be subject

---

[7] HI, one of the three "new institutionalisms" (Hall and Taylor 1996) in the social sciences, is sometimes extended and referred to as comparative-historical analysis (Mahoney and Thelen 2015).

to "lock-in" along the path for long periods of time. Such postcritical juncture "lock-ins" to specific arrangements are followed by "policy feedbacks" which produce "increasing returns to scale" to a set of institutional arrangements (Pierson 2000; Katznelson, Skocpol, and Pierson, 2002). In evolving incrementally in this fashion, they set the stage for the next juncture, in which the "policy paradigm" can seemingly rapidly shift (Hall 1983, 1993).

Thelen has led a group of political scientists in detailing four such pathways through which evolutionary institutional and policy change unfold over time: drift, conversion, layering, displacement/exhaustion (for a review, see Van Der Heijden 2010; cf. Thelen 1999, 2004; Hacker 2004; Hacker, Pierson, and Thelen 2015; Mahoney and Thelen 2010, 2015; Schickler 2001; Orren and Skrowonek 2004).[8] Definitions of these four pathways are offered in Mahoney and Thelen (2010, 15–16). Building on Thelen's prior affirmation of North's (1990, 3) definition of institutions as the "rules of the game" which become a "shared script" (Thelen 1999) for actors, "layering" is defined as the introduction of new rules, on top of or alongside existing ones. "Conversion" occurs when existing rules are strategically redeployed, effectively altering them in practice. "Drift" describes the impact of changes in the external environment on existing rules, which are not updated to reflect new conditions. Finally, "displacement" removes existing rules via the introduction of new ones which supplant them.[9]

This literature also articulates a vocabulary to describe the environment in which such evolutionary processes occur: competing and discordant institutions operate in "political space" (Thelen 2000), where they can overlap and co-occur via institutional "intercurrence" (Orren and Skrowonek 1996, 2004). The implications and interinstitutional dynamics of intercurrence, however, are not fully developed in this literature. Similarly, beyond acknowledging that institutions typically have their origins through "forging coalitions and thus mobilizing various social and political actors in support of particular institutional configurations" (Thelen 2004, 31), how institutions do *or do not* emerge has not been fully developed in HI.

Related institutionalist scholarship, however, has attempted to extend theorization on this front in promising ways. Mair and Marti (2009, 422) showed that new institutional models can emerge through "institutional voids," situations where "institutional arrangements . . . are absent, weak, or fail to accomplish the role expected of them," which can be "an opportunity space for

---

[8] With respect specifically to policy evolution, Hacker (2004) distinguishes between these pathways based on implementation discretion and structural political constraints to change (e.g., veto points).
[9] Steinlin and Trampusch (2012) have suggested shrinkage as a fifth pathway, one which bears some similarity to displacement.

motivated entrepreneurs" who engage in forms of entrepreneurial and institutional bricolage (Mair and Marti 2009). Separately, Friedland and Alford (1991) and Thornton, Ocasio, and Lounsbury (2012) conceptualized the existence of institutional logics, which might explain the motivations for actors who drive evolution both within and across various institutional models and forms. This latter work, however, has not been effectively incorporated into HI, nor does it explain where such institutional logics come from, or how they relationally fit together with other relevant macro-social processes and structures. This, among other limitations, has become a source of critique for field theorists.[10]

Strategic action field theory. As developed by sociologists (Fligstein and McAdam 2011, 2012; Kluttz and Fligstein 2016; Scoville and Fligstein 2020), SAF (or simply "field theory")[11] takes a somewhat different approach than HI.

Born of a different "new institutionalist" school, that of sociological institutionalism (Hall and Taylor 1996), field theory is linked to a broader corpus of literature at the intersection of markets and movements, drawn from organizational studies, social movement studies, and various prior sociological efforts to define organizational fields (Fligstein and McAdam 2019; cf. DiMaggio and Powell 1983; Bourdieu 1990). In attempting to offer a more general and dynamic theory of social change and agency, Fligstein and McAdam (2012, 64) conceive of SAFs as "constructed social orders that define an arena," each with its own internal field logics, bounds, and practices. Fields may have different internal logics, but all are organized such that actors, beliefs, and rules matter to their members. As these authors note, "[I]n times of dramatic change, new ways of organizing 'cultural frames' or 'logics of action' come into existence. These are wielded by skilled social actors, sometimes called 'institutional entrepreneurs,' who come to innovate, propagate, and organize strategic action fields" (Fligstein and McAdam 2012 ,4). Frames and frame development are among the most widely studied social movement processes (Benford and Snow 2000) and also apply well to fields and institutions, which is one reason why Fligstein and McAdam describe field development as involving "movement-like" processes.

Beyond frame development, such field organizing efforts typically involve other movement-like or movement-based processes, such as resource mobilization, leveraging of cycles and opportunities, and strategic deployment of repertoires, tactics, and practices, which may include making demands on the state for legal or policy change (cf. McAdam 1982; McAdam, Tarrow, and Tilly

---

[10] Personal communication with Fligstein, May 2019; see also Kluttz and Fligstein (2016); Scoville and Fligstein (2020).
[11] There are different varieties of field theory (Barman 2016). SAF theory is the most recent comprehensive iteration and claims to remedy shortcomings of prior versions.

2001; Davis and Kim 2021). In so doing, although this has not always been explicitly stated by field theorists, it is presumed that they may also engage with and deploy other processes established by the literature on organizations and movements, from which field theory is drawn. For example, they may deploy the same multiscalar processes of "scale shift" as do movements, which typically begin organizing locally, before diffusing laterally or horizontally to other places, and subsequently scaling vertically to larger jurisdictions, such as provincial/state/regional, national, and the transnational or global scale (Soule 2013; Schneiberg and Soule 2005; McAdam, Tarrow, and Tilly 2001). They may also establish "organizational archetypes" (Greenwood and Hinings 1988, 1993) and "organizational repertoires" (Clemens 1993) through which to codify, institutionalize, and further diffuse and disseminate their approach. Finally, they may conceivably form what are called meta-organizations (Arne and Brunsson, 2005), or voluntary organizations of other organizations, to help them further institutionalize and develop into a field (Berkowitz and Dumez 2016).

After initially focusing on *intra*field dynamics, field theory has subsequently additionally articulated a grammar to conceptualize *inter*field relations, showing how new fields relationally emerge and subsequently evolve through specific agentic processes. As Fligstein and McAdam (2012, 18) noted in further developing their theory of fields, "Virtually all of the previous work on fields, however, focuses only on the internal workings of these orders, depicting them as largely self-contained, autonomous worlds." And yet today, when SAFs have been extensively developed and connected across our entire social world, change often emerges from the agency found in the relationship *between* existing fields: "The main theoretical implication of the interdependence of fields is that the broader field environment is a source of routine, rolling turbulence in modern society. A significant change in any given strategic action field is like a stone thrown in a still pond sending ripples outward to all proximate fields" (Fligstein and McAdam 2012,19). Specifically, fields can be hierarchically nested, like "Russian dolls" (19), and can also *overlap* (Evans and Kay 2008). Where fields relationally overlap, great change can be generated to both generate new fields, most often during periods of field rupture or crisis, as well as to drive evolution during periods of relative "field settlement."

Developing this grammar by articulating the "architecture of field overlap" (Fligstein 2001; Evans and Kay 2008; Spicer, Kay, and Ganz 2019), field theory has examined how specific individuals and entities can exert agency at the intersection of fields by using their relative position to effect change and outcomes. Skilled social actors from one field, for example, can encroach on, co-opt, or outright displace another field, resulting in conflict in the broader field environment between challenger and incumbent fields (Fligstein and

McAdam 2012, 2019; Spicer, Kay, and Ganz 2019). They can also take advantage of shifts in the field environment, which may create adjacent field openings (or voids), to construct new fields. This does not mean agents will necessarily successfully leverage these opportunities to effect change; structural opportunities are necessary, but not sufficient, conditions for change. Effective agents must leverage them, often making use of movement-like processes and practices to do so.

A field theory approach thus also seems promising for understanding co-operatives: the historical formation of co-operatives as a result of movements and movement-like processes is clear, as discussed earlier (e.g., Schneiberg, King, and Smith 2008; Schneiberg 2011). Co-operatives are both a business model and the product of a movement (Upright 2020), and it is the co-operative movement which has historically ultimately undergirded the development of most key organizational archetypes of co-operative business models: worker, consumer, producer, and hybrid variations of these. These forms also developed and emerged alongside of—and often in competition with—the other modern enterprise forms that have come to dominate economic life, most notably the IOF.

Comparison and application of SAF and HI to the co-operative case: Toward a theory of cooperation at scale. While SAF starts from a different vantage point and disciplinary tradition than HI, the two approaches nonetheless share many common traits. For reference purposes, Table 2.4 offers a general, comprehensive translation dictionary for use across the conceptual frameworks.[12] We can accordingly use any number of commensurate terms and concepts from these frameworks to understand how the factors which correlate with co-operative prevalence at scale today, as reviewed earlier, have emerged to condition how co-operative enterprise, as a field and as an institution, emerged and evolved over time. As the cases will variably show, these factors have acted not only to both undermine and enable the bases of solidarity which undergird the scaling and coordination mechanisms of co-operatives, but to shape the external field and institutional environment in which co-operatives operate.

Despite the seeming commensurability of HI and SAF, however, there are differences in their explanatory grammar, which will become more apparent through their joint application to the comparative co-operative cases. Such application, as the cases will show, suggests SAF may be both more

---

[12] Not all concepts in the dictionary will be of central importance or use in this book, as certain dynamics are more applicable than others to the co-operative case. As such, I do not discuss all the concepts shown in the dictionary. I offer them in the interest of comprehensiveness.

Table 2.4 Translating Conceptual Vocabularies: Historical Institutionalism and Strategic Action Field Theory

		Field Theory	Institutionalism
Intrafield Dynamics		movement-like process: scale-shift 　vertical 　horizontal	
		layering	layering
		drift	drift
		co-optation	conversion
		displacement/encroachment	displacement, shrinkage
Intrafield Elements		cultural frames	shared scripts/institutional logics
		logics	
		bounds	
		practices	
		skilled social actors	political actors; institutional entrepreneurs
Broader Dynamics and Traits		incumbents	incumbents*
		challengers	challenger coalitions*
		field rupture/crisis/ unsettled period	critical juncture/policy window
		field settlement	punctuated equilibrium
		field emergence	institutional origins/ emergence
		field overlap	intercurrence
		hybrid fields	institutional recombination and bricolage
		field architecture, field relations	institutional arrangements
		field environment	political space
		field opening	institutional void

Sources: Thelen (1999, 2004); Streeck and Thelen (2005); Orren and Skrowonek (2004); Pierson (2004); Hacker (2004); Schickler (2001); Fligstein and McAdam (2011, 2012); Grabher and Stark (1997); Mair and Marti (2009); Evans and Kay (2008); Hall (2016); Spicer, Kay, and Ganz (2019), Emmenegger (2021); Balsiger (2021); Steinlin and Trampusch (2012).
*HI scholars such as Emmenegger (2021) appear to now be borrowing these terms directly from Fligstein's work.

comprehensive and flexible than HI, as its creators have claimed (Scoville and Fligstein 2020).

Institutionalism is, to be sure, a powerful analytical tool. As applied to co-operatives, HI's framework can help describe how different macro- and meso-level structural factors, such as those reviewed earlier in this chapter, manifested over time and influenced institutional and policy development paths for co-operatives in different country contexts. It can also perhaps help us understand how individual institutional models like the co-operative evolve over time, both through incremental changes that occur over long periods of "punctuated equilibrium" and the periodic "critical junctures" which interrupt and reset these long periods. By incorporating related and extended work in institutionalism, we might also start to conceptualize how or why co-operatives emerged when they did in these different countries; as the "success" cases will show, national co-operative movements were initially able to leverage "institutional voids" to construct a robust co-operative sector better than did their counterparts in the United States.

But the HI approach, even when extended to encompass relevant insights like those of Mair and Marti's (2009) on institutional voids and bricolage, has significant limits. It does not offer a fully developed, dynamic model of interinstitutional change. That is, its proponents have not developed a well-articulated grammar or syntax to enable comprehensive understanding of how institutions overlap, relate, and change together in response to their contexts, or why institutions may—*or may not*—develop at all. Given how and why HI was developed—in response to a mechanistic model of punctuated equilibria as the key driver of change in existing political institutions—such limits are not surprising. These limits may inhibit our ability to construct as compelling an explanation to the co-operative question using HI, as subsequent chapters will show and as I will synthesize and review in the concluding chapter.

Nonetheless, the two frameworks can begin to help us move toward building and testing a theory of cooperation at scale: we can systematically examine how co-operatives can achieve widespread prevalence at scale by organizing as a field or institution. Based on the various literatures reviewed above, this process will likely involve the development of a stable, organizational archetype—the co-operative model itself—based on a shared script and institutional logic. It will also require repeated, successful implementations of that archetype in practice and promotion of its diffusion across different domains into varying industries, populations, and areas. Its successful implementation will likely require that its adherents deploy shared cognitive or cultural frames as part of their shared script, so as to help animate solidaristic bonds between co-operative members as a generative substitute for the profit motive. It will also likely require a field opening or institutional void in the organizational environment, which adherents of the co-operative model can use to conduct these activities, so as to develop the model to scale. Finally, such institutional or field development will accordingly also likely involve coordinating these successful implementations across supply chains, industries, and areas, and further involve coordinated meta-organizing by advocates to achieve appropriate enabling policies from the state. By "appropriate enabling policies," I mean those which respect the archetypal form's purpose and logic and affirm its operating organizational definitions, rules, and bounds.

The presence or absence of the relevant conditioning factors in the institutional or field environment may variably undermine or advance these various processes. For example, the greater presence of industries with a high degree of economic homogeneity, which reduces the costs of economic democracy and cooperation among firm members, may yield a more fruitful environment for co-operatives to achieve scale. A more socially homogeneous population may advance such efforts as well, easing the co-operatives' ability to generate frames which animate solidaristic bonds. Similarly, the greater presence of liberal institutional arrangements may undermine co-operatives' ability to individually develop and collectively coordinate to scale, as reviewed above, while geographic features, such as small size and remoteness, may also play a conditioning role.

Method: Process Tracing a Field, or Field Tracing

To determine if field theory enables better explanation, I apply both frameworks to the comparative cases using a form of process tracing, which is an established method deployed in comparative-historical work (Bennett and Checkel 2014). I further develop a variant of this method, which elsewhere I have referred to as field tracing (Spicer, Kay, and Ganz 2019).

Process tracing bears some resemblance to other multicase comparative analytical approaches associated with institutionalists, such as "contextualized comparisons" (Locke and Thelen 1995). The method's roots in political science and sociology date back to the late 1970s, to the work of Stanford political scientist Alexander George (1979; George and Bennett 2005). Originally applied to micro-level phenomena by George, who studied political psychology, it has subsequently been applied to macro-level phenomena. As defined by Bennett and Checkel (2014, 7), process tracing

> refers to the examination of intermediate steps in a process to make inferences about hypotheses on how that process took place and whether and how it generated the outcome of interest. In previous work together with George, one of us defined process tracing as the use of "histories, archival documents,

interview transcripts, and other sources to see whether the causal process a theory hypothesizes or implies in a case is in fact evident in the sequence and values of the intervening variables in that case" (George and Bennett 2005: 6). We added that "the process-tracing method attempts to identify the intervening causal process—the causal chain and causal mechanism—between an independent variable (or variables) and the outcome of the dependent variable" (ibid.: 206).

Such an approach requires an extraordinarily large amount of information (Bennett and Checkel 2014), but "by analyzing process-level evidence on causal mechanisms, process tracing can claim, in principle, to increase the internal validity of causal inferences dramatically and thereby strengthen our causal interpretations of both single case studies and studies based on co-variation" (Schimmelfennig 2014, 102). In outcome-based process tracing (Beach 2017), the focus is on identifying the causes of a specific outcome. Field tracing (Spicer, Kay, and Ganz 2019) is simply a subvariant of this type of process tracing, which applies this general approach to trace the causes which might explain an outcome in the development of a field, either in a single case or comparatively across multiple cases.

By using this approach to trace the co-operative field's comparative-historical development across the four case countries, I thus seek to enable both within-case and cross-case comparison (Mahoney and Thelen 2015; Gerring 2016) and generate both case-specific and generalizable insights about the causes of differences in outcomes in comparative co-operative development. Relying on primary and secondary source historical documents (N = 1,186) and interview transcripts (N = 173),[13] which were fixed-coded (Allen 2017) to capture the various potential causal factors identified as germane in existing literature (capitalist family, industry mix/economic homogeneity, social homogeneity/homophily, and geography), I trace how and why a comparatively more enabling environment for co-operatives developed in the success cases, from the mid-1800s forward, when the modern co-operative model was first institutionalized in stable form, largely in the United Kingdom, whence it diffused around the globe (Wilson, Webster, and Vorberg-Rugh 2014). I then trace how in the United States a comparatively hostile and restrictive field environment came to develop over time. In the comparative field tracings, consistent with the process tracing approaches reviewed above, I examined evidence which might indicate how or if the

---

[13] Interviews were conducted from a purposive, stratified sample of all relevant classes of co-operative stakeholders across the case countries, with materials from more than 30 physical libraries and archives across seven countries; countless digital collections were also utilized.

presence or absence of the posited macro-scaled causal dimensions (which have been statistically associated as germane to co-operatives' meso-scaled systemic development to scale, as reviewed earlier in this chapter) might have influenced co-operatives' institutional development.

In selecting interviewees, I engaged in purposive sampling of key strata of stakeholders and participants in the co-operative field (e.g., different types and industries of co-operatives, large and small businesses, failed and successful co-operatives, local and national government officials, co-operative apex organizations). To achieve this coverage, I arranged interviews clustered in "high-activity" regions (as affirmed by statistical data analyzed in Spicer 2022 and by the historical record) in all four countries. Using semi-structured interviews, I questioned participants on what they believed to be the most critical issues to achieving lasting scale in their respective co-operative systems. In all four country cases, interviewees additionally alerted me to the existence of policies and field environment features which I otherwise would not have identified via document analysis or archival research alone. Individual formal interviews were supplemented by participant-observation ethnographic data and informal interviews at global and/or international co-operative sector events held in Québec and New York, as well as within-country, local co-operative events held in Paris, Wellington (New Zealand), Boston, New York, and Oakland (California).

In the United States, interviewees (N = 87) were selected across three regions, established by other research as "high-activity" regions (Spicer 2020; Jackall and Levin 1984) to allow maximum coverage of both national and state/local co-operative actors, as well as account for the diffuse and multipolar/regional structure of the U.S. economy: the Northeast Corridor, focused on Boston, New York, and Washington, D.C. (the D.C. area containing many national representatives); the San Francisco Bay Area in Northern California; and the Upper Midwestern regions of Minneapolis–St. Paul (Minnesota) and Madison (Wisconsin), as the two neighboring states have a shared co-operative history. A small number of interviews in all three regions were conducted in Spanish or mixed English-Spanish (Spanglish), but most were conducted in English. In France, in-person interviews centered on the Paris region (N = 25), which dominates national economic, political, cultural activity in general. Of note, interviews in France were mostly conducted in French, with some in "Franglais," a mix of the languages, and very few in English. A small number (N = 7) of additional supplemental interviews were conducted with nationally prominent co-operative actors in Rennes, Lille, and Lyon. I manually completed the English translations of French interviews and French historical document source materials; any errors in these translations are my own. In Finland, interviews (N = 23) were clustered in the greater Helsinki region, which accounts for nearly one-fourth of the national population. A small number of supplemental interviews were conducted in two cities outside of the Helsinki region, Tampere and Turku, which are also part of the "six-aiki," Finland's six largest cities (three of which are in the Helsinki region—the cities of Helsinki, Espoo, and Vantaa), with national coverage thus achieved via interviews in five of the six principal cities. All interviews in Finland were in English. In New Zealand, the Auckland region accounts for roughly one-third of the national population and is the business center of the country, while the national government is based in the second largest region, Wellington, which is also on the North Island. Christchurch is the third largest region and the hub of economic activity on New Zealand's South Island. Given the dispersion of actors across these regions, interviews were conducted in all three (N = 26), which combined account for more than half of New Zealand's population.

Additional information on interviewee coverage is included in the appendix, as is information on the various archives (N = 37) consulted in person; many co-operative ephemera and historical documents have not been digitized, nor are they available digitally. Before proceeding to the historical analysis of the central U.S. case, I first cover the comparative success cases, beginning with Finland, the rich democracy with the greatest prevalence of large-scale co-operative enterprise.

3
Finland, the Co-operative Commonwealth?

> We have no Rockefellers or Carnegies . . . but we have co-operatives.
> —A. I. Virtanen, 1939, Finnish Nobel laureate in chemistry
> (quoted in Kuisma, Wynne-Ellis, and Pellervo-Seura 1999)

As I sat guardedly enjoying my soft-serve vanilla cone at the end of Helsinki's Esplanadi Park, I looked up to witness what had already become a familiar sight: seagulls dive-bombing an American tourist couple's ice cream. Though the spot was a draw for visitors, it also appealed to locals, and after several battles with Helsinki's highly aggressive and hungry seagulls, I had learned to immediately cover my ice cream, just as the locals did, to guard against surprise attacks from above. "That's why we are all covering our ice cream," I said to the couple. They went back for two more cones, then came and sat next to me, perhaps drawn by the familiarity of my North American accent. "I've never seen such aggressive seagulls! They weren't like this in the other Scandinavian countries!" said the couple, who had disembarked from a cruise ship docked for the day.

During my time in the country, I quickly became accustomed to hearing tourists refer to Finland as a Scandinavian country. Scandinavian countries are often associated with democratic socialism and a more enlightened form of capitalism (Sanders 2016; Lakey 2016), often called a "cuddlier" capitalism (Thelen 2012, 8), consistent with classifications of their economies as operating with a robust, universalistic state welfare regime (in Esping-Andersen's 1990, 1999 Worlds of Welfare Capitalism framework), which in turn complements their coordinated market economy model (Hall and Soskice 2001), as reviewed in the previous chapter. Given this reputation, it perhaps is no surprise that Finland has more large co-operatives per capita than any other high-income democracy, including its Scandinavian neighbors.

Technically, however, Finland itself is not Scandinavian. I weighed how to say this to the tourists, hoping I didn't sound like some pedant who starts every sentence with "Well, *actually.*" The best I could muster was "Well, you are not in a Scandinavian country," eliciting a confused look from the Americans. "You are in Finland. Finland is not Scandinavian," I clarified. My eyes met those of a local woman sitting across from me on the Esplanadi. She approvingly smiled at my gentle corrective. (Most Finns speak better English than I do, and it is my native tongue.) Scandinavia, a term first popularized by the 19th-century pan-Scandinavian movement (Kirby 2006), encompasses the three Germanic-language kingdoms of Denmark, Sweden, and Norway, which share a common root tongue and have a tightly conjoined political history. I explained to the couple that Finland is *Nordic*, a broader term which encompasses the Scandinavian countries, as well as Finland, Iceland, and the Faroe Islands. But Finland stands apart from Scandinavia, a point often lost on visitors, and its distinctive identity matters in understanding the historical source of its co-operatives' strength.

Finland is also not a "mixed" case with respect to the presence of features posited to enable or inhibit co-operative development at scale. It is a nearly "perfect" case, the mirror image of the United States. It possesses only pro-co-operative features, at least with respect to the structural traits identified in prior research as enabling cooperation at scale, reviewed in Chapter 2. It is a small, geographically and oftentimes politically isolated country, distant from world markets. Its factor endowments have supported economic strength and advantage in readily co-operativized industries, such as natural resource industries and export-oriented agriculture. Finland operates with comparative capitalism archetypes which are institutionally more congruent with the co-operative model, having developed a CME with a robust, social-democratic welfare state, setting a "high floor" to constrain enterprises and support labor, and creating a more level playing field for all enterprise types, while having normalized the types of interfirm coordination mechanisms that co-operatives rely on to scale. And finally, it has a high degree of social homogeneity and homophily, as it is populated by a people whose national identity has historically activated a strong sense of social solidarity, reflecting historical marginalization and oppression over centuries by different neighboring foreign powers who shared neither their language nor their heritage.

Given these traits, it is perhaps not surprising that if any country can lay claim to having successfully built a "co-operative commonwealth" and a robust co-operative ecosystem, disproving Naomi Klein's claim that the dream of co-operatives has never been tried, it is Finland. Even today, one can stay in a co-operatively owned hotel, shop only at co-operatively owned grocery stores and department stores, eat out and grab a pint only at co-operatively owned restaurants and pubs, and eat co-operatively grown food at home, in a house made with co-operatively processed lumber, while listening to music produced by co-operative artists, paying for it all using a co-operative bank account and co-operatively owned investment funds (Figure 3.1).

Yet even here, in the "perfect case" for national cooperation at scale, the co-operative model's success cannot be fully understood through a mechanistic

Figure 3.1 Helsinki's consumer co-operatives. North, east, and west around Helsinki's main center and rail station, you find anchor businesses like the sleek Radisson Blu hotel (bottom left), a branch and prominent signage of OP bank (bottom right) which is Finland's largest domestic financial institution, and SOK's Sokos Department store, restaurant, and hotel complex, which includes the flagship Marks & Spencer. All of these businesses are consumer-owned Finnish co-operatives, whose profits go to their user-owners. Only in Finland are Radisson and Marks & Spencer operated as co-operatives. Photos by the author.

analysis of the pro-co-operative factors present. Instead, it requires a historical and temporal grounding, which reveals how these factors came together to produce a "big bang" moment during the co-operative movement's initial development in Finland. Such grounding is also necessary to understand why, in what would seem to otherwise be extremely fertile soil for the co-operative model, co-operatives have faced obstacles and setbacks here. Its take-up and use are still limited in some key areas, with fewer large worker co-operatives, though they are generally rarer at scale in other countries, too. In some industries, co-operatives have also experienced a long-term decline, as this chapter will detail.

Still, Finland today has more large co-operative enterprises than any other rich democracy on earth, normalized for the nation's size. How and why did this come to be? The answer reveals how and why field theory can help enable compelling explanations. While HI can describe how Finnish co-operative policy evolved with changing conditions over the 20th century, it does not help us understand how and why the co-operative movement became so powerful to begin with and remained so, thereby enabling it to secure accommodative policy change. Nor does it explain why the movement initially developed and organized so rapidly in the particular moment that it did. Extending HI by applying other institutionalists' work on "institutional voids" (Mair and Marti 2009) partly remedies this issue, but still does not quite do the job. Field theory, however, enables us to answer these questions, identifying the solidarity mechanisms co-operatives leveraged to occupy these voids, while also helping identify the underlying factors that shaped the evolutionary changes to the co-operative field over the longue durée.

It is difficult to overstate the role that the co-operative movement played in establishing Finland as a modern political and economic entity, and more broadly in stabilizing and developing its national economy during the 20th century. Over the century, Finland went from having a GDP per capita less than half that of Britain or Sweden, to being nearly on par with them (Ojala, Eloranta, and Jalava 2006), the outcome of a development process in which co-operatives played a pivotal economic and political role.

Between 1899, when Russia attempted to revoke the Grand Duchy of Finland's self-rule, and 1917, when Finland successfully declared independence in the wake of the Russian Revolution, Finland went from having almost no co-operatives to having more than most any other country (Parker and Cowan 1944). The pace of co-operative development over these two short decades was rapid and stunning. How and why did this come to be? At first glance, Finnish co-operatives' origin story would seem to be consistent with the very thinking about revolution that HI scholarship arose to critique, as noted in Chapter 2. HI critiqued the notion that "critical junctures" and revolution alone yield extraordinary and lasting institutional change. A field theory reading, however, reveals a more nuanced story, one that is still consistent with HI's evolutionary approach, while going beyond it. Field theory exposes a prejunctural institutional and field environment which was ideally suited for the co-operative to enter and thrive in. Unlike the United States, unencumbered by neither a well-developed population of IOFs nor by a racialized economic and social system which undermined social solidarity, Finland's co-operative advocates were able to leverage the emergent political force of national social solidarity to economically organize and to procure robust political support for co-operative enterprise at a pivotal moment in time: the moment of Finnish political independence.

As a poor, underdeveloped territory that had been colonially occupied and dominated for centuries by Sweden and Russia, Finland's fledgling co-operative movement faced few competitors or well-established incumbents in its field environment from other modern enterprise forms in the final years of its suzerainty at the fin de siècle. Consistent with its political and economic underdevelopment at this time, competing organizational models like the joint stock corporation/IOF were limited in their development and strength. Unlike France—where revolutions yielded a destabilizing field rupture in a comparatively more well-developed economy, creating new field openings or "institutional voids" (Mair and Marti 2009) for challenger organizational forms to leverage—in Finland there was less, economically, to be destabilized or ruptured by the Finnish fight for independence to begin with. The field environment of private economic organizational models was poorly developed and sparsely populated. The co-operative model was able to claim and establish strong occupancy of the voids in this underdeveloped field space. How?

Reflecting the co-operative's nature as a hybrid field, which combines logics from the first-order fields of both civil society and the economy/market, pro-co-operative skilled social actors established a central role for the model in the Finnish nationalist Fennomen movement (Figure 3.2). They did so by connecting co-operative organizing to an emergent, nationally based social solidarity, thereby enabling the direction and application of this emergent social solidarity into an action-oriented economic and political consciousness to procure independence, with the co-operative as its institutional vessel. In Finland, the co-operative thus became a critical, and arguably central, tool in the Grand Duchy's achievement of formal political and economic independence from Russia in 1917. By building and owning co-operatives, the Finns could control the local economy and, with it, their political destiny. Legally enabling such co-operatives, and constructing an organizational system for them, was among the first actions political leaders undertook as they attempted to establish their independence.

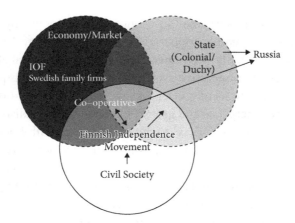

Figure 3.2 Finnish co-operatives—field environment, 1900.

With the onset of the Cold War, however, the field environment shifted, as the Soviet Union emerged to assert a degree of dominance over Finland in matters of foreign policy and trade; Finland would thus come to have a partially closed economy in this era, at least with respect to these two functional domains. During this period, at the height of Finnish co-operatives' strength, co-operative-enabling legislation was repeatedly updated and amended (consistent with HI's concept of layering, which, as reviewed in Chapter 2, also applies to fields). But why did this layering occur? What motivated and sustained the solidarity underlying Finnish co-operatives? Geography and geopolitics offer an answer. Finland may have been influenced by the Soviets in this era, but it nonetheless remained an independent democracy with economic and diplomatic ties to the West, which it also physically abutted. Co-operatives, as a middle way between the LME-style capitalism of the United States and United Kingdom and the state collectivism of the Soviets, helped defensively secure a domestically and "locally" controlled, financed, and owned economic base. They assured the nation's continued independence, delicately balancing on the geographical edge of the Iron Curtain. As such, their continued health was of great political and economic importance in this era, assuring their continued relevance to citizens, and providing impetus to update the laws governing them.

When the Cold War ended and Finland integrated into the EU and adopted the euro, however, co-operatives and the overall economy faced "modernization" (i.e., liberalization) and restructuring in what was effectively another period of field destabilization. The role of large co-operatives accordingly declined, as some demutualized and converted to IOFs, were sold in bankruptcy, or were surpassed in economic prominence by new entities, typically IOFs, in less readily cooperativized industries (e.g., Nokia, the telecommunications firm). Many co-operatives' explicitly political elements were also lost in this era. Co-operative evolution and history in this period is thus consistent with HI notions of conversion, as well as with field displacement, resulting from the emergence and growth of economic liberalism via EU integration and the growth of IOFs. Co-operatives' battles with liberalism in this era also reveals another value of adopting a field theory approach. The clash between the CME-congruent coordination approach of co-operatives and the LME-style approach of IOFs during the period of EU integration shows how the arrangements of multiple comparative capitalism archetypes can exist side by side in a given context, as embodied through the prevailing mix of firm types, their comparative and relational dominance shifting over time. A field theory lens thus suggests that LME and CME archetypes can be understood as embodying two particular field configurations in the economy, which reflect varying degrees of IOF dominance over other firm types, including the co-operative.

Nonetheless, today Finland remains the most co-operative-dense, high-income democratic nation on earth. Its producer, consumer, worker, and hybrid co-operatives play substantive roles in the markets for banking, insurance, healthcare/hospitals, grocery/retail, hotels and hospitality, agriculture, natural resources, utilities, housing, student employment, and the arts. In the 2020s, as its neighbor Russia again asserted itself on the global political stage, co-operatives appeared to be playing a new institutional role in the economy, performing a "globalization insurance" function, the importance of which has only been heightened by the supply-chain disruptions generated by the COVID-19 crisis, and as the value of domestic control over enterprise in key industries again becomes clear. In the remainder of the chapter, I trace the origin story and subsequent field evolution of the Finnish co-operative movement in greater detail, from the period preceding Finnish independence through World War II; the Cold War and through the fall of the Soviet Union; and through the current era of EU-Finnish integration and the return of Russia as a political threat.

Co-operatives as an Offensive Strategy in Finnish Nation-Building, 1800s–1945

As noted, Finland has a distinct and separate socioeconomic, cultural, and political heritage from other Nordic countries. Its language is not descendant from their shared Germanic Old Norse tongue, either. Finnish is not even Indo-European, a category which includes almost all other European languages, from Russian to English to the Romance languages, as well as Hindi, Urdu, Bengali, and Farsi. Finnish is in the completely separate Uralic family of languages, alongside Hungarian, Estonian, and various lesser-spoken languages of ethnic minorities in northern Russia. None of these languages was historically spoken on the land masses physically adjacent to Finland. Finns are arguably not even genetically linked to other Europeans: a recent global study on genetic populations, published in *Nature* (Lek et al. 2016), divided world populations into genetic "families" and partitioned the European population into "Finns" and "Non-Finns." This is because the Finns are not closely genetically related to the rest of the modern European population.

Why does this matter? Co-operatives often rely on social solidarity as a generative substitute for the profit motive. Finns, who have a distinct social identity consistent with their genetic and linguistic isolation from their historical neighbors, possess a long-standing and deeply rooted social solidarity on which to base cooperation. Much like the Basque region of Spain, whose solidarity in the face of historical oppression has undergirded the Mondragon co-operative system (Whyte and Whyte 1991), as well the highly co-operative and similarly marginalized Québécois (Lévesque cited in Bouchard 2013), the Finnish people have long stood alone and apart, in tension with their neighbors. For more than a millennium, the Finns have been surrounded to the east (Russia), south (Germanic), and west (Scandinavian nations) by peoples with a markedly different heritage, peoples who forcibly occupied and colonially controlled Finland for much of its settled history. These groups also shaped the historical field context which would enable the rise of the co-operative model in Finland at the dawn of the 20th century.

Finland in the age of empire: Prefacing the emergence of the co-operative movement. As compared with most other countries classified today as rich democracies, Finland's modern economic and political institutions were not well developed by the late 19th century, after centuries of Swedish and Russian occupation.

The Swedes had occupied southwest Finland (where most of the nation's population and economic activity is still concentrated) from the Northern Crusades through the Middle Ages. From the 1300s onward, a small, Swedish-speaking minority controlled the Finns' historical territory. Economically, through both the Kalmar Union (Danish-Swedish crown) and Swedish Empire periods, Finland had been free from many traditional European feudal economic arrangements or Russian-style serfdom. But this is not to say that standards of living were high. While a significant minority of Finnish farmers owned homesteads, most land and other resources were controlled by Swedish nobles and merchants (Skrubbeltrang 1964), who imposed high taxes. To economically provide for themselves, Finns often relied on *talkoot*. A word borrowed from Sweden but virtually unknown and unused by Swedes today, *talkoot* refers to the tradition of Finnish peasants engaging in shared communal work in rural villages, and embodies a premodern form of cooperation which presages the institutional development of the co-operative. While interviewees I spoke with often mentioned this concept, such traditions are not unique to Finland. They appear everywhere, from America's pioneer communities' spirit of "circling the wagons" and related tradition of rural cooperation, to New Zealanders' related cultural trope of the Number Eight Wire (see Chapter 5).

Finns also had only limited political control throughout the Swedish Empire's reign, achieved at varying times either locally through the Riksdag (Diet or Parliament) of Helsinki, held from 1616 forward, or via limited direct representation in Stockholm (Kirby 2006). Sweden finally ceded Finland to Russia in the Napoleonic Wars, in 1809, concluding a long period of wars between the two powers which had decimated the Finnish population. Mindful of the ongoing political revolutions throughout the Western World in the 19th century, Russia initially allowed Finland comparatively more political autonomy (Kirby 2006) in its domestic affairs, but through bureaucratic, not democratic, means. Upon assuming control of Finland from the Swedes, the Russians dismissed the Riksdag of Finland in 1809 and did not assemble a Diet or new legislative body until 1863, with an appointed Senate of Finns administering the nation instead.

But as the fledgling Fennoman nationalist movement took hold and Russia lost the Crimean War, Russia's position with respect to Finland changed. It began to exert more control over Finland, with the goals of increasing its economic development and improving its political integration with Russia (Kirby 2006). In 1864, the Finnish Diet was finally reinstated, and regularly assembled thereafter. It soon passed legislation to empower joint-stock companies, which previously had not been authorized; most enterprises had been held by individuals or families (Ojala, Eloranta, and Jalava 2006), who led small industrial enterprises or larger forestry-related businesses. Forestry and lumber were by then already leading industries and commodities, well on their way to becoming Finland's "green gold" (Ojala, Eloranta, and Jalava 2006). Finland was thus not only comparatively late in industrializing; even more so than France, it was also late in enabling the IOF as a legal form, which accordingly was still limited in prevalence in the late 19th century (Ojala, Eloranta, and Jalava 2006).

Meanwhile, Finnish identity continued to evolve to center an oppositional stance which focused on the Russians rather than the Swedes. By the late 1860s, the Fennoman movement was well formed, its adversarial, nationalist ethos embodied by an adage that achieved long-standing cultural recognition: "Swedes we are no longer, Russians we do not want to become, let us therefore be Finns," attributed jointly to the Fennoman movement leaders Arwiddson and Snellman (Tarkiainen, cited in Klinge 2003).

The movement was not merely a cultural one; it also stoked a nascent Finnish political and economic consciousness. Though peasants had enjoyed mixed land access and ownership rights, control over the land and the economy had remained largely concentrated in the hands of the crown, the church, and the Swedish-speaking noble and merchant classes (Kirby 2006; Skrubbeltrang 1964). Political representation in the Diet in this period was still based on the legacy Swedish "four estates" system, which by then had been largely abandoned in Sweden, as had corollary feudal political systems elsewhere in Europe. Political parties had thus not yet effectively been developed in Finland, in contrast to much of the rest of Europe.

Nonetheless, the Finnish "agrarian question" and "labor question," as in the other cases examined in this book, yielded a strong nascent farmers' movement. The landless, agrarian laboring population, which had increasingly migrated to cities like Helsinki, also supported the burgeoning labor movement. Given their comparatively later timing, these movements in Finland drew on the social movement and organizing experiences occurring in the rest of Europe (Kirby 2006). In the face of harsh conditions in Finland, emigration to the United States was strong and was often supported by many in the Finnish labor movement (Jalkanen 1969), yielding significant migration flows which would continue through the early 20th century (giving rise to a strong Finnish-American co-operative movement in New York and the Upper Midwest; see Chapter 7; cf. Alanen 1975; Kercher, Kebker, and Leland 1941; Rodgers, Petersen, and Sanderson 2016).

Connected to Finland's nationalist and labor movements was a fledgling interest in co-operatives. As early as 1860, a Rochdale-style co-operative store was planned in Helingsfors (today, Helsinki), but it was never founded; a few rural co-operative stores were created in the 1870s but did not last long (Gebhard 1916). Several co-operative dairies were also founded in the 1880s and 1890s. There was not, however, any organized or systematic effort to develop co-operatives throughout Finland at this time, one of many ways Finland's economy lagged behind those in Western Europe. Indeed, by the end of the 19th century, though signs of urban development and industrialization were beginning to appear, the nation remained largely agricultural, with a subsistence economy. Hjerppe and Pikhala (1977), in producing the first historical estimates of Finnish GDP by sector, found that Finland was effectively 40 years behind neighboring Sweden in its development, and GDP per capita, as noted earlier, was far below that of most European countries and the United States. Large, joint-stock company employers, which, as noted above, were comparatively new, remained fairly uncommon, with the limited number of industrial enterprises in existence typically owned by families of merchants and Swedish nobles (Ojala, Eloranta, and Jalava 2006). This is in sharp contrast to the U.S. case, where, as I will show in Chapter 6, joint-stock companies were well developed (Gomory and Sylla 2013; Sylla and Wright 2013) and organized (Voss 1993) by the time both industrialization and the modern co-operative movement emerged, a factor which played a role in the demise of the pro-co-operative Knights of Labor there (Voss 1993).

Of course, for an institutional innovation like the co-operative to take root, it is not enough to simply have fallow ground, through the existence, for example, of significant field/institutional voids. This is necessary, but not sufficient. The ground must also be fertilized and sown; skilled social actors must take advantage of the opening in the field environment to construct a new domain of action. In Finland, there is no question who these skilled social actors initially were: the married couple of Hannes and Hedvig Gebhard, who were not only the founders of the modern Finnish co-operative movement but were towering figures in Finnish independence and national politics, writ large.

The Gebhards had traveled to Europe, where they learned of co-operatives (Hilson 2017), and Hannes produced a study on the model and its potential application to Finland in 1899. This came on the heels of an 1898 Finnish translation of a book on co-operatives by Axel Granstrom, then secretary of the Board of Industry and Trade in Finland (Marshall 1958). Tireless as co-operative advocates, intellectuals, organizers, politicians, and historians, in founding the Finnish co-operative movement and its apex organization, Pellervo, the Gebhards took advantage of Finland's late development and turned it into an asset. Rather than flounder through rounds of failed institutional experimentations in the dark, as even the early British cooperators had, the Finns were able to draw on the successes of the movement elsewhere and synthesize lessons from its experiments, acting as institutional or field bricoleurs. They imported and skillfully combined the best ideas from various European co-operative movements, particularly those of the Irish agricultural co-operatives and its apex organization (Gebhard 1916), as well as the federating approaches of the Raiffeisen banking co-operatives of Germany. And when the political opportunity arose to put their co-operative development plan into action, they struck.

The co-operative big bang: 1899–1917. In the face of rising agrarian, nationalist, and labor movements, and in response to concerns over a possible German invasion of Russia via Finland, in 1899 Tsar Nicholas II issued the

February Manifesto (Jussila 1984), which began a series of "Russification" measures that dramatically reduced Finland's political autonomy (Kirby 2006). This single decree would set into motion events which would animate not only the co-operative movement but the larger movement to achieve national independence. In the wake of the February Manifesto, the authority of the Finnish Senate was restricted vis-à-vis the Tsarist governor, Russian became the official language, and mandatory military conscription measures were introduced.

These policies directly activated the solidarity of the Finnish people, yielding a swift and united response: despite the existence of historically typical class cleavages between farmers, workers, and the fledging bourgeois class, the Finns organized a comprehensive resistance movement, which included the nation's first political parties, newly formed (Kirby 2006).

Also in direct response to the February 1899 Manifesto (Gebhard 1916), in that same year, the Pellervo-Seura (Pellervo Society) was created, the central coordinating apex organization for the co-operative movement in Finland, as a means by which to advance the standard of living and economic independence for the Finnish people as a *nation* (Gebhard 1916). The name "Pellervo" itself reflects the nationalistic roots of the co-operative movement: Pellervo is the god of fertility, the forests, and agriculture in Finnish mythology and in the *Kalevela*, the national epic poem of Finland written in 1849, and a key work in the Fennoman nationalist movement. The Pellervo Society thus sought to effect the national economic independence advocated by Snellman, a founder of the Fennoman nationalist movement and the Finnish political party in the mid-19th century (Skurnik 2002).

Unlike the other case countries, where a co-operative apex organization eventually followed the creation and development of co-operatives from the bottom up, in Finland it was the reverse. Pellervo was founded first and proactively constructed the co-operative ecosystem from the top down. This was strategic and intentional. Hannes Gebhard, in providing an account of their work, noted that Finns were predominantly either landless or a smallholding agrarian people, geographically spread out and isolated from one another. Coupled with the nationalist concerns regarding economic and political independence, the co-operative model seemed ideally suited in these conditions as a way for Finns to coordinate and pool their economic activity for mutual gain (Gebhard 1916). Having learned from the experiences of other national co-operative movements, their efforts were systematic from the start, with explicit plans for three pillars of co-operative development (Simonen 1949; Skurnik 2002): a federated model of organizing co-operatives into larger co-operatives, a comprehensive national legislative framework, and a central ideological/educational umbrella organization.

Led by Pellervo and the Gebhards, this systematic approach to building a co-operative ecosystem spread through Finland's economy, with a "co-operative commonwealth" developing at an unparalleled and breathtaking pace. After founding Pellervo in 1899, the Gebhards immediately worked with members of the Finnish Diet to pass a law in the newly restrictive, but also emboldened, political climate. Because of their efforts, a Finnish law enabling co-operative enterprises was implemented in 1901, alleviating co-operative participants' fears of Russian censure and persecution for what would have otherwise been illegal activity. Juho Paasikivi, Pellervo's first legal secretary who later became the seventh president of Finland (1946–56), noted in Pellervo's flagship periodical when the legislation was passed:

> Finnish farmers! You now have a law that will fortify the weapon hitherto found the strongest and most rewarding from experience gained elsewhere, and which will secure your income and improve your occupation. . . . But ultimately it is up to you as to whether this law, which in itself is but a framework, will remain still-born or receive that content, that spirit and inspire that activity, which the friends of this ideal expect of it, and *which could play its own role in pumping new, fresh blood into the recently petrified and strangled body of our people*. (Paasikivi 1901, quoted in Skurnik 2002, 108, emphasis added)

The link between the co-operative legislation and the budding nationalist sentiment in the face of Russian oppression was thus quite clear. It should be noted that the co-operative movement was also present in Russia at this time, though its success was mixed there (Gebhard 1916). Given the political climate, the presence of co-operatives in Russia (Lenin 1910; Spence 1993) perhaps made Finnish co-operatives less of a problematic development from the perspective of the occupying Russians.

Pellervo, which had also obtained state grants to subsidize its start-up and operating costs (Gebhard 1916), held schools for co-operative training, and its early classes of 150+ national participants immediately diffused the co-operative model across the Duchy (Power 1939). In Tampere, which was Finland's early industrializing equivalent of Manchester, the workers at the Finlaysons factory founded one of the first stable Rochdale-style consumer co-operatives in 1900–1901 (Power 1939). By 1902, 15 such co-operatives had been founded, as had another 28 dairy co-operatives. The Gebhards had spearheaded state funding and a law to help capitalize the creation of the OKO central co-operative bank (Osuuskassojen Keskuslainarahasto Osakeyhtiö, or Central Lending Fund of the Co-operative Credit Societies Limited Company), a co-operative lender to be owned by smaller, local co-operative banks. Today, OKO Bank is OP Group, a co-operative banking group that is the largest domestic bank in Finland (see Figure 3.3). By 1903, a total 189 co-operatives had been founded, including 24 co-operative banks (Power 1939).

Figure 3.3 OP Bank headquarters, Helsinki. In the heart of Finland's Wall Street, at Gebhard Square, is the largest office of the nation's largest, most financially sound, and innovative bank. It claims to have been the first European bank to have online services, and it is aggressively moving into open bank p2p platforms, runs a car-sharing service and electric car leasing program, and is building large hospitals for its health insurance clients. A co-operative, it is owned by more than 25% of the Finnish people as customers, founded a century ago with the help of Hedvig Gebhard (photo bottom left) and her husband, Hannes. When Finland became the first place to allow women to run for parliamentary office, Hedvig was elected. Photos by the author, or by permission from the Pellervo Society.

In 1904, Pellervo spearheaded a meeting in Tampere of 37 consumer co-operatives to coordinate the creation of a co-operative store wholesale society, Suomen Osuuskauppojen Keskuskunnan, or SOK, a co-operative of co-operatives (Power 1939). SOK today is the largest grocery store and retailer in Finland by a wide margin, and is part of the S Group, a diversified, horizontally and vertically integrated consumer co-operative encompassing restaurants, pubs, hotels, gas/petrol stations, department stores, insurance and credit, owned by its customers. In 1905, the farmers' movement founded a co-operative (called Labor, this entity was actually a co-operative conversion of an organization founded in 1897), and Pellervo also spearheaded the creation of Hankkija, a wholesale society for 47 farmers co-operatives (Power 1939), to supplement the Labor co-operative (Gebhard 1916). By 1906, the Valio central co-operative dairy/butter society, a co-operative of dairy co-operatives, had been created, which would coordinate Finland's rapidly developing butter export industry; by the 1910s, Finland's Valio, like New Zealand's dairy co-operatives, had emerged as a major butter exporter to the United Kingdom (Gebhard 1916).

By 1905–6, in just six short years under Pellervo's leadership, over 2,000 co-operative societies (Power 1939; Gebhard 1916) were operating and formally registered as such in Finland. Their efforts largely fed into these five critical "co-operatives of co-operatives" in retail/grocery, banking, agriculture, agricultural supply, and dairy, the development of which Pellervo had also coordinated: SOK, OKO Bank, Hankkija, Labor, and Valio (Power 1939). Hundreds of co-operatives were formed across every activity imaginable, from fishing to threshing to peat-moss growing and gathering (Gebhard 1916).

Domestic unrest in Russia produced the October 1905 general strike, which also spread to Finland. The tsar's October Manifesto introduced widespread reforms in response, temporarily ending Russification measures and radically restructuring the Finnish Diet, which was still based on the four estates, for which fewer than 5% of the population could vote (Goldstein 1983). Even within the 5%, the three "upper estates" were heavily overrepresented; most Finns were not represented in the Diet at all. Russian reform introduced a 200-seat proportional representation-based, universal suffrage, unicameral parliamentary body, the Eduskunta. This reform included women, making Finland the world's second self-ruling territory, after New Zealand, to allow women the right to vote and stand for election.

In the subsequent 1907 elections under the new laws, both of the Gebhards were elected to the new Finnish Diet, apparently the first husband and wife to be freely elected to a modern parliamentary body for either a nation or an autonomous region. They represented the late Snellman's Finnish Party (which, after the 1918 post-Independence Finnish Civil War, would birth the National Coalition Party. Hedvig Gebhard continued to serve in the Diet for this successor party through the 1920s, a center-right party which remains one of the "big three" parties in the nation today. For details on her political career, see Hallsten and Gebhard 1933).

Beyond the Gebhards, a host of other co-operative supporters and members were elected through multiple political parties, assuring continued and broad political support of the movement (Kuisma, Wynne-Ellis, and Pellervo-Seura 1999). Co-operative leaders would thus play prominent roles in government from the nation's beginning, and they would continue to do so over much of the 20th century. Russia would reverse some reforms in the following years and repress or limit the co-operative movement at times. Labor unions also began to create a national infrastructure at this time, led by the forerunner organization to today's SAK (Suomen Ammattiliittojen Keskusjärjestö), the largest union, now representing approximately one-fifth of the population, which formed in 1907 in Tampere (Kirby 2006). As World War I continued and the Russian Revolution unfolded in February 1917, an increasingly independent Finland took advantage of the crisis to officially declare its political independence.

A tale of two co-operative movements, 1917–1945. By the time of Finnish independence in 1917, less than two decades after formal, systematic efforts to develop a previously nonexistent co-operative sector, Finland had become one of the most, if not the most, co-operative-dense countries on earth (Parker and Cowan 1944; Gebhard 1916; Gide 1922). A civil society–led movement, organized and led by the Gebhards and Pellervo, had worked with direct legislative and financial support of the embattled and limited Finnish state to develop a co-operative economy, and, despite other challenges, these dynamics would continue to mark the postindependence period.

From the beginning of Finland's independence, co-operative leaders held high-level political positions: the first Finnish president, Stahlberg (1919–25), had been on the Board of Directors of Elanto, the largest consumer co-operative society in Greater Helsinki (Parker and Cowan 1944). Its subsequent prime minister (who shared some executive power with the president) was Vaino Tanner (1926–27), who had authored much of the initial co-operative legislation and state support in the early 1900s. Tanner would hold Finnish cabinet posts through the 1940s and was the global leader and president of the ICA from 1927 to 1945. His 18-year leadership of the global co-operative apex organization is the longest anyone has held the position; he relinquished it just before being imprisoned after World War II for his role in leading the wartime German-allied Finnish government.

Though co-operatives had played a critical role in harnessing rising Finnish nationalism and securing its political and economic independence, the co-operative moment was directly affected by the dynamics of the Russian Revolution. Just as a White Guard versus Red Guard cleavage had unfolded in the Russian Revolution, in Finland the social cleavages both across and within the old four estates (nobles, clergy, merchants, farmers/peasants) remained, and the divide between the White Guard (bourgeois) and Red Guard (socialist) elements led to a schism in the co-operative movement in 1917, and the brief Finnish Civil War in 1918. The White forces, with assistance from the Germans, prevailed (Kirby 2006).

Many of the "red co-operatives," as several Finnish interviewees referred to them even today, had broken off from the White-associated SOK to form OTK (Osuustukkukauppa). OTK served as a "progressive" socialist co-operative central wholesale society and had its own educational/coordinating body, the KK (Kulutusosuuskuntien Keskusliitto).

Despite initial clashes, both groups would grow markedly in the decades between the two world wars, executing the "co-operative commonwealth" strategy of the British Co-operative Wholesale Society in parallel, each constructing an entire co-operative ecosystem and supply chain, with co-operative stores supplied by subsidiary co-operative manufacturing and production operations, in turn utilizing co-operative agriculture and inputs, all financed through the co-operative banking system. Co-operatives thus quite literally built the modern Finnish consumer economy. Their warehouses, manufacturing facilities, and office buildings still stand across not only Helsinki but the countryside as well. By World War II, Finland's co-operatives accounted for almost all agricultural output and 30% to 40% of retail trade (Parker and Cowan 1944; see Figure 3.4).

Alongside the development of the two rival consumer co-operative conglomerates, another wave of co-operative development after World War I and the Finnish Civil War further broadened the base of support for co-operatives, as additional central organizations were created for eggs, meat processing, and agrarian production and forestry (Gebhard 1916; Kuisma, Wynne-Ellis, and Pellervo-Seura 1999). Co-operatives would come to dominate forestry, long Finland's leading export, in part due to state action. The Finnish Parliament enacted major land reforms, restricting the ability of traditional private enterprises and foreigners to buy forest land, while increasing the forestry ownership of smallholding tenant farmers (*torppari*), in acts largely drafted between 1915 and 1925 (Palo and Lehto 2012). In direct response to these legal changes, forestry co-operatives developed, and a central association, again with assistance from Pellervo and the Gebhards, was

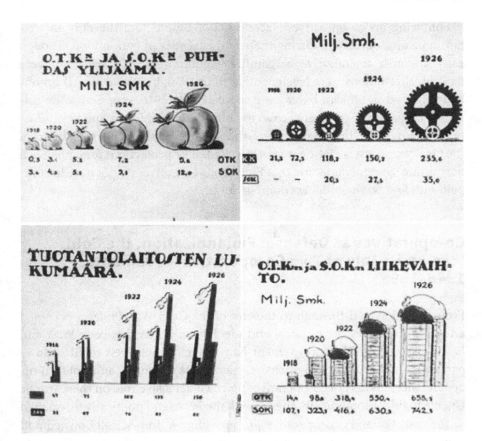

Figure 3.4 The Red and White co-operatives' rapid growth. These early, art-deco style, proto-"data visualizations" from the 1920s show the rapid growth in industry, agriculture, and commerce in Finland's two rival consumer co-operative groups, SOK and OTK. Photos taken by the author at Co-operatives Exhibition, Finnish Labor Museum, Tampere.

formed. Though the smallholder forestry co-operatives faced various challenges and setbacks, through association with central co-operative MTK they became the basis for Metsäliitto and Metsä Group, today the second-largest co-operative in Finland after SOK Group, and the largest producer co-operative in Europe, broadly owned by roughly 100,000 smallholding Finnish forest owners. Metsä Group is one of the largest forestry and paper/wood advanced materials suppliers and manufacturers in Europe, and leads Finland's forestry industry. After Canada, Finland has long been the second-largest exporter of forestry-related goods globally (Peltola 2003).

Following on co-operatives' success, labor unions and the Finnish welfare state also developed during these early decades of nationhood. Though early attempts at collective bargaining beginning in 1924 were not very fruitful, after unions were briefly outlawed in 1930, by World War II unions had achieved significant bargaining successes. By 1946, economy-wide collective bargaining agreements covering most large employers and key industries were in place; these agreements, though amended, remain today, part of the broader, robust social-democratic welfare state protections for labor. Such bargaining agreements assure that Finnish co-operatives do not have to compete with low-wage producers domestically.

Co-operatives as Defense: Finlandization, the Cold War, and a Tale of Two Co-operative Movements, 1946–1995

From World War II through to the end of the Cold War, Finland occupied a tense position on the physical and ideological border between West and East. If the co-operative movement had originally achieved rapid scale as part of Finland's attempt to offensively secure its economic and political independence, in this era co-operatives played a defensive role on these fronts. Unable to fully economically engage with the West, and politically threatened to the east, Finland's co-operatives, in providing a domestically owned and controlled supply of goods and services, helped defensively secure Finland's continued economic and political independence during the era, and thus attracted continued popular and political support, with enabling laws and regulations updated as required.

"Finlandization" and the Cold War economy. Finland had occupied a peculiar position in World War II. Invaded by the Soviets multiple times, most notably in the "Winter War" of 1939–40, Finland, with limited resources, had beaten back the far larger Soviet forces. To secure its position, Finland sided with its former ally Germany, without fully cooperating with it. Due to its relationship with Germany, Britain had also declared war on Finland in 1941. But by 1944, Finland was negotiating a settlement with Russia, which it had effectively fought to a draw. It would pay reparations for nearly a decade after World War II's end and cede contested land in eastern Finland, which the Russians had attempted to seize in an earlier invasion.

Finland lost significant territory and had to resettle its dislocated population as per the peace agreement with Russia, temporarily straining the operations of both co-operatives and traditional enterprises. But alone among the

Baltics and Eastern European nations, Finland escaped becoming an occupied or satellite state of the Soviet Union. Auguring the emerging East-West tensions and Finland's delicate position, the United States provided aid and loans to Finland but carefully limited the amount of the loans: too much aid might invoke a Soviet response (Pihkala 1999). A 1952 U.S. National Security Council study noted, "The key to U.S. policy (toward Finland) is to avoid any steps which would threaten the delicate balance of Finnish-Soviet relations" (declassified 1986, 1759). Finland, which declined Marshall Plan aid, found itself in a precarious position in the Cold War era, walking a "political tight rope" (Standish 2016), joining neither NATO nor the Warsaw Pact, despite pressure from both sides for it to do so. Over the next several decades, Finland would develop a response that outside political analysts came to call "Finlandization," a term of revived interest today, given Russia's current role in regional and global geopolitics (Standish 2016; Reynolds 2023). Often viewed as a pejorative by Finns (as confirmed by three interviewees), "Finlandization" involved deferring to Soviet wishes on foreign policy. In exchange, Finland was allowed to remain an autonomous and democratic nation. It was not occupied like the Baltics, nor was it forced into the Warsaw Pact.

Finlandization did not only mean walking on a political tightrope; it also involved balancing on an economic one. Though the United Kingdom would remain Finland's leading trading partner over much of this period (alongside Sweden and West Germany), the Soviet Union emerged as one of Finland's major trading partners, just as Russia had been when it ruled Finland. By 1953, the Soviets had temporarily surpassed Britain as Finland's largest partner (U.S. Department of State, Office of the Historian 1989). Trade with the Soviet Union before the war had been almost nil, but by the 1950s the Soviets accounted for roughly one-fourth of Finland's international trade (Ollus and Simola 2006). Beginning in 1947, Finland, alone among Western democracies, had a formal, bilateral trade agreement with the Soviets, renegotiated every five years. Eight such agreements were negotiated, the last commencing in 1986. Though companies in other Western nations traded with the Soviets, they rarely did so under formal bilateral agreement. Finland, meanwhile, by the 1970s had become the Soviets' second-largest trading partner after West Germany, a country nearly 15 times more populous than Finland. While Finland exported a diversified range of products to the Soviets, they imported mostly oil and energy products from the Soviets. Finland also had bilateral trade agreements with other nations, and over the course of the 1950s and 1960s joined the General Agreement on Tariffs and Trade, the UN, the Nordic Council, and in 1973 the European Economic Community. Nonetheless, its economy remained heavily protected by a range of import quotas and licenses, tariffs, restrictions, and limitations on foreign direct investment (Ojala, Eloranta, and Jalava 2006). These restrictions were allowed by the European Economic Community due to Finland's unusual international position (Paavonen 2001, 2004). A historical account of this era by the Bank of Finland noted:

> The junctures of domestic policy and labour market relations are essential to understanding the monetary and exchange rate policies of the Bank of Finland, but a national perspective alone is not enough. The activities of the Bank of Finland must also be seen in an international context.... At the end of the Second World War, the *country was economically isolated* and had to entirely rebuild its trading relations, creditworthiness and international liquidity.... *Economic integration with western market economies was regarded in Finland as an important objective, even though the process was hindered by the suspicious attitude of the Soviet Union.* In the words of Juhana Aunesluoma, an authority on the subject, *Finland's trade and integration policies paint the picture of "a small figure walking the tightrope between economic necessity and political possibility."* (Kuusterä and Tarkka 2012, 16, emphasis added)

Co-operatives as economic independence and as a "middle way." The political contrast with the United States in this period is also instructive. In the United States, as I will explain in Chapter 7, co-operatives came under political attack during the Second Red Scare. Fear that communism was surreptitiously at America's doorstep, infiltrating its institutions, activated antico-operative sentiment in response. In Finland, there was no such Red Scare, but rather a Red Reality: totalitarian communism was literally next door, with invasion possible at any moment. Finland's Communist Party, legalized in 1944, achieved popular support as high as 25%. The 783-mile eastern border with Russia was also physically close to key Soviet military and population centers.

Finland's leaders could ill afford to alarm the Soviets by liberalizing its economy too much, thereby becoming economically and materially beholden to Western trading powers. Ideologically, it could not afford to fully adopt a "free market"–style economy either. Located at the Soviet border, it risked alarming its neighbors that liberal capitalism—as embodied by the form of the IOF—was reaching ever closer. Finland was trapped between Scylla and Charybdis: ideologically, materially, and physically, it sat wedged between totalitarian communism and free-market, liberal capitalism. The co-operative model, as a "third way" (Skurnik 2002; Kuisma, Wynne-Ellis, and Pellervo-Seura 1999; Childs 1936) between the two, helped navigate this dilemma. Just as the Argonauts carefully navigated between the proverbial rock and the hard place of the sea monsters Scylla and Charybdis, so too did the Finns, their *Argo* propelled by co-operative ownership. Finland, physically situated at the border of East and West, thus relied on an economic model which straddled the economic worlds of East and West. To the East, the economy/market field was largely subservient to the state. To the West, this relationship was reversed. Co-operatives, generated out of the civil society field with state-enabling legislation and support, offered a compromise.

Finns had entered the Cold War with a strong co-operative sector, which also made explicit political room for both bourgeois (White) and socialist (Red) elements of cooperation through the SOK and OTK, respectively. The interests of the rural agrarian and natural resource–based population, meanwhile, were well represented in the sector's other large central co-operatives. Co-operatives also provided key nonexport (i.e., "nonbasic" industries, in the language of economic trade) consumption goods for the domestic economy, thereby reducing the need for such goods to be obtained in politically charged international markets. And co-operatives produced goods and materials, notably forestry goods, which were readily exported.

Unable to fully participate in the financial liberalization, free trade, and transnational integration that began in the 1950s and 1960s, if the Finnish economy was to continue to develop, it would be on the basis of domestically controlled institutions and arrangements, leveraging those which were already in place. Co-operatives thus continued to play a leading role in the Finnish economy during this period, and the state continued to act in ways which supported their health. Consistent with institutionalists' notion of layering, Finland's center-left-led Parliament comprehensively updated its co-operative-enabling statutes in 1954 and repeatedly amended co-operative acts as needed to reflect changing conditions in numerous other years, while also continuing to use the form in new ways; for example, during this period the state helped create road co-operatives in rural areas (Isotalo 1995; Heggie and Vickers 1998) as well as co-operative water systems (Katko 2016).

Consumer co-operatives' first-mover advantage, in having gained 30% to 50% market share prior to the Cold War, also gave them a head start on domestic, investor-owned rivals. Detailing the co-operatives in the Cold War era, Komulainen and Siltila (2015, 6) noted that even as "private retailers established their own wholesale companies and started to compete fiercely with the co-ops, the Finnish co-ops had centralized much earlier. Already in the 1910s, HOK and Elanto had their own wholesalers and ideological associations."

Beyond playing a critical stabilizing role for the nation's delicate position in the international political economy, the co-operative movement provided institutional room for this tension to play out within the country, as noted above. In detailing the rivalry between HOK and Elanto, respectively the local consumer co-operative societies of White SOK and Red OTK in Helsinki—a city which by then was rapidly urbanizing and playing a dominant role in the national economy—Komulainen and Siltila (2015, 8) note that "the competition between HOK and Elanto escalated again in the 1950s, at the same time as did the Cold War. The international juxtaposition between the communists and the capitalists was reflected by the toughening competition between the co-ops."

HOK, the bourgeois/White society, became Helsinki's and the nation's largest restaurant owner-operator, in part by aggressively moving to include highly profitable alcohol sales after Prohibition ended in the 1930s, while Elanto remained dry, in solidarity with the temperance movement, which was closely affiliated with labor (Komulainen and Siltila 2015). HOK also became a key hotel owner-operator, as it moved to develop hotels for international travelers to the Helsinki Olympics in 1952. Elanto, reflecting the needs of its labor movement–associated, working-class member-owners who did not travel as much, did not yet enter the hotel market but focused on being a grocery and retail conglomerate, introducing self-service stores during this era to save its working-class members time when shopping (Komulainen and Siltila 2015; cf. Komulianen and Siltala 2018).

Notably, the Red co-operatives in particular were overtly political, their internal elections often seen as a barometer for national left-of-center parties' elections (i.e., the SKP/SKDL and SDP, respectively the major national communist party/coalition and social democratic parties, the latter of which remains one of the nation's three major parties today).[1] In this era, the Red co-operative stores also began to fall behind in terms of investment, quality, and selection, auguring problems to come (Brazda and Schediwy 1989). Nonetheless, the existence of two robust co-operative movements—one left, one right—meant that the co-operative movement, and co-operatives themselves, were not inherently associated as right or left, but appealed to both.

---

[1] See Brazda and Schediwy (1989) for detail on the links between the Red co-operative movement and these parties during the Cold War.

Co-operatives as Globalization Insurance: Liberalization, European Integration, and the Return of Russia, 1995–Present

In the late 1980s and 1990s, the demise of the Soviet Union sent Finland's economy, already in a recession due to the ongoing Nordic banking crisis, into an extraordinarily severe decline, arguably the worst in its history. GDP declined by roughly 13%, and employment fell by approximately 20%. Unemployment increased from under 4% to over 18%. For comparison, U.S. GDP declined by 4% and employment decreased by 7% in the Global Financial Crisis (GFC). Even at the height of the COVID-19 pandemic, U.S. unemployment did not reach such levels.

With the Soviet Union's collapse, there was nothing to stop Finland from pursuing closer ties to the West. In 1992, Finland swept away many of its economic regulations and introduced dramatically stronger competition laws, which eliminated the old system of price and import regulations. It joined the EU in 1995 and adopted the euro when it was introduced in 1999. Integration with the EU meant further opening and liberalizing Finland's closed, heavily regulated economy, and was not without its costs; the co-operative sector was directly affected. Co-operatives had developed the "co-operative commonwealth" strategy of interlocking production in part through various interfirm agreements, which ran afoul of the new liberal, atomistic approach to interfirm competition, which is a key element of LMEs' institutional arrangements, as noted in Chapters 1 and 2.

In a key account of co-operatives in the period, Kuisma, Wynne-Ellis, and Pellervo-Seura (1999) explained how liberal notions of interfirm competition and antitrust regulations, previously fairly limited in Finland, were dissonant with the co-operative coordinating logic. As the field environment shifted with Finland's EU integration—which involved the advance of the liberal market and the retreat of the state—these antico-operative logics grew stronger, yielding an increasing institutional incongruency between co-operatives and the changing dynamics of the Finnish economy. The following lengthy passage effectively shows how the co-operative model came to clash with the liberal archetypes of today's comparative capitalism families in the Finnish case, where liberalism had long been constrained due to geopolitics, before being quickly unleashed on the economy:

> Although the government had tightened up competition laws at the end of the 1980s, it was when these were brought into conformity with EU practice that the real blow was struck at Pellervo co-operation. Inter-company price agreements,

production restrictions and territorial divisions were forbidden if they did not simultaneously make production and distribution more efficient, encourage technological and economic developments, or if the ensuing benefits did not mainly accrue to the customers or consumers. The Pellervo idea of co-operatives working together had been in existence for almost a century. In the eyes of the competition authorities, collaboration between the co-operative dairies within Valio amounted to a forbidden horizontal cartel, whereas Pellervo saw it as an economic alliance of milk producers that was also beneficial to the consumers. In the opinion of the Pellervo Society and co-operative enterprises, too little attention was paid to the special nature of co-operation in the preparation of competition legislation. They wished a co-operative group or central society, its member co-operatives and individual members, to be treated as a group within the meaning of the law. When this failed, Pellervo enterprises applied to the authorities for a permit exempting horizontal co-operation, but only the service co-operatives were partly successful. The Office of Competition even forbade co-operative banks from price agreements, although they considered that the group should be treated as a single entity. On the other hand, the authorities did consider that agreements over prices and logistics within the S Group (SOK and its member societies and their subsidiaries) as promoting the production and distribution of goods, so long as uniform prices were not binding on the societies and that they were also free to buy from others. It was the co-operative slaughterhouses, however, that came under the closest scrutiny. The authorities noticed that, despite the dismantling of TLK, co-operation in this sector involved agreements on territories, prices, and production. Officials struck at the slaughterhouses but failed to find evidence of lawbreaking. They considered that cross-territorial sourcing, meat importation and producer-price competition were acceptable evidence of genuine competition. In this way supranational competition policy succeeded in destroying co-operation between Pellervo enterprises, thus making illegal the century-old Pellervo ideal of co-operatives working together for the common interest. Competition legislation also changed the marketing of the Metsäliitto Group's products when the forest companies were forced to abolish their sales associations Finnpap, Finncell and Finnboard. (Kuisma, Wynne-Ellis, and Pellervo-Seura 1999, 117)

Given these challenges, some co-operatives struggled to adapt and died out, effectively displaced by IOFs. Others survived by pursuing more market-facing partial/hybrid investor ownership models, while still ultimately remaining co-operative in their majority ownership. But the government, though rarely acting to provide significant subsidies, acted in other ways to enable the continued utilization of the co-operative structure.

It is worth reviewing these developments in slightly greater detail, for they also help clarify how field theory can both incorporate and go beyond not just HI but comparative capitalisms as well. A field theory treatment of Finland's co-operatives in this period reveals how competing varieties or families of capitalism can exist side by side in a country, as embodied through competing, firm-type-based fields of action, with their comparative positions strengthening or weakening over time. It is not as simple as Finland being a CME and the United States an LME. Each country contains both systems in simultaneous operation. The difference is the degree to which one dominates, both economically and politically. What the co-operative's evolution in Finland shows, at least in the era of EU integration, is that the degree of dominance shifted over time, one coming to partially displace the other, effectively reflecting a partial field displacement (Figure 3.5).

As noted above, many of Finland's leading co-operatives faced new challenges in the economic environment; some would effectively die out, most notably its Red consumer/retail co-operatives. With the threat of EU and global competition, Finland's co-operatives faced a stark reality. As an interviewee from one of the nation's largest co-operatives stated regarding this time, "We had to adapt and change, or die. We still wanted to be a co-operative, but we knew we had to be a business first. The business had to run. Finland's protected, export-oriented businesses had been able to charge more to Soviet enterprises and operate with an accordingly lower degree of economic efficiency (Ollus and Simola 2006). This was also an issue in the domestic, consumer-oriented market, where co-operatives dominated; as early as the 1960s, both White and Red co-operatives were experiencing economic challenges, relying increasingly on debt to finance their development and

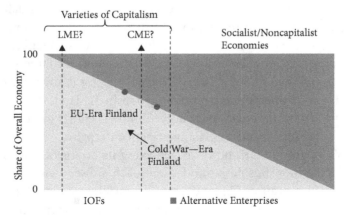

Figure 3.5 Finland's EU integration and co-operatives: partial field displacement.

operation (Brazda and Schediwy 1989). They also continued to operate in less profitable rural areas as part of their "national duty" (Komulainen and Siltila 2015). Structural crises had thus been slowly brewing in the previous era. The end of the "featherbedding" system of import controls and guaranteed prices (Kuisma, Wynne-Ellis, and Pellervo-Seura 1999), coupled with rising interest rates, led to the dramatic restructuring and sale of groups like Hankkija, the long-standing farmer's co-operative, and TLK in meat processing, part of which would remain a co-operative through a successor firm, a going concern today, as HKScan.

The greatest trauma for the co-operative movement in this transition was the loss of the historic Red consumer co-operatives. OTK and KK, whose stores by this time were known as the "E-group" stores, ultimately went into bankruptcy, their operations sold to an investor group. For Finland's labor movement and socialist populations of a certain age, the loss still resonates, painfully so. One interviewee said, "My family's social life had historically revolved around the Red co-operatives. Our town's life revolved around it. My uncle is still angry that it closed and was sold, and that was over twenty years ago"

The remnants of the co-operative E-group, however, persist. On the basis of the remaining assets after its consumer operations were wound down and sold (some became investor-owned, some were sold to rival SOK), it has evolved into a sustainable investment company owned by its long-standing customers, called Tradeka. Such an investment model is not foreign in Finland: it has a two-tiered pension system, with a state system of "social security" supplemented by a compulsory, employer-coordinated, and insured pension. This pension and benefit system, though it developed late (Van der Linden 1996), makes some use of the co-operative/mutual ownership structure. The supplemental investments are largely held by one mutually owned/co-operative pension insurer, Varma. With over 70,000 customer-owners, Varma manages the pension investments for nearly 900,000 Finns, effectively one-third of the national labor force, and bills itself as the largest single private investor in Finland today. Thus, if Varma's success is any indicator of the potential for a co-operative investment group in Finland, the remnants of the former Red co-operatives may succeed in their efforts to find new life as Tradeka, a consumer-owned social investment enterprise.

Rival White group SOK, however, reflecting its bourgeois history and its long pursuit of a more business-minded approach, subsequently rebounded in the face of EU integration. Under extreme financial duress itself in the 1990s, the group undertook a range of operational and management improvements to enhance its efficiency, and its market share rebounded from 16% to 47%, as confirmed by SOK itself in an interview. It is perhaps not surprising some Finns today see SOK as "like any other store." Five interviewees remarked on this, one noting that SOK was "not really a co-operative, in the sense of the word: it is simply a store like any other." But SOK objects to that characterization. One SOK interviewee said:

> It is both true and not true that we are run like any other store. We are run like any other business. Because we are a business. But we continue to serve areas of the country, regions of the country, with our operations even if they are not very profitable, because we are a Finnish co-operative. We serve the needs of our members, who are the Finnish people, all of them. We are not here to maximize profit. We keep operations going in places where a company, an investor would say, "Tskkk ... no, no profit, not enough profit here." ... Yes our stores and our regions, which own us, the children own the mother, all need to stand themselves, to make a surplus. But we do not run to the stock market to make decision[s]. We do not close a store because an investor wants more. We are different ... we are a co-operative.

Since EU integration, Finland has experienced a few outright demutualizations: Elisa, the telephone co-operative, for example, demutualized, and Red-associated insurer Kansa was merged into mutual insurer Sampo, which has also demutualized. Several of Finland's large agricultural co-operatives also pursued a hybrid or "next generation" model, as has also occurred in the other case countries, in which minority ownership shares were sold on the stock exchange, or a subsidiary was traded on the stock exchange, while ultimate control and ownership remained with the owner-members (farmers). Reflecting the history of land smallholding in Finland and the historical legacy of early 20th-century land reforms (reviewed earlier), most farmer-members of these co-operatives are family-run enterprises with few employees (in contrast to New Zealand, where increasingly the farmer-members of Fonterra, for example, include large, investor-owned farms).

Despite these challenges, the state has repeatedly undertaken actions to assure the continued health of the nation's largest co-operative enterprises, revising general co-operative legislation in 2001 and 2014 and passing special legislation to bolster the co-operative banks in the 1990s. The co-operative structure itself was also used, as it had been in the other case countries, as a means by which to address unemployment in the 1990s recession, with some limited state support. Co-operatives today, however, receive little if any state subsidy, pay comparable tax rates, and their incorporation law is similar to that of a limited liability company, with the notable exception that a co-operative costs less to form (Spicer 2022).

Unlike other Nordic countries, which allowed and encouraged large co-operative banks to be restructured into investor-owned enterprises in the aftermath of the 1990s banking crisis, the Finnish state created legislation to strengthen and secure the co-operative banks. Today the OP Group is extremely well capitalized and returns healthy profits to its owner-members. Competitor POPPankki Bank, which separated from the main OP Group during the Nordic crisis to form its own co-operative consortium, is another significant co-operative bank. Together they account for roughly half of the banking market in Finland today.

Though the original producer co-operatives for food and resources were effectively worker-owned by the farmers and land/forestry smallholders, these are not the same as what are typically called worker co-operatives, in which workers own industrial or service-based businesses. Such worker co-operatives did not have a significant history in Finland until their emergence as a "make-work" strategy for the underemployed in the 1990s (cf. Kalmi 2013). They have since evolved to become a tool for a wide range of types of employment. Students often form co-operatives to engage in part-time work or entrepreneurial ventures (such as Kajak Games, a co-op which publishes student-created video games), and artists and gig-economy workers also form co-operatives to organize their activities (such as Lilith, a large artists co-operative). Though some employment co-operatives initially received some Ministry of Labor support in the 1990s, today they receive no "special treatment." In fact, as of the late 2010s, there were over 1,300 of these "new generation," small co-operatives, according to the Pellervo Society's data, breathing new entrepreneurial life into the co-operative model and reversing the long-standing trend toward ever-larger consolidations among co-operatives in Finland.

Ultimately, Finland's increasing integration with Europe has meant economic liberalization. As such, it is not entirely clear if co-operatives will continue to thrive. But as affirmed by the re-emergence of Russia as an unexpected force, as well as Brexit and the appearance of contentious populist parties in significant positions in parliaments across Europe, nationalism has not yet been relegated by globalization to the dustbin of history, nor have geopolitics disappeared. Such dynamics became only more pronounced in the COVID-19 crisis, as supply-chain disruption and vaccine nationalism undescored the importance of domestic control of key industries and the role co-operatives can play in accomplishing this.

This has not escaped the notice of the Finns, who have survived such periods before, in part through cooperation. Skurnik and Egerstrom (2007) have argued that since its EU integration, co-operatives have served as a form of "globalization insurance" for Finland. Beyond using co-operatives in this way today, Finland had previously used co-operatives as a form of Cold War "insurance," as reviewed earlier. Co-operative policy and law thus were not allowed to institutionally "drift" (Hacker 2004) into irrelevance. Such laws have repeatedly been updated as underlying conditions changed, allowing the co-operative as a field to evolve with shifting conditions. As one interviewee noted:

> People tell stories about co-operatives in Finland. This is because we know that these co-operatives are different, part of what makes Finland different. I am sure you have heard these stories. We cooperate in Finland because of *talkoot*. . . . Do you know *talkoot* . . . our peasant tradition of cooperating to work together in poor farms and villages? . . . We cooperate because we believe in equalness of people, too, socialism! There may be some truth in these things. . . . But I think America had peasant traditions, too . . . and America also believes in equality, too, yes? . . . I have spent fifty years in co-operatives, and I know that we cooperate because we have to, because it is smart. We have always had to be smart. We were between Sweden and Russia. Then we were between Russia and Germany, even in my lifetime. Then it was the Soviets and the Americans, the West. . . . Many thought that because of the European Union, the co-operatives would slowly go away. But Russia again breathes heavy. The European Union does not look so promising as it once did. America, Britain . . . look at what you have done, too! I will not mention this. The past is here again. Nations still live. And co-operatives do, too.

I interviewed this informant before Russia's invasion of Ukraine, a development which finally enabled Finland's invitation to join NATO. In a recent communication over email with this informant, she affirmed the value of domestic ownership and control given these subsequent events.

Finland's Co-operatives, Geography, and the Evolution of Fields

Finland has spent its entire existence on what Sir Halford Mackinder, a founding figure of modern geopolitics and the second director of the London School of Economics, in 1904 called "the geographical pivot of history." Mackinder's crude theory was that the great Eurasian landmass was so large and rich in resources, it constituted a "global heartland," and that modern human history could be understood as a fight for control of it, hinging on a "pivot area" at its center: Russia. Though this work fell out of favor with the demise of the Soviet Union and Francis Fukuyama's (1989) claim that this collapse marked the "end of history," recent events have brought a renewed focus on Mackinder's idea, which again graces the pages of outlets such as *The Economist* and *Foreign Policy*, serving as a sign of the times and of the shortsightedness of Fukuyama's proclamation a generation ago.

For Finland, however, this notion has never been far away, staring at it from across a 783-mile border, providing a stark and daily reminder of the benefits of domestic ownership and control through solidarity, and the role of co-operatives in securing peace. This is not the only factor that explains Finland's co-operatives' initial strength and subsequent evolution to endure: social and economic homogeneity to engender solidarity and a history of less liberal politics/policies also played a role, as the case history elucidates. But it is only by examining how these factors came together, in the formation of co-operative enterprise as a *field*, that a coherent narrative unfolds.

Co-operatives emerged in an underpopulated field environment at a particular moment in time, when there was a weak, "embryonic state" and body of law (Kirby 2006). Joint stock companies had a late-developing and limited history, the historical economic institutions of slavery and serfdom were not present, and political parties and labor bargaining institutions were crude and just beginning to form. In this spartan field environment, pro-co-operative actors were able to leverage a nascent national solidarity, partly rooted in geography and geopolitics, to construct a robust co-operative field, enabled by national policy. Finnish co-operatives, modern Finnish political parties, and the nation of Finland itself thus emerged and developed together, forged in the same crucible of forces. Even after this initial establishment, to coordinate and control some of Finland's most exportable and consumable goods in a way which was politically palatable given its geographical positioning between East and West, the co-operative continued to be utilized by Finnish economic actors. This resilience was further supported by the fact that Finland's resources lent themselves to industries which were readily cooperativized (e.g., agriculture and natural resources). As a result, national co-operative-enabling legislation was repeatedly supported by political actors who amended and layered new laws onto the existing co-operative legal framework. Some co-operatives, however, were displaced by encroaching IOFs with the rise of economic liberalism and EU integration, their displacement showing how multiple comparative capitalism archetypes can exist simultaneously within a place, operating side by side, their comparative dominance over one another shifting over time. Nonetheless, as Finland has moved closer to its Western neighbors, the historical geopolitical legacy of co-operatives has remained, repurposed today as "globalization insurance," mindful of Finland's historical precarity in the shadow of empires, which still loom large today.

HI notions of evolution—of drift, displacement, and layering—well describe how co-operative policy evolved in Finland. But, as developed in the previous chapter, and as the paragraph above makes clear, field theory can also capture these subprocesses of field transformation, while also helping us identify how or why co-operatives were not only able to obtain such policy treatment but were also initially able to emerge in Finland with such strength and speed, leveraging national solidarities not present in the same way in the American case, as we shall see. Furthermore, field theory as applied to the Finnish case helps us understand why it is that revolutions may only sometimes bring about unexpected and lasting institutional change or field transformation. When revolution destabilizes or ruptures the field environment in ways which create a new opening or enhance the appeal of an existing void for a preexisting institutional or field challenger to leverage, as occurred in Finland with co-operatives, dramatic institutional change or field transformation can ensue. But not all revolutions will necessarily or always have this effect on the field environment in question.

Finally, the Finnish case shows how field theory can account for the ways in which geography shapes fields' development, by conditioning the nature and structure of the field environment. Finnish co-operatives' emergence, evolution, and endurance cannot be fully understood without geographical insight. The strength of the co-operative field's "middle way" appeal in Finland partly rests on the nation's geographical position. Finland lies on one of the world's most significant geopolitical fault lines, on the border of the geographical pivot of history, a border which even today demarcates the territory of competing political and economic models. If one wants to fully understand how and why fields are constructed in the way that they are, consideration of geography is thus essential, as the New Zealand case (Chapter 5) will also affirm.

4
Co-operatives as the Heart of France's Social and Solidarity Economy

> There are two worlds. One world is about using money . . . to make more money . . . the "classic enterprise" model. Another world is about using money . . . to serve people's needs. . . . You still want to make money, enough to cover your costs with some reserves for security and reinvestment, but it's not about money for more money. That's not the primary goal. It's about turning money into something else. This second world is the world of the social and solidarity economy, with co-operatives at its heart.
> —French national co-operative meta-organization director, Paris, 2017

The co-operative meta-organization director's face puckered into a mixed expression of amusement and disdain. In my schoolboy French, I had asked her to answer my questions as if I was truly as stupid as my meager language skills suggested. "Are you as stupid as you sound? I pray not!" she snapped in reply. The first of my French interviews was not off to an auspicious start.

But I was as wise to beg stupidity as I was to apologize for my clumsy French: the complexity of French co-operatives can rapidly overwhelm the uninitiated outsider. The director tore an enormous sheet of paper from an easel and placed it on the boardroom table, quickly covering both sides with an array of French co-operative legal forms. There are nearly 30 such forms (Hiez 2017), each enshrined in French law, each with its own incorporation requirements, tax treatments, institutional history, and government councils; many have their own distinct sources of financing and national advocacy organizations, and in turn are often built up from regional organizations. All of these forms are knitted together, formally, into a broader French economic domain legally recognized as the social and solidarity economy, or *l'économie sociale et solidaire* (ESS), which also has its own meta-organization,

ESS France, which liaises with the government minister of the ESS, who is a member of the cabinet of the minister of the economy, who is in turn on the Council of Ministers (i.e., the Cabinet in Anglophone governments).[1]

Unsurprisingly, given this complex structure, co-operatives and the ESS are included in a host of policy mechanisms which American cooperators "can only dream of," as U.S. co-operative leaders remarked when I shared policy-related findings from the French case with them.[2] French workers, for example, have a right to buy their company if it is going to be shuttered (via the Florange Law), and often select the co-operative structure to do so; in many cases, they may be taking over a still-profitable business, closed simply because it was not profitable enough or because it lacked strategic corporate importance to an investor.[3] When the French government decides to sell off a state-owned business, it may mutualize it, turning it into a co-operative, as occurred in the local banking system at the end of the 20th century. Demutualization typically requires ministerial approval, which is rarely given, and the firm must typically demonstrate it cannot otherwise remain in business as a co-operative, as several interviewees relayed. Incentives for co-operatives to demutualize are reduced by the legislated use of indivisible reserves, a form of co-operative retained capital which cannot be captured by windfall exit sales to private equity, as occurred with U.S. mutual insurers and banks beginning in the 1980s. Many workers, even at traditional businesses, can allocate their retirement savings into co-operatives and related forms via "90/10" funds, the equivalent of American 401(k) accounts, but where 10% is earmarked to ESS firms; the law requires most workers to be offered such options.

Such contrasts with the United States are startling. Of particular note, worker co-operatives, rare even in France, are nonetheless far less rare than in the United States. As of the early 2020s, there were just over 600 documented worker co-operatives employing roughly 7,000 individuals in the United States, according to data from the U.S. Federation of Worker Co-operatives.[4] France, a country one-fifth the size, had over 2,600 such enterprises, employing upward of 58,000, according to the French co-operative movement's data,[5] and include large entities such as Groupe UP, with 3,500 employees, which is led by a gender-balanced management council. Adjusting for each country's size, worker co-operative employment, while still rare in both countries, is by my estimate roughly 35 times more prevalent in France than in the United States.

---

[1] For a useful review of the major ESS forms and families and their policy frameworks, see Jeantet (2016) (with forward by former President Hollande, available in French only).
[2] For key policy differences, see Spicer (2022), which are also briefly reviewed in Chapter 2.
[3] CECOP/CICOPA Europe (2013); Les Scop (2012).
[4] See Chapter 7.
[5] https://serre.grainesdesol.fr/wp-content/uploads/2023/02/RA-2022-CGSCOP.pdf.

Despite all of my preparatory research, it was thus daunting, in that first interview, to face the extraordinary institutional complexity of French co-operatives. The array of codified legal forms available to co-operative entrepreneurs, I commented to that first director I interviewed, reminded me of the slogan of a certain technology giant for its app store: "There's a co-op for that." She did not react. Was the phrase "There's an app for that," which I had translated very literally, not in use in France, I asked? Stone-faced, she responded, "It is perfectly clear. We know this expression. Like most American translations, though, it sounds stupid." Without missing a beat, I replied, "Like me, in French?" After a moment, a smile spread across her face, followed by a guttural noise, one that does not exist in English but which conveys a distinctly French sense of amusement. Perhaps I would be able to break through the cultural distance between us after all.

Unlike my breakthrough with the director, co-operatives in France had not historically had such a quick breakthrough in their own development. One might presume that French co-operatives' strength, as in Finland, could be traced back to a big-bang event, perhaps to one of the nation's various well-known socialist revolutions or uprisings. But this was not the case. There is a link between France's many revolutions and its co-operative development, but France's *mille-feuille* co-operative field structure emerged and evolved gradually, over time, as this chapter will trace.

Meanwhile, co-operatives and the ESS were seemingly everywhere in France. After leaving the interview, I collapsed in exhaustion. I was unsure if this was residual jet lag, having only recently arrived from the United States, or due to the seven flights of stairs I had climbed to reach my front door, or from having spent the entire day speaking a language not my own. To resist the temptation to revert to English, I turned on the television for background noise as I made dinner. A leading national evening news program featured a story on schools' Week of the Social and Solidarity Economy. Facilitated by yet another meta-organization, L'ESPER (L'Économie Sociale Partenaire de l'École de la République, itself a partnership of 43 ESS organizations), thousands of children in more than 200 schools across France today receive instruction about co-operatives and related organizational forms. Students form many such enterprises each year within their own schools as well.

My food started to burn as I stood, slack-jawed, staring at the television. How could I not be gobsmacked? Even the proverbial school bake sale was a co-operative in France, as part of a formal government–civil society partnership program, and it was covered *on the national news*. I would later come to learn from the leader of yet another French ESS organization, Rencontres Mont Blanc, that this educational component was not a new development: during his

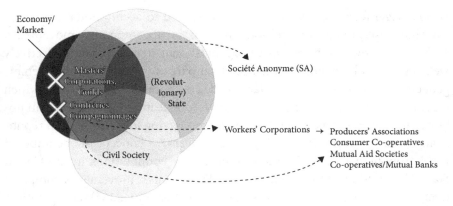

Figure 4.1 The French Revolution, 1790s→Second Revolution/Empire, mid-1800s field architecture.

own childhood, he had participated in school co-operative businesses, which might purchase supplies or run the student newspaper.[6] Co-operatives and the ESS were just a part of everyday life in France. They could be found in schools, and they could also be found occupying industry-leading positions across the banking, insurance, agriculture, and retail/wholesale industries, among others. If not directly through revolution, how had France come to be so different from the United States with respect to cooperation at scale?

As in the United States, France's co-operatives developed and evolved slowly. But they did so from a markedly different starting point, in response to different contextual forces, and along a very different path. Over two centuries, across multiple French revolutions, empires, and republics, the French state only gradually allowed co-operatives to develop into the institutional voids/field openings produced by the first French Revolution, which had abolished feudal corporations and all other economic intermediaries between the people and the state (Figure 4.1).

Emerging out of the recombined[7] remnants of both feudal and revolutionary forms, and initially operating in a legal twilight as the state remained conflicted about granting economic liberty to "associational" forms, co-operative advocates gradually but consistently achieved national legal recognition through an evolutionary process. Especially during the long Third Republic (1870–1940), through repeated rounds of institutional layering,

---

[6] While the United States, for example, does have the North American Students of Cooperation, it primarily focuses on university student housing co-operatives.
[7] Consistent with Grabher and Stark's (1997) notion of institutional recombination.

various legal forms and policies were developed to accommodate four distinct but closely linked and well-organized national co-operative movements, each with its own comprehensive organizational structure, and collectively well supported by major national political parties, reflecting France's emergent class formations. In particular, the idea of producers' associations, which would evolve into the worker co-operative, long featured prominently in political upheavals and associated utopian plans, giving form to national republican/socialist visions of escaping "wage slavery," a concept unencumbered in Metropolitan France[8] by the chattel slavery connotations in the United States. In so doing, and drawing on the French labor movement's comparatively "deeper reservoirs of class solidarity" (Moss 1994, 334), co-operatives cemented their position as a third pillar of French socialism and became increasingly legally well-integrated into France's associational life and territorial mode of economic development and social protection.

At the end of the 20th century—and again as a gradual, time-released response to another upheaval, that of 1968—co-operatives continued to evolve into the linchpin subfield of the legally defined ESS field, which joins together all social-purpose enterprises and enjoys a formally structured relationship with the state. Encompassing co-operatives, mutuals, foundations, nonprofit associations, social enterprises, and solidarity enterprises, today's ESS was forged out of a revived Socialist Party's efforts to reinvigorate a decentralized Jacobin France. ESS was built directly on an old French economic idea, that of the social economy, repurposed for a new era.[9] This enabled co-operatives to recover and reinvent themselves, as at the same time, economic liberalization contributed to the collapse of France's leading consumer co-operatives, their remnants acquired by merchant-owned producer co-operatives and IOFs.

Ultimately, the modern French government has repeatedly granted sanction and legitimacy to France's co-operatives through enabling legislation, specialized public economic development tools, and access to mainstream financing programs. In exchange for bestowing legitimacy and reflecting historical revolutionary legacies of concern over intermediaries between the people and the government, the state subjects the field to exhaustive oversight and comprehensive regulation, carefully proscribing its bounds. While such an approach, which involves an active and coordinating role for the state, is incongruent with the institutional arrangements of LMEs, as reviewed in Chapter 2, it *is* congruent with the CME variety of capitalism which prevails

---

[8] Slavery outside of Metropolitan France—that is "Mainland" France—in the French Empire was outlawed in 1794, reinstated by Napoleon, and banned again in phases between 1815 and 1848. In Metropolitan France, slavery was outlawed in 1315.

[9] Consistent with notions of institutional bricolage (Mair and Marti 2009).

in France and which emerged in parallel to these co-operative developments, as we shall see.

Given these dynamics, if there is a single case HI should handle well, it would be the slow-evolving French case. The case's contours align well with HI's focus on incremental evolutions—rather than revolutionary punctures and critical junctures—as being key to explaining big changes and differences in institutions across places and times. Indeed, HI does handle the case fairly well. It helps us understand how, despite clear links to revolutionary events, the emergence of France's complex co-operative framework reflects gradual interregnum evolution. Just as HI posits, co-operatives emerged and repeatedly evolved out of prerevolutionary elements which were picked up and slowly refashioned for postrevolutionary realities.

But HI does not provide us with a *grammar*—an architecture of relational positions—to understand *why* this occurred and how or why French co-operatives have retained such comparative strength, particularly given that France, unlike Finland, is a mixed case with respect to features which support wide-scale cooperation.

In contrast, field theory not only accommodates description of the evolutionary dynamics which HI catalogues, but its grammar enables us to identify three factors explaining French co-operatives' comparative strength. First, it enables positional identification of the initial field rupture and associated field opening that co-operative actors leveraged and captured to construct their own field. This opening was created by French revolutionary abolition of all economic associations and corporations. Co-operative actors deployed an emergent working-class solidarity to capture this field space; they imprinted this void with co-operative organizational experiments. This rupture *also* reduced the comparative field incumbency advantages of the IOF over co-operatives, diminishing their comparative head start. Second, field theory enables relational conceptualization of the co-operative field as a nested subfield within the broader ESS field, an architecture which has bolstered co-operatives' access to resources. Strategic action fields, as described by Fligstein and McAdam (2011, 3), "look a lot like Russian dolls: open up an SAF and it contains a number of other SAFs." This describes co-operatives' nesting within the French ESS, the latter field constructed around the former. Finally, field theory also helps explain French co-operatives' ability to sustain policy and organizing attention over time: the field space which co-operatives initially leveraged, and which ESS has subsequently evolved to claim, was long at the very core of the French national project itself, which wrestled with the question of which organizations and institutions can permissibly come between the individual and the state. The unique associational, federated business model of co-operatives, built on solidaristic bonds between people rooted in places, placed it at the center of this question, which is bound up not only with ideas contesting economic liberalism but with different approaches to regulating and coordinating capitalism as well.

France's co-operative history is so rich that this chapter could be an entire book itself. I therefore focus on those high-level features of the case which best help us understand how France came to have such a well-institutionalized co-operative field. The remainder of this chapter thus traces the evolution of France's co-operatives as a field, focusing on their emergence in the transition from feudalism to postrevolutionary France, their coalescence into a state-sanctioned field in the Third Republic through to the Trente Glorieuses, to their post-1968 reinvention as the linchpin subfield of the ESS today.

The French Evolution? Co-operatives' Slow Emergence in Modern France, 1780s–1860s

To understand how co-operatives emerged in France, one must begin with the transition from feudal to revolutionary France, before examining how co-operatives evolved over the subsequent 80 years. The French Revolution of 1789 ripped France's economy apart, producing an extraordinary field rupture, destroying key organizational forms and associated fields. With respect to the emergence of co-operatives, it also established a pattern, one which would hold across the Second (1830) and Third (1848) French Revolutions. Providing fertile ground for organizational and field experimentation, all three revolutions were marked by the outsized presence of fledgling co-operative forms, which were built from the repurposed remnants of prerevolutionary organizational models. These models repeatedly captured the imagination of the emergent French working classes, thereby imprinting themselves onto the long-lasting institutional voids or field openings left by the initial French Revolution. Though such revolutionary experiments with co-operatives were typically either abolished or restricted by postrevolution governments, their remnants would persist, as former participants would continue to work to slowly develop and organize the forms during the long periods between revolutions.

It would take nearly a century for a recognizable and stable field settlement to be reached, in which co-operatives—along with other forms of association—would achieve some semblance of formal, state-recognized legitimacy. During this long period of instability, distinct strains of French co-operation slowly emerged, operating in a legal twilight without official state permission, gestating as a proto-field. Critically, other organizational forms, such as unions and in fact the modern IOF, *also* struggled to achieve full state legitimation in this period, undermining their ability to establish field incumbency by denying them as strong a "first-mover" advantage as they were able to establish in locations like the United States.

The French Revolution's long shadow: From abolished feudal corporations to the emergence of societies. The word "revolution" is used so casually today that it is worth stating, unequivocally, that the French Revolution of 1789 was a revolution in toto, constituting a complete rupture of the entire field environment, "the most astonishing thing to have hitherto happened in the world" (Burke 1790, 7). The existing state and its associated political institutions were swept away and replaced by a new republic (Skocpol 1979). Existing social and economic institutions of daily life in the nation, from the Church to industrial structures, were dramatically restructured, abolished, or heavily reregulated (Sewell 1980; Tilly 1975). Excluding its Civil War, it would be difficult to identify any singular postfounding national event in the United States with such a lasting and institutionally transformative effect. With respect to economic life, it may be difficult for some modern readers to comprehend how revolutionary this event was, because the ancien régime of the feudal system which had hitherto prevailed is so completely foreign to us today. As this system's rupture affected co-operatives and most other forms of economic organization, a brief review of it is warranted.

At the time of the Revolution, France was primarily an agricultural society (Skocpol 1979), which accordingly did utilize some co-operative-like agricultural organizational structures. Prerevolutionary rural cheesemakers (*fruitières*) in Franche-Comté, for example, had long deployed a co-operative-like collective association, to turn pooled milk into gruyère cheese.[10] Despite being primarily an agricultural society, French cities had emerged as centers not only of agricultural administration and trade (Tilly 1975) but of burgeoning craft and industry, as part of an industrial "evolution" in which small-scale firms and family enterprises dominated (Sewell 1980; Price, 2006). As such, the emerging commercial and industrial economy was largely organized around a model of corporatism achieved through city-chartered local trade corporations (*corps métiers*), which had oversight of most trade

---

[10] Many Anglophone co-operative researchers, when recounting the history of global co-operatives, often note that the first co-operative was a French cheesemaking producer co-operative in Franche-Comté in 1750; each invariably cites Shaffer's (1999) *Historical Dictionary of the Co-operative Movement*, as this information appears on the very first page of his global co-operative timeline. Yet I could find no such record in the Francophone literature, in France or elsewhere, and Shaffer offers no citations for his claim. Based on his description, he appears to be referring to the *fruitières*, which had a history going back several centuries (Seeberger 2014; Mélo 2012, 2015; Gagneur 1839).

and commercial activity (Sewell 1980; Tilly 1975). Individuals had no right to freely incorporate, but required explicit government permission and approval to form an enterprise, led by a master craftsman. A master's corporation might consist of one master (*maître*), a journeyman (*compagnon*), and apprentices (*apprentis*); the largest grew to have over 70 workers under a single master (Sewell 1980). The masters had legal right to control the trade through the corporations, which were organized into *jurandes* or guilds, another feudal corporate form consisting of many masters' corporations. As France grew, masters' privileges became increasingly harder to obtain from the state (Sewell 1980). Lifetime journeymen, who had no legal personhood in the corporation (only the master did), were subject to increasingly limited opportunities. They bettered their condition through *confréries*, mutual aid societies which provided health and sickness benefits and assurance, a French equivalent of the English "friendly society," forerunner to the modern mutual co-operative society. *Compagnonnages*, a mutual aid form similar to *confréries*, typically included a greater focus on worker training, development, and placement (Sewell 1980).

The French Revolution abruptly ended this economic system. It explicitly abolished the feudal organizational forms mentioned above, via 1791's Allarde Decree and Chapelier Law, giving life to calls by the Declaration of the Rights of Man (1789) to eliminate the corporation and allow the "right of every citizen to acquire, possess, manufacture and sell" in their chosen trade (Sibalis 1988, 719).[11] This was not a secondary or marginal issue in the French Revolution; it was *central* to French ideas of liberty. The corporation had come under attack during the Enlightenment for being against the laws of nature and free labor, with philosophers and radicals arguing that *no corporate body or organizational form* should come between a citizen and the state, and that individuals should be free to make their own living without requiring a corporate privilege (Bairoch 1989). Critically, these laws did not just abolish corporations and guilds; they also *forbade any type of replacement*, outlawing associations of workers of any kind (Bairoch 1989). The laws "produced a major redefinition in the structure of work, as labour in France became more unfettered than it had been in centuries. Indeed, within a few years nearly all distinctions between journeymen and masters had been blurred, beginning the formation of what would later be known as the 'working class'"

---

[11] As part of an effort to reform the prerevolutionary set of institutional arrangements, a temporary abolishment of corporations had been enacted in 1776 by Turgot, who had also eliminated government control over grain production and trade as part of the new laissez-faire thinking of physiocrat economists (Bairoch 1989). These reform efforts were short-lived, however, and Turgot's attempts to reform if not eliminate the corporation failed and were reversed.

(Fitzsimmons 1996, 149–50). While other countries, such as the United Kingdom, would also forbid workers' associations, such efforts were repealed after a fairly short period (Thompson 1963).[12] In France, these laws would not be fully repealed for over a century, effectively making the formation of organizations of employers or employees illegal for generations.

Also included in the 1791 abolitions were the new revolutionary "workers' corporations" (Sewell 1980), which had briefly openly flourished between 1789 and 1791–92, in which workers freely associated to self-regulate, train, and advance their trade. These were effectively a temporary substitute for the feudal corporation, built upon the goodwill and logic of the feudal *confréries'* and *compagnonnages'* mutual/friendly society forms. If not these workers' corporations, what would be allowed to permanently replace the feudal forms? France could not go entirely without economic associations and organizations: economic disruption and unrest were widespread as a result of the abolitions (Sibalis 1988). But given the nature of the Revolution, entities which were framed via their name or their formal operating structure as a corporation, given the word's ancien régime connotations as a liberty-constraining entity, were not tolerated. Voluntary "associations," a new framing "idiom" (Sewell 1980), were also not tolerated, as they were interpreted as conflicting with the supreme dual authority of the individual and the state in the postrevolutionary environment. Coalitions or associations of more than 20 persons for striking or any other purposes were also not allowed, as clarified under the 1810 Napoleonic Code, unless specifically authorized by the government for a restricted purpose (Archambault 2001).

To solve this problem of organizing an economy with feudal corporations, the government repeatedly granted exceptions for certain individual organizations, and sometimes certain classes of organizations, case by case. Through a long period of field experimentation, a host of forms thus developed over the 19th century to fill the institutional void/field opening created by the French Revolution. These forms were incubated by interregnum institutional evolutions, as well as by the political revolutions of 1830–33 and 1848, as will be explained in greater detail in the next subsection. Government regimes variably repressed and accepted these new and emerging forms, which expressed controversial new ideas about free association, often referred to in shorthand as "associationism" (Sibalis 1988; Chanial and Laville 2005; Moss 1976a, 1976b; Sewell 1980). For example, partial substitute organizations for the corporations and guilds, such as the Paris butchers' and bakers' employers

---

[12] The U.K. Combination Acts of 1799, which effectively forbade workers' associations, were functionally repealed by the 1825 Bubble Act (Thompson 1963).

associations, or *syndicats*, were readily and quickly exempted by Napoleon's administration from revolutionary corporate bans, in the name of securing food supplies and public order (Sibalis 1988). Many other employment-related associations across the trades quickly sprang up, alongside those such as the Paris butchers and bakers organizations, and were sometimes tolerated (Sibalis 1988; Sewell 1980). "Trade union" functions of such associations, however, were not technically fully enabled and legalized until 1884, when the French Parliament enabled trade unions, after having previously allowed the right to strike in 1864 under the Loi Olivier, which had partially abolished the prohibitions on coalitions (e.g., strikes).

In general, what replaced the abolished corporation, after fits and starts and as consolidated in the Napoleonic Code beginning in 1807, were various forms of the *société*, or society. This form would be used both to develop the modern IOF and to organize co-operatives/mutuals. In the postrevolutionary world, France was a society, with nothing between the state and the individual. The state could, however, authorize "societies" to operate in the public interest, with its express permission and on its behalf. Thus the "society" today remains the parent form of all ostensibly "corporate" economic ownership forms in France, encompassing not only co-operative subtypes but the IOF model most commonly associated with traditional capitalism: the *société anonyme*, or SA, introduced in 1807.

To be sure, the society form of ownership was not entirely new, nor was the SA a complete break with the ancien régime: other types of capital-raising and economic societies had existed in the ancien régime as entities of a specific form granted for specific and narrow purposes by the state (Braudel 1982a; Price 2006). The *société en comandite* (*simple/par actions*), a partnership form, for example, had been used to raise capital, as had similar limited partnership forms (*société en nom collectif*), granted carefully as a privilege by the state in the 17th and 18th centuries (Cameron 1961; Guinnane et al. 2008; Haveman 2022). But large-scale incorporations using the SA, even after 1807, remained comparatively rare and typically smaller-scale (Haveman 2022; Rochat 2009; Cameron 1961; Braudel and Labrousse, 1976). Government administrators sometimes denied incorporations and would suggest other forms as more appropriate (Rochat 2009). Even then, traditional businesses, which were typically owned by families, often would place voluntary restrictions on the shares of an SA so as not to allow the free trading of shares, reflecting their wish to retain control over who had ownership (Rochat 2009). Free incorporation of profit-seeking businesses was not fully allowed in France until 1867, decades after the United Kingdom had lifted such restrictions (Thompson 1963). This same 1867 law also legally enabled the co-operative society (*société coopérative*).

Thus, while the SA legally emerged before the modern co-operative in France, incorporation permission was still not freely granted to enterprises, and not all types of activities were tolerated. In practice, SAs, as a successor to masters' corporations, *remained comparatively rare in this period in France* (Haveman 2022; Sylla and Wright 2013; Guinnane et al. 2008), in part reflecting the contentious politics of the era. France was marked by tension between the conservative remnants of the old regime, the revolutionary ideals which resisted issuance of both special privileges and corporations, and emerging "free market" liberal thinking, which sought reduced state intervention in enterprise to allow free incorporation (Rochat 2009; Braudel 1982a; Braudel and Labrousse 1976; Price 2006). This tension manifested through state actions such as the above-referenced restrictions on SAs and co-operatives alike. Indeed, Sylla and Wright (2013) and Haveman (2022) note the role of explicit state restrictions on IOFs in explaining the lateness of the development of the IOF in France when compared to contemporaneous incorporation levels in the United States and United Kingdom. What this meant, in practice, was that while the IOF had a modest first-mover advantage over the co-operative in France, it was denied the type of runaway lead achieved in the United States, which contributed to establishing its field incumbency there. Meanwhile, vis-à-vis the United States and United Kingdom, France was comparatively late in industrializing its economy, which was dominated by small/family firms through the mid-19th century (Haveman 2022; Sylla and Wright 2013; Price 2006).

A proto-field emerges, 1820s–1860s. The new SA form, which pooled capital among many investors, did not serve all enterprise needs. Other society forms, some entirely new and others directly building on abolished prerevolutionary forms (Chanial and Laville 2005), sprang up to fill the void to coordinate economic activity, in ways which neither conformed with economic liberalism nor ran afoul of evolving French republican conceptions of allowable organizational economic intermediaries between the individual and the state. Specifically, alongside the prerevolutionary tradition of agricultural cooperation, and building on the rich French utopian socialist traditions of thinkers such as Saint-Simon, Fourier, and Proudhon,[13] four other co-operative and mutual forms begin to take shape and evolve in this era: consumer co-operatives, mutual and co-operative bank/credit institutions, mutual workers'

---

[13] These various thinkers each advanced slightly different utopian socialist schemes, often short on implementable detail, which all typically led, in theory, to a complete transformation of society to be run on some type of co-operative basis. But their work also birthed targeted and specific forms of institutional experiments in France.

aid societies, and producers' associations/worker co-operatives.[14] Various forms of these four co-operative enterprise families, located in what Sewell (1980) might have termed "the margins of the law," appear in the historical record with frequency during the 19th century's first half, before eventually becoming collectively legible as part of a comprehensively coordinated co-operative framework. I trace the development of each below.

Though consumer co-operatives could trace their lineage as far back as 1793 to brief revolutionary-era experiments related to workers' corporations (Gaumont 1924; Gide 1904), the first sustained effort appeared in 1830s Lyon, a key center of early French artisanal silk production. Lyon had been a center of revolt after the July Revolution (the Second French Revolution of 1830), with labor radicalism and mutualism efforts sparked by the revolts of silk spinners, or *canuts*, in 1831 and 1834. The first of these, in 1831, Engels (1880, ch. 2) described as "the first working-class rising" to occur under capitalism. Here, an early consumer co-operative inspired by Fourier's (1808, 1822, 1829) writings, specifically his utopian *phalanstère* communities, was founded in 1835, called *le commerce véridique et social* (truly equitable and social business). After several years, this enterprise faded; reflecting the government's sentiment at the time, it was deemed illegal. Brazda and Schediwy (1989, 678) note, "From the point of view of the law, Commerce véridique et social was not a company; there were no articles of incorporation and the public prosecutor regarded the founding as an unlawful speculation." Often, these mid-19th-century co-operatives were appendages to the workers' corporations and producers' associations (Gaumont 1924; Lambersens et al. 2017; Brazda and Schediwy 1989). Consumer cooperation of the Rochdale variety, though it would not fully develop in France until the Third Republic, was thus present in fits and starts in this era, several cities hosting such short-lived efforts as had occurred in Lyon (Gaumont 1924).

Co-operative banking forms had similar false starts: until the Second Empire of the 1850s and 1860s, French banking was dominated by the state and state-related banks and the Haute Banque, a loosely defined term used to refer to roughly 20 private family-led banking houses (Plessis 2003). These houses were generally incorporated as partnerships (*société en nom collectif*) or limited partnerships (*société en commandite simple*) of the "society" parent family of organizational forms, still granted only by special permission of the state. In

---

[14] In the French context, where the concept of associationism looms large, worker co-operatives and producers' associations were long near-synonymous. A producers' association is thus not equivalent to the modern Anglophone producer co-operative, which can consist of IOFs forming co-operatives. In France, such co-operatives, which emerged much later, are called merchant or industrialist co-operatives, as will be covered later in the chapter.

the aftermath of the 1848 Revolution, however, state restrictions on banking were loosened during the Second Empire, often referred to in French as the "Empire Libéral" due to its conflicted effort to allow a degree of liberalism so as to appease republican sentiment, which also allowed mutual banks to emerge. In fact, the idea of mutual banks would be central in the 1848 Revolution, with Proudhon's idea for a People's Bank included in the revolutionaries' plans and implementation efforts. Though Proudhon's Banque du Peuple was never fully realized as initially planned, the idea persisted, and by the 1860s the first mutual and co-operative banks were in operation. In 1863, Jean-Pierre Beluze, a follower of French and American utopian socialist and co-operative developer Etienne Cabet, created the Société du Crédit au Travail, designed to serve the worker co-operatives of Paris (Karafolas 2016). In 1864–65, classical political economists Leon Walras and Leon Say helped create and work in the Caisse d'escompte des associations populaires, also designed to serve the producers' associations and worker co-operatives (Ros 2001), which was followed by an imperially approved version, the Caisse d'escompte des Associations co-operatives (Hubert-Valleroux 1884). These banks each lasted only a few years, but would act as demonstration projects for the modern co-operative banking system in France.

The two most well-developed strands of cooperation to emerge in this early period, however, were the mutual aid societies and the producers' associations/worker co-operatives, which also eventually achieved greater degrees of state legitimacy.

Though most of the journeymen's *confréries*, the fraternal mutual aid entities that had prevailed under the corporate and guild system, were shuttered after the 1790s, a few survived the original French Revolution in altered form, reorganized as societies of mutual aid (Sibalis 1989). They also took on the charitable functions that some of the *compagnonnages* had provided, as well as those previously provided by the Catholic Church, which saw only some of its prior privileges restored by various early 19th-century French governments. These governments—including both Napoleon's and the subsequent Restoration government—were generally tolerant of these mutual aid efforts (Sibalis 1989), granting them allowances to operate, albeit they were not technically or legally recognized as mutual aid societies per se. The state occasionally even offered financial support (Sibalis 1989). Philanthropists of the era supported their growth, particularly in Paris. Some employers were supportive and encouraged workers to join mutual aid societies (Sibalis 1989), which were often organized by trade. Over the first half of the 19th century, the number of mutual aid societies in Paris would grow from virtually none to nearly 300, counting tens of thousands of workers among their members, who claimed death benefits for funeral expenses, a sick benefit, and pensions (Sibalis 1989). These societies were a direct outgrowth of their predecessors: "The mutual aid societies of Paris thus continued to evolve, but their quantitative explosion in the first half of the nineteenth century was built on models elaborated, piece by piece, across the preceding hundred years" (Garrioch 2011, 29). After the July Revolution, a law in 1835 formally allowed these entities to make deposits into the savings and loan banks (*caisses d'epargnes*) (Gibaud 1986, 1998), offering them partial legal recognition and increased financial stability. During the Second Empire, in 1852 Louis Napoleon would remove from the penal code the legal ban on forming mutual aid societies, giving rise to an "imperial mutual" system of semiformal recognition.

These mutual societies ultimately developed into today's employer-centric and mutual/co-operative-intensive insurance, social security, and retirement systems in France (Dreyfus 2016; Van der Linden 1996; Bennet 1975). Unlike in the United States, United Kingdom, and many other rich democracies, which have a single-payer "Beveridge-style" public social security scheme complemented by supplemental private retirement and old age social security, France's publicly mandated, primary social security system is more Bismarckian, with private and employer-based systems. A significant portion is administered by mutually owned insurers and related organizations, which descend directly from the surviving, if adapted, feudal logic of the *confréries* and *compagnonnages* by way of these early mutual aid societies.

The fourth strain, the worker co-operative, most clearly demonstrates the role of both evolution and revolution in forming the co-operative field in France. Transforming in stages, from the postrevoluntary workers' corporations and surviving mutual societies into the producers' association or workers' association of the post–1830 Revolution (the Second French Revolution), it would further evolve to occupy the central position in the coordinated economic strategies proposed and implemented in the 1848 Revolution (the Third Revolution), each time carried forward by participants from the prior revolution. By the period's end, the worker co-operative occupied a central ideological position within French socialist and labor movements. They often featured prominently in both their proposed and actual implemented political programs, as a means by which to free workers from "wage slavery" (Andrews 2013; Roediger 1991); as the key "method of trade emancipation from the wage system (Moss 1976a, 73), the form enabled "skilled workers [to] pool their meager resources and become their own masters of machines in co-operative associations" (Moss 1976a, 73).

Specifically, elements of the feudal *compagnonnages*' various worker training and coordination activities, organized by trade and region, persisted after the revolutionary workers' corporations into the early 19th century; some operated clandestinely, others in groups of fewer than 20 to be in accordance with the laws which restricted associations of more than 20 (Sewell 1980). Sparked by the 1830 Revolution, and working from the ideas of Saint-Simon, a generation of French intellectuals, journalists, workers, and politicians, led by Philippe Buchez and Louis Blanc, worked collectively to transform these organizations into producers' associations or workers' associations (initially *contrat d'association de travailleurs* and then *l'association ouvrière*). Acting as institutional innovators, or "skilled social actors" in field theory language, they developed and codified, in an iterative and specific fashion, governance rules and models for this emergent form and disseminated information around the country about these associationist experiments.

Their ideas initially flowered during and in the months immediately after the July Revolution of 1830, during which time radical political programs, put forward by groups like the Society of the Friends of the People, called for "voluntary co-operatives or associations of production" (Loubére 1959, 321; cf. Cavaignac 1832). Sewell (1980, 203–5) notes, "By the fall of 1831 his (Buchez') schemes for workers' associations had been radically transformed—from an initial plan for mutual insurance societies to a plan for producers' cooperatives" (cf. Hubert-Valleroux 1884; Frobert and Lauricella 2015). Buchez, a medical doctor and avowed Catholic and Christian Socialist, put forward and published a plan for the workers' association based on indivisible capital reserves, in which the net profits of the co-operative could not be divided for distribution to individuals, and calling for initial financial aid from the state (Sewell 1980; Hubert-Valleroux 1884; Frobert and Lauricella 2015). Parisian workers sought to enact these associational and co-operative plans, as "beginning around 1831, workers in various trades began to recast their corporations as associations" (Sewell 1980, 204). The plan included not only co-operative production efforts but also strikes and calls for organizing across industries collectively. Efforts would again be short-lived, suppressed by the state after the 1834 Lyon uprisings, tightening restrictions on even smaller associations, making these experiments again illegal, though a few survived (Hubert-Valleroux 1884).

The institutional effects of this brief period were nonetheless significant and long-lasting. Across two revolutions, feudal remnants had been transformed into workers' associations and informed the emergence of a French class consciousness, with worker co-operatives at its center. As Sewell (1980, 209, 211) writes, "[I]t was in this confluence of corporate and republican agitation in the fall of 1833 that the Parisian workers developed the idiom of association into a coherent framework of collective action," which did not "designate workers' co-operatives as a separate kind of association but as one aspect of the generation association or corps for each trade." This led to ideas for association and solidarity across trades as a united working class, through federations of workers' associations (Hubert-Valleroux 1884).

Buchez and Blanc, both of whom would come to occupy prominent government positions in the 1848 Revolution, continued to experiment with other workers' associations, deploying their plans, helping to develop implementable models for worker co-operatives throughout the 1830 and 1840s (Hubert-Valleroux 1884), setting the stage for their reappearance in grand fashion in the next revolution, in 1848. Buchez would expand his plans for workers' associations, which initially focused on highly skilled urban workers, to encompass many other types of workers (Guentzel 2022; Buchez and Roux-Lavergne 1836), while Blanc would author *L'Organisation du travail* (1839), which would lay out the case for the co-operative workshops that were central in the 1848 Revolution, which was part of a revolutionary wave across Europe and which collectively caused Marx and Engels to pen that a "spectre was haunting Europe."

Indeed, it was in the 1848 Revolution that the producers'/workers' associations came to take center stage in France's labor and socialist movements. Led by Blanc, who was appointed by the provisional French government after 1848 to examine the "labor question," his Luxembourg Commission, in conjunction with Parisian workers, called for the creation of an entire economic exchange system centered on national, co-operatively owned workshops across the trades. Articulating a French variant of the "co-operative commonwealth" idea of interco-operative coordination, the Luxembourg Commission yielded proposals, briefly implemented, for interlocking institutions based on the workers' corporations, including both the co-operatively owned National Workshops (Les Ateliers Nationaux) and Proudhon's mutualist Bank of the People, backed with initial government funds to be sourced from railway profits.[15] Ultimately, these efforts were only partially implemented during the Second Republic due to political infighting, arguably set up to fail by a conflicted government (LaMartine et al., 1851; Hubert-Valleroux 1884). Nonetheless, while in the provinces the workers' associations were either forcibly shuttered by the local government or preemptively closed to avoid arrest, a significant number in Paris persisted past 1852 and into the Second Empire.

---

[15] Marx would mock Buchez's proposal for state aid to workers associations. Marx, letter to Schweitzer, October 13, 1868. (Marx, 1868).

Indeed, as of the mid-1860s, at least 16 such associations which had sprung from the 1848 Revolution were in operation across a wide range of industries and trades, as then covered in the *New York Times* (1864); countless others continued to form, with coordinated funding and development activities (Tombs 1984). Lacking explicit legal recognition prior to 1867, they appeared to operate on paper as fraternal societies or traditional business societies to avoid government prohibitions (Hubert-Valleroux 1884).

Notably, by this time it was well established among the various strains of French socialism and labor movements that workers' associations were key to ending slavery, both with respect to its "wage slavery" form (a term slowly borrowed from the English before appearing with more frequency after 1848; Roediger 1991) as well as in its "chattel slavery" form in the French colonies. Slavery there had been abolished in 1794, was partially reinstated by Napoleon, then abolished again in 1848. As Andrews (2013, 511) notes, "Although not uniform in their approach, Charles Fourier, Charles Dain, Désiré Laverdant, and Jules Lechevalier all suggested some form of co-operative labor association as the solution to the problem of slave emancipation." They did so as part of broader socialist efforts drawing on the French workers' "deeper reservoirs of class solidarity than were their US counterparts" (Moss 1994, 334), as has been affirmed by quantitative studies of Third Republic socialist strikes, which were ideologically broader and straddled greater swaths of workers (Friedman 1988a, 1988b).

Thus, by the end of the Second Empire and the famed Paris Commune of 1871, worker co-operatives were established as central to the labor movement. Indeed, the April 16, 1871, decree of the Communards called for the handing over of abandoned factories to co-operatives, an idea which has continued to inspire co-operative efforts to "recover businesses" around the world, from Chicago's recent window-producing worker co-operative to well-known efforts in Argentina (Vieta 2019). Such efforts arguably all trace their lineage to France and this long 19th-century evolution, which established worker co-operatives as central to a broader co-operative strategy. Tombs (1984, 970–71) succinctly summarizes:

> Workers' co-operatives in 1871 had already a long history in France; they were the essence of French socialist aspirations for most of the nineteenth century. The idea of co-operation as a means of escaping the undesirable consequences of capitalism and industrialization had been widely propagated in the 1830s, and indeed it inherited something of a much older corporate tradition. Elaborated in a variety of ways by Buchez, Fourier, Proudhon and Blanc, by the 1840s ideas of 'association' as a solution to social problems had become commonplace even

among moderate republicans. Consequently, the 1848 Revolution saw attempts to put them into practice, including the ill-fated National Workshops. Their closure, and the June insurrection, were by no means the end of co-operatives. Nearly 300 were set up in Paris during the Second Republic, from 120 trades, and they had perhaps 50,000 members; there were still about 200 in existence in the harsh climate of 1851.

During the Second Empire, and especially during the 1860s, the establishment of co-operatives, both of consumers and of producers, became a central part of the organized activity of workers. Chambres syndicales, which were tolerated by the regime from the middle 1860s, commonly devoted part of their funds to establishing producers' co-operatives, which were regarded both as a way of employing members during strikes and as a long-term solution to the problem of wage slavery. By 1865, about 50 Parisian chambres syndicales were accumulating funds for this purpose; by 1868, there were over 50 producers' co-operatives in Paris and a similar number in the provinces. Their appeal was not limited to socialists and trade unionists. Prominent radicals and liberals also favoured them. Victor Hugo and Georges Clemenceau, for example, were supporters, and the leading liberal economist Leon Say was chairman of the Caisse d'Escompte des Associations Populaires. Naturally, therefore, the republican Government of National Defence encouraged the establishment of several important producers' co-operatives during the Prussian siege of Paris in the winter of 1870–1, and gave them large contracts for the making of uniforms. The tailors' co-operative gave work to some 35,000 people, mostly women working at home. A newspaper, L'Ouvrier de l'Avenir, "Organe des Chambres Syndicales et des Associations Ouvrieres," set up in March 1871, listed 50 producers' co-operatives that existed in Paris in the weeks before the outbreak of the insurrection which established the Commune. They were mainly small enterprises in the traditional skilled trades of the city, such as jewellery, tailoring and hat making. In short, by the time the Commune was set up, the idea of producers' co-operatives was familiar and widely approved, though there were diverse interpretations of their significance—a minor element in a mixed economy or a practical step towards the eventual emancipation of labour.

These ideas persisted well beyond the Second Republic and the 1871 Paris Commune: "As Bernard Moss has shown, a vision of the future socialist society as a federation of democratic self-governing trades that collectively owned the means of production dominated the French socialist and labor movement right down to World War I" (Sewell 1980, 275). Moss's (1976a, 1976b) seminal accounts of this aspect of France's particular labor history and its central role in 1848 and beyond in shaping French socialism, labor, and unionism is worth reviewing:

> The original form of trade socialism revolved around the producers' association or co-operative, a social workshop owned and controlled by members of a trade. Arising along with the trade union in many industrializing nations, the producers' association became the main project and ultimate goal of the French labor movement. From the beginning, it was part of a larger socialist strategy for the collectivization of industrial capital and emancipation of trades from the wage system. Mechanisms were developed to prevent the formation of an emancipated elite in one trade or among the collective trades. Associations were originally designed with expanding funds of collective capital to ensure the continual admission of new members without capital and emancipate the entire trade. To give associations an advantage in competition with larger capitalist enterprise, workers looked to the establishment of a democratic and social republic, which would provide leverage in the form of public credit and contracts. Representing the interests of the industrious classes—workers, peasants, and tradesmen—against the privileged bourgeoisie, the republic was expected to supply the credit that was restricted under a regime of privilege. Even without the help of the state, workers could begin to finance themselves by organizing mutual credit and exchange in a federation of trades or universal association. With the help of a social republic and universal association, workers could accumulate capital, outcompete capitalist enterprise, and lay the foundations of a socialist economy administered by a federation of trades. (Moss 1976a, 72–73)

More generally, by the end of the Second Empire and the establishment of the Third Republic in 1870–71, most of the main co-operative organizational forms which would come to form the field were thus visible and partially organized and attaining increasing and substantial degrees of legality and state support, and with it, legibility and legitimacy as a field. The Second Empire had seen the first significant enabling acts for co-operatives and mutuals, giving them their first, sustained official sanction under the law. In 1852, the prohibition on mutual aid societies was removed from the penal code, By the Second Empire's end in 1870, mutuals could register without seeking case-by-case state approval; the overwhelming majority of mutual aid societies registered, numbering in the thousands (Gibaud 1998). In 1867, the *société de capitaux variable* was introduced, which allowed the *société co-operative* for workers and consumers to be legally formed. This latter act in particular would establish the beginnings of a national legal framework for the consumer co-operative, which would come to prominence in the Belle Époque of the Third Republic.

Alongside competing, capitalist economic forms, a proto-field of distinct types of co-operatives and fledgling interfirm coordination strategies had thus finally emerged out of a lengthy period of institutional and field experimentation, initially stoked by the field rupture generated by the first French Revolution. Efforts to wipe the field environment in the economy clean had, in the long run, arguably been a failure: variations of old forms had returned to intervene between the people and the state.[16] But new substitutes, including the co-operative, had been imprinted and incubated in the void, and ultimately achieved partial recognition by the state, framed by field-building skilled social entrepreneurs who sought linguistic idioms and forms which governments could accept. Though it was sometimes hostile to the co-operative in this era, the French state had limited the development of other forms as well. Thus, by the dawn of the Second Industrial Revolution and the First Globalization in the 1870s and 1880s, France's co-operatives were paradoxically still limited in their reach, while also being comparatively well positioned with respect to other institutional forms in the late-industrializing French economy.

A Field in Full: From "the Co-operative Republic" to Les Trente Glorieuses, 1870s–1960s

Throughout the Third and Fourth Republics (1870/71–1940, 1946–58), the co-operative field continued its slow evolutionary emergence in a process marked by two dynamics. First, though not always successful, co-operative actors generally experienced repeated organizing and legislative success, procuring direct and indirect state sanction and support and a comprehensive enabling legal framework. After specifying the co-operative as a form in national law in 1867, other significant legislative acts passed in 1894, 1898, 1899, 1901, 1906, 1908, 1910, 1915, 1923, 1947, and 1949; many of these acts were amended in other years, consistent with processes of institutional layering. By 1918, a formal council liaising between all co-operatives and the government was in place. Smaller, industry-specific co-operative councils and various government ministries were also instituted, and by the late 1940s a comprehensive national enabling framework for most major types of co-operatives was in operation, specifying their legal status, their ability to access public funds,

---

[16] This is consistent with Thelen's (2004) findings in the German case of education/training institutions, regarding the persistence of institutional forms and logics to survive highly disruptive "critical juncture" events.

appropriate tax treatment, and a formal liaison role for a range of co-operative meta-organizations.[17]

Second, at the same time, co-operative actors continued to organize to claim and develop a well-defined field space in the French economy. This was not a top-down, comprehensive strategy of the variety attempted, for example, in the 1848 Revolution. Instead, they repeatedly built local and regional co-operative networks and organizations into national federations—obtaining legal sanction as they went—by organizing with respect to key emergent bases of both social solidarity and social cleavage. Where possible they bridged divides with respect to worker class, religion, or political orientation, while at other times organizing efforts remained separate and distinct, resulting in four distinct co-operative movements, which were only loosely coordinated: agricultural, workers/consumers, educators/public employees, and merchants/industrialists. Borrowing from various co-operative and mutual models and coordination strategies in the United Kingdom and Germany (Jeantet 2016; Laville 2010), to varying degrees these different fronts of cooperation also developed their own commercial, banking, and social protection/insurance functions. I review each of these developments in greater detail below.

Co-operatives achieve full legal legitimacy: The Third Republic's "effervescence of special provision." The Third Republic remains the longest uninterrupted political regime in modern France. Its key electoral and political institutions persisted from the end of the Second Empire (and the collapse of the Paris Communes of 1871) until Vichy France, the Nazi-occupied government of World War II. Continuing France's postrevolutionary history, in which organizations and associations coming between the individual and the state required particular and evolving permissions, during this period the co-operative field's state-sanctioned legitimacy continued to develop incrementally, slowly transitioning from requiring special permission to receiving explicit state sanction and support. Though co-operative actors sometimes unsuccessfully proposed legislation, they were frequently successful in procuring enabling laws and other forms of direct and indirect support. Ultimately, as Seeberger (2014, 63–64) notes in his history of the evolution of French co-operative policy and law, "Two important markers shape its evolution: the law of 24 July 1867 which recognised, although only indirectly, the existence of co-operative societies, and the legislative framework of the law of 10 September 1947, which defined the legal form and gave it its full legal identity. The slow genesis of a law specific to co-operatives began with the first

---

[17] Co-operative taxation in France is extremely complex and varies by co-operative subtype. In general, co-operatives appear far less subject to double taxation (at the corporate and member levels) because their retained funds promote prosocial employment development.

attempts at forming co-operatives and culminated with the lasting consolidation of co-operative legislation. . . . Co-operative law required patient and rigorous efforts for almost one century, until it found its place in the French legislative structure." Between the key acts of 1867 and 1947, however, the government repeatedly passed enabling legislation and offered supportive policy treatment, as well as sometimes offering financial support, in what Seeberger called "an effervescence of special provision" (68). Among the myriad legislative developments in this interval, many of which I review below, three notably eased the co-operative field's continuous development: the complete legalization of labor unions and strikes, which occurred by 1884 (unions were frequently key supporters of different types of co-operatives; see prior section and the next subsection); the charter of mutuality in 1898, which moved from tolerance to encouragement of mutual societies in providing primary social protection; and the explicit 1901 recognition by the government of a right of two or more people to form an association for any socioeconomic purpose. This last development finally clarified that the revolutionary-era Chapelier/Allarde restrictions on free association were dead.

Though the names of the political parties changed frequently, as did the composition of the ruling coalitions, these acts were all passed under parliaments with republican-led coalitions, typically consisting of moderate republicans ruling in coalition with more radical republicans and socialists. Ultimately, the state worked with co-operative actors to develop a formal policy structure and governing body, through which the co-operative field and the state could mutually communicate, a structure which has evolved but remains in place to this day. The High Council for Mutuality, developed after the Charter of Mutuality in 1898, and the High Council of Cooperation, tripartite bodies with co-operative, parliamentary, and executive branch representation, created in 1918 after World War I, remain important bodies for such communication regarding the policy needs of co-operatives.

As noted by Duverger (2016a, with forward by Hamon), this legal structuring allowed a great compromise: the state would end revolutionary prohibitions on civil society organizations by defining their activity, providing them with loans, and conditioning how they could raise and spend their funds:

> This effort of structuring the co-operative and mutualist movements was made during their progressive institutionalization during the Third Republic, which gave them specific statutes. The Chart of Mutuality was adopted in 1898, while special laws multiplied to recognize the different families of co-operatives: agricultural credit and agriculture by 1899, low-cost housing co-operatives in 1908, maritime mutual credit in 1910, worker co-operatives in 1915, consumer co-operatives

in 1917, popular banks and surety/safety mutual societies in 1917, and artisans co-operatives in 1923. . . . . [T]his adds to the end of the a priori suspicion with regard to the associations that had come with the 1901 law ending the prohibition on association. . . . [T]he negotiation of these statutes is the culmination of an institutional compromise between the State and these movements. . . . The State accords advances (loans) to the co-operatives, obliges the mutual to invest their funds and reserves in the public funds, and gives grants to the associations. *The social economy is therefore tied to the State, which organizes its funding circuits, and subjects them to regulation in exchange for their legitimation.* (Duverger 2016a, 26–27, translated by author, emphasis added)

By 1947, a thorough enabling framework for the co-operative field was thus in place, with the laws of 1947 and 1949 also enabling co-operatives to participate in postwar economic reconstruction projects (Seeberger 2014). These laws continued to be amended, as needed, through Les Trente Glorieuses.

Four movements of modern French cooperation: Agricultural, workers/consumers, educators/public employees, and merchants/industrialists. The legislative flowering under the Third and Fourth Republics of France did not reflect a unified co-operative movement per se. To be sure, as reviewed earlier, co-operatives had clearly captured the national imagination during repeated revolutions and upheavals, through revolutionaries' repeated demonstration projects in the original field void left by the first French Revolution; there would have been few who were unfamiliar with co-operatives as a result. But rather than reflect the efforts of some unified plan, co-operative advocacy and usage developed across four major substantive groups during this era—peasants/agricultural interests, workers/consumers, educators/public employees/intellectuals, and merchants/industrialists. One cannot claim, on the basis of the historical evidence, that these constituted distinct subfields of the co-operative field, but they were not fully coordinated either, instead exhibiting greater connections within, rather than across, these four fronts.

Agriculture, arguably the oldest French co-operative type, had been among the last to develop. This was largely because agriculture itself had been late to modernize and develop. As Desigauz (1940, 31) notes, "French agriculture, slower in its development than either commerce or industry, had to wait until the close of the last century before being equipped with any credit organisation corresponding to its requirements and capable of providing it, by means of a rational employment of scientific progress, with the resources necessary to its expansion and to the betterment of its production." Previous efforts, including those of the state-backed Crédit Foncier as a land and mortgage lender in the 19th century, had failed due to institutions' physical remoteness from local agricultural production, according to Desigauz. The solution for both agricultural production and finance was to build a locally dispersed national infrastructure from societies initially restricted by department, which were ultimately allowed to federate, merge, and expand. Notably, the model that agricultural cooperation ultimately adapted—of "territorial" local and regional networks federated into a national network—represents the general approach that other various types of co-operatives also utilized to achieved scale in France in this era.

Disagreements between the traditional agricultural co-operative societies in the mid-19th century were evident in case law, which attempted to resolve their disputes despite their lack of enabling legislation, leading to failed attempts in the 1860s to explicitly enable them in France's rural code of law (Seeberger 2014). Finally, in the 1880s, the recently legalized trade and labor unions (1884) would lead the way in advocating for agricultural producer and credit co-operatives. Specifically, future prime minister René Waldeck-Rousseau's 1884 act legalizing trade and labor unions would immediately and intentionally be used for this purpose by the most prominent farming organization, the Société des Agriculteurs de France. The group was dominated by conservative and Catholic interests and also backed by landowners, and in response to the law immediately developed local "agricultural syndicates," which ultimately rolled regional bodies into a national, federated structure (Cleary 1989), securing an "agricultural peace."

They were not clear on exactly what they were creating, however: "[T]he precise shape and character of these new organizations was not immediately apparent to society activists" (Cleary 1989, 34). Their efforts were matched by a rival republican/socialist effort, led by the Société nationale d'encouragement à l'agriculture, created in 1880 with express government support, and they sought to develop agricultural co-operatives, insurance, and credit institutions locally and nationally. The government had immediately followed on this effort by creating a formal Ministry of Agriculture to further support the development of such institutions, and laws explicitly enabling agricultural credit and cooperation soon followed, enhanced by provision of public loans, in 1894 and 1906. The co-operative elements of the two rival syndicalist factions— one Catholic, one socialist—would be joined together in the Fédération nationale de la mutualité et de la coopération agricole in 1910, at which time France had more than 5,000 agricultural syndicates with nearly 800,000 members (Simpson 2011, 64–65). Though the tensions between the Catholic and socialist agricultural groups would persist into the 1940s and beyond, the Fédération eventually incorporated other national coordinating groups for agricultural co-operatives. These too were also often birthed with direct and indirect state political and financial support, including those for agricultural credit and insurance. Today this umbrella group is the Confédération Nationale de la Mutualité, de la Coopération et du Crédit Agricoles, which works alongside the High Council of Agricultural Cooperation, which mediates between the agricultural co-operative movement and the state to advance agricultural co-operatives' interests in policy/law.

Critically, agriculture would also develop its own social security, insurance, and financial institutions: the law of July 4, 1901, exempted mutual agricultural insurance from restrictions that dated to 1867, and Catholic and socialist agricultural insurance groups were created. This was part of a broader expansion of mutual societies in providing primary social protection after passing the 1898 charter of mutuality, creating a Bismarckian system of employment-based, mutually owned social security. When France finally developed universal social security in the 1940s, though mutuals were demoted to a supplemental/secondary role in many industries, farmers refused to cede control via the agricultural mutual insurers, which continue to own and administer their primary system of publicly mandated social security benefits in France today. These various agricultural co-operative insurance and retirement programs are now led by Crédit Agricole's assurances division, Ag2r La Mondiale, and Groupama (Groupe des Assurances Mutuelles Agricoles). In parallel, a national network and federation of agricultural credit societies, enabled by multiple parliamentary acts, would also develop in this period, over time turning into Crédit Agricole, France's global agricultural banking co-operative and one of the five main banking groups in the country.

Meanwhile, the labor, workers, and socialist movements would also develop their own co-operative organizations, in the second strain of French cooperation which developed in this era. They would continue to develop producers' associations and worker co-operatives, which formed in varying collaborations with both consumer co-operatives and urban labor unions, while also giving rise to their own banking institutions: in 1893, la Banque coopérative des associations ouvrières de production (Workers' Production Associations Bank) would be founded. By 1938, this had evolved into today's Crédit Coopératif, France's leading social economy business bank, for worker and consumer co-operatives, and ESS enterprises (Dreyfus 2013). The bank is also a member of Groupe BPCE, one of France's five largest banking groups, and an umbrella co-operative banking group.

Again reflecting how upheavals seed postcrisis evolution, participants from the 1871 Paris Commune would develop worker co-operatives throughout the 1880s and beyond, taking advantage of the 1884 law legalizing unions to found a Consultative Chamber to help develop worker co-operatives (la

Chambre Consultative de sociétés coopératives ouvrières de production; Martin 1947).[18] By 1885, there were approximately 40 worker co-operatives in the country (Antoni 1980, 18). Eventually, the Law of 18 December 1915 would establish the specific legal form of worker co-operatives (today known as *sociétés coopératives et participatives*), which henceforth benefited from their own national legal statute. At the time of World War I, there were at least 100 worker co-operatives in France, some accounts claiming 120 (Antoni 1980) and others as many as 400 (Parker and Cowan 1944, 86). In 1936, worker co-operative development experienced an uptick, numbering more than 400 and including more than 20,000 workers in total (Parker and Cowan 1944; Antoni 1980), and by 1937, worker co-operatives had transformed the Consultative Chamber into the Confédération générale des Coopératives ouvrières de production, which remains the national organizing and liaising meta-organization for worker co-operatives (as Confédération générale des SCOP).[19] Observers at the time noted significant national development of co-operatives in the book publishing industry and select development of worker co-operatives in other industries, such as the Paris construction industry, some having as many as 800 employees, as reported by Edmond Briat, architect of the Confédération Générale, at the National Co-operative Parliament of 1938. By that year, the worker co-operative movement had also created a central fund at Crédit Coopératif to finance development of new co-operatives, with the government contributing matching funds (Lasne 2001); new development would continue apace after World War II, gaining speed in 1947 (Martin 1947).

Critically, though worker co-operatives continued to form and develop in this era, the key front of development was the consumer co-operative movement, which created a strong national operating footprint and framework during the Third Republic. The 1915 law for worker co-operatives referenced above was followed by the Law of 7 May 1917 to better enable consumer co-operatives to obtain credit and expand. As noted earlier, consumer co-operative efforts had often been appended to the worker co-operatives and producers' associations but initially lacked full support of the labor movement and socialists. Though adopted as one of the "three pillars" of the French socialism and labor movements,[20] many participants saw the consumer-related efforts as a transition model to a worker/producer co-operative economy

---

[18] Cf. testimony of Briat at the National Co-operative Parliament, Revue des études coopératives 67, 193–95.
[19] SCOP is the modern worker co-operative society. The acronym has changed over time: *société coopérative de production, société coopérative ouvrière de production,* and *société coopérative et participative.*
[20] Alongside trade unionism and political party organization (Furlough 1991).

at best, or as being at odds with worker and production co-operatives at worst, given consumers' focus on lower prices, possibly at the expense of fair compensation of labor. This is, in some ways, similar to the early U.S. labor movement's experiments with consumers' cooperation (see Chapter 6). But in France, unlike in the United States, the consumer co-operative movement established a national framework and achieved explicit support of the labor movement. After a decade of rapid growth, in 1885 nearly 90 consumer co-operatives would come together to form the Fédération de Coopératives de Consommation (Lambersens et al. 2017), a national coalition for the sector, which had birthed France's first chain store (Lambersens et al. 2017).

As with French agriculture, and reflecting the consumer versus worker tension noted above, two national consumer co-operative movements developed. There was a socialist movement of "red co-operatives," La Bourse coopérative des sociétés socialistes de consummation ("La Bourse"), led by Marxist Mathieu Basile, aka Julian Guesde, which would splinter from the main Federation in 1895. The main Federation, renamed L'Union Co-operative, would take a more bourgeois-friendly, nonviolent approach embodied by the "yellow co-operatives," associated with Protestantism and the emergent Christian socialism. In fact, Charles Gide would be a leader in both the Christian socialist movement and in the more bourgeois consumer co-operative societies in the south of France, which adopted Gide's School of Nîmes approach. They sought emancipation from profit-maximizing, liberal capitalism without resorting to violence or statism by adopting the distributive/consumer co-operative model at the heart of a solidarity-based, "social economy" (Gide 1905a, 1905b) to construct a "co-operative republic" (Furlough 1991). In 1921, Gide, whose concept of the social economy would come to prevail across the co-operative and ESS movements, also established the *Revue des études coopératives*, an academic and applied journal, to disseminate information about experimentation in the co-operative field, nationally and internationally.

In order to work together to advocate for themselves and avoid being taxed in the same way as explicitly profit-seeking enterprises, the two unions would merge in 1912 to form the FNCC, Fédération Nationale de Coopératives de Consommation. In three short decades, the number of consumer co-operatives had grown from approximately 300 in the 1880s to over 3,000 in the early 1910s (Brazda and Schediwy 1989; Lambersens et al. 2017), with roughly one million members. The FNCC in 1914 represented approximately two-thirds of consumer co-operatives in France, placing it fourth in the ICA's rankings of national consumer co-operative memberships at the time (Brazda and Schediwy 1989; Lambersens et al. 2017). As in the United Kingdom, they would develop a robust production capacity, creating their own goods in their own factories, and become a major force in French consumption through the mid-20th century, with a double-digit market share in groceries/home goods. They also enjoyed significant trade union support, particularly after 1920, when a union charter was included in the national collective agreement of consumer co-operatives (Lambersens et al. 2017). Consumer co-operatives also featured in the postwar rebuilding of France, engaging directly with the state to secure cost-efficient food and supplies (Parker and Cowan 1944).

Educators, teachers, intellectuals, and public-sector workers constitute a third front of cooperation. They not only developed their own consumer co-operatives in the early 1900s; they also developed their own insurance/social security and banking institutions. Today Mutuelle d'assurance des instituteurs de France, which advertises itself as *l'assureur militant*, or the "activist insurer" of the social and solidarity economy, traces its history back to the 1930s, when teachers coordinated the development of their own automotive insurance mutual. This would expand and develop over the following decades, ultimately growing to administer their own supplemental social security and retirement systems, as delegated by the state. They would also develop their own bank, first as an association in 1951 called Caisse de Prêts de l'Education Nationale de Seine et Oisein, which would be redeveloped by the 1960s as a co-operative called CASDEN, Caisse d'aide sociale de l'Éducation nationale. Today CASDEN serves as a bank for all public employees and has become part of the larger Groupe BPCE, one of the five principal banking groups in France. The educators/public co-operative network also includes Mutuelle générale de l'Éducation nationale, which not only offers health insurance for educators but also owns hospitals and medical facilities for its subscribers' and member-owners' use.

As part of the educators' movement, a student co-operative movement also developed during this era: in 1928, L'Office Central de la Coopération à l'Ecole (OCCE) was created, which works with students and teachers to develop co-operatives in classrooms to finance and run student projects. The OCCE operates in public schools with direct approval of the Ministry of Education and sometimes receives grants from various levels of governments (e.g., city, region) on specific projects. Today, such co-operatives have over 5 million members across 51,000 schools, grouped by region/department. In addition, Henri Desroche, who developed the "action research" model for social economy experimentation, aided in developing a system of Collèges Coopératifs at the end of this period, founding the first in Paris in 1959 to promote higher education on co-operatives. By the 1970s, these various entities were coordinating their interests in activities through the newly created Comité de coordination des œuvres mutualistes et coopératives de l'Éducation nationale.

Finally, the fourth front of cooperation was that of bourgeois merchants and industrialists regrouping to form purchasing co-operatives. In France, this developed in direct response to the consumer co-operatives of the 1880s. As Holler (1992, 83) describes it:

> In Reims on May 29, 1885, the first joint purchasing society in France is constituted: la Société rémoise de l'épicerie vins et spiritueux. This society, voluntarily born from the action of independent merchants and grocers, was a reaction to the appearance of a new form of distribution, the consumer co-operative, which newly threatened their activity through competition, and constitutes the first society of purchasing in common, in France. Although they had not yet used the term "co-operative" to qualify and refer to their activities, the "Rémoise" must nevertheless be considered the precursor to retail merchant co-operatives, which would not operate with a specific legal statute until 1949. (author's translation)

Not all merchant and industrialist co-operatives were defensive reactions to consumer co-operatives, as Holler details, and the approach spread throughout France rapidly in the early 20th century as merchants and manufacturers used co-operative structures to scale purchasing, advertising, and other aspects of their businesses. Beyond coordinating their businesses co-operatively, these merchants/industrialists also developed their own co-operative financial institution, Mutuelle d'assurance des commerçants et industriels de France et des cadres et des salariés de l'industrie et du commerce, which was founded in 1960 for supplemental insurance, retirement, and other social protection for the sector. It subsequently created SOCRAM, the mutual/co-operative bank for the sector. This fourth strain, notably, emerged after the others, largely after the world wars: three of today's six leading French grocers, structured as co-operatives of individual stores, were founded in the 1920s (Systeme U, originally Unico), the 1940s (E. Leclerc), and the 1960s (Intermarché). Curiously, these co-operatives would provide competition to the consumer co-operatives and may have played a role in their decline (Lambersens et al. 2017).

By the Fourth Republic, co-operative actors had thus achieved complete legal recognition, and the co-operative model was fully operational as a field of action, with significant uptake and use in a wide range of industries throughout the country and across wide and varied socioeconomic groups and associated union and movement-based organizations. But the strategy had not emerged whole cloth, guided by some overarching entity, as in

Finland. Although, as noted earlier, by the middle of this period co-operatives had the ability to speak to the government with a single voice via the High Council of Cooperation, it would be disingenuous to suggest that this entity (or any of the other such sectoral or co-operative subtype-specific meta-organizations) had somehow acted to orchestrate the widespread use and legislative successes of co-operatives which had transformed it into a recognizable field. Indeed, such entities appeared to be the consequence, not the cause, of long, slow, and deliberate efforts by local cooperators to construct dense, multitier national and cross-cutting sectoral networks to coordinate their activity, in piecemeal and partially organized fashion.

The Rise of the Social and Solidarity Economy, 1970s/80s–Present

As in other rich democracies, including the case countries in this book, a field shift occurred in the French economy in the 1980s, one which involved a degree of liberalization, as the period of state-led "dirigiste" economic development which had marked the postwar growth and rebuilding of the Trente Glorieuses ended with the 1970s' inflation, low growth, and high unemployment, which also produced a welfare-state crisis (Duverger 2014). But if the shift involved a process of liberalization, it had a distinctively French character, reflecting the nation's long-standing ambivalence toward economic liberalism, which would enable a renewed role for co-operatives as part of a vision for a decentralized and Jacobin France. The new field configuration emerged over the course of the 1980s presidency of François Mitterand, which also saw the generational rise of 1968's socialists to national power; the socialists led the government for four terms, 20 years in total, between 1981 and 2017.

Socialist leaders had been profoundly influenced by the May 1968 riots and their aftermath, in which a generation rediscovered worker co-operatives, producers' associations, and other solidaristic and self-managing forms of economic organization as an alternative to the IOF or state enterprise models (Duverger 2016a, 2016b). Reflecting the combined effects of both crisis and evolution in shaping the field environment, in the decade after the 1968 riots and before coming to national power, the left would slowly incubate a series of plans and models to bring life to an old French idea: the social economy. Continuing to experiment even after they came to power, they repeatedly passed enabling laws and funding initiatives to bring this new model to life, birthing the modern ESS field in the process, with a reinvented co-operative subfield at its heart. Consistent with processes of institutional layering, legal changes in 1978, 1983, 1992, 1999, 2001, 2003, 2008, 2012, and 2014 (Seeberger 2014) enabled both the creation of the ESS and the continued evolution of co-operative models.

Nonetheless, the period was marked by tension between the political and economic necessity of a reduced role for a top-down central state in steering the economy and a desire to avoid relying solely on the IOF in lieu of the state. The net result was a new field configuration which saw an increasingly decentralized state play a more indirect role, funding and enabling social and economic development and cohesion initiatives generated by the regional and territorial governments and nongovernmental partners, with an explicit role for the newly created and institutionalized ESS field in the process. Co-operatives, which had already developed into a field through a host of regional-to-national federated coordinating bodies, were accordingly well-positioned to play a significant role in such a shift. Though co-operatives did not navigate this broader field transition without loss or hardship (notably, with institutional/field displacement of consumer co-operatives), they were nonetheless able to leverage their position of relative and comparative institutional strength to claim as secure a space in the new field configuration as in the old.

The emergence of the ESS. At the time of the May 1968 riots, the idea of the "social economy" was not new. The phrase had existed in France even before the French Revolution (Duverger 2016a, 2016b), and over the 19th century would be developed as an economic philosophy and fledgling social science (e.g., Le Play's efforts in 1856) and most closely associated with Charles Gide. The concept was often contrasted with "political economy" (Gueslin 1998). If political economy was primarily concerned with the role of the state in the economy and the economic development process, social economy was concerned with using solidarity and the bonds of civil society and community as a force and factor in the economic domain (Duverger 2016a, 2016b) to improve daily life. Accordingly, the idea of the social economy had been popular at the end of the 19th century. Attempting to explain the concept's newfound popularity, Gide (1905b, 2) wrote, "Political Economy, that superb science of riches and wealth, has said nothing to the people of their pains, nor of the manners by which to cure them, while the Social Economy speaks of nothing else" (translated by the author).

But the idea of social economy, despite its association with Gide and co-operatives, had not been articulated as a comprehensive socioeconomic development strategy, as operationalized through specific politics, programs, and organizational forms. In the 1970s, however, the social economy was politically rediscovered and was actively recovered and incorporated into politics and plans by the political left, which had been reinvigorated by the events of 1968 and their participants. The major political parties of the left, most notably the previously moribund Parti Socialiste, would begin to articulate the social and solidarity economy as a comprehensive, institutionalized alternative to the IOF and the dirigiste state.

The French left had already begun to update co-operative legal structures, inspired by events such as the high-profile Lip watch factory occupation in Bensançon in the early 1970s (Reid 2018). In 1968, efforts to form a nongovernmental meta-organization for co-operatives (the High Council for Cooperation is quasi-governmental), which had been underway since at least 1945, finally succeeded, resulting in the creation of the le Groupement national de la coopération (today CoopFR), while a counterpart organization for all third-sector forms, Comité national de liaison des activités mutualistes, coopératives et associatives formed in 1970 (Duverger 2014). In 1978, a centrist government facing increasing electoral threats from the left and responding to pressure from these groups, passed a law (Loi no. 78-763 du 19 juillet 1978) updating the 1915 worker co-operative statute. Both the 1915 statute and other interim and amended laws were substantively superseded by a new, modernized, and more comprehensive statute, clarifying the range of activities and capital structures that could be deployed.[21] By 1980, there were 800 worker co-operatives active in France (Antoni 1980). But beyond these, there was a growing awareness by the left that France had a host of such associational and self-management structures, all operating under different rules and in different ways but sharing a common purpose and common treatment under the law:

> The juridical statutes of co-operatives, mutuals, and associations as they had been formed at the end of the nineteenth century possess at least one common trait: these organizations were all prohibited from obtaining profit-seeking capital on the open financial markets, but were instead given access, as a counterparty, to the public institutional circuits for the collection of savings and distribution of credits (e.g. savings banks). If these institutions over the last fifteen years have tended to recognize one another and to be recognized in modifying some of their regulations, it is probably because the public authorities, since the end of the 1960s, have encouraged them to obtain for themselves the resources that they need, which leads them to defend their respective identities to become more in

---

[21] Cf.« Manifestes Coopératifs », , *Revue des études coopératives* 193. Institut français de la coopération (1978) : 179–82.

solidarity, while also using financing procedures analogous to those of other (traditional) enterprises. (Vienney 1986, 2, translated by the author)

As had occurred with the original co-operative movements, ESS was subsequently and slowly developed, with the dominant conceptualization in practice[22] led by Les Rocardiens, the more reformist wing of the ruling Socialist Party affiliated with Michel Rocard, a leading French socialist politician from the 1960s through the 1980s, who would eventually become Mitterand's prime minister, and who was also a key political actor in advancing a legislative agenda for France's social and solidarity economy. In the 1970s, when he was considered a possible presidential contender, Rocard had articulated the idea of a social economy rooted in self-managed enterprises such as co-operatives, mutuals, and associations, as a middle way between capitalism and statism. He also rearticulated the view that cooperation was, alongside unions and the Socialist Party, one of the three pillars of socialism, and in 1977 he stated that the social economy and decentralization were to be "two pillars of the revitalization of civil society in a Jacobin France" (Duverger 2016b, translated by the author).

When Mitterand's administration came to power in 1981, Rocard was named minister of territorial cohesion and minister of (economic and financial) planning. As the social economy did not exist as a ministerial mandate or legally recognized concept for use in policy implementation, he led four critical actions to create it and subsequently manage it in the new government (Duverger 2016b). First, in 1981 he established a delegation to organize the social economy's key actors. Second, in 1983 he created the Institute for the Development of the Social Economy, which would have oversight of new debt and equity tools, such as the legislation of 1983's newly created *titre participatif*, effectively a former of preferred equity/mezzanine debt for co-operatives and some other social economy forms. The Institute would evolve to become part of today's ESFIN Gestion, effectively a social economy/co-operative private equity/preferred debt investment house for France's social economy. Third, he spearheaded passage of the first formal social economy law of July 20, 1983, which, in addition to enabling the items noted above, updated various co-operative acts while creating a preliminary and interim

---

[22] There were competing conceptualizations of ESS, with a more militant and revolutionary variant, associated with Chevènement and his Center for Socialist Studies, Research, and Education. Adherents of this variant accused Rocard's vision as being too accommodating of actually existing capitalist relations, which would result in a limited social economy operating in parallel to, rather than replacing, capitalism, and which did not involve nationalizing industries and avoiding the market economy (Escalona 2016). Critiques maintain that the Rocardian version of ESS also too readily accepts neoliberal "offloading" of the state onto ESS, reflecting a degree of liberal accommodation.

social economy form, the Union d'Économie Sociale. Fourth, he introduced the social economy as one of three pillars of the economy in the Ninth Plan of 1982–83 (a national economic development plan), alongside the public and private sectors, in Mitterand's vision for a "mixed economy."

After Mitterand left office, the ESS continued to evolve through a series of legislative acts and related economic organizing and experimentation in implementation, ultimately laying the groundwork for the comprehensive ESS law of 2014, which effectively did for the ESS what the comprehensive 1947 law had done for co-operatives. This law grouped co-operatives, nonprofit associations, mutuals, foundations, and the newly defined certifications for "social enterprises" and "solidarity enterprises" into a legally defined category, ESS. It not only formally defined the constituent forms of the social and solidarity economy; it affirmed they must all adhere to many co-operative-like governance, capital, and ownership restrictions. It also affirmed the importance of ESS's overall and subconstituent national and regional federations, and the role of the national High Council of the Social and Solidarity Economy, through which ESS actors can liaise and communicate with the French government. Specifically, the law defines the legal subtypes of entities as those with a social utility to improve employment, social cohesion, and respect for the environment. It also assures and, in some cases, improves their access to various public and retirement investment funds, new financial structures, and favorable tax treatment. The new social and solidarity economy law also enhanced the ability of worker co-operatives to effectively utilize a form of venture capital, *amorçage*. The act also imposed requirements to develop regional/territorial strategies, as affirmed in local congresses where local ESS actors leverage their face-to-face solidarity to work together to achieve their goals.

In the interim, new types of enterprises, including new multi-stakeholder and specialized forms of co-operatives, had also been created through a process of institutional experimentation by co-operative organizers and various meta-organizations, and subsequently given legal sanction and support. These include the *coopérative d'activités d'emploi* (CAE), a type of business incubation and employment-generating co-operative, which was given legal standing as a business form in 2001 in national law, and the *société coopérative d'intérêt collectif*, effectively a multi-stakeholder community co-operative, which benefited from legislation in 1992 and 2001 allowing direct outside minority-stake investment into co-operatives. Legal changes in 2001, among other years (2003, 2008, 2014), also allowed the development of *fonds communs de placement d'entreprise solidaire*, or "90/10 funds," in which 10% of a mutual fund can be dedicated to funding co-operatives and other social economy businesses. Laws require all major employers to offer at least one such fund as an employee retirement investment option. France's *Banque Publique d'Investissement* (BPI France), which serves similar functions as the U.S. SBA, also developed a large (500M euro) lending program to the social and solidarity economy sector, with co-operative lending prominently featured. Consistent with the transition of the co-operative field's nesting within ESS, the *Revue des études coopératives*, the long-standing academic/applied journal for diffusing information about co-operative development, was renamed *Revue des études coopératives, mutualistes et associatives* in 1986, then again renamed *Revue internationale de l'économie sociale*.

Liberalization, decentralization, and ESS. The development of the ESS as a field, with co-operatives as a nested subfield, was part of a broader social and economic development strategy that involved a degree of decentralization and liberalization as well. As with liberalization elsewhere, this did not always benefit co-operatives. In the early 1980s, facing rapidly declining membership and serious financial losses, the consumer co-operative movement turned to Mitterand's new socialist government seeking aid and support for recovery. None was given. As France began to stop picking *champions nationaux* in different industries as part of both a reduced role for the central state and liberalization (Palier and Thelen 2010), the leading consumer co-operative conglomerate was allowed to fail. By 1986, the main central consumer co-operative body, the FNCC, was in extreme financial difficulty; most of its major regional consumer co-operative federations were being sold or liquidated, as were many employer-based consumer co-operatives. As an example of the latter, the famed Consumer Co-operative of Mining Workers, which had long been affiliated with France's Communist Party and had supported communist organizations, was liquidated in 1986.

What had gone wrong? The consumer co-operatives had failed to evolve with changing market conditions. As France suburbanized in the 1960s and 1970s, new retailer-owned co-operatives (e.g., Leclerc) and IOFs (like Carrefour) expanded by developing hypermarkets. Consumer co-operatives rapidly came to be seen as small, limited, and outdated (Brazda and Schediwy 1989; Lambersens et al. 2017). The merchant co-operatives also outcompeted the consumer co-operatives by "stealing consumer co-operatives' thunder" (interviewee), borrowing the dividend concept and transforming it into what today are standard corporate loyalty reward programs (Lambersens et al. 2017, 113). But the state also appears to have played a role: a legal change in the Law of 11 July 1972 allowed the merchant co-operatives to further expand their joint operations, and then in 1973 the Jean Royer Law limited the opening of large shops. Though this was intended to help small stores (and consumer co-operatives) survive, perversely it had the opposite effect: "[I]n fact what the law did was protect the larger retailers Carrefour and Leclerc from new competitors, as they already had the best business locations. These restrictions, on top of internal management mistakes such as extravagant investments to acquire materials and equipment at high interest rates, overhead costs that were too high and low rates of return per square meter, caused the downfall of many consumer co-operatives. . . . Consumer co-operatives gradually declined to [the] benefit of other types of co-operatives" (Lambersens et al. 2017, 114, 116). To be sure, some legacy consumer co-operatives survived for a time: of the 20 regional consumer co-operative federations active in 1980, 4 remained into the 2010s, in Alsace, Champagne, Normandie-Picardie, and southwest France, as national membership dropped from 3.5 million to 1.4 million between 1980 and 2010 (Lambersens et al. 2017). Co-op Alsace, however, was effectively acquired by competitors by 2016, while the other three have joined other distribution societies: two operate as part of Systeme U and E. Leclerc, consumer-owned divisions of these central retailer-owned distribution co-operatives, and are effectively what would, in Anglophone terminology, be called "hybrid" consumer/producer co-operatives. A few employer-based co-operatives, serving the employees and families of specific employers, most notably a few public utilities, also survived; though the teachers' consumer co-operatives (e.g., CAMIF) ultimately failed, those for the French post and French telecom remain in operation (Lambersens et al. 2017). These developments are wholly consistent with France's liberalization: the more "liberal" co-operative structures—those of the merchants, whose structure allows for a greater focus on profit-seeking investment—had outcompeted the traditional consumer co-operatives and had also more successfully leveraged their position under the law in the 1970s.

As part of the ESS evolution, new hybrid forms of consumer co-operatives, however, have emerged, using new multi-stakeholder co-operative models: the 400+ store Biocoop network, a French equivalent of Whole Foods, is owned by a mix of its food suppliers, co-operative investors/banks, consumers, and workers. One of its regional co-operatives in Brittany (Bretagne) has deployed holocracy, a flat, nonhierarchical management structure, and is touted as one of the largest European co-operatives of its kind (see Figure 4.2). Reflecting the importance of cooperation among co-operatives, Biocoop is partnering with Enercoop to obtain renewable, co-operative power. Enercoop, founded in 2004–5, is a new national co-operative network of "militant energy" or "citizen energy," that is, 100% renewable energy, multi-stakeholder co-operatives. Owned by a mix of consumers, producers, and solidarity investors, it is a co-operative of 11 regional co-operatives. Like many other legislated co-operative

Figure 4.2 Scarabée Biocoop. One regional co-op member of the nationwide Biocoop grocery chain is Scarabée Biocoop in Bretagne. Scarabée started out of a basement 30 years ago to become the largest consumer co-op in western France and one of the largest in Europe. Their stores, which include cafés, sharing libraries, and high-tech, environmentally conscious refilling stations for a wide range of goods, are powered by Enercoop, a 100% renewable national co-operative of local energy co-ops. The stores have been financed in part through France's co-operative equity/investment banking house, ESFIN Gestion. Photos by the author.

models in France, such a structure is not enabled as a distinct legal form in countries like the United States.

Other new co-operative models also enable or accommodate a degree of economic individualism. The CAE, for example, has enabled independent artists, artisans, and entrepreneurs to collectively pool their business and support operations via co-operative structures, all while maintaining their own small business, often with indirect state financial support. In the arts, for example, the French government has a long-standing public investment program, commonly known as *l'exception culturelle française*, which refers to public supports and grant programs (*les subventions*) created by France's first minister for culture (André Malraux) in the 1960s. These grants are available to a wide range of visual and performing artists and artisans. But as interviewees noted, there are more applicants than there are grants, and the grants are not sufficient to permanently support an artist's livelihood. Besides these grants, some working artists with irregular income can, if they meet certain minimum activity criteria, be eligible for public subsidy and support between artistic engagements (*le intermittent du spectacle*), a public support which the artists' unions have repeatedly helped negotiate, as noted by one interviewee.

Many artists and artisans, however, are not eligible for this "intermittence benefit," or, as noted above, cannot sustain themselves with general French cultural grants. In order to develop their capabilities and be self-sustaining, new forms of co-operatives have been created, cultural co-operatives like CAE Clara in Paris being a large and prominent example. CAE Clara helps artists and artisans use these various grants and subsidies to develop their artistic work into a sustainable career, providing business development, marketing/branding, financial, training, and other career and entrepreneurial support services. With roughly 150 artists affiliated as either permanent or trial basis members, CAE Clara grew so large that demand for its services has expanded beyond the arts. It thus formed a spinoff co-operative, CAE Clara-bis, to provide similar services for young professionals working in design, digital programming and computer services, and other high-tech or professional services (Figure 4.3). Other CAEs, such as Coopaname in Paris, which has several hundred cooperators, enable the use of the model beyond the arts for a wide range of entrepreneurial projects and professional service activities, with participants able to initially leverage unemployment and start-up entrepreneurship grants from the state.

These new uses of the co-operative model reflect the effect not only of liberalization but also of decentralization and how these two forces fit together to shape cooperation in France today as part of the ESS. Indeed, ESS's locally federated or decentralized "territorial" orientation, as the French speak of it, has been key to its usage and implementation across France. The national French government would come to delegate and decentralize functional responsibility in three stages beginning in the 1980s, with departments and regions possessing primary capability and responsibility for the execution and implementation of social protection, as well as economic development, with

Figure 4.3 France's "creative class" co-operatives. CAE Clara is a business co-operative for creative professionals in Paris. It spun off Clara-bis as a co-operative for digital economy workers. Photos by the author.

a central role for ESS. One regional actor in ESS in Rennes in the region of Bretagne (Brittany) stated in an interview:

> Rennes is not Paris. We have a distinct and quite separate history, as you well know. We are also not Alsatians. We have particular difficulties and issues, and we have our own local organizations with which to manage them. Some are co-operatives, yes. But some are not. Why should the government tell us we cannot have an association do something, that a mutual or co-operative must, or that the government must, when we have a local association of a nonprofit, democratic nature, that is perfectly capable of solving a problem? Let us decide what are goals are, and who and how to meet those objectives. Do not tell us from Paris that it must be a co-operative or not. No, of course not. ESS gives us a framework with which to do that.

Throughout the Trente Glorieuses, France had explicit regional development policies which sought to improve standards of living in lower-income regions. But they had implemented the policies through top-down regional social and economic development programs led by central government planners, which did not grant local control to set priorities for development of local resources or to deal with local problems (Pasquier 2003). But in the 1980s' field shift, the state would modify this approach, decentralizing functions to local governments (in contrast to the privatization that had occurred in Britain; cf. Le Galés 1993).

By the early 2000s, a second stage in this shift, asserting fiscal autonomy for the departments and regions, had begun. The words "decentralization" and "region" were formally added into the French Constitution, stating that France is a "decentralized Republic" effective as of 2003. In 2015, decentralization entered a third stage, with the Law NOTRe (Nouvelle Organisation Territoriale de la République; the word *notre* means "ours" in French, in a play on words) of August 7, 2015. This law increased substantive autonomy for the local state and enabled a greater role for ESS as well. Local and regional social and solidarity economy actors have been explicitly authorized to work with local governments to implement various social cohesion and economic development policies and must frequently hold agenda-setting convenings. How and where they are involved is determined by each regional ESS chamber, which encompasses the local/regional co-operative infrastructure. (See Figure 4.4 for details on some of these efforts in Paris in the late 2010s.) In conjunction, social clauses in national public procurement specify favorable treatment for worker and artisanal co-operatives (Borzaga and Becchetti 2010). Relatedly, there are cases of cities also implementing similar policies at a local level; an interviewee who worked as the social and solidarity economy minister for a major French city government noted they had informal programs to target procurement for such businesses.

There nonetheless remains a tension between the decentralized ESS field developments and liberalization. Notably, demutualization was not allowed at all until 1992, when a legal change made it possible, in rare or exceptional circumstances, to convert to another ownership form. Such cases remain rare, according to several interviewees, and require approval of the minister of the economy on advice of the counsel body liaising between the co-operative sector and the government (Naett 2015). Typically, approval to exit the co-operative sector is granted to the enterprise only when there are few or no other options for the co-operative to otherwise remain a going concern, that is, avoid bankruptcy. Further, for some co-operative subtypes, the French law specifies the use of "indivisible reserves," a co-operative-sector

Figure 4.4 The ESS in regional action: Paris. In the Paris region, ESS has had strong support from Mayor Anne Hidalgo, who with Nobel Peace Prize winner Muhammed Yunus, built a conference center/house for ESS, Les Canaux (upper left). The city also turned a closed hospital into a temporary utopian village for ESS, Les Grands Voisins, or The Great Neighbors (upper right). From 2016 to 2018, this modern "Paris commune" housed people and 100+ social, cultural, and training organizations and co-operatives, complete with a cinema, farm, apiary, urban manufacturing, and restaurants. The jump-start provided by this low-cost space and network enabled some of these groups to be self-sustaining by the demonstration's end, when the campus was redeveloped into an affordable housing ecodistrict. In St. Denis, one of the city's economically disadvantaged banlieues, an empty three-story garage building became Coopérative Pointcarré (bottom right), a multi-stakeholder-owned co-operative boutique, café, fab lab, digital coworking space, and artisan/entrepreneur professional development lab, part of the larger Coopaname co-operatively owned network of "employment co-operatives," a new legal form. Last, Solidarité Étudiante, which organizes student housing, food, and services co-operatives and social economy entities at universities (bottom left), worked with the participatory budget program of the city and mayor of Paris and a consortium of co-op bank lenders to build a co-operatively owned coworking space and café for students and co-op companies, ESSPACE. Solidarité Étudiante, the organization itself, is in turn a 50-50 gender-balanced, multi-stakeholder-owned co-operative, another newer legal form. Photos by the author.

term which refers to co-operative capital that cannot be divided for distribution or payout to individuals. It also does not comparably restrict internal rates of return on co-operatives, reducing financial incentive to demutualize. Demutualization also, as noted by one interviewee involved with co-operative policy work in France, embodies a logic that is "against the nature and purpose of co-operatives. The capital value of the co-operative has been built up over a long time, by generations of cooperators, the surpluses reinvested. Why should today's generation have the ability benefit from this, in some 'windfall' from an exit or demutualization, as is said in Britain? Past generations did not do this so that they could benefit today.... This is against the logic of co-operatives." This logic was why French co-operatives organized to fight against more liberal demutualization policies. The 1992 legal change allowing demutualization had worried cooperators, according to several interviewees. They were concerned that widespread Anglo-American-style demutualization could occur. Indeed, when the French government passed a law mutualizing the state-owned local savings branches (*caisses d'epargnes*) with Law #25 in 1999 (Karafolas 2016), the initial legislation contained provisions which would have allowed greater demutualization in general. The co-operative meta-organizations rallied to successfully amend this legislation to prevent this (Naett 2015).

At the same time, the French government has encouraged various co-operative and social economy institutions to form federated umbrella groups to realize efficiencies, enhance financial operations, and improve their cohesion; in the wake of the Global Financial Crisis, for example, various co-operative banks and mutual assurers were allowed to keep their divisional identity but were effectively merged into larger banking and mutual groups. Groupe BPCE, for example, is the co-operative holding group which includes many of the formerly state-owned savings banks that were cooperativized in the 1990s, along with Crédit Coopératif, CASDEN, Crédit Maritime, and several other divisions. The co-operative educational entities have also more broadly regrouped under the banner of L'ESPER, which, as noted earlier, seeks to more broadly educate and promote the concepts of the ESS sector in schools.

Meanwhile, again reflecting broader limits on economic liberalism in the coordinated market economy context of France, IOFs remain subject to a degree of co-operative-like constraints. All firms with over 50 employees have a workers' committee, called the enterprise committee (*comité d'entreprise*). For all workers in each union's trade, the firm must also have union representation on the workers' committee and the health and safety committee. The firm must consult with these unions and committees on a wide range of decisions pertaining to wages and job control. This applies to all workers (in that trade) at firms with over 50 employees, even if those workers are not members of the union. The impact of these costs and controls is significant on IOFs. The result is a "distortion," as documented by economists (Garicano, Lelarge, and Van Reenen 2016), in the number of 49-person firms, with many firms clustered just below the 50-employee threshold, the level at which many regulations apply. There are comparatively few firms just above this threshold size. These regulations, which may equate to a 10% increase in wage costs, create a "strong disincentive to grow" (Garicano, Lelarge, and Van Reenen 2016), reducing economies of scale for IOFs today. Due to this, the "additional restrictions" of a co-operative—on capital raising, for example, or on governance—voluntary restrictions of co-operatives, are comparatively less of a restraint on co-operatives' ability to grow in countries like France, because such restraints apply to all businesses, reducing differences in the field environment between firm types. As a Paris-based co-operative banker noted, when asked about regulatory challenges:

> This is not a big problem for co-operatives in France. Of course not! No, in France, this is a problem for all of the businesses! This is not the Silicon Valley. I tell you? I went to school there. Start up here, hire people there. No, as I told you, that's crazy. This is France. We have workers' councils, health and safety committees, collective bargaining, and many other things for any company with fifty or more employees! Any company! These regulations are not so different than those of a co-operative, very restrictive compared to the U.S. Somewhere around forty or so rules become effective on any company when it has fifty employees. Fifty is not very many. Growth comes with costs.

The net result is that, even after a sustained period of decentralization and liberalization, co-operatives are able to effectively organize and often compete against the IOF, which is also subject to significant intervention from the state. Unlike in the U.S. case, where there is clear institutional incongruency between the liberal variety of capitalism and the co-operative field, in France there is instead complementarity and congruency, reflecting the fact that its variety of capitalism has historically been shaped by a suspicion of liberalism and an interventionist state.

Co-operative Development: A French Evolution

Co-operatives in France today thus continue to maintain a well-defined and -developed field space. While this reflects clear links to the country's repeated revolutions, which have long animated a national solidarity that inspires use of the co-operative model, co-operatives' field development is not primarily a mechanistic result of revolution. Nor does it reflect the outsized influence or leadership of a single institutional or individual leader. France's co-operatives' success has accordingly unfolded along a markedly different developmental path than in Finland and is instead marked by incremental evolution and piecemeal development. In round after round of crisis and change, through revolution and evolution, co-operative proponents have invented and reinvented their field space to adapt to new conditions imposed by the state. Skilled social actors acted again and again as field bricoleurs; they variably experimented with new models by working with remnants of precrisis forms, which were then refashioned for new conditions and imprinted into crisis-generated field voids. In the interregna, as co-operative advocates and each prior crisis's participants would rise to nationally prominent political positions, they would champion these models and obtain state legitimation, and eventually built a comprehensive framework. In exchange for such state sanction, co-operatives have submitted to control by the state, while also reducing the burden faced by local and national governments, by providing resources to the state to meet its responsibility for implementing programs to achieve social and economic development goals.

As noted earlier, while this process is consistent with HI's notions of institutional evolution, it is only by applying the grammar of field theory that one can understand why and how this happened and how co-operatives have been able to evolve to maintain their field position. They did so by continuing to leverage their location at the core of the initial field rupture, which has long defined the French national project, which centers the role of intermediaries between individuals and the state and motivates a long-standing national ambivalence toward economic liberalism. This same concern shapes national policy toward IOFs as well and undergirds the congruency between co-operatives and France's interventionist approach to regulating and coordinating capitalism. Co-operatives, rooted in the ESS associational model of federated, bottom-up decision-making and local autonomy, have been able to claim the contested field space shaped by these forces by offering their model as a compromise, one which respects state control while channeling national solidarity as an animating substitute for the profit motive. This is a solidarity based on economic democracy, equality, and collective flourishing. That such a solidarity, through co-operatives, has not come to outright dominate the economy vis-à-vis the IOF is not the point. Rather, the point is that the comparatively greater strength of that solidarity, as an animating force, has been sufficient to enable and sustain a more coherent national field of action for French co-operatives.

5
Liberalism and Co-operatives

New Zealand's Strange Bedfellows

> All people think that New Zealand is close to Australia or Asia, or somewhere, and that you cross to it on a bridge. But that is not so. It is not close to anything, but lies by itself in the water. It is nearest to Australia, but still not near. . . . It will be a surprise to the reader, as it was to me, to learn that the distance from Australia to New Zealand is really twelve or thirteen hundred miles, and that there is no bridge.
> —**Mark Twain (1897)**

When I was initially choosing the cases for this study, a distinguished U.S.-based scholar cautioned me against selecting New Zealand, despite the clear methodological rationale for its inclusion. New Zealand is a mixed case with respect to the presence of traits which condition the ability of co-operatives to scale, but if there is a single critical case which might be able to counter the claim that co-operatives cannot succeed at sustained scale in liberal, individualistic cultures and LMEs like the United States—or, to put it another way, that economic liberalism is neither a sufficient nor a necessary condition to impede widespread cooperation at scale—it is New Zealand. The country was named the world's most co-operative economy by the United Nations in 2014 (Dave Grace and Associates 2014; cf. Garnevska et al. 2017), with large co-operatives evident across many industries, including agriculture, retail/wholesale, grocery, insurance, banking, and energy (Figure 5.1). The largest domestically headquartered firm of any kind in the country, Fonterra, is a dairy co-operative and a major exporter. Its gleaming headquarters, with a ground-floor welcome center celebrating its farmer-owned, co-operative history, helped anchor the redevelopment of Central Auckland's Viaduct and Wynward Quarter areas. In so doing, it serves as a symbol of New Zealand's continued economic development, and of co-operatives' prominent role in the process, a point noted by several Auckland-based co-operative informants.

Figure 5.1 Co-operative businesses keep New Zealand's wealth local. Merchant/producer co-operatives, a reverse franchise in which the stores own the parent company co-operatively, are common in many New Zealand industries, including wholesale/retail distribution (pictured). They often feature signage touting New Zealand ownership. Photos by the author.

Nonetheless, the distinguished U.S.-based scholar had cautioned me against including New Zealand in this study, saying, "New Zealand . . . is quite marginal, as a location to study. You are already working . . . on a marginal topic, on co-operatives. Choosing New Zealand makes it doubly marginal . . . all the more difficult to get anyone's attention." There is no doubt that New Zealand is often marginalized and treated as an afterthought on international and global stages. It is so often left off world maps, for example, that an entire sub-reddit documents such instances, as do articles in major news outlets (Figure 5.2).

But in fact, its marginality is the entire point, at least for the purpose at hand. For it is New Zealand's marginality and remoteness, a trait which also struck American essayist Mark Twain when he visited, that have enabled its co-operatives to thrive and persist. It is this geographic marginalization that explains why liberalism alone is not enough to sink cooperation at scale. If it were, New Zealand would not be home to so many large co-operatives. Despite the wholesale importation of British economic liberalism into colonial New Zealand, liberalism's effects have, time and again, been diminished and offset by the nation's geographic remoteness and small size, which creates costs and externalities which undermine New Zealand's ability to maintain a stable economic base of domestically owned IOFs. The nation has thus repeatedly relied on IOF alternatives like the co-operative to manage its geographic

Figure 5.2 New Zealand's frequent omission from world maps reflects its persistent remoteness.
Sources: Frost (2018); Evans (2019).

marginality, at the expense of liberal ownership forms and associated institutional arrangements.

Understandably, though, Kiwis (as New Zealanders are sometimes called) might not appreciate being referred to as marginal. Perhaps the more apt term to use is "antipodean." Historically developed to refer to places on the opposite side of the earth from Britain (such as New Zealand and Australia), the terms "antipode" and "antipodean" are more generally used today to refer to any polar opposite. Within the set of developed countries which are typically labeled economically liberal (LMEs), New Zealand seems to be a polar opposite with respect to cooperation at scale, a land of seemingly abundant co-operative success. Indeed, New Zealand is the only LME which ranks in the top group of developed nations with respect to the prevalence of cooperation at scale today (Spicer 2022), suggesting that liberalism and cooperation at scale are often strange bedfellows, with New Zealand acting as a curious exception.

Many other aspects of the New Zealand case are not only antipodean but disorienting, especially when making comparisons to other liberal nations. Whereas the history of utopian socialism looms large in U.S. co-operatives' development, utopian *capitalism* appears more significant in New Zealand;

reflecting its liberal heritage, New Zealand was explicitly founded on a *capitalist* utopian plan—not a utopian socialist one. But these efforts unexpectedly failed, creating a field opening for proponents of alternatives like co-operatives. Relatedly, and again markedly different from the U.S. case, here the Knights of Labor did not fail but were ultimately quite successful in helping to generate one of the world's strongest early welfare states and a system of state-led socialism, one which persisted throughout much of the 20th century and which helped support cooperation at scale.

In fact, from its initial industrial development in the late 1800s through the 1980s, the nation had one of the most state-dominated economies among the rich democracies (Nagel 1998), a fact perhaps surprising given New Zealand's categorization today as an LME. When co-operatives finally did face the bogeyman of economic liberalism, via "Rogernomics," which was 1980s New Zealand's equivalent of Reaganism or Thatcherite liberalization, it was paradoxically and ostensibly initially led by the party of New Zealand's political *left*—the Labour Party, which ultimately transformed New Zealand into something approaching a recognizable LME. Co-operatives, which were directly and explicitly politically threatened by this liberalization process, were ultimately able to organize and leverage a backlash to effect policy, enabling their continued viability and competitiveness today.

How can one make comparative sense of such antipodean dynamics? The grammar of field theory again enables construction of a more complete and robust explanation than HI. As in the other cases, HI is useful in describing the *how* of the evolutionary path of co-operative development. New Zealand's co-operatives emerged into the institutional void left by failed colonizing investors. They repeatedly evolved through processes of layering, as co-operative and alternative models were enabled by the frequent updating of policy and law. In the 1980s, co-operative actors were threatened, as state policies enabled what HI would label displacement and conversion of both co-operatives and other IOF alternatives in the aftermath of "critical juncture" events. Ultimately, co-operators were able to institutionally reorganize and obtain supportive state treatment, activating layering processes, thereby avoiding institutional/policy drift into irrelevance.

But beyond describing *how* all of that happened, HI does not help us craft an explanation as to *why* these dynamics developed and unfolded as they did: *Why* were co-operatives able to leverage critical juncture opportunities? *Why* were co-operatives able to initially emerge at all, given New Zealand's distinctively liberal character at its founding? *Why* is it that New Zealand's co-operative population today includes so few worker co-operatives? Field theory again enables an explanation. The abundance of co-operatives and other alternatively owned firms reflects how economic liberalism's banner-bearer enterprise model, the IOF, has historically been constrained in New Zealand by its geography. In contrast to the U.S. case, where liberalism's negative effects compounded with racial dynamics to create obstacles in co-operatives' immediate field environment, in the New Zealand case the initial force of liberalism was blunted by geography, yielding field openings which co-operatives and other IOF alternatives leveraged in partnership with a supportive "developmental state" (Johnson 1982), as this chapter will trace.

Specifically, New Zealand's geographic remoteness undermined IOFs' initial efforts to succeed at scale, yielding transaction costs and uncertainty premiums which undermined both the ability and desire of distant joint-stock companies to enter the market, thereby creating an opening in the field environment for co-operatives and other IOF alternatives to leverage and to take root. Furthermore, distant investors had misjudged the nature of New Zealand's resources, that is, factor endowments, which were ideally suited to grow different inputs than they had expected, ones better suited for co-operative-prone industries. With competition diminished in the wake of IOFs' failures, cooperators were thus able to take advantage of New Zealand's factor endowments to develop into incumbents in key export-oriented industries. During this era of state- and co-operative-led economic development, co-operatives—alongside other IOF alternatives, including state-owned enterprises—thus became a key institutional tool of a steering developmental state through which to root domestic control and ownership of the economy, while also enabling connection and coordination of production and distribution to geographically distant export markets, showing evidence of CME-like interfirm coordination strategies as they performed this function.

Subsequently, after the crisis induced by the loss of New Zealand's largest trading partner, Britain, the state attempted to renegotiate its approach to steering the economy, through a program of liberalization, destabilizing the field environment. This period was one of active retreat by the state from direct economic activity, which can be conceptualized through field shift (Figure 5.3), in which the withdrawal of the state and promotion of economic liberalization yielded opportunities for IOFs to advance at the expense of other forms: to encroach on their previous field space. This period was accordingly marked by explicit and direct political threats to co-operatives, alongside widespread privatization of formerly state-owned and trust-owned firms. But the privatization did not merely increase the prominence of IOFs in New Zealand; it increased the prominence of *foreign* IOFs. Many of these large domestic firms came to be acquired by foreign investors, who sometimes

132 Co-operative Enterprise

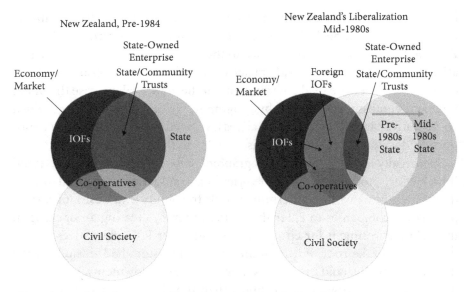

Figure 5.3 Field shift: New Zealand co-operatives and 1980s liberalization.

discontinued or diminished service provision, thereby threatening New Zealand's economic sovereignty.

But this new field configuration quickly proved unstable. As liberalization activated geopolitical concerns that unfettered investor ownership could result in foreign economic control, it yielded a backlash co-operatives and other alternative enterprises leveraged to survive and arguably thrive, organizing to achieve policy changes and other supportive state action which enabled their continued incumbency in key areas, against advancing IOFs. As in the Finnish case, New Zealand's co-operatives thus came to serve a geopolitical role, domestically rooting economic ownership and control, and reducing the ongoing threat of acquisition by larger neighbors Australia and China. Nonetheless, to keep foreign investor ownership at bay, New Zealand has relied more on producer co-operatives, which are decidedly far more consonant with economic liberalism[1] than other co-operative forms. This, too, is not surprising, given the legacy of New Zealand's founding liberal character in shaping the field environment.

For co-operatives, New Zealand's institutional and field environment has thus been historically marked by a tension between the economic liberalism of its British roots and state efforts to manage its geographical remoteness.

---

[1] The link between co-operative forms' varying degrees of consonance with liberalism is reviewed in Chapters 1 and 2.

This tension has frequently manifested in an uneasy relationship between governments of various political stripes and economic development programs built on both: (a) direct or indirect state ownership and investment in the economy and (b) co-operative and related alternative ownership models, including consumer and charitable trust ownership. By organizing to capitalize on this tension, co-operatives have been able to carve out, claim, and defend a substantial field space in New Zealand. Below, I trace the historical field development of New Zealand's co-operatives, from their emergence during the colonial founding period in the mid-1800s, to the field settlement which characterized its state- and co-operative-led, export-oriented development for a century through the 1970s, to its subsequent experiments with liberalization since 1984, which threatened co-operatives' incumbency in key industries.

New Zealand as a "Utopian Capitalist" Experiment Gone Awry: 1840–1870

All of today's LMEs, including both the United States and New Zealand, reflect, in varying ways, the economic traditions, institutions, policies, and laws of British economic and political liberalism, which were exported to its colonies. And yet the economic contexts and timing of these importations were quite different. By 1840, as reviewed in prior chapters, the First Industrial Revolution in the United States and United Kingdom was in full swing, and in response, co-operative institutional experiments abounded in both countries. At the same time, while Australia had already been a British penal colony for 50 years, its closest neighbor, New Zealand, had virtually no European settler-colonists. The North and South Islands of New Zealand's population consisted of approximately 90,000 to 100,000 Maoris and just 2,000 Europeans, who were largely a mix of whalers, sealers, Australian migrants, and missionaries. In 1840, the Maori signed the Treaty of Waitangi, which gave Britain the exclusive purchase right to their land. Two decades later, the Maori population had declined by 35% and been surpassed by British settlers, as treaty-related conflicts known as the New Zealand Wars had weakened the Maori, and as settler colonization had begun in earnest and at scale (Smith 2005).

In field theory terms, such wars, which enabled settler-colonization, involved supplanting and usurpation of Indigenous populations and their social, economic, and political systems, effectively leaving extraordinary institutional voids or field openings in their wake. As with biological systems, invasive species may destroy native ones, destabilizing the field environment and creating room for colonizing orders to take hold. Through their wholesale importation of primarily British ideologies and institutions, settlers brought with them the potential to replicate a host of colonial fields and associated organizational forms with which to repopulate the voids of this destabilized field environment. Which imported forms took root?

As early colonization in New Zealand was explicitly liberal and capitalist in nature, one might expect that joint-stock companies and IOFs would quickly come to dominate. Indeed, the original intention for New Zealand's colonization, as developed by Edward Gibbon Wakefield in his plans for "systematic colonization" (Bunker 1988), was to comprehensively construct a decidedly "capitalist utopia" (Ellis 2013), primarily White in racial composition,[2] the "fairer Britain of the South Seas" (Ip 2003). Industrialization-induced economic dislocation in the United Kingdom in the 1830s and 1840s—which had helped to birth both the U.K. and ultimately the global modern co-operative movement—also fueled interest in out-migration from Britain (Phillips and Hearn 2008) to locations like New Zealand. The economic winds thus might have seemed as if they were at Wakefield's back.

But his efforts failed, disastrously so. Between 1840 and 1860, British colonization across New Zealand was initially led by Wakefield's New Zealand Company, a U.K. joint-stock company (i.e., an IOF) organized in 1840 in London by Wakefield, who was also involved with British colonization plans in Australia and Canada. He would spearhead efforts while based in Britain and did not set foot on New Zealand until the 1850s, by which time his efforts would be beyond salvage. While Wakefield had conceived of New Zealand as a utopian experiment, it was one that was very different from the utopian socialist models which had birthed the U.K. co-operative movement, and which subsequently diffused across the world (Fogarty 1990). New Zealand was to be built on a utopian *capitalist* model (Olssen 1997), constructed on a logic of economic liberalism, where capitalist investors owned large plots of agrarian, crop-producing land closely settled around urban land. These capitalist investors—largely absentee investors who were to remain in the United Kingdom—would employ immigrant laborers who were to be assisted by the New Zealand Company in relocating, a capitalist colonization plan memorably analyzed in *Das Capital* (Marx 1867, ch. 33).

---

[2] New Zealand's immigration was fairly racially homogeneous in the 19th century, and it maintained de facto Whites-only immigration policies throughout the early and middle 20th century (Thomson and Trlin 1970). Though Maori social movements since the 1960s directly linked to the development of some worker co-operatives, as reviewed later in this chapter, there is little in the historical record to suggest racial difference as a social cleavage which undermined cooperation at scale in much of New Zealand's history. New Zealand, unlike the United States and some other U.K. settler colonial societies, lacks a substantive history with race-based slavery as a domestic economic institution (Thomson and Trlin 1970).

To be sure, the New Zealand Company's vision in some ways directly influenced other utopian socialist plans, which would later become highly influential in the co-operative movement in the United States and United Kingdom, such as Ebenezer Howard's (1898) Garden City plan, which embodied the same vision of an agrarian utopia, free from the problems of industrial society in both Britain and the United States (Olmsted 1928, 27, cited in Olssen 1997, 207). Wakefield sought to "to effect the transfer of a vertical slice of pre-industrial English rural society to the colony" (Phillips and Hearn 2008, 46). But unlike the Garden City and other utopian socialist plans, Wakefield's vision did not include co-operative/associational business and housing elements. It advanced a solely capitalist ethos and organizational model which was "backward-looking and conservative" (Coleman 1987, 18), one which explicitly sought to keep colonists working for capitalists. In developing his colonization plans, Wakefield explicitly drew on the liberal ideas of Adam Smith (Birchall 2022) and also stated how such employment dynamics acted as a substitute form of slavery, that is, wage slavery (Cazzola 2021).

Wakefield's New Zealand Company founded several distinct New Zealand settlements, including the national capital and second largest city, Wellington, in 1840. His company also created spinoffs or joint ventures to found other colonies in partnership with the Church of England and Free Church of Scotland. These joint efforts would produce the two largest cities/regions on the South Island today, which are the third- and fourth-largest cities in New Zealand: Canterbury (Christchurch) and Otago (Dunedin) in 1850 and 1848, respectively (Thorns and Schrader 2010). The New Zealand Company was thus behind the development of three of the four principal cities in the country today. Auckland, the fourth and largest city, was founded by the British in 1840 and had a similar capitalist ethos. As John Logan Campbell, founder of Auckland, said of his new city, "[T]he whole and entire object of everyone here is making money, the big fishes eating the little ones" (quoted in Fischer 2012, 64).

Ultimately, however, the New Zealand Company, which had brought over 15,000 settlers to the colony over a decade, was not financially viable and was "hopelessly impractical" (Coleman 1987, 22). Their plans had shown "a substantial ignorance of New Zealand conditions," as they "had come with the intention of engaging in arable farming, without consideration of whether this was suitable to New Zealand conditions" (Alley and Hall 1941, 35, 37). Their original legal claims to the land were imperfect, and absentee speculative investors, rather than farmers or others directly motivated to economically develop the territory, had dominated purchases (Hawke 1985; Tai Awatea n.d.). Wakefield, meanwhile, never actually visited New Zealand either prior to or during the Company's implementation efforts. There was also no clear export market for wheat, grain, or similar higher-density agricultural production, as originally financially planned to support investor returns, yielding a "desperate search for exportable cash products" (Coleman 1987, 22). And while the land was unexpectedly well-suited for pastoral purposes such as wool (Peden 2011), this could not provide the expected financial returns. The Company also struggled to attract British investors and workers, who were deterred by the danger and great cost of the voyage, a function of the distance and remoteness.

By the 1850s, the New Zealand Company was bankrupt and under British Colonial Office state administration, its debt forcibly transferred to settlers (Hawke 1985). As Maori wars and economic uncertainty continued to plague the colony in the 1850s and 1860s, emergent provincial governments found it difficult to individually raise money for infrastructure development. In 1870, New Zealand's premier Julius Vogel proposed raising £10 million to advance a national infrastructure development program (approximately $2 billion today). Over the decade ahead, the New Zealand government would ultimately borrow £20 million ($4 billion) on the London financial markets, then a very large sum, to finance development of roads, state-owned railways, and a state-owned telegraph, postal system, and postal banking[3] (Dalziel 1975; Smith 2005). As these plans unfolded, New Zealand's Parliament abolished provincial governments in order to centralize and coordinate development efforts, affirming its decision to continue to play a role that investor-led markets had, to that point, failed to successfully perform (Dalziel 1975; Smith 2005). The government also retained significant arable land it had acquired; through various land reforms in the 1870s, it promoted long-term leases rather than outright land sales to further encourage settlement (Dalziel 1975; Smith 2005). This contrasts sharply with the land strategy in the United States, where the government had given away large swaths of land for nominal cost via the Homestead Acts.

Alongside the strong state sector, which emerged to fill the voids left by the failed New Zealand Company, were fledgling experiments with co-operative organizational models. Early settlers had imported these models into the field environment from the United Kingdom. Here, the timing of New Zealand's colonization may have been serendipitous: unlike in the United States, for example, where colonization and development had occurred long before the emergence of stable co-operative forms, colonization occurred in New

---

[3] The brief foray in postal banking in the United States, for purposes of comparison, would not start until much later, in 1911.

Zealand as these forms had taken hold and were diffusing via the U.K. and international co-operative movements and were already forming into a stable and recognizable field.

Indeed, almost as soon as New Zealand was formally colonized by the British in the 1840s, co-operatives and mutuals appear in the historical record. In 1844, the same year a stable, replicable co-operative business model was first institutionalized in Rochdale, England (Wilson, Webster, and Vorberg-Rugh 2014), the first consumer co-operative in New Zealand appeared. Backed by the man who would become the second premier of New Zealand, William Fox, the co-operative provided goods to colonists working for the New Zealand Company in Riwaka (Balnave and Patmore 2008). The first chapter of the Manchester Unity Independent Order of Odd Fellows, a British friendly society/mutual society, was formed on a ship passing from the United Kingdom to Nelson, New Zealand in 1841 (Gourlay 1942). Manchester Unity would ultimately take root and thrive throughout the colony (Olssen 1996), with chapters established in quick succession in the 1840 and 1850s in Wellington, Auckland, Dunedin, Lyttleton, and Christchurch (Gourlay 1942), claiming thousands of adult male members by the 1870s (Neison 1877), with membership rolls higher in absolute numbers in New Zealand than in the United States, which was far larger in overall population (Neison 1877). By the end of the 19th century, nearly one-quarter of New Zealand's adult men were members of this friendly/mutual benefit society, which provided social insurance (e.g., sick pay) services (Olssen 1996). Manchester Unity would later sponsor one of New Zealand's earliest credit unions, which would eventually become the basis for the country's credit union industry today (McAlevey, Sibbald, and Tripe 2010; McLauchlan 2002; Runcie 1969). The Ancient Order of Foresters, another early mutual benefit society with a similar purpose, which was originally founded in Rochdale in the 1830s, also rapidly grew in New Zealand and claimed several thousand members there by the 1860s and 1870s (Neison 1877), similarly representing a far greater penetration rate than the society had managed to achieve in the United States (Neison 1877).

By the 1870s, it was clear that if New Zealand was a liberal colony, as planned, it was one with a central state-led economy, and specifically, strong state-related ownership, with imported, newly developed U.K. co-operative models also taking root. State ownership in particular stands in marked contrast to other modern LMEs like the United States and United Kingdom, where IOFs were comparatively more well developed early on (Gomory and Sylla 2013; Sylla and Wright 2013), reducing opportunities for alternatives to take root and thrive. In contrast with New Zealand, where the government oversaw the development and ownership of key infrastructure systems which would undergird the nation's subsequent industrialization and development in the late 1800s, in the United States private ownership of the Second Industrial Revolution's railroads, telegraph, and banking industries was substantial and would come to fuel America's Gilded Age inequality (Gomory and Sylla 2013; Sylla and Wright 2013). This striking contrast did not go unnoticed at the time: the comparative lack of U.S. public and co-operative ownership was observed by international social reformers, who sought to bring such ownership models from New Zealand to the United States, so as to "New Zealandize" the United States by replacing its "vicious system of private ownership" (Coleman 1987, 65).

Field Settlement: Alternative Ownership in the Making of Modern New Zealand, 1870–1970

Colonial New Zealand's economy ultimately developed in response to two parallel advancements in the late 1800s, which together proved critical in establishing a degree of field incumbency for co-operatives in certain industries. These developments supported a field settlement and configuration which would remain in place for a century and would transform the nation from a largely undeveloped settler colony into a highly developed nation. This configuration, as noted earlier, was one in which an interventionist state not only played a direct ownership role in the economy but actively enabled and promoted large-scale co-operatives, which would come to dominate key export-oriented industries.

First, as noted above, in the wake of the failure of the "capitalist utopia" model of colonial development led by the New Zealand Company, a strong, centralized state emerged to steer and guide the economy. In conjunction, a powerful labor movement, which included dramatic political wins in the 1890s by the pro-co-operative Knights of Labor and their successors and allies as part of a Liberal-Labour governing alliance, reinforced a unique New Zealand model of "state socialism" (Le Rossignol and Stewart 1910; Coleman 1987). This model was marked not only by policies to enable co-operatives but by extraordinary state ownership, strong labor rights, and one the world's most advanced early welfare states, with "a level of state regulation unparalleled in most other Western economies" (Massey 1995,7). Second, major government land reforms, coupled with the time-space-compressing technological advances of the Second Industrial Revolution (Combes, Mayer, and Thisse 2008), enabled and aided development of readily cooperativized export industries like dairy and meat (Evans and Meade 2005). If, by the mid-20th century, New Zealand had economically developed to become "Britain's farm," it was a co-operative one, in turn supported by up- and downstream co-operative and state-owned businesses, all undergirded by "high-floor" labor policies of its robust welfare state.

The Knights of Labor and the Liberal-Labour alliance: A pro-co-operative developmental state takes root. While the co-operative movement and its models may have been imported from Britain, American institutional and field influences also diffused to New Zealand: the Knights of Labor, the American organization which played such an important role in the late 1800s in the U.S. co-operative movement, spread to New Zealand in 1887 (Salmond 1950), just after the Knights' U.S. peak. As in the United States, the Knights's New Zealand organization would not last long. But unlike in the United States, where its co-operative efforts and anti-"wage slavery" ideology interacted with race-based slavery and strong resistance by IOFs to limit its effect, in New Zealand the Knights' efforts were not undermined by such dynamics.

Here, their efforts were directly incorporated into the national labor movement's legislative victories, as noted by the U.S. Knights in their official publication, the *Journal of United Labor* (Weir 2009). Weir has argued that these victories were made possible by the later development of political parties in New Zealand, as the Knights were initially able to directly advance their cause unmediated by a party system. Thus, as the U.S. Knights were fading, the New Zealand Knights' agenda, which included enabling support for co-operatives, was being advanced by the parliamentary members of the emerging Liberal-Labour political alliance; at least 25 Knights were known to have been in the New Zealand Parliament in the 1890s. Given the Knights' membership secrecy, the actual number is believed to have been higher (Weir 2009). The Knights' membership was geographically diverse as well; as New Zealand's first national labor organization, it grew from strong local assemblies in Auckland on the North Island and Christchurch on the South, and developed a local presence throughout both islands (Weir 2009).

New Zealand's parliamentary government was not organized along party lines until 1891, when the new Liberal Party, operating with explicit Labour movement support, won a majority. This "Lib-Lab" alliance would rule New Zealand for two decades, from 1891 until 1912, and would create the foundation for New Zealand's welfare state and state-led economy that would reach its peak under the first Labour government, which held power from 1935 to 1949. In the 1890s, the Liberal-Labour alliance secured industrial peace by enacting world-leading labor and social welfare reforms, producing one of the most robust welfare states of the era (Le Rossignol and Stewart 1910; Coleman

1987). Many reforms had been promoted by the Knights and their elected supporters in Parliament.

In 1892, New Zealand's Parliament enacted land reforms, including a progressive land tax meant to discourage large estates, a land-repurchase scheme, and a progressive income tax. In 1893, New Zealand became the first self-governing territory to give all women the right to vote. In 1894, it enacted the Industrial and Reconciliation Act, led by a Fabian socialist and minister of labor for the Liberals, William Pember Reeves. New Zealand became the first self-ruling territory to recognize industrial and trade unions and impose a binding system of national labor arbitration and minimum wage agreements by industry. By 1898, a New Zealand–wide old-age means-tested pension system was introduced (albeit one which excluded Chinese immigrants; Le Rossignol and Stewart 1910), and in the early 1900s state housing development began with the Workers Dwelling Act of 1905.

Alongside these reforms, direct state intervention and investment into various sectors of the economy continued apace, building on the previous government-led and -owned efforts in rail, postal banking, and communications (Coleman 1987). In another high-profile IOF failure, the private Bank of New Zealand was bailed out by the government in the 1890s and would become wholly owned by the government in the early 1900s. In 1903, the government introduced the State Coal Mines Act to develop state-run coal mines "to succeed where private enterprise had failed" (Telegraph—Press Association 1902), according to the premier who signed the act. By the early 20th century, all utilities and natural resource sectors, including forestry, electricity, railways, and banks, had developed as state-run or quasi-state-run entities; the state actively owned shipping lines, airlines, hospitality/tourism properties, and a winery as well (State Services Commission 1996).

State-led co-operative programs and legislation were introduced: in 1894, W. H. Clarke promoted a plan for 14 state-supported co-operative farms to put the unemployed to work (Weir 2009; Sargisson and Sargent 2017). While the full plan was not implemented, some 2,200 people were ultimately settled in such farms (Sargisson and Sargent 2017). In 1908, shortly after becoming a dominion of the British Empire (enabling it greater autonomy and legal self-determination), New Zealand would pass its own version of the United Kingdom's Industrial and Provident Societies Act, providing a stronger legal framework for co-operatives and mutual/member-owned societies. Consistent with HI's processual notions of institutional and policy layering, it would repeatedly update its Friendly Societies Act, most notably in 1908–9, to enhance regulation for friendly societies, which had become a key provider of health insurance and sick care, as noted earlier.

Co-operatives and the economic development of New Zealand. At the same time, the colonial economy, originally focused on subsistence, export to Australia, and wool production, shifted between the 1870s and 1890s into dairy products and mutton, primarily for export to the United Kingdom. Both industries came to be dominated by co-operatives. These industries, enabled by development of direct long-distance shipping lines, refrigeration techniques, and dairy processing mechanization and technology, rapidly overtook all other sectors to dominate New Zealand economic activity. The United Kingdom overtook Australia as New Zealand's primary trading partner, and by the early 20th century, between 80% and 90% of New Zealand's exports were accounted for by the United Kingdom (Nixon and Yeabsley 2010).

These infant export industries were economically coordinated and organized primarily through co-operatives, which were available as a legal form through imported British law: New Zealand's Parliament had clarified in the English Laws Act of 1858, which applied retroactively back to 1840, that all English laws—including both statutory and common law—applied in New Zealand. Britain, as noted in Chapter 2, had passed comprehensive enabling legislation for co-operatives by the 1850s and 1860s as part of the Industrial and Provident Societies Act, which had enabled member-owned co-operatives to own real property (not allowed under the Friendly Societies Act they had previously used to incorporate; see introduction to Brazda and Schediwy 1989).

Notably, wool production, which had been rapidly supplanted in economic importance by dairy and mutton, had not been particularly conducive to cooperation. To the naked eye, wool is of a highly heterogeneous and nonstandard quality, reducing the homogeneity of economic interest among producers in pooling their products co-operatively to sell to market (Evans and Meade 2005). Dairy products and mutton are comparatively more homogeneous and amenable to co-operative organizing: it is difficult for a buyer to distinguish between two gallons of milk or two cuts of mutton (Evans and Meade 2005). And New Zealand's geography and topography—particularly its rolling green hills—were well suited to these two products, which were readily cooperativized. New Zealand's British settlers were also familiar with co-operative models, which had become widespread in Britain well before technological advances enabled the growth of readily cooperativized industries in New Zealand. In 1871, New Zealand's first dairy co-operative was organized in Otago on the South Island, 11 years before refrigeration enabled long-distance export of dairy products in 1882. By 1890, 40% of the country's 400 dairy farms and factories were organized as co-operatives (Stringleman and Scrimgeour 2008); 85% of the nation's 600 dairy farms and factories were structured as co-operatives by 1920, achieving an incumbent position retained today (Pearson and Thorns 1983; Trampusch and Spies 2014). Co-operatives similarly held a leading market share in mutton (Evans and Meade 2005).

IOFs in such industries found themselves unable to compete. The New Zealand and Australian Land Company, an IOF of this era, did not succeed in its refrigeration-related production efforts; it sold its New Zealand operations in 1903, as "the state energetically evangelized for co-operatives" (Belich 2001, 61). The co-operative market shares in dairy and mutton were also no doubt partially aided by government land policy. Preexisting "large estates," which had been assembled during and immediately after the New Zealand Company era, were broken up, culminating in the new Liberal government's 1890s policy of "closer settlement," which sought to increase population living in and around the town settlements and a "one man, one farm" approach to agricultural production (McAloon 2008; Lucas 1966). Specifically, so as to encourage a "one man, one farm" society, land acts in 1892 and 1894 had imposed significant taxes on large land estate holdings and limited the size of land lots which could be sold, while also imposing tenure restrictions. These policies, which had eased by the 1950s (Fairweather 1985) and had been removed by the 1990s (Massey 2016), impeded the assemblage or maintenance of large-scale, investor-owned farms (dairy or otherwise). The government also actively acquired, through legal expropriation, if needed, large estates and subdivided them for resale to individual farmers, reducing heterogeneity in estate size (Massey 2016).

I have not identified any historical sources which explicitly connect the intent of these land policies to the flourishing and development of New Zealand co-operatives in this era. But there is an isomorphic symmetry between the institutional logic of the government's "one man, one farm" land policy and that of the "one man, one vote" co-operatives which sprang up to produce and market the products created by the farmers on this land. Given this congruency, it is not surprising that these small-lot farmers viewed co-operatives—the formation of which the state actively encouraged—as the most viable way to pool their products to reach the U.K. market.

Critically, these initial producer co-operatives in commodity export industries also supported development of other co-operatives as part of the emergence of co-operative interfirm coordination strategies[4] in the industrializing agricultural supply chain during the 20th century in banking, insurance, and farm supplies. Farmers Mutual Group, the dominant rural and agricultural insurer in New Zealand today, was founded in 1905 (Standing 2005), after

---

[4] And again, concordant with what is today viewed as a CME-style interfirm coordination strategy.

the Farmers' Union (or "Farmers' Parliament") lobbied the New Zealand Parliament for the Mutual Fire Insurance Act of 1903, which enabled its formation as a mutual (i.e., consumer co-operative). Farmlands, one of the five largest New Zealand co-operatives today, is a retail supply store chain with 82 locations, owned by its 64,000 farmer shareholders. Farmsource, a subsidiary of the nation's largest co-operative, dairy producer Fonterra, is a similar retail chain, focused on dairy supply. Two other large co-operatives today, Ballance Agri-Nutrients (named after the 1891 Liberal-Labour premier John Ballance) and Ravensdown Fertiliser, are agricultural supply co-operatives. Rabobank New Zealand, a subsidiary of the Dutch global banking co-operative, is a dominant agricultural lender and banker.

Liberalism as a constraining force on New Zealand cooperation. While the industrialization of "Britain's farm" may have been marked by leading co-operative enterprises and their associated coordination strategies, which in turn were supported by an interventionist and developmental state, this is not to say that economic liberalism was nonexistent, nor that it did not negatively affect co-operatives. Three points from the period are clear in this regard: New Zealand's co-operatives historically were primarily accounted for by those operating with a "more liberal" form; relatedly, central co-operative apex or meta-organizations to coordinate development across diverse co-operative forms struggled and died out; and finally, more liberal governments exhibited ambivalence toward co-operatives.

First, the ranks of New Zealand's co-operatives have historically been dominated by producer co-operatives. As reviewed in Chapters 1 and 2, producer co-operatives, where the co-operative members can be IOFs, are far more consonant with the logic of economic liberalism than either consumer or worker co-operatives (Kaswan 2014). Alongside the development of the agricultural co-operatives and the Knights of Labor's successes, British-style, Rochdale consumer and worker co-operatives did develop somewhat in this period, but they were decidedly more marginal and less central in the New Zealand economy. Beginning in the 1880s, there were sustained attempts by "old British co-operators" (Balnave and Patmore 2008) in Christchurch to create a "co-operative commonwealth" using the Rochdale interlocking system of different types of co-operatives but centered around the consumer model. Ultimately, after some successes, these efforts did not achieve lasting scale (Balnave and Patmore 2008). The British co-operative wholesale society, which had initially been a supportive partner to New Zealand's consumer co-operatives, ultimately withdrew support over the balance of export-import trade with the New Zealand co-operatives. Only in Palmerston North did a significant Rochdale-style grocer/consumer retail co-operative succeed, the largest such entity in Australasia (Coy and Ng 1989), before it failed in the liberalizing 1980s.

As consumer co-operatives struggled to compete, an IOF and a producer-owned co-operative[5] came to dominate the grocery industry. In place of consumer co-operatives, the dominant two grocery chains became Four Square, a producer co-operative of independent store owners which developed into today's Foodstuffs, the largest grocery chain in New Zealand (and second largest co-operative in the country), and Self-Help Co-operative Grocery, which was not actually a co-operative. Having started the business before the term "co-operative" was legally restricted to use by actual co-ops, Self-Help had aspired to be a co-operative but could not interest potential consumer co-operative participants in its efforts (Sutherland 1947). The firm would eventually be bought out by an Australian firm—exemplifying how New Zealand's larger and closest neighbor has been a constant threat to domestic ownership and economic control—and eventually evolved into today's Countdown, the number 2 grocer in the New Zealand grocery market duopoly.

During this era, a National Party–led government nonetheless allowed for the development of what is today one of New Zealand's largest mutual benefit and member-owned organizations, effectively a consumer co-operative: Southern Cross. It provides secondary health insurance as a supplement to the national universal healthcare service. The organization also owns hospitals through a separate but linked charitable trust ownership structure. Southern Cross's initial development, which involved an eventual National Party prime minister, intentionally selected a mutual society ownership structure, aware of its prior history and usage in healthcare in the country (Smith 2000). Though friendly societies had effectively been replaced by a universal healthcare system in the late 1930s, public healthcare was not comprehensive in terms of benefit, and such societies had not entirely died out (Smith 2000; Olssen 1996).

Work trusts and worker co-operatives also had a sporadic but long-standing history in New Zealand as either a "make-work" unemployment-reduction strategy or as a government public works contracting strategy ("co-operative contracting") (Hare 1945; Derrick 1993; Chile 2006; Scotts 2011). Beginning in the mid-20th century, unemployment-reducing work trusts received not only National Party government support but the support of local council (city) governments in Auckland and Christchurch (Hutt 1978), then the two largest cities. These programs were similar in purpose to both the 1930s wave

---

[5] Auguring the challenges consumer co-operatives would face later in France, which enabled co-operative grocers to emerge.

of Depression-era self-help work co-operatives in the United States and the "community economic development" worker and consumer co-operatives in the 1960s through 1980s in the United States (Spicer 2020).

While these programs were effectively viewed as marginal and stop-gap measures to employ the poor and/or workers displaced by factory closures, National Party governments nonetheless sometimes supported them because they sought to put people to work. As National's minister of justice then said, "The notion of the work co-operative—something that I might tell the house is now attracting international attention—is working in a viable way to solve the problems of alienation, lack of job opportunities . . . and above all, the feeling that society offers nothing and gives nothing to these young people" (quoted in Gilbert 2010, 341). Directly inspired by the U.S. civil rights movement, one Maori-led social movement group explicitly and directly adopted the U.S. "Black Power" name and formed worker co-operative trusts (Gilbert 2010, 2013) in association. Some other worker co-operatives and trusts also had affiliations with Maori liberatory social movements (Gilbert 2010, 2013). As Scotts (2011) found, early 1980s estimates of the number of small work co-operatives and/or work trusts ranged between a low of 86 and a high of 300 (McCalman and Evans 1982; Fitzsimons 1982; Co-operative Workers Trust 1985). Virtually none of these, however, seems to have survived beyond the 1980s.

Second, given these constraints and challenges for the less liberal forms of co-operatives, it is not surprising that efforts to form a central co-operative meta-organization and apex body, to act as an institutional and field organizer and coordinate development across co-operative subtypes, met with limited success over this period. Individual producer co-operatives were largely able to obtain accommodative policy without relying on such intermediary bodies. Efforts to construct a coordinating national co-operative wholesale society in conjunction with (and based on investment support from) the British co-operative movement failed (Balnave and Patmore 2017). The development of some other national advocacy organizations were initially successful, yielding the Co-operatives Women's Guild, the New Zealand Co-operative Alliance, and the New Zealand Federation of Co-operatives (Brickell 2006), but none of these groups survived after World War II.

Finally, the post–World War II rise of the fledging National Party, which had formed out of the conservative remnants of the defunct Liberal Party,[6]

---

[6] The Liberal Party had been unable to find a constituency, further evidence of the challenges that liberalism faced in its development in the New Zealand context. Its proponents decamped into the Labour and National parties, infusing economic liberalism to a degree into both parties.

demonstrates and affirms the ambivalence of liberalism toward co-operatives. Coming to power in 1949, for the next 35 years it would hold power in all but six years (during two three-year Labour governments, 1957–60 and 1972–75). Through the late 1940s, the Labour government had attempted to promote and support consumer co-operatives in its housing and urban development schemes (Schrader 1996), even as it maintained consumer rations implemented after it had sent supplies the United Kingdom in World War II. This came under attack by the National Party as "centralized planning" which was reducing "consumer's standards of living" in the postwar era (Brickell 2006, 137). Though the National Party discontinued such programs and introduced some reforms to liberalize the economy, they ultimately maintained the strong welfare state and direct state-run enterprises built by Lib-Lab and Labour governments over the preceding half-century. They also repeatedly passed laws to update or expand co-operative-enabling legislation, again consistent with processes of institutional layering. Under the National government, an updated Co-operative Companies Act was introduced in 1956. The National government also later introduced the Credit Union and Friendly Societies Act in 1982. As late as the 1970s, New Zealand was creating new state-owned enterprises because "the New Zealand farmer has always been at the mercy of the overseas shipping companies" (Hayward 1981, 148), which was the government's justification for creating a state shipping line in 1973. New state interventions thus continued during this period, reflecting the ongoing role that distance played in structuring outside investment into the economy and the threat of foreign control.

As noted earlier, the National Party also offered some support for a consumer co-operative/mutual supplemental medical enterprise, which still exists today, and offered modest support for small worker co-operatives in the 1970s. Shifts in government control thus did not fundamentally tinker with the long-standing New Zealand formula of direct use of state ownership and power alongside use of co-operative structures to connect to the global economy and to develop domestically controlled and owned enterprises. Ultimately, the deeply protectionist policies of the National government of Robert Muldoon in the 1970s through the early 1980s and a fixed U.S. dollar exchange rate were increasingly unpopular in a period of economic malaise. New Zealand continued to struggle to adjust to the decline of the British Empire and ascension of the United Kingdom to the European Economic Community (EEC, now the EU) in 1973, which cost New Zealand its major trading partner, as exports to Britain were displaced by products from within the EEC. By 1982, the New Zealand government had imposed wage and price controls, and the economy was undergoing a prolonged, severe recession, setting the stage for field rupture and a realignment of the state-led configuration which had held sway for a century.

Field Rupture: Co-operatives Adapt to the Liberalization of New Zealand, 1984–Present

When its leading foreign export market, the distant Britain, entered the EEC in 1973, the economic effect on New Zealand was nothing less than an economic shock. It ended Britain and New Zealand's bilateral trade agreements and threatened the nation's prime exports of sheep and dairy products, both of which were heavily cooperativized. As severe recession took hold under Prime Minister Muldoon (1975–84), his National Party's center-right government introduced programs to reduce unemployment and stimulate economic growth, as noted. These programs, which ultimately maintained New Zealand's long-standing field settlement (marked by a state-led and pro-co-operative economic model and an associated set of field arrangements), did not seem to work. Labour thus proposed a more radical strategy in the 1984 election cycle: jettisoning the model entirely.

From the Labour Party's election in 1984 through the end of the National government in 1994, New Zealand went from being "the most protected, regulated and state-dominated system of any capitalist democracy to an extreme position at the open, competitive, free-market end of the spectrum" (Nagel 1998, 223). Reaganomics and Thatcherism in the two leading LMEs, the United States and the United Kingdom, were *neo*liberal movements, or liberal recapitulations in these countries. But New Zealand's corollary development of "Rogernomics" (Menz 2005) in 1984, and subsequently "Ruthanasia" in 1990, named after Finance Ministers Roger Douglas and Ruth Richardson, were effectively the country's original and first period of sustained, significant, and "successful" liberalization. The reforms of Rogernomics, one scholar observed, made "Thatcher look timid" by comparison (Menz 2005,49).

These efforts, however, were not wholeheartedly accepted by the public, and the new, post-rupture field configuration, in which IOFs were coming to play a far more dominant role, was unstable. New Zealand had long managed its trade relationship with Britain, its largest trading partner, through state and co-operative ownership, tools which had enabled domestic retention of both wealth and decision-making control. As that relationship ended, and the state withdrew from enterprise ownership and from co-operative support, foreign IOFs filled the field opening/institutional void, consistent with notions of field encroachment, as well as institutional conversion and displacement. As they came to control an increasingly wide swath of New Zealand's economy, it activated economic sovereignty concerns, a function of New Zealand's remoteness and size. It ultimately produced a political and economic backlash, which co-operatives leveraged by reorganizing for policy change, enabling them to adapt and arguably thrive.

The liberal revolution and its backlash: 1984–2001. Curiously, the liberalization and deregulatory revolutions in New Zealand were led not by the right but by the center-left: when Roger Douglas became finance minister in 1984, he was serving on behalf of a Labour government, which had come to power by defeating the center-right National Party. Though the Labour Party was socially progressive, its economic reforms, following a policy paper by Douglas, were stark and all-encompassing: it devalued the New Zealand currency by 20% and removed many export incentives, state-led sectoral development policies, and import restrictions (Smith 2005). Most notably, it sold off some state assets entirely and transformed some government departments into arm's-length, state-owned enterprises run with a focus on private-sector efficiency. It also eliminated policies which had restricted the sale of state-owned or state-controlled assets, which covered a wide range of industries, including timberlands, petroleum, airline operations, telecommunications/utilities, hotels, banks, insurance, steel, shipping, railways, broadcasting/communications, computing, and housing (Boston 1991). It introduced the nation's first antitrust or competition law in 1986 (Ahdar 2020), a critical legal element which supports LME-style institutional arrangements, which paved the way for the first Australia–New Zealand free trade agreement in 1990 (Ahdar 2020). National Party Finance Minister Richardson (1995, 2016) in particular made no secret of her desire to see more IOFs play a leading role in the economy, explicitly attacking co-operatives on various grounds as part of this policy position; co-operatives were unsurprisingly excluded from her government's various policy reforms, neglected, for example, in the update to the Companies' Act of 1993. Such attacks on co-operatives from economic liberalizers were not surprising: in other LMEs, this era's liberalization generally went hand in hand with demutualization (Martin and Turner 2000; Davis 2007) as liberal policies sought to unlock co-operatives' value by encouraging conversion to IOFs (Chaddad and Cooke 2004; 2007; Patmore, Balnave, and Marjanovic 2021).

Ultimately, however, many aspects of this liberalization program were met with negative voter sentiment and a backlash (Soederberg, Cerny, and Menz 2005), particularly as Australians and foreign investors came to own privatized former state- and trust-owned assets, and as some privatizations failed and required government intervention to avoid service disruption or closure. Air

New Zealand, for example, had to be renationalized; most major banks were acquired by Australian firms, and underperforming branches were closed. Again reflecting New Zealand's balancing act between geography and liberalization, this reactivated historical concerns regarding national economic independence and economic security, as relayed by several interviewees.

One Wellington interviewee, who actively lobbied New Zealand governments on behalf of co-operatives, described this era:

> We are very far away from everything . . . so we have this history of building and owning our own businesses because we have to, and then if Australia comes and buys them, we don't always like that. Every schoolboy learns that we were once part of the same colony [as Australia] and decided . . . to go it alone. There's a tension there. We don't want to be owned by the Australians, we have our own identity and value our independence. . . . Yes, independence economically and politically, also culturally. . . . But we are so far away from everyone else, what do we do? That's where co-operatives and trusts come in. . . . It becomes a government issue for us . . . on the basis of economic independence.

Though the center-right National Party government continued to hold power in the 1990s, it undertook actions responsive to the backlash. In that decade's push to deregulate energy markets, the aforementioned failed or troubled government privatizations enabled the mutualization of the regionalized energy system and, to a lesser extent, banks as well, through co-operative and co-operative-like structures, such as consumer/community trusts that effectively operate as co-operatives. The regional energy system includes both legal co-operatives and community trust-owned structures, variably reflecting local preference (Kalderimis 2000; Hoicka and MacArthur 2018). This system prevails across all of New Zealand, not just in rural areas (as in the United States). Auckland, the nation's largest metropolitan area, has a consumer trust, Entrust, at the center of its energy system; residents vote for the organization's leadership and receive dividend rebate checks each year (their surplus share). In parallel, Indigenous-owned and -managed trusts also operate, with similar community benefit (Hoicka and MacArthur 2018).

In addition, the Co-operative Companies Act was updated in 1996, allowing for outside minority equity investment (Evans and Meade 2005), enabling up to a 40% public sale of common nonvoting stock.[7] The New Zealand

---

[7] New Zealand's co-operative apex body/meta-organization continues to advocate for legal action related to this act, securing waivers, as recently as 2016, from securities filing provisions which would impose equity-raising costs on small-scale co-operatives availing themselves of outside investment options.

Companies Act had been updated and modernized in 1993, and co-operatives had not been included. The concern was that if their statute were not similarly updated, co-operatives would be disadvantaged. The government could have declined to support the 1996 act; this would have been tantamount to institutional/policy drift, in which a policy or statute is not updated to reflect changes to underlying conditions, and therefore becomes less effective or relevant (Hacker 2004). But instead, New Zealand's co-operative advocacy organization led efforts to lobby for such changes and shepherded the act to passage.

Of note, this advocacy organization, today known as Co-operative Business New Zealand, was registered and created in 1984, as the nation's liberalization began, to advocate for co-operatives' interests, with an explicit recognition that changing political conditions warranted such action, as affirmed by an interviewee. As this period of change began, co-operatives still did not have a strong national organizing body—prior ones had died out, as noted earlier—and so they formed one to advocate for their interests. Early challenges for the newly organized group included privatization of the Apple and Pear Marketing Board (McKenna, Le Heron, and Roche 2001; McKenna and Murray 2002): in the 1990s, the government was unresponsive to efforts to formally convert this entity into a producer co-operative (Stevenson 2000), and the organization was ultimately reorganized as an IOF, further stimulating the privatization backlash, as interviewees affirmed. Under Helen Clark's new Labour government, however, Parliament passed the 2001 Dairy Industry Restructuring Act, allowing the merger of New Zealand's largest dairy co-operatives to form Fonterra, today the nation's largest private enterprise, and still a co-operative. The rationale was to allow for a single, unified dairy export firm capable of competing in global markets (Lind 2014; Rydberg 2009). To offset the merger's monopolistic effects—and in response to newly enacted antitrust/competition laws, referenced above—new regulations allowed and encouraged formation of new dairy companies, and several smaller co-operatives and IOFs have thus been formed. At the request of co-operatives themselves, the state has also on occasion directly acted in specific instances to reduce the risk of the loss of domestically owned co-operatives to demutualization: a 2007 amendment to the special enabling law for New Zealand's largest agricultural insurer (a consumer-owned co-operative/mutual) which lobbied to make it more difficult to demutualize by requiring 75% member-owner approval, was motivated in part out of desire to preserve domestic ownership, according to interviewees.

This backlash to liberalization also affected the banking sector, with partial state support for co-operative and mutual banking assets somewhat reemergent. In 1984, the government had owned or directly guaranteed more than half the commercial banking sector (M3 financial institutions; Brash 1996). Many of these were deregulated in "Rogernomics" experiments, with state and community asset privatization resulting in a partial loss of its trust-owned banking sector (which held bank equity on behalf of local communities, which received the profits) to Australian investors. The sector has been partially rebuilt in the two decades since, through market and state action: TSB, the one remaining major community trust bank, has grown significantly to become the seventh largest bank. The state, too, reintroduced a public bank, Kiwibank, under Clark's Labour government,[8] which has become the fifth largest bank over the past decade; co-operative-sector actors interviewed noted calls for it to be cooperativized (O'Neill 2010). A public investment/retirement agency, the PSIS, was mutualized, with government assistance, into the Co-operative Bank, which has become the sixth largest bank, just behind the four major Australian-owned banks and Kiwibank. Small credit unions in New Zealand have coordinated under the "Co-op Money" banner (consistent with the co-operative coordination model), sharing services in their back office and support operations in order to scale their operations and to compete with larger financial firms.

Co-operatives in New Zealand today: The continued tyranny of distance. New Zealand's co-operatives have succeeded, to a degree, in adapting to and thriving in the liberal era. They have organized to secure legislative treatment which allows them to continue to compete and serve their members.

Producer co-operatives, which are more consonant with the logic of liberalism and its arrangements, still dominate the ranks of New Zealand's large co-operatives; many of them have thrived by accepting outside equity investment, enabled by recent decades' legal changes, to make outside/external minority stake investment easier. Though this further diluted the democratic, member-driven nature of the co-operative form, it is how these co-operatives have been able to persist and compete. Not all producer co-operatives have survived, however; the New Zealand Honey Producers' Co-operative, for example, was finally demutualized in 2016, while in the wake of the Christchurch earthquakes, AMI, the mutual insurer, had to be demutualized because of the catastrophic losses. Nonetheless, many persist: FTD/Interflora, known the world over as a leading company for floral delivery with nearly $1 billion in annual revenue, remains a co-operative in New Zealand, owned and controlled by its member florists nationwide, even though the networked firm has demutualized everywhere else around the world. FTD/Interflora's individual

---

[8] Clark was elected in 1999 under a newly introduced mixed-member proportional system.

florist owners, said one interviewee, have observed the loss of control that investor ownership has brought for the rest of the global organization and have no interest in demutualizing.

Such "reverse franchise" producer co-operatives are not unusual in New Zealand and include its leading grocery chain, home improvement store chain, and agricultural supply store chains. Fonterra and Silverfern, the mutton co-operative, in recent years created a co-operative joint venture to form Kotahi, a "cooperation among co-operatives" shipping and logistics company, to connect their products to world markets, reflecting the persistence of CME-like co-operative coordination strategies and their value in enabling New Zealand to manage its remoteness.

There remains, however, little direct national-level government support, via subsidies or lending programs, for worker or consumer co-operatives, consistent with the nation's founding liberal character and heritage. These types of co-operatives have struggled to achieve sustained, national scale, and instead remain (as in the United States) "trapped" in localized pockets. In field theory terms, they have not been able to construct a defendable field space. With a few notable exceptions, major consumer co-operatives largely disappeared, either before or during the Rogernomics programs of 1984, while the Muldoon-era work trusts and co-operatives faded with the rise of the Labour-led liberalization and reforms. There are few registered worker co-operatives in existence today, though new entities are forming. Loomio, founded in 2012 out of the Occupy movement (see Figure 5.4), is a platform technology company which has built a decision-making and consensus-building app which seeks to reduce governance and decision-making costs for other enterprises. Another worker co-operative, Tui Bee Balms, is structured as part of several alternatively owned enterprises near Nelson on the South Island, long a center for "bohemians," as several interviewees noted. As in the United States and other case countries, city governments have nonetheless recently taken limited action to incorporate co-operative enterprise where appropriate as a local economic development tool, as in decades past. Auckland, for example, introduced co-operative business incubation in the 2010s in its Southern Initiative, a community economic development model in South Auckland, as one interviewee noted.

What persists are a host of other non-IOF forms alongside the co-operative. State-owned enterprises, such as Kiwibank, remain prominent, and sizable community- and consumer-owned energy systems and banks are also common. Unlike in the United States, where the tax war in the 1950s against co-operatives led to ring-fencing of what operations could be conducted as a tax-exempt nonprofit (see Chapter 7), in New Zealand the lines are less clear.

Figure 5.4 Wellington offices of Loomio, a joint U.S.–New Zealand high-tech worker co-op born out of the Occupy movement that uses technology to enable collaborative, consensus-based decision-making in nonprofits, governments, co-ops, social enterprises, and social movements around the world. Photos by the author.

Charitable trusts (as distinct from community or consumer trusts), for example, sometimes own large, for-profit businesses which are tax-exempt. The most well-known example is Sanitarium, New Zealand's largest cereals manufacturer. Sanitarium is a for-profit charitable trust exempt from income tax. The trust is 100% owned by the Seventh Day Adventists; all cereal profits are reinvested in the hospitals and healthcare facilities it operates. Because this reduces the burden on the state to meet these costs, they are exempt from taxes on profits. Reflecting how such non-IOFs coordinate and partner to achieve prosocial goals, Sanitarium also coordinated with Fonterra, the milk co-operative, and the New Zealand government to create Kickstart. This formal, state-sanctioned, public-private partnership brought breakfast to at-risk children at more than 1,100 schools. Such arrangements affirm New Zealand's continued use of co-operative, community, and state ownership in prominent social and economic development initiatives.

The closest major land mass to New Zealand is Australia. And yet, again as Mark Twain observed, the two countries' closest cities of Auckland and Sydney are separated by 1,340 miles of ocean, comparable to the distance between London and St. Petersburg, Russia, or New York City and Dallas. Affirming how the continued costs of distance can constrain global IOFs and enable alternatives to succeed in their absence in places like New Zealand, Amazon lacks New Zealand operations and initially would not even ship to it from their new Australian hub, which opened in 2017 (*The Register* 2018). Further reflecting cost and distance, items from Amazon's main U.S. site did not become available for New Zealand shipping until 2018, at a minimum cost of $20. It is not surprising that co-operatives like Interflora should persist alongside other co-operative-like and state-related enterprises in New Zealand, while the presence of globalizing, footloose IOFs like Amazon is limited. Ultimately, New Zealand's economy developed as part of the "First Globalization" (Berger 2003, 2017) in the late 19th century, using the time-space-reducing technologies of the Second Industrial Revolution (Combes, Mayer, and Thisse 2008), such as long-distance shipping, telecommunications, and refrigeration, to become "Britain's farm." Co-operatives established a defensible field space in New Zealand's economy by playing a critical role in overcoming the tyranny of distance to organize this economic activity, a role which they continue to play today.

The persistence of New Zealand's large co-operatives thus reflects the tyranny of distance, not just as an economic force but as a political one. Because of its remoteness, New Zealand faces a stark choice between domestic economic control and economic ownership by their larger closest neighbors, Australia and China. To avoid the latter, New Zealand still relies on a range of IOF alternatives like the co-operative to keep its wealth domestically owned and controlled. As a result, the continued viability and health of the co-operative as an organizational form becomes a compelling national policy issue, earning the attention of the government. As in the other cases, the deployment of field theory enables us to understand not just *how* this arrangement came to be but *why*: due to New Zealand's size and remoteness, the nation has been unable to realize a stable economic field settlement predicated solely or primarily on programs of economic liberalism and its associated enterprise model, the IOF. The state thus must explicitly support and stoke what Schneiberg (2010) has called an "organizationally diverse ecology" of enterprise types, with co-operatives and related forms playing a central role, to both generate and retain wealth in the domestic economy. Field theory thus helps us explain not just *how* but *why* New Zealand's co-operatives remain liberalism's long-running, strange bedfellow.

6
American Cooperation in the 19th Century
A Field Denied

> Ever since its commencement, the co-operative movement in the United States has never been satisfactorily organized.
> —Ira B. Cross (1905–6), professor of economics, UC Berkeley

Paradoxically, co-operatives in America are simultaneously abundant and scarce: though co-operative enterprises have been abundant throughout U.S. history, those of lasting scale are comparatively scarce. To be sure, there have been specific niches where American co-operatives have long been seemingly successful and have endured to the present day: electricity, agricultural marketing/distribution, and consumer credit are the most obvious areas.

But even on these fronts, the story of American cooperation is one of restriction and limits on both scale and scope, as briefly reviewed in Chapter 2 (cf. Spicer 2022). U.S. electrical co-operatives are generally small and rural, by design. American credit unions are common, but almost entirely small-scale, restricted in geography and financial scope. Some agricultural co-operatives are quite large but are defined by exception, their existence possible by an exemption in early U.S. antitrust law, which protects agricultural marketing and distribution co-operatives from prosecution for unlawful coordination. Over the decade I spent conducting research for this book, American co-operative participants repeatedly affirmed this paradox of scarcity and abundance. One New York City cooperator dryly told me that American co-operatives seem to have a knack for "snatching defeat from the jaws of victory." And yet, a few minutes later, he was extolling the rich history and use of the model in the United States.

Indeed, the U.S. historical record is rich with promising, wide-ranging experiments with co-operatives, first incubated in the early 19th century by a broad spectrum of socioeconomic groups and movements. But by that century's end, figures like UC Berkeley labor economist Ira Cross were already bemoaning the U.S. co-operative movement's comparative failures. As a contemporary of Cross put it, co-operative stores were an "almost utter failure" and "to the ordinary commercial mind a term of derision" (Barnard 1881, 109). Cross's statement about co-operatives' lack of organization provides a clue as to why: the American co-operative movement has never satisfactorily organized itself into a *field* at national scale, one with clear definitional bounds and state-legitimated modes of operation and coordination, as established and defended by skilled social actors. The result, despite cycles of effort, is an incomplete field, often trapped at the subnational, local scale, always in a state of partial organization.

What Cross never offered, however, was a compelling empirical explanation as to *why* exactly co-operatives could not organize themselves nationally as well as they had elsewhere. American cooperators faced the foe of co-operatives everywhere: economic liberalism and its banner-bearer model, the IOF. They accordingly faced some of the same competitive challenges as co-operatives elsewhere: of attracting capable businesspeople; of learning, through experimentation, how to develop, implement, and coordinate replicable models at scale for use in the local context. It is true, as this chapter will review, that IOFs developed earlier and with more force in the United States, imprinting themselves into the field environment in the economy with greater heft. In so doing, they more quickly established a strong incumbent position in the economy, adding to co-operatives' American challenges.

But American co-operatives did not just face the IOF as a competitor. They faced another competing ownership model, one absent elsewhere through industrialization: the race-based system of chattel slavery. Proponents of both of these two competing ownership models blocked the co-operative from establishing a field space from which to organize itself, constraining cooperation from the very beginning (Figure 6.1). In fact, it nearly destroyed American cooperation before it began.

While antebellum labor movement organizations did include fledgling efforts to support co-operatives, the key movement driving cooperation in that era was that of the communitarians, whose efforts struggled to penetrate the South. And the central problem the communitarians faced in promoting co-operatives, which nearly destroyed the movement nationally, was how they framed their opposition to industrial capitalism and the IOF as a fight against "wage slavery." This framing directly interacted with the brewing controversy over race-based chattel slavery.

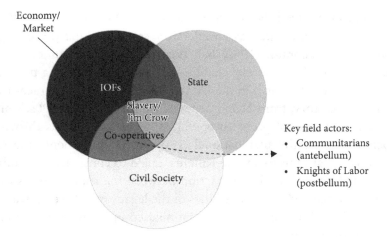

Figure 6.1 American co-operatives: field architecture, 19th century.

These issues foreshadowed the problems which plagued the communitarian movement's successor in promoting co-operatives, the multiracial Knights of Labor, which led the first full-fledged co-operative field-building effort by a national labor organization in the United States. At their 1886 peak, they represented an estimated 20% of all American workers (Kaufman 2001). In their effort to claim the institutional void or field opening once occupied by slavery, their co-operative drive into the South ended in racialized violence, as they triggered what we would today recognize as fears of a "great replacement": the replacement of White ownership of Black laborers with multiracial collective ownership of workers' own labor, via the co-operative model.

The failure of the Knights, and their replacement by century's end by the all-White American Federation of Labor (AFL) as the leading labor organization, is often cast as the critical moment in which American exceptionalism, especially with respect to labor, takes hold (Kaufman 2001; Voss 1993). In that larger story in the emergence of American exceptionalism, however, co-operatives play a significant role. For with the Knights' demise, and their replacement by the AFL, co-operatives lost their status as one of four key planks of the American labor movement (Ware 1929).

As the labor movement's leadership passed from the Knights to the AFL in the 1890s, the co-operative movement was accordingly left without a major organizational champion on the national economic or political stage. It would continue in the 20th century to be characterized by partially organized field-building efforts, splintered into subfields by industry/co-operative subtype, region, and race, as will be shown in Chapter 7. As a result, American co-operatives never developed as an effective "countervailing power" against capital—a role Galbraith (1952) had theorized that both unions and co-operatives could play—thereby enabling the entrenchment of a particularly virulent strain of liberalism in the United States. This chapter traces the beginning of this story, from U.S. independence through the 1890s, from the antebellum diffusion of proto-co-operative forms and models through the postbellum rise of the first national co-operative movement. The champion actor of that movement, the Knights, failed to construct a national co-operative field, felled by the interaction between the framing of its fight as against "wage slavery" and the realities of the legacy race-based slavery. This interaction had nearly destroyed its national co-operative predecessor, the communitarians, as well.

A Field in Formation? Four Strands of Antebellum American Cooperation, 1790–1860

Despite the rapid proliferation and diffusion in the United Kingdom of the Rochdale system of interlocking co-operatives in the 1840s, the system did not appear in the United States until the Civil War's end, when it established its first toehold in the North (Leikin 2004; Commons et al. 1918). In the midcentury decades immediately before and after the co-operative's emergence as a coherent field in the United Kingdom, however, four distinct proto-co-operative strands were nonetheless visibly in formation in antebellum America: mutually owned financial enterprises, productive associations, co-operative stores, and communitarian socialist communities (sometimes historically referred to as co-operative colonies).[1]

Experiments across the three of these four strands which were most closely linked to the emergent communitarian and labor movements—that is, all the strands save mutually owned financial enterprises—were small-scale, short-lived, and poorly coordinated throughout the antebellum period. In his account of American socialism, Kipnis (1952, 2) writes, "Co-operative colonies were not the only utopian solutions attempted by dissatisfied members of society. Producers' and consumers' co-operatives flourished sporadically for over forty years as utopian alternatives to the production and distribution

---

[1] There were a handful of short-lived antebellum experiments in co-operative agricultural marketing/distribution which were either only partly implemented or failed in the 1820s and 1830s. See Knapp (1969, 12) for details.

relations of capitalism. With every new industrial crisis, with every failure of the trade unions to alter materially the conditions of labor and the standard of living in pre- and post-Civil War America, farmers and workers turned anew to co-operatives as a way to beat the capitalists at their own game." Moreover, the three fledgling strands of cooperation which were most directly movement-based—again with mutually owned financial enterprises as the fourth strand and arguable exception—were not substantively national in coverage. All four remained primarily organizationally articulated at the local and regional scale and did not penetrate all regions. Specifically, they failed to make substantive headway in the American South, which was not an insignificant portion of the country; by the eve of the Civil War, the 1860 census enumerated nearly 9 million souls in what would become the Confederate States, accounting for more than one-fourth the U.S. population.

This lack of national development is not surprising, given that the issue of slavery nearly destroyed the major movement directly associated with at least three of these proto-co-operative strands: the communitarian movement. By the 1840s, this movement was led by Associationists, who were proponents of the American version of Fourierism (see Chapter 4) and the immediate successors to the Owenites (the forerunners to the Rochdale model). As put by Guarneri (1991, 253) in his authoritative historical account of the 19th-century American communitarian movements, "By the latter half of the 1840s the escalating sectional controversy over slavery not only precluded any Fourierist 'solution'; it was threatening to break up the communitarian movement itself."

While the short-term, limited-scale experiments across these three co-operative strands may have carried outsized symbolic importance to the fledgling communitarian and labor movements at the time, the U.S. economy was simultaneously and quickly industrializing, marking the beginning of a rapid, early 19th-century shift in the population, from being majority self-employed to working as employees in organizations (Haveman 2022, 30). These organizations were disproportionately corporations operating as IOFs, which were developing at a comparatively greater pace than elsewhere (Wright and Sylla 2011; Sylla and Wright 2013; Hannah 2014).

As Hilt (2017, 40) explains, however, incorporation was a distinctly post-independence phenomenon, corporations being rare in the American colonies: "[F]rom the colonial era up through 1791, only thirty-two businesses received corporate charters from the American states." This changed after American independence:

One area of financial development in which the United States most differed from European precedents was that of the business corporation. In Europe, corporations tended to be privileged monopolies, and there were relatively few of them. The first promoters of U.S. corporations may have had the European model in mind, but increasingly found themselves overwhelmed by democratic political forces that insisted upon the extension of corporate privileges to nearly all white males who desired them. It was in the United States, therefore, starting in the 1790s when about 300 corporations were chartered, that the old European idea of the corporation as privileged monopoly began to be transformed into the modern idea of the corporation as a competitive enterprise. Between 1790 and 1860, U.S. state governments chartered some 22,000 corporations under special legislative acts and another 4,000 or so under general laws of incorporation. Assuming that exit rates did not drastically differ between continents, by 1830 the United States had at least 15 times more corporations per capita than Britain did (Harris 2000, 288; Sylla 2009, 226–28). France, Germany, and Russia lagged even farther behind (Thieme 1961; Freedeman 1979; Owen 1991). (Wright and Sylla 2011, 231–32)

In field theory terms, IOFs were thus developing a first-mover advantage and position of comparative field incumbency in the emerging industrial U.S. economy. The traditional joint-stock corporation, which was the legal form the IOF took in the United States, was rapidly proliferating across the country, including in the South (Wright and Sylla 2011). Against this backdrop, four early strands of cooperation were developing, reviewed below.

Mutually owned financial enterprises. The most well-developed early strain of cooperation in antebellum America was the mutually owned financial enterprise, which arose in the late 18th century. Led by mutual fire insurance, which by the mid-1800s would directly give rise to and inspire mutual life insurance, savings banks, and savings associations, these quickly became substantial in scale and number. Critically, unlike the other three strains of cooperation reviewed here, some of these models were in substantive use across the United States, including in the South. As much as legally allowed, predecessor versions of these forms were in wide use among the Black population as well.[2]

As in the United Kingdom, there were links between the development of mutually owned financial enterprises and friendly and mutual aid/benefit societies, a predecessor form. Though a friendly society in Charleston, South Carolina, sponsored the first fire insurance company in the United States

---

[2] Mutual savings banks specifically, however, remained an almost entirely Northeastern U.S. phenomenon, accounting for 95% of deposits in that region even at the 20th-century peak of their development (Moysich 1997). They were largely established by wealthy philanthropists (Moysich 1997).

in 1735, it was defunct by 1740 (Wainwright 1953). Also in 1735, Benjamin Franklin helped found Philadelphia's Union Fire Company "as an association for mutual assistance" (Knapp 1969, 8), which would lead to his cofounding the first long-term, stable fire insurance company in the United States in 1752, which was structured as a mutually owned enterprise. This particular mutual insurance firm, the Philadelphia Contributionship, remains in existence today as a mutual. Its initial success marked a rare occasion when a co-operative or mutual form established a first-mover advantage. The success of the firm "encouraged the formation of a number of similar mutual fire insurance companies prior to the formation of the first stock company in 1794. There were some ten mutual fire insurance companies in existence by 1800 as compared with four companies organized on a stock basis. Thus it was in the field of mutual insurance that the co-operative form of business enterprise first took definite form in the United States" (Knapp 1969, 9). These urban fire insurance mutuals directly fueled the development of farmers' mutual fire insurance beginning in the 1820s. By 1850, more than 100 such firms had spread from New England across the Northern states, typically incorporated under special charters (Valgren 1924). Relatedly, by the 1830s and 1840s, both mutual savings/building and loan associations and mutual life and other general mutual insurance companies were beginning to take root and grow to scale, spreading primarily throughout the Northern states (Barnard 1881; Clough 1946). Mutual life insurers began to proliferate in the 1840s (Wright and Kingston 2012), as joint-stock companies had performed poorly during and after the Panic of 1837, and mutuals required little start-up capital (Murphy 2010). They also introduced a number of institutional innovations which enhanced their success, some of which can be traced to the efforts of New England Mutual's Elizur Wright, an abolitionist and Associationist mathematician and reformer (Murphy 2010; Guarneri 1991). Though many Northern antebellum mutual life and property insurance companies eventually refused to insure the lives of the enslaved, this was a core business for some Southern mutual insurers, such as Greensboro Mutual Life and North Carolina Mutual Life (Murphy 2005), neither of which survived the Civil War.

Gordon Nembhard (2014) synthesizes research which affirms that the forerunners to these various types of mutually owned enterprises, the friendly and mutual aid societies, were in widespread use by Free Black people throughout the antebellum United States. Though more common in the urban centers of the North, she draws on Berry (2005), Weare ([1973] 1993), and Jones (1985), who established that such mutual aid societies were also in use throughout Southern cities with Free Black populations. Weare ([1973] 1993, 9), reviewing primary historical accounts, found that "despite laws in slave states inhibiting the assembly of free Negroes, there is evidence that the free Negro populations of Richmond, New Orleans, and Charleston openly organized several benefit societies, including New Orleans, Charleston, and Richmond." It is unclear, however, if these were mutually *owned* enterprises, in which Black individuals would have owned shares in the association or company, as is the case with the emergent mutual insurance and banking enterprise forms reviewed above, which were in wide use among the non-Black population by 1860. Weare, who describes mutual benefit societies as a "rudimentary instrument" (7) from which mutual insurance evolved, concludes that Black mutually *owned* insurance, particularly in the South, was unable to develop until after the war due to the institution of chattel slavery, which would have precluded formal legal ownership rights (10).

Nonetheless, it is clear that by 1860, mutually owned financial enterprise was the most well-developed form of co-operative in the United States: "On the eve of the Civil War the best rooted form of co-operative enterprise was the farmers' mutual insurance company. At that time there were well over a hundred associations of this type located principally in New England, the Middle Atlantic states, and as far west as Illinois . . . while in the eastern cities the building and loan associations which had caught hold during the 1850s were gaining in popularity and were rapidly perfecting their methods" (Knapp 1969, 27).

Productive associations: The worker co-operative's forerunner. Today, in Anglophone contexts, the term "producer co-operative" typically refers to business co-operatives, in which the member-owners are other firms, which themselves may be IOFs. Historically, however, scholars and cooperators alike used the terms "industrial or producer co-operatives," "producers' associations," or "productive associations" to refer to what today would be most often recognized as worker co-operatives.[3] These entities were formed by working producers who pooled their labor into a collectively and democratically controlled workshop or store (Jones 1977; Aldrich and Stern 1983). Typically, these were formed by journeymen working in a skilled trade or craft; antebellum examples are carpenters, shoemakers, coopers, tailors, and iron smolders, among others (Jones 1977; Aldrich and Stern 1983; Commons et al. 1918).

Though there purportedly had been prerevolutionary instances of striking journeymen workers setting up temporary "make-work" and "retaliatory" co-operatives (Rayback 1959, 17), the first such entity in the independent United States seems to have been formed in 1791. As with these predecessors, this

---

[3] The reasons and timing for this evolution require further study and are beyond this book's scope.

was a temporary retaliatory entity against masters in Philadelphia by striking journeymen carpenters, created the year before the first formal trade union in the United States was created (Commons et al. 1918, 94, 127–30). The second co-operative workshop, set up by Philadelphia journeymen cordwainers (shoemakers) in 1806 after they had been convicted of conspiracy, was intended to be permanent; it was not set up as a retaliatory, stop-gap measure (Commons et al. 2018; Jones 1977).[4] At least three more such associations were established in the early 1830s (Commons et al. 1918; Jones 1977), and by 1836 the fledgling National Trades' Union, the first entity of its kind and arguably the first substantive national labor movement organization in the United States, proposed co-operatives as a way to end strikes permanently (Ware 1929), reflecting interest in cooperation by the emergent American labor movement. Unfortunately, "the first American labor movement was, in fact, destroyed, along with its experiments in co-operation, by the panic of 1837" (Leikin 2006, 321). The pace of co-operative formation appeared to quicken again by the late 1830s, however, as the American labor movement redeveloped in the wake of the long 1837–44 depression (Shirom 1972; Stockton 1931; Jones 1977; Aldrich and Stern 1983; Curl 2009; Commons et al. 1918).[5]

Philadelphia and other dense settlements in the Northeast and Midwest, such as Boston, New York, Buffalo, Detroit, Pittsburgh, and Cincinnati, all played host to these early producers associations, the formation of which was often linked to labor unrest and organizing (Shirom 1972; Stockton 1931; Jones 1977; Aldrich and Stern 1983; Curl 2009; Commons et al. 1918). Some were associated with recent German immigrants (Commons et al. 1918, 568) who "were inspired to co-operate by the movement in their home country" (Leikin 2006, 321) and who would come to play a significant role in postbellum socialist movements nationally (Kipnis 1952). German interest was catalyzed by German immigrant Wilhelm Weitling, who by 1850 had proposed, in a national convention of German-American workers, to coordinate producers' co-operatives with a labor exchange bank, building on English and French ideas from Owen and Blanc; the proposal was not enacted (Bell 1996, 19). Outside of the larger cities, producers' associations "met with better success among the English-speaking workmen" in smaller cities, particularly in the Midwest (then called the Old North-West or Middle West), where a small

---

[4] The labor-related conspiracy conviction of these cordwainers, which necessitated the founding of this second co-operative association, was one of a series of such conspiracy cases tried in the early 1800s, which at the time were highly controversial in that they hinged on whether English common law applied to such labor combinations.
[5] All of these works explicitly note the timing of formation as co-operatives' cyclical response to upheaval.

co-operative shop could accommodate a greater share of the local skilled workers operating in their given occupation (Commons et al. 1918, 569).

Not all of these productive associations, which were sometimes endorsed and supported by the emergent city industrial congresses (Commons et al. 1918), would be recognizable to modern eyes as a worker co-operative, reflecting the fact that producer co-operatives and worker co-operatives had not yet emerged as stable or distinct institutionalized forms. Indeed, "many of the so-called productive associations of laborers outside New York would be better called associations of small capitalists or master workmen, as there were not a few such corporations formed in which each member contributed several hundred or even a few thousand dollars" (Commons et al. 1918, 569). Meanwhile, the city industrial congresses and councils were ambivalent toward co-operative efforts; they held internal debates over whether to support organizing and unionization efforts against capitalist-owned firms (Commons et al. 1918), that is, IOFs, which were already then ascendant in leading the First Industrialization's continued transformation of the American economy (Sylla and Wright 2013; see below).

Aldrich and Stern (1983) created a database of all such productive associations in the United States in existence starting in 1835, when an observable increase in the formation of such co-operative associations appears in the historical record. For the decade between 1835 and 1844, they identify 12 such entities. Eight were located in the Northeastern states, and four in the Midwest and Plains states. There were none in the South. In the following decade, 1845–54, as the labor movement reemerged and new National Industrial Congresses were formed and supported cooperation (Ware 1929), 32 such co-operatives formed nationally, according to Aldrich and Stern's data. In the Northeastern region, including in New England and the Mid-Atlantic states, were 23 such enterprises; 8 were spread across various Midwestern and Plains states. Just one was formed in the South (Aldrich and Stern 1983).

Few of these entities appeared to last more than a few years or to achieve any meaningful scale (Aldrich and Stern 1983; Jones 1977; Shirom 1972), though some did grow to have as many as 80 members (Commons et al. 1918, 569). A few did attempt, with limited success, to coordinate their efforts with not just city industrial councils and congresses but with fledgling ideas for co-operative stores, warehouses, and banks, reflecting their links to the emergent American communitarian movements of the Owenites and the Associationists (Commons et al. 1918). Jones (1979, 343), analyzing data from this period, finds that while "most early producer co-operatives were in the East . . . for later groups we see a drift to the West," a finding he reiterated in a later, extended study (Jones 1984).

While Aldrich and Stern (1983) offer regional-level descriptive statistics by decade, they did not provide any mention of specific detailed cases of antebellum producers' associations in what would become the Confederate South; neither their data nor the related data set of Jones (1977, 1979, 1980) is still available at the individual record-level.[6] Most of the standard academic sources of the American labor and co-operative movements of the era which do provide such case-level detail also do not mention any specific Southern instance (Commons et al. 1918; Jones 1977, 1979, 1980, 1984; Shirom 1972; Aldrich and Stern 1983; Bemis 1888; Jackall and Levin 1984; Horner 1978; Lichtenstein 1986). In Randall's (1888) history of cooperation in the South, written as a chapter in the first exhaustive national study of American cooperation (Adams 1888),[7] he notes the scarcity of such co-operative associations before 1884, at which time a national revival in cooperation associated with the Knights of Labor bore fruit in the South. This is consistent with Aldrich and Stern's (1983) data, which observes a rapid increase in the national presence of such entities in the postbellum period, particularly after 1884. Jones (1979) estimated that nearly 44% of all such co-operative associations formed in the United States between the 1840s and 1950s were accounted for by Knights of Labor–related efforts. He later estimated the Knights' efforts accounted for 54% of all such enterprises formed in the 19th century, and over 25% of the total created through the 1970s (Jones 1984).

Antebellum efforts were aided by high-profile champions such as Horace Greeley, who by the 1840s was promoting productive association in the Northeastern states: "Although advocating other reforms, the *abolition* of the wage system was his leading hope, and for this reason he may be considered the exponent of productive co-operation" (Commons et al. 1918, 508, emphasis added). Greeley was also an advocate of Fourier's Associationist phalanxes, a form of utopian socialist community (Griffin 2018). A successful editor of the *New York Tribune* and cofounder of the *New Yorker*, Greeley regularly featured Karl Marx as a columnist (Tuchinsky 2005). A future congressman and the losing candidate in the 1872 presidential election for the new Liberal Republican Party against incumbent and Radical Republican Ulysses Grant, Greeley was transparent in connecting his support for co-operative enterprise

---

[6] As per emails between the author and both Jones and Aldrich; Stern is deceased.
[7] The first specific documented instances of productive associations for which I can find records occur in the non-Confederate, border states. Randall details instances in Maryland from the postbellum era, in 1871 and approximately 1875. The first, which lasted three years, was not technically set up as an association but as a traditional joint-stock corporation with profit-sharing, and in the second, five cooperators quickly sold out to the sixth who bought the firm (Randall 1888, 493). We also know of an antebellum instance in today's Wheeling, West Virginia (then Virginia) established by Horner (1978) and referenced by Leikin (2004) and Lichtenstein (1986). Wheeling was never part of the Confederacy.

among Northern White workers to the issue of race-based chattel slavery, on the basis that White wage labor constituted a form of slavery which similarly required abolition (Griffin 2018; Guarneri 1983). His connection of the two issues made him a visible, high-profile target for Southern pro-slavery political actors and media (Griffin 2018).

Notably, while there were significant numbers of Free Black workers in skilled occupations during this era, particularly in the North (Foner 1974), where they sometimes also engaged in organized labor campaigns and unionization efforts (Foner 1974), I find no record of any racially integrated or Black worker co-operatives in this era.

Co-operative stores. The second antebellum strain, co-operative stores, had direct links to the same movements—that of the communitarians, as well as the fledgling labor movement—which had incubated productive associations. Co-operative stores in meaningful scale first began to take root in the mid-1840s, when a labor movement–related organization emanating out of New England rapidly built a large-scale network of stores spanning at least 10 states (Cowling 1938, 81), mostly in New England and the Northeast, and also in Canada (Ford 1913). There are no known instances of an antebellum co-operative store in the future Confederate States.

Arguably there had been a previous, limited effort in 1829 to create such stores, in places such as New York on the Owenite plan (Parker 1956), as well as in Philadelphia and Cincinnati under a co-operative marketing plan developed by "the first American anarchist," Josiah Warren, whose "time stores" were designed without profit and were based on a contributed labor model (Commons et al. 1918, 96, 511). But it was the New England–based Working Men's Protective Union which oversaw the only significant antebellum effort to create widespread consumer cooperation in the United States. Their rapidly created networks of stores lasted roughly a decade before experiencing an equally rapid decline. Interestingly, this network was not based on the Rochdale consumer co-operative model established in 1844, but rather on Rochdale's immediate predecessor models in the United Kingdom (Cowling 1938, 38) espoused by King and Owen; a wave of such stores had collapsed in rapid fashion in the United Kingdom in the early 1830s (Wilson, Webster, and Vorberg-Rugh 2014; see Chapter 2).

The New England Association of Farmers, Mechanics, and Other Working Men had formed in Boston in 1831 and immediately began discussing the benefits of creating a co-operative store system (Cross, 1906, 9; Ford 1913, 14). The Association was one of many such local labor movement organizations, as neither the labor movement nor unions had yet scaled up to emerge as a nationally coherent institution or field. Indeed, "what has been called the labor movement of the period from 1827 to 1837 consisted of varied organizations with all-embracing social programs" (Pessen 1956, 434) and is sometimes referred to by historians as the working men's movement of the Jacksonian era (Pessen 1956). In different cities, the movement variably took the form of city-level industrial congresses and councils, such as those reviewed above as supporting productive associations, as well as general trade unions and political parties, such as the various local working men's political parties (Pessen 1956), which often included leaders with links to the communitarian movement. It also included Working Men's Associations such as the one in Boston (Pessen 1956).

Like many such regional labor movement–related entities, this New England organization was largely wiped out by the Panic of 1837 and subsequent depression, but in 1844 a direct successor organization was formed, the New England Working Men's Association, which included the same constituencies as before and would come to be associated with the emergent labor reform movements of the 1840s. As Early (1980, 35) notes, it also included a number of utopian socialists, such as Fourier's Associationists: "Though Associationists proselytized for phalanx living . . . they also supported the drive for the ten-hour day and . . . consumer co-operatives."[8] The new association quickly supported the development of a "sort of Fourier association" called a protective union (Commons 1910, 263; cf. Early 1980, 43). By 1845, closed (i.e., members-only)[9] stores in New England had begun operation, and by 1847 they were of sufficient number and scale to warrant the creation of "a federation for purposes of general co-operative purchase and propaganda" (Ford 1913, 14). Formed that year as the Working Men's Protective Union, the central federation would change its name to New England Protective Union in 1849 (Ford 1913), and its individual shops were referred to as union stores. These co-operative stores would soon come to dominate the entire organization and crowd out all other activities (Cowling 1938, 80). Though they adhered to a number of operating rules and coordination strategies which characterize the Rochdale model, these member-owned stores were neither

---

[8] Reflecting the intellectual marginalization of the co-operative in the United States, Early goes on to extensively note how these connections between different strands of Associationist cooperators and the nascent labor movement had long been discounted by American labor historians, most notably the dominant Wisconsin School of labor history led by Commons, whose framework was also deployed by Ware and Foner, because this school of American labor history viewed any deviation from the trade union as regrettable, finding utopians particularly "contemptuous" (Early 1980, 34–35), and viewing the AFL as having freed the U.S. labor movement from its native "producer consciousness" (Sanders 1999, 72). Most of the major historical accounts available today, which include details on the American co-operative movement reviewed above, are from these Ely-Bemis Wisconsin School scholars.

[9] They would later be open to nonmembers (Ford 1913, 15).

technically nor legally co-operatives, which, as of this date, had no formal, legally specific form available to them in the United States.

The Working Men's Protective Union ultimately grew to a significant scale, which "increased rapidly throughout the northeastern states in the [18]50's" (Ford 1913, 15), with 700 to 800 U.S. locations at their peak (Ford 1913). By the 1860s, due to a combination of business strains created by the Civil War and organizational infighting, the central wholesale association split into two rival unions and wholesale societies (Rozwenc 1941). Most stores either collapsed and closed or were sold and converted into IOFs (Cross 1906, 11), causing the model to disappear. By century's end, fewer than five stores from the Protective Union were still in existence, (Cowling 1938) and only two, both located in New Bedford, Massachusetts, had retained co-operative governance and organizational features (Ford 1913, 16–19). Other, limited attempts at forming co-operative stores, unrelated to the Protective Union, occurred during the Civil War, but these were highly localized efforts in the Northeast that were limited in scale (Cross 1906, 12–13). In 1863–64, the Rochdale co-operative store system was formally introduced in Boston and Philadelphia and would begin to develop thereafter (Leikin 2004, 2006).

Despite the Protective Union's reach across 10 states, and despite interest in the model reaching into the rural Upper Midwest, where it would inspire separate and independent efforts to start co-operative stores (Keillor 2000), I can find no instance of any store being opened in what would become the Confederacy. Bemis (1888, 23) documents the existence of Protective Union stores in the six New England states and in New York, Ohio, Illinois, and Oregon, as well as operations in Canada. Rozwenc, who draws on Bemis in his 1941 treatise on antebellum co-operative stores, documents 776 known locations of the Protection Union stores in his appendix (125–32); he also identifies antebellum stores which were either wholly independent or affiliated with local Protective Union movements that never federated with the central organizations. Of these nearly 70 stores (137–38) the only two located south of Pennsylvania or Ohio are in Maryland and Washington, D.C. He lists no stores in the future Confederacy. Though he does explicitly consider the regionalism of the Protective Union movement (116–19), he never mentions the South. There are no references to Black Americans in his work either.

Communitarian socialist experiments. Perhaps the most visible of the antebellum strains of cooperation were the utopian socialist communities associated with the French and English models of Fourier and

Owen,[10] which were direct forerunners of modern co-operative enterprises in those countries. American historians and historical social scientists refer to this particular subset of utopian socialist communities as "communitarian socialist" experiments (Bestor [1950] 1970) formed by the American "communitarian movement" (Bestor [1950] 1970; Guarneri 1991). Sometimes the Shakers or Shaking Quakers are analytically considered alongside or in conjunction with these secular utopian experiments. These groups' settlements were typically comprehensively planned, with residents living and working collectively, utilizing co-operatively pooled property and labor. Sometimes they acquired or occupied existing properties, around which they constructed additional buildings; at other times, the communities were developed from the ground up. Their methods and history have been extensively documented (Fogarty 1990; Bestor [1950] 1970; Hillquit 1903; Noyes 1870; Kumar 1990; Guarneri 1991; Pitzer 1997).

There were other varieties of utopian communities at the time, but they are often treated as distinct from the communitarian socialist projects. Of the approximately 130 utopian communities founded before 1860, roughly 80 to 100 were of these other varieties or strains, while approximately 30 to 50 were communitarian socialist in nature.[11] Typically these other kinds of communities were religious and separatist in nature, led and populated by "foreign-language speaking" (i.e., non-English speaking) residents and directly created through religious-oriented direct foreign migration, typically involving Continental European Anabaptists and Pietists. They did not always or necessarily feature collective or community property and labor, though some did incorporate such elements (Fogarty 1990; Kumar 1990; Bestor [1950] 1970; Kanter 1972; Hillquit 1903). Though largely located in the Northeast and Midwest, some half-dozen were created in the Southern states, including in North Carolina, Louisiana, Arkansas, and Texas, based on my analysis of existing inventories of these communities (Fogarty 1990; Bestor [1950] 1970; Hillquit 1903).

In contrast to these foreign migration-dominated communities, the communitarian socialist projects, or "co-operative colonies," as they were sometimes called in the postbellum era (Kipnis 1952; Fogarty 1990;

---

[10] Etienne Cabet of France was another key figure, whose philosophy inspired a small number of U.S.-based communities.

[11] I list a range of values because there is some debate over what counts as a settlement; some settlements, for example, collapsed as they were attempting to establish themselves and were never meaningfully constructed, settled, or occupied.

Pitzer 1997), of the Shakers, the Owenite villages of cooperation, and the Fourierian phalanxes were typically and primarily drawn either from current, local residents in the area who were living in a preexisting town or settlement, or from U.S. residents who were resettling from another region, most typically from the Northeast/New England to the Upper Midwest. With a few notable exceptions, these communities were typically not led or populated by newly arrived settlers or immigrants, nor were they typically drawn from farmers or "pioneers" (Bestor [1950] 1970; Guarneri 1991). Utilizing Bestor's catalogue of documented American communitarian socialist communities, I can find records of only two which were established in what would become the Confederacy: Nashoba, in Tennessee, and La Réunion, in Texas. Both were initially led and conceived offshore by foreigners and lasted barely a year before beginning to collapse. The latter was populated by new immigrants who sailed from France (Kagay 2010). The former, led by Scots émigrée Frances Wright, was focused on buying Southern enslaved people (and readying them for recolonization in Liberia or Haiti) to live in an interracial community of equality and co-operative labor, one which allowed interracial sex as well. Wright had to immediately abandon the co-operative labor aspects of the plan because they proved unworkable, in part due to the plan's "radical" ideas on race (cf. Bestor [1950] 1970, 218–25).[12]

I thus can find no record of any constructed communitarian socialist communities which were led by or drawn from the populations of the existing surrounding settlements of the Southern slave-holding states which would form the Confederacy. These communities, which were typically formed primarily from existing settled, local populations, were entirely contained in what we would today call the Northeast and Midwest (see Figure 6.2). Thus there were few utopian communities of any kind in the American South, and fewer still associated with the communitarian movement, which, as reviewed above, played a clear role in the development of productive associations and co-operative stores and which played a central role alongside the labor movement in developing the co-operative model in the United Kingdom, France, and beyond (Wilson, Webster, and Vorberg-Rugh 2014). Indeed, Fourier's American followers, the Associationists, whose efforts were led by Greeley and Albert Brisbane, were staunch advocates of other types of co-operatives

---

[12] Wright's experiment was not of marginal importance but was widely covered and discussed in the news media of the day: "[U]ntil her death in 1852 she was a favorite topic of conversation; her utterances made headlines; her actions created scandals; her ideas intrigued the intellectuals and reformers of two continents; she counted as friends some of the most famous people of the world. Her experiment at Nashoba ... commanded attention on both side of the Atlantic" (Emerson 1947, 291).

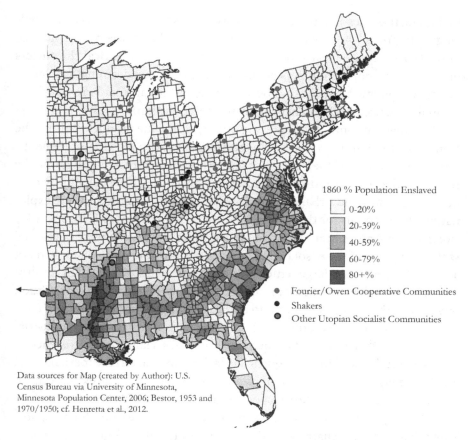

Figure 6.2 Co-operative communities and slavery. Antebellum utopian socialist/communitarian developments and slavery were rarely found together. There were no Fourierian/Owenite co-operative developments in areas where slavery was significant. Sources: U.S. Census Bureau via University of Minnesota, Minnesota Population Center (2006); Bestor (1953, [1950] 1970); cf. Henretta et al. (2012).

(Early 1980). These other types, as reviewed above, were also rarely found in the South.

The Role of Slavery in Constraining Antebellum Cooperation

What explains the relative lack of antebellum Southern cooperation? Curiously, despite the glaring lack of co-operatives in the Antebellum South, and despite the extensive historical documentation of American co-operatives in this era, this question has rarely been asked. In social science, it can be challenging to prove "the negative case" (Ragin 1987), that is, the counterfactual, or the lack of some expected outcome. Nonetheless, the historical chroniclers of American cooperation repeatedly noted the regional strength of antebellum cooperation outside the South, and the historical record provides substantial evidence which can help us answer this question.

Given that the communitarians were not typically the product of either the frontier or foreign migration and were associated with existing settlements, one might wonder if their lack of Southern communities might simply be related to the region's industrial and urban structure, specifically its level of industrialization and urbanization. One might wonder if this simple explanation also accounts for the lack of productive associations and co-operative stores in the Antebellum South, given that these efforts also were developed with the support of the Associationists and Owenites and more often than not appeared in towns and large settlements and were not associated with rurality. The very first exhaustive academic effort to document American cooperation offers the only attempt I can find to address the question of the comparative lack of Southern cooperation, and it makes exactly that argument: "Industrial life in the Southern states is unique in its newness, claiming an existence of but two decades, and in consequence is lacking in industrial experience.... The South lay largely in a state of stagnation, socially and industrially, from colonial days until the outbreak of civil war" (Randall 1888, 489).

Yet this explanation seems wholly inadequate for two reasons. First, we now know that historical characterizations of the Antebellum South as primarily a pre-industrial, rural, and agricultural region were inaccurate. By 1860, the South had experienced a comparatively substantial degree of town settlement and development, industrialization, IOF incorporation, and labor unrest. Second, there is a far more plausible explanation for the lack of Southern proto-co-operatives, one on which the evidence is clear: co-operative ownership was framed as a direct threat to the race-based ownership of slaves as a social and economic system, and this nearly destroyed the antebellum communitarian movement.

On the first point, Starobin's (1970a, 1970b) work on industrial slavery upended the prevailing economic historiographic wisdom that the South had not been substantively industrialized by the Civil War and that slavery was incompatible with industrialization (Lichtenstein 1991). Starobin had attempted to answer a speculation posed by his UC Berkeley doctoral supervisor Kenneth Stampp (1956, 397), whose seminal work on slavery as a "peculiar institution" concluded, "[I]t is doubtful ... that slavery in any decisive way retarded the industrialization of the South." Starobin (1970a, 1970b) calculated that by 1860, 15% of U.S. industrial capacity was accounted for by the South, as was 20% of its invested industrial capital. He documented the development of substantive mills, factories, foundries, and processing operations across wide-ranging industries, including the industrial processing of cotton, tobacco, hemp, turpentine, and lumber, as well as textile manufacturing, coal, and ironworks, throughout the Southern states, particularly in the Atlantic states east of the Piedmont fall line, Virginia, the Carolinas, and Georgia, and in the hill country of the Gulf Coast states of Alabama and Mississippi.

He found significant levels of industrial slavery across all these Southern industries and states, estimating that by 1860 about 5% of the Southern enslaved—nearly 200,000 persons, a figure larger than the entire population of Boston at the time—were employed in Southern industry. He exhaustively documented the use of both full-time industrial slavery by industrial capitalists, as well as for-hire industrial enslaved labor, temporarily rented by industrial capitalists from plantations. The latter category constituted just 20% of the industrial slave population, according to Starobin. Later work by Murphy (2005, 2010), detailing the rise of a substantial slave insurance business in the Antebellum South offers a clue as to why: the enslaved were a great source of property ownership wealth for Southerners, so much so that they increasingly became less willing to rent them out for such purposes (Starobin 1970b, 128–37). Starobin also detailed the use of enslaved Black persons in all-Black workplaces, on segregated teams in interracial workplaces, and, occasionally, in fully integrated industrial workplaces. He documents how and under what conditions industrially enslaved Black persons were supervised and managed by other enslaved Black people and examines the varying degrees of racial animus relating to the use of the enslaved in both single-race and multiracial workplaces (Starobin 1970b; Starobin 1968). In some specific industry-city combinations, industrial enslaved labor was outright dominant:

> Prospering throughout the antebellum period, southern tobacco factories employed slave labor almost exclusively. Richmond's fifty-two tobaccories employed 3400 slaves in the 1850's, Petersburg's twenty establishments worked more than 2400 slaves, and Lynchburg's forty-seven companies used more than 1600. In 1860, Danville had thirteen tobacco factories employing almost 500 slaves; eighteen other plants in the surrounding county used 400 bondsmen. "Down the centre of a long room," wrote one of the many visitors to Richmond's tobaccories, "were twenty large presses, at each of which some dozen slaves, stripped to the waist (it was very hot), were tugging and heaving at long iron arms which turned screws, accompanying each push and pull by deep-drawn groans." (Starobin 1970b, 16–17)

As a result of this pronounced industrial slavery, in some Southern cities and settlements Starobin (1970b, 9) found substantially greater degrees of urban slavery than would otherwise be expected: "Slaves formed substantial portions of urban populations, amounting to as much as 50 per cent in Charleston by 1850."

Notably, Starobin makes no mention of co-operative associations. A University of Wisconsin labor history professor, Starobin was associated with the 1960s American New Left and was a "red diaper baby" (Lichtenstein 1991), a term used to refer to children of parents who were members of the American Communist Party. Given the interest of the New Left in co-operatives, and given Starobin's own efforts to contest the prevailing historiography of American labor, which had long been dominated by the anti-co-operative Ely-Bemis/Wisconsin School (Early 1980; Sanders 1999), if he had found a record of any antebellum co-operative in the countless Southern archives he consulted to construct his data, it stands to reason he would have mentioned it, but he makes no such mention. He does, however, repeatedly review Southern labor unrest, including slave revolts and strikes by non-Black workers (often, immigrants), during the antebellum era.

This is not to imply that all Black people in the Confederacy were enslaved. As noted earlier, Free Black people throughout the South engaged in wide-ranging business activities, including business ownership and entrepreneurship (Schweninger 1989; Walker 1986). By 1860, the Confederate states were home to at least 1,500 Black-owned businesses, more than two-thirds of which were nonagricultural, covering every business activity imaginable, including manufacturing and industry (Schweninger 1989). Louisiana accounted for more than one-third of these businesses, New Orleans being a key center "with its Spanish and French traditions, its racial intermixing, and its long history of free black enterprise" (Schweninger 1989, 30).

These findings, which suggest a substantial industrial South, are consistent with the subsequent analysis of Wright and Sylla (2011, 233), whose exhaustive database of U.S. incorporations through the 1860s shows that "by the 1850s, if not the 1830s, entrepreneurs in the South and West chartered in per capita terms about as many corporations as did entrepreneurs in the North." Such accounts of the South, where IOFs were clearly developing hand in hand with rapidly growing industrial activity and urbanization well before 1860, is wholly inconsistent with an undeveloped, rural, and agricultural South. It is therefore simply not plausible to claim a wholesale lack of Southern cooperation due to a lack of the necessary level of industrialization, incorporation, or settlement.

What, then, if not industrialization, explains the paucity of antebellum Southern cooperation? A simple argument and a key first-order point is that many working Southerners—in some places, an outright majority—were not free to associate and join co-operatives because they were enslaved. Even Free Black people lacked full rights of assembly and association in the Antebellum South, likely limiting their ability to form mutual or associative enterprises (Weare 1993). However, the Free non-Black population of the South was *also* constrained by slavery from cooperating. As noted earlier, the predominantly White communitarian movement, which was a common driver of interest in at least three of the four fledging proto-co-operative strains in the rest of the nation, was nearly broken up as a national movement by the issue of slavery, which "strained relations among Associationist leaders almost to the breaking point" (Guarneri 1991, 261). The communitarians, a national movement with documented adherents in the South (Guarneri 1991; Tregle 1979), faced two interrelated issues which made slavery a central problem: one pertained to the West and the question of the institutions of the emerging frontier, the other to the South-North divide and the question of race-based slavery versus "wage slavery." Together, these two intersecting questions inhibited Southern communitarians' ability to implement co-operative experiments and undermined general interest in the co-operative model in the South, in ways which presaged later challenges for the Knights of Labor.

For the communitarians, as for Americans in general at the time, the West was of outsized importance. Drawing on Frederick Jackson Turner's (1893) famed frontier thesis, historians Bestor (1953, [1950] 1970) and Guarneri (1983, 1991) established this point. If one recasts their historical accounts into the language of field theory or institutionalism, in the West's undeveloped[13] field space and institutional environment small-scale experiments or "patent-office models of the good society" (Bestor 1953) could take root and develop into an ultimately dominant position, allowing the realization of a truly new world. Bestor ([1950] 1970, 246) reviews the centrality of these intersecting issues of Western expansion and slavery to American society and the communitarians: "The violence of this controversy becomes explicable only if one grasps how important in the climate of opinion of the day was the belief that the society of the future was being uniquely determined by the small-scale institutional beginnings of the present. From the Missouri crisis of 1819–21 onwards, practically every major battle in the long-continued contest was fought over the question of whether slavery should go into, or be excluded

---

[13] Regrettably, most of these sources do not pay much attention to the troubling treatment of Indigenous peoples in these settler-colonial formulations.

from, territories whose social institutions had not yet crystallized." For the communitarians specifically, "[a]nnexation would add virgin territory where co-operative communities could take root. . . . [E]xpansion would generate popular enthusiasm for the principles of a truly democratic society and thus rekindle discussion of social reform" (Guarneri 1991, 260). And in seeking to address the West with their models, this meant the communitarians had to face head-on the question of slavery. Guarneri (1991, 253) begins his chapter "The Problem of Slavery" in his magisterial book *The Utopian Alternative*, an exhaustive account of the 19th-century American communitarians:

> A key part of the Associationists' organizing campaign was their attempt to win rival reformers to Fourierism. The greatest challenge came from abolitionism, the crusade against slavery which predated the Fourierists and in some respects had been a model for their propaganda efforts. At first a fairly abstract problem of morality and economic theory, the question of what to do about slavery became increasingly urgent as slaveholders encouraged war with Mexico and the South's peculiar institution spread to new western territories. Confronting the problem of slavery in the mid-1840s led Associationists to clarify important philosophical differences with abolitionists over the nature and merits of "free" and slave labor systems. But the issue also produced serious internal divisions in the Fourierist movement: was "chattel slavery" or "wage slavery" the worse evil, and which should be attacked first?

Specifically, as Guarneri goes on to detail, in directly considering the issue of existing race-based slavery in the South, the communitarians faced internal disagreement over how the sequencing and method of ending slavery was to be incorporated into their various co-operative plans. On the question of sequencing, they debated whether race-based slavery should or could be abolished before the elimination and replacement of wage slavery with co-operative labor systems. On the question of method, they debated whether and how to directly utilize their co-operative models as a possible way to end slavery as a complement or as a substitute for abolition, as the abolitionists' plans in this regard had been critiqued as poorly thought out. Guarneri writes, "Even historians sympathetic to abolitionism have criticized 'the almost total failure of the antislavery movement as a whole to provide any direct, organized, sustained, and practical assistance in training the Negro for freedom in white society.' Associationists frequently pointed out that immediate emancipation would leave the slaves adrift with few skills and no education, ripe to become dependent 'hirelings of Capital' " (254).

In general, Northern Republican communitarians argued that race-based chattel slavery had to end first, while Southerners and Democrats took the view that co-operative models could be used to gradually end race-based chattel slavery, and that this need not occur before the transition away from wage slavery (Guarneri 1991, 258). To that end, communitarians developed specific co-operative emancipation proposals. Though Northern leaders such as Greeley "merely voiced the hope that if free blacks formed successful co-operative townships in the North or became productive members of existing phalanxes, the public would be convinced that peaceful emancipation benefited blacks and would then pressure masters to release their slaves" (254), Southern communitarians did develop some concrete plans. Two in Louisiana, led by Southern communitarians who originally hailed from Washington, D.C., and North Carolina, attracted significant attention. The plans were likely given advice by future Louisiana state attorney general Thomas Jefferson Durant, a communitarian who called his region "peculiarly unsusceptible to the influence of associative doctrines" (263). These plans, which were not implemented and which involved significant elements of White paternalism, realized the "gradual replacement of slavery with an alternative labor system, the introduction of co-operative arrangements in transitional colonies, and . . . the reliance upon voluntary participation by slaveowners" (265).

Neither plan involved developing multiracial settlements, which were exceedingly rare during the Civil War, with just two in the historical record: a Northampton, Massachusetts, settlement which counted Sojourner Truth among its Black members (Gordon Nembhard 2014) and Nashoba, reviewed earlier.[14] This lack of multiracial cooperation is unsurprising, given that even some Northern Associationists had "stated that mixed-race communities would 'always produce incompatibility' between members" (Guarneri 1991, 257). Given that even many Northern Associationists expressed skepticism over multiracial communitarian settlement, it is also not surprising that, excluding Nashoba, there is no record of a viable plan for a Southern multiracial communitarian settlement. I also cannot find any plan to populate a Southern communitarian settlement by local residents of any race. One notable 1850 plan by a Southern communitarian for a Southern settlement, for example, called for populating it with *Northern* emigrants (266). Indeed, given the communitarian movement's antislavery links and its direct attacks on wage slavery, the idea that any significant number of Southerners,

---

[14] An entirely Black utopian antebellum community did, however, develop in Canada: Wilberforce was founded by Free Black people from Ohio (Pease and Pease 1963; Gordon Nembhard 2014).

where urban residents would surely have been well aware of the existence of both Black industrial slavery and business ownership in their midst, might embrace the anti–wage slavery of "the most reviled of northern 'isms'"—Associationism—"seems little short of bizarre" (263).

Ultimately, beyond the brief Nashoba experiment, the communitarian movement was constrained in putting its co-operative philosophy into operational practice in the Antebellum South by the institution of slavery. Because the communitarian movement, which played a direct, national role in so many types of co-operative experiments in the antebellum United States, was so severely constrained in the South, so, too, was cooperation overall in the country. Meanwhile, the institution of slavery was not the only incumbent field that cooperators were then facing. As noted earlier, by 1860 the IOF was rapidly proliferating across the United States, including in the South, and at a world-leading pace:

> In the period from the 1790s to the 1860s, the United States led the world in modern corporate development. Recent research provides the first comprehensive look at corporate development, revealing that U.S. states from 1790 to 1860 chartered 22,419 business corporations under special legislative acts and several thousand more under general incorporation laws that were introduced mostly in the 1840s and 1850s. (These totals far exceed the number of corporations created in any other country (most likely in all other countries combined) during that time. The United States thus became what might be called the first corporation nation. (Gomory and Sylla 2013, 2)

Notably, when controlling for the total size of these incorporations, the United States and the United Kingdom were well-matched in lead position globally (Hannah 2014). While this is unsurprising given that both these nations led the First Industrialization, the level of activity in the United States clearly also reflected a liberal philosophy with respect to the issues of business corporate charters. Though business corporate charters of the antebellum era were initially available under special charters often subject to restrictions of geography and activity scope and level of capitalization, they were nonetheless widely and freely granted to White males (Wright and Sylla 2011). Furthermore, by 1860 roughly 90% of the U.S. population lived in states where the special chartering system had given way to general incorporation laws, and the remaining few that did not offered "liberal access" to their special charters (Hilt 2017, 174). "Many Southern states enacted particularly liberal statutes, but sometimes also prohibited non-Whites from incorporating businesses" (Hilt 2015, 1). Meanwhile, apart from mutually owned financial institutions, lasting, at-scale co-operative enterprise throughout the United States was by comparison muted in its development, nowhere more so than in the South. Accordingly, at the Civil War's outbreak, there were no co-operative-specific legal incorporation forms or policies available in any state.

Postbellum American Cooperation: "Wage Slavery" and the Knights of Labor, 1865–1880s

Although the communitarian movement declined in significance in the postbellum era, "it did not suddenly end with [the] coming of the Civil War" (Guarneri 1991, 386). Communitarian socialist experiments continued to form, eventually reaching the South (Fogarty 1990). But their prominence on the national stage in general, and with respect to the development of co-operatives specifically, was ceded to the labor movement, which carried forward the long-awaited fight against wage slavery in a country in which race-based chattel slavery had ostensibly and finally ended:

> The critique of wage slavery ... resurfaced as craftsmen and factory workers linked protests against their conditions with the Radical Republican movement to eliminate oppression in the South. Associationist predictions that the bloody extinction of chattel slavery was simply "clearing the ground" for the peaceful destruction of the wage system suddenly appeared prescient. Prewar agitators ... who had denounced the subordination of slaves and championed the cause of "honest industry," made an easy transition into labor reform. For the Fourierists it was a case of renewing the old struggle. Once again utopian socialists, some of them veterans of antebellum labor campaigns, allied themselves with labor-reform associations, trade unions, and labor parties and came together in omnibus conventions akin to the National Industrial Congresses of the 1840s. *For three decades after the war the course of the labor movement remained unsettled*, with various voices advocating collective bargaining ... producers' co-operatives ... or even revolutionary violence. Amid the confusion several former Fourierists remained active, their efforts usually aimed at steering labor organizations not toward the phalanx but into co-operative schemes to combat industrial capitalism with ever widening circles of associated workers. (Guarneri 1991, 391, emphasis added)

Guarneri's choice of words—that the course of the labor movement remained "unsettled" for three decades—is apt, for it would take this long for a postbellum field settlement to be reached in the aftermath of the central instance of full-scale field rupture or institutional crisis in postrevolutionary American history: the Civil War.

The war had disrupted the key social, economic, and political institutions of the South and the entire nation. Slavery had also been the lifeblood of the Northern economy, and of U.S. international trade as well. At the dawn of the postbellum period, there was thus a sense of optimism and opportunity in the American labor movement in general, and with respect to cooperation specifically. Could the demise of race-based chattel slavery be followed by the end of wage slavery? Suddenly this was not a hypothetical question. Building on the Associationists' legacy, "as the labor movement reemerged in the 1860s . . . co-operation . . . captured the imagination of postwar labor leaders" (Leikin 2004, 3).

Though stand-alone, mutually owned financial institutions such as mutual life insurers and savings and loan associations continued to develop apace in this era (Knapp 1969), there were a number of movement-based organizations which attempted to holistically organize and coordinate co-operatives at scale. One rose above all others in national prominence, success, and failure: the Knights of Labor. If one seeks to idenify a singular moment which shapes the field path for American co-operatives, it is the rapid demise of the multiracial Knights in the late 1880s and their replacement by the all-White AFL, which would soon come to be aligned with the Democratic Party. After the AFL's rise, cooperation was permanently relegated to footnote status in the American labor movement. By the 1890s, postbellum optimism about wage slavery's end had faded.

In the wake of the Knights' demise, co-operative development efforts would come to rely on movement-based organizations that were more limited in scale and scope and fragmented along racial and regional lines; they would also be politically associated for several decades with various failed efforts of populists and socialists to form a viable national labor party. Co-operatives would thus enter the 20th century without a clear field organizer and without strong enabling laws or accommodative policy in place. Meanwhile, the IOF was continuing to consolidate its leading position in organizing the American economy. As the Knights and co-operatives were fading from the American labor movement, corporate personhood became enshrined into law. States also engaged in what Supreme Court Justice Louis Brandeis would refer to ex post facto as a "race to the bottom" to remove any and all restrictions on incorporation, so as to attract investment dollars, further cementing the IOF's status as field incumbent.

The end of slavery: Field rupture and the rise of the American labor movement. To understand the rapid rise of the Knights requires situating their development in a postbellum context of economic field rupture. Slavery had been economically important not just to the South but to the entire U.S. economy and international trade flows of the day. Its demise constituted a severe rupture in the field environment and institutional structure of the economy, one which would take some time to crystallize into a clear field settlement given the upheaval created by the war (1860–65) and Reconstruction (1865–77). Beyond the industrial slavery of the South, industrialization elsewhere had *also* completely relied on slavery. In the United States, while race-based chattel slavery of both an agricultural and industrial nature had supplied a significant component of the region's economic output, it had *also* spurred and enabled U.S. Northern and British industrialization: the cotton of their mills was picked and produced by Southern enslaved labor. On the eve of the American Civil War, "Britain, the most powerful nation in the world, relied on slave-produced American cotton for over 80 percent of its essential industrial raw material. English textile mills accounted for 40 percent of Britain's exports. One-fifth of Britain's twenty-two million people were directly or indirectly involved with cotton textiles. The British textile industry was concentrated in one region, Lancashire [Manchester], and Britain was thoroughly vulnerable to a disruption in the supply of cotton" (Dattel 2010, 61).

Slave-produced cotton, according to 1993 Nobel laureate in economics and new institutionalist Douglass North (1966, 67), "was the major independent variable in the interdependent structure of internal and international trade," a point which echoes Hobsbawm (1968, 34) on the primacy of cotton to the First Industrial Revolution: "[W]hoever says industrial revolution says cotton." As Marx (1847, ch. 2) also observed:

> Direct slavery is just as much the pivot of bourgeois industry as machinery, credits, etc. Without slavery you have no cotton; without cotton you have no modern industry. It is slavery that gave the colonies their value; it is the colonies that created world trade, and it is world trade that is the precondition of large-scale industry. Thus slavery is an economic category of the greatest importance. Without slavery North America, the most progressive of countries, would be transformed into a patriarchal country. Wipe North America off the map of the world, and you will have anarchy—the complete decay of modern commerce and civilization. Cause slavery to disappear and you will have wiped America off the map of nations. Thus slavery, because it is an economic category, has always existed among the institutions of the peoples. Modern nations have been able only to disguise slavery in their own countries, but they have imposed it without disguise upon the New World.

When counted as property or assets, which is how America's enslaved were treated under the law of the period, these individuals had an economic value of $3.5 billion, making them the most valuable owned asset in the United States, exceeding that of manufacturing or railroads (Coates 2014). Their value

> was roughly three times greater than the total amount of all capital, North and South combined, invested in manufacturing, almost three times the amount invested in railroads, and seven times the amount invested in banks. It was also equal to about seven times the total value of all currency in circulation in the country, three times the value of the entire livestock population, twelve times the value of American farm implements and machinery, twelve times the value of the entire U.S. cotton crop, and forty-eight times the expenditures of the U.S. federal government that year. Needless to say, the domestic slave trade had made human property one of the most prominent forms of investment in the country, second only to land. In fact, by 1860, slave property had even surpassed the assessed value of real estate within the slaveholding states. (Deyle 2006, 60)

This was not an obscure or unknown fact: "most Americans at the time were aware of the immense value of the slave property" (Deyle 2005, 60). It is thus difficult to overestimate the centrality and importance of the end of slavery to the U.S. and global economy of the time.

In the wake of this upheaval and crisis, the American labor movement would suddenly appear to make significant advances in its own field development. Millions of workers had just been freed from one system of labor—the race-based chattel slavery system—and would need to be incorporated into others, potentially into the emergent "wage slavery" system of capitalist firms. While the structure of the American labor movement and the strength of the wage labor system itself both now seem a fait accompli, this was not the case as the postbellum era dawned. This was contested, via the era's emergent labor movement.

It is therefore neither an accident nor a mistranslation from the German that Marx, in the passage quoted above, called America "progressive," a view shared by other Europeans, including French workers and labor organizations, who were variably impressed by how comparatively *advanced* the U.S. labor movement was during this period (Fink 1983, 5–6). Engels himself, writing at the peak of U.S. labor tensions in 1887, which involved the Knights of Labor as the central organizing labor body, observed that the U.S. labor movement had advanced far more rapidly compared to its slow, gradual development in Europe. Indeed he observed of America that "the working class passed through . . . two stages in its development in ten months" (Engels and Wischnewetzky 1887). This view, as Fink asserts, was held not just by those sympathetic to the labor movement but also by forces hostile to it at the time. Such perceptions did not shift until *after* the demise of the Knights (Voss 1993).

The strength of the postbellum American labor movement is directly attributed to the Knights (Voss 1993), the first universalistic and national U.S. labor organization focused on organizing the "industrial masses" without regard for race, gender, religion, or national origin. Their sweeping, inclusive approach would not be successfully replicated in the United States for nearly a century (Gourevitch 2015). Their approach not only included Black workers to a degree that would not be seen again in organized labor until the 1970s (Marable 1983), but it also included a central role for co-operative enterprise.

The Knights of Labor: Central postbellum co-operative field organizers. Initially, various labor movement–based organizations attempted to advance postbellum field-building efforts across different strains of co-operative enterprise, with varying degrees of success. Almost all of these organizations eventually adopted variations of the Rochdale plan, attempting to establish both co-operative stores and linked productive/worker co-operative associations (Cross 1906; Knapp 1969). These orders, which varied in their success with respect to their consumer versus worker cooperation, their geographic reach, and their degree of organizational sophistication, included the Sovereigns of Industry, the Patrons of Husbandry (the Grange), Farmers' Alliances, and the Industrial Brotherhood, which all appeared more successful with consumer cooperation (Cross 1906), as well as the Knights of St. Crispin and the Iron Molders' International Union/National Labor Union, which were comparatively more active in developing productive associations (Aldrich and Stern 1983).

Through their various co-operative experiments, these field-building organizations set the stage for the Knights. The labor movement group the Sovereigns of Industry, at their early 1870s peak, operated either co-operative stores or buying clubs across 450 local councils (Leikin 2006, 322). The Knights of St. Crispin, an order of shoemakers, operated 40 co-operative shoe factories and a number of linked co-operative stores, primarily to serve their members (Leiken 2006); some of these stores endorsed the Rochdale co-operative model. The Iron Molders' Union created 36 co-operative foundries and operated linked co-operative Rochdale stores, again for their members (Leiken 2006). Finally, the Grange, primarily a White rural farming organization with particular lasting strength in Ohio, Kansas, Missouri, and Texas (Cross 1906, 16), would operate state-level collective buying and selling schemes, through which they came to operate "five steamboat lines, thirty two grain elevators, and twenty two warehouses." Before the Grangers' collective buying efforts began to fail, profits were reinvested into fledgling manufacturing co-operative efforts, which were not successful. Profits were then used to develop at least 500 co-operative stores on the Rochdale plan, and they proposed a joint consumer-producer venture with the United Kingdom's Co-operative Wholesale Society (Cross 1906; Knapp 1969). The Grangers' legacy would help spur the late 19th- and early 20th-century development of farmers' co-operatives across multiple industries, particularly in the Upper Midwest (Schneiberg, King, and Smith 2008; see next chapter). The Grangers, which had few Southern Black members (Hild 2007, 13), largely faded as a national organization by the mid-1870s (though a revival would occur in the early 20th century) and was succeeded in 1886 by the Farmers' Alliances (see end of this chapter and next chapter). Most of these various efforts to establish co-operative enterprises, however, quickly faded with their sponsoring movements, which often disappeared in the wake of various financial panics. The rural Grangers, for example, began to fade after the Panic of 1873, in part because "there were no social ties to hold the members together" (Cross 1906, 17).

None of these efforts, however—not even those of the Farmers' Alliances, the remnants of whose efforts would carry the torch of cooperation forward after the Knights' demise—was as comprehensive in its national scale or scope as the Knights, whose multi-racial coalition to organize and coordinate a co-operative commonwealth of interlocking co-operatives produced an "unknown" number of consumer and producer co-operatives. The number of such co-operatives reached a number "totaling possibly in the thousands" (Leikin 2006, 322), supported not just by local assemblies but by the national organization as well; by 1880, 70% of the Knights' general fund was earmarked for co-operative ventures and education (McLaurin 1978, 53).

At the Knights' peak in 1886–87 in Northern cities such as Minneapolis, "62% of the 593 working barrel makers in the city operated seven barrel co-operatives and dominated the industry. They also opened a co-operative store and inspired the formation of at least 15 other co-operative businesses in Minneapolis, including a laundry owned and operated by women. The labor press heralded this success as a model for workers to learn from and emulate" (Leikin 2006, 322). In many states where the Knights (and their predecessors) organized co-operatives, however, they did so without the help of enabling laws, particularly in Southern states, where no such laws existed:

> Many of the associations of the Protective Union, Grange, Knights of Labor, and Sovereigns of Industry had to operate without specific legal authorization. If they

incorporated, it was under the general corporation act, making it difficult to follow co-operative principles. If not incorporated, members were jointly and severally liable for any debts of the co-operative. This latter was a serious drawback, for it tended to keep out the more well-to-do families which had a good deal to lose if the enterprise failed. Michigan has the honor of passing, in 1865, the first State law specifically authorizing the formation of co-operatives. Massachusetts followed in 1866, Ohio in 1867, Minnesota in 1870, and New Jersey in 1881. Three States enacted a co-operative law in 1887—Connecticut, Pennsylvania, and Wisconsin. In New England (the region which had been particularly receptive to co-operation), even as late as the turn of the century Connecticut and Massachusetts remained the only States with permissive legislation. (New Hampshire still has no such law.) Some of the early statutes were obtained through the efforts of the Grangers, Farmers Alliance, and other movements above mentioned. (Parker 1956, 360)

By 1890, however, the Knights had faded, as had postbellum optimism about cooperation. Not only were most co-operative ventures started by their predecessors defunct, but the Knights were in full collapse, felled in part by the growth of employers and the IOF (Voss 1993), but *also* by the same interaction of wage slavery and race-based slavery that had nearly destroyed the communitarians, as we shall see.

The Knights have been repeatedly analyzed by labor historians and social scientists.[15] Built into a national organization from local assemblies federated into district-level and state assemblies, the national Knights were formed in Philadelphia in 1869. They would dominate American labor organizing from the late 1870s to the late 1880s (Foner 1947–94), after taking over as the lead labor organization from the National Labor Union (NLU) and the Colored National Labor Union, two segregated efforts to form a national labor organization in the late 1860s. Both of these organizations in principle had supported co-operative development, but they established few such enterprises and had largely evolved into political organizations by the 1872 elections, in which their efforts to establish labor reform parties were unsuccessful. (Pro-co-operative Horace Greeley ran for the new Liberal Republican Party, siphoning away much of the NLU's base; the Colored National Labor Union remained loyal to the Republicans; Hild 2006, 286.) The Knights attempted to establish interlocking production/worker co-operatives and consumer co-operatives, as a Jeffersonian labor republicanist and producerist "co-operative

---

[15] Key social and political science accounts come from Gourevitch (2015); Voss (1993); Hallgrimsdottir and Benoit (2007). General labor historian accounts include those of Fink (1983); Leikin (2004); Foner (1947–94, 1974); Ware (1929); McLaurin (1974); Hild (2006); Marshall (1967); Grob (1961); Meyers (1940); Black (1963); Kann (1977).

commonwealth" alternative to the union-based collective bargaining approach, which engaged directly with the wage labor system on its own structural terms. Though the Knights did unionize and strike, they believed such efforts were of limited, short-term effectiveness; their overarching goal was to move to the co-operative model. Historian McLaurin (1978, 39) explains, "[T]he order rejected the wage system and the separation of labor and capital. . . . Instead the order proposed a program of arbitration, education, and co-operation. Arbitration would settle disputes between labor and capital before the wage system was abolished."

Unlike the AFL that succeeded them, the Knights adopted a pluralistic approach, engaging with all four of Ware's (1929) "main strands" of the American labor movement; the variable importance of each strand had not yet reached a state of field settlement.

> Four main strands are discoverable in the American labor movement: fraternalism, collective bargaining, co-operation, and politics. While it is assumed today that collective bargaining is the major function of a labor union, it took nearly half a century of agitation and experiment to reach this assumption, and even now it is accepted in some quarters with reservations and in a few, not at all.
>
> The reluctance of the labor movement to accept collective bargaining as its major function was due largely to the fact that this involved an acceptance of the wage system. Before the Civil War the wage system was a fact, but not necessarily an irrevocable one, and attempts to escape from it or replace it by something else were not so obviously hopeless as they later became. Thus the communities of Owen and the Associationists were less fantastic in their time than they may seem today, and the co-operative tradition which derived from them, seemed to make sense in an industrial community of small shops and stores. (320)

With respect to the politics strand, the Knights in the 1886 municipal elections ran "labor tickets" in 189 towns and cities in 34 of 38 states and four territories (Fink 1983, 26), winning in many of them.[16] In that year's federal elections, "the Knights claimed to have elected a dozen Congressmen (usually in fusion with one of the major parties)" (Fink 1983, 27). The Knights also substantially attempted to organize and engage with agricultural workers, making them one of the rare entities of the era to attempt something resembling a "farmer-labor" organizing strategy. They substantially organized across racial lines,

---

[16] Fink's data confirm that two of the four states where they lacked candidates were South Carolina and Louisiana.

unlike the NLU. As Marable (1983, 31) notes, in his account of how capitalism underdeveloped Black America:

> [B]y 1970 black trade union membership totalled . . . one-tenth of all union members. Ironically even this figure does not indicate a historic breakthrough in bi-racial labor co-operation. In the late 1880s and 1890s the Knights of Labor had practiced a policy of building an effective biracial organization and claimed black workers as almost 15% of its 600,000 membership. In the assessment of political economist Victor Perlo, the Knights of Labor "represented a high point of an approach in industrial unionism and of black-white labour unity." In short, organized labor had only begun to reach the level of numerical parity for blacks within its own ranks and equality that had existed for a brief moment a century before.

This included efforts to establish both multiracial as well as Black-led and -owned co-operatives in the South, reflecting the fact that "the most significant of all the Order's objectives in the South was inter-racial solidarity" (Black 1963, 205). As Kann (1977, 56) notes, "Richmond's Black and white district assemblies also organized a co-operative soap factory, a co-operative building association, and a co-operative underwear factory." Drawing on records from the Knights' *Journal of United Labor*, he lists other Black co-operatives, "like the co-operative grocery stores established in Selma and Hot Springs. On a larger scale the Black Knights of Vicksburg and Macon organized building associations to construct their own homes. In Alabama an entire town, Knightsville, was established by and for Black Knights" (58).

What went wrong for the Knights? Historically, much is often made of 1886's Chicago Haymarket riots as the watershed for the U.S. labor movement, leading to the decline of the Knights of Labor and the rise of the more conservative AFL. The demise of the Knights is the moment, according to Voss (1993), when "American exceptionalism" in the labor movement takes hold and the American labor movement is put on a different path than elsewhere. If one deploys the framework of institutionalism, Voss effectively casts the moment as a "critical juncture," even if she did not use this language, referring to it as the "second moment" of American class formation.[17] In the framework of fields, this is the moment where the long postbellum period begins to move toward a fairly durable labor field settlement, focused on the role of collective bargaining via unions. Indeed, one might argue that this is the moment that

---

[17] In personal communication with Voss in 2018, she concurred that the "critical juncture" term seemed appropriate.

drives the answer to Sombart's (1906) age-old question: Why is there no socialism in the United States?

Voss (1993), in developing the orthodox social science account of the Knights' failure, rejects arguments that the outcome reflected any unique structural weakness on the part of U.S. labor. Rather, she argues that the issue was one of comparative employer strength. Specifically, her explanation is that U.S. employers' capacity to counterorganize was greater than in France or England. This was in part due to the earlier development of "employers" in the United States. As the data developed by Sylla and Wright (2013) have subsequently shown, Voss's argument seems borne out by the fact that the IOF developed earlier in the United States than elsewhere. But even if employers had greater capacity to counterorganize, as Voss claims, that does not mechanistically translate into action. What motivated employers to act with comparatively greater force in the United States than elsewhere? Was it the simple profit motive? This is not addressed by Voss. Further, in testing her hypothesis, Voss (1993, 202) uses data from the *New Jersey* Knights, which she assumes was representative of national efforts, an assumption she acknowledges to be potentially imperfect. In making this assumption, Voss overlooks the potential role played by race-based slavery and its successor institutions, and with it, the role played by co-operatives as a polarizing, antislavery institutional form in the juncture. Other than a passing consideration of ethnicity as a possible contributing factor in New Jersey, she ignores racial difference within the United States as playing a possible causal role. Race and slavery do not appear in her analysis at all.

This is curious, given that racial tensions within the Knights' Southern assemblies in particular, as well as racial tensions within the organization in general, were already well documented by respected labor historians at the time of Voss's work. Fink, whose work Voss substantially relied on, gave ample consideration to the racial question of the Knights of the South, as had Foner (1974) in his volume on Black workers in American labor. Southern Knights historian McLaurin (1978) and historians Grob (1961) and Marshall (1967) had addressed this by Voss's writing as well. So, too, had Meyers (1940), Black (1963), and Kann (1977) in their historical articles on the Southern Knights. These scholars showed that even as the Knights' membership figures peaked nationally in 1886, their numbers were still rising in the South, particularly in rural areas: the growth in Southern membership continued through 1887, offsetting Northern declines, and rose in some Southern states through 1888 (McLaurin 1978, 170–71). This despite the fact that "the Knights faced the extremes of national racial and labor problems in their Southern organizing drives" (Kann 1977, 49). These data are strongly suggestive of regional differences in the Knights' efforts and success and undermine the national representativeness of New Jersey as a case from which to draw causal arguments.

This is not a controversial critique, nor is it a new idea. Though it has not been applied specifically to co-operatives, the role of race-based slavery has been examined in explaining the historical weakness and "American exceptionalism" of the limited U.S. labor movement (Foner 1947–94; Fink 1983), lack of a major socialist or labor party (Sombart 1906; Lipset and Marks 2000; Archer 2007), weak welfare state (Alesina, Glaeser, and Sacerdote 2001; Williams 2003), and limited unions (Katznelson 2013). That the same issue might plague co-operatives, particularly efforts to advance their development through the Knights of Labor in the postbellum era, warrants consideration.

Wage slavery, race-based slavery, and the marginalization of co-operatives in American labor. In criticizing Voss's otherwise exceptional work for its oversight of race, I do not intend to disparage or discredit her argument, but rather build from it.

Causation is rarely attributable to a single factor nor of an "either/or" nature: it is typically multifactorial and of a "both/and" nature. Voss's argument is not wrong: employer strength as manifest by the ever-growing IOFs surely mattered and is a necessary factor in understanding what became of the American labor movement in general, and co-operatives specifically. But if one postulates necessary and sufficient conditions, her argument seems an insufficient explanation on its own, particularly for my narrower question, which focuses on co-operatives. Conversely, it would be disingenuous to argue that only race-based slavery, and not the emergent IOF-based system of wage slavery, felled the Knights and, with them, efforts to construct cooperation as a well-defined field in the United States.

Both factors are necessary to understand what happened to American co-operation with the demise of the Knights. It was the interaction of these two items—of the emergent strength of the wage-slavery system through IOFs, coupled with the simmering remnants of race-based chattel slavery through the Jim Crow system[18]—that on the margins set American cooperation, and arguably the broader American labor movement and American socialism, on a different course than elsewhere, leaving co-operatives without an effective national political and economic organizing champion. This interaction, which had been brewing as an issue throughout the antebellum period, reached a climax with the Knights, whose efforts in organizing Black workers

---

[18] This was achieved through various ownership and financial arrangements, such as sharecropping, convict lease systems, payment in company scrip, and refusal to enact eight-hour workdays or 40-hour work weeks in the South.

not only exposed the challenges of coordinating a national labor movement in the face of the solidarity cleavage generated by race but also exposed the same force of race in animating Southern employers to counterorganize.

Specifically, the Knights ran headlong into racial divisions and violence when they attempted to organize Southern Black workers on "the co-operative plan" (DeSantis 2016; Gourevitch 2015). Moving deeper into the South, the Knights attempted to organize workers to strike as a first step toward the ultimate goal of organizing the formerly enslaved into co-operatives, through which they might own and operate former plantations. This strategy, which echoed the Reconstruction era's "labor companies" approach, was met with extreme hostility in the South, particularly among the planter class in Louisiana (DeSantis 2016; Gourevitch 2015; McLaurin 1978; Kann 1977). It culminated in the massacre at Thibodaux in 1887, one of the largest episodes of violence of its kind, which led to a decimation of the Knights in Louisiana and permanently damaged their efforts in neighboring Mississippi (Hild 2007, 130; McLaurin 1978). Given the timing of these events, it likely hastened the decline of the Knights of Labor nationally as well (Gourevitch 2015).

To reiterate, the Knights did not just *include* Black workers; at their peak, they explicitly began a campaign which *focused* on them.[19] In 1886, the year of the Chicago Haymarket riots, the Knights commenced a new organizing campaign in the South, announced at their general assembly meeting that year in Richmond, Virginia. Auguring the tragic events to come, the assembly was surrounded by controversy. A Black Knight was set to introduce the governor of Virginia as a speaker to the assembly; this nearly ended in bloodshed, as recounted by one of the leading Knights, Terence Powderly, in 1889. They nonetheless persisted in having a Black member introduce Powderly, and the announced Southern expansion proceeded:

> The Knights' expansion into the American South began in 1886 at their general assembly meeting in Richmond, Virginia. In a conspicuous show of racial solidarity, a black Knight named Frank Ferrell took the stage to introduce the Knights' leader.... In defense of his controversial decision to have a black Knight introduce him, Powderly wrote "in the field of labor and American citizenship we recognize no line of race, creed, politics or color" (Powderly, 1889). After the assembly, a number of Knights met with local contacts in Southern states such as South

---

[19] This is not to paint the Knights as a perfect organization with respect to race: some Black organizing campaigns were initially led by Whites; many Southern local assemblies were segregated by race, though typically integrated at the district level. The Knights also generally experienced internal divisions over the extent of their inclusion of Black workers due to their poverty and presence in many lower-skilled professions. See McLaurin (1978).

Carolina, Virginia, and Louisiana to organize workers and set up local assemblies. Their plan in southern Louisiana was to organize the sugar workers and to present plantation owners with a choice: raise wages or face a crop-threatening strike. After the summer growing season, sugar had to be cut relatively quickly or be lost to frost, so a threat to withhold labor carried real weight. The Knights' organizing drive in Louisiana quickly turned into one of the boldest, and most catastrophic, challenges to the plantocracy since the end of Reconstruction ten years earlier (Scott, 2009). Initial letters from local organizers in the sugar parishes showed little awareness of the looming danger. (Gourevitch 2015, 2)

The lack of awareness over the danger seems particularly curious: even after Reconstruction had ended, biracial third-party farmer-labor tickets (e.g., the Greenback Labor Party, backed by Northern Louisiana Grangers and New Orleans labor; Hild 2007, 39–40) were met with election violence and murder in the late 1870s, with the loss of an estimated 50 lives (Hild 2007). In fact, "this bi-racialism . . . prompted a ferocious barrage of intimidation, violence, and fraud from White Democrats in Louisiana," with threats of intimidation directed not just at Black people but explicitly at Whites who offered support (Hild 2007). Similar incidents, directed at third-party farmer-labor candidates, occurred at the time of the Knights' Southern drive in North and

Figure 6.3 Former Co-operative Wholesale Society headquarters, East London (Whitechapel). This building's façade, constructed in 1885–87, features the cooperative's motto "Labor and Wait." The U.S. spelling of labor, in solidarity with antislavery American abolitionists (Berk and Kolsky 2016), affirms that the centrality of race in the U.S. co-operative movement was then well-known internationally. Photos by the author.

South Carolina, where "intimidation, murder, and inflammatory rhetoric worked well" (Hild 2007, 41).

The Southern campaign nonetheless proceeded. The Knights initially succeeded in organizing Black-owned, Southern co-operative plantations (Gourevitch 2015), as recorded in their official record, the *Journal of United Labor*, efforts which were widely known internationally (see Figure 6.3). Using records from this journal and other sources, Gourevitch traces how campaign frames referred to "wage slavery," explicitly building on notions of "labor republicanist" liberty, to link the condition of the formerly enslaved to that of workers nationally. The hope and optimism over initial Southern successes of 1886 would quickly turn by the following year. The governor and militia of Louisiana threatened to crush any sugar cane strike by thousands of Knights-organized Black farm workers. When 10,000 workers struck in November 1887, the governor declared a state of martial law. Military action was supplemented by White "paramilitary" groups (i.e., mobs/gangs), which included at least one leader who later became a U.S. congressman (DeSantis 2016). Black movement in cities and towns was restricted. The total death count is unknown; though the state government played a direct role in the event, the deaths were not well-recorded, unsurprising given the declaration of martial law and racial nature of the massacre.

Official record of the massacre, formally recorded as eight deaths, survive because a Black Civil War veteran was injured in the attack, forcing the federal government to record this in his pension claim. Though estimates as high as 300 have been produced, the baseline estimate is that at least 60 were murdered and buried in shallow, often unmarked graves (Rodrigue 2007; DeSantis 2016) during the period of martial law. Black workers eventually returned on plantation owners' terms, and Southern sugar cane workers would not engage in any such organizing efforts again for 60 years, when the Congress of Industrial Organization's "Operation Dixie" also failed (Griffith 1988). The failure of the Southern campaign further undermined the Knights' central leadership, robbed them of badly needed resources and legitimacy, and likely hastened their decline and co-operatives' overall standing in the labor movement (Gourevitch 2015).

The Louisiana incident was not an isolated one: that same year, 1887, the Co-operative Workers of America, a primarily Black offshoot of the Knights started by Hiram Hoover (aka Hiram Hover), a former Knight in the Carolinas, began organizing Black co-operative schools and stores in South Carolina. White vigilantism quickly stamped out what became known as "the Hoover scare," and the organization disbanded (Gordon Nembhard 2014, 52–53; Baker 1999). Similarly, one of the Farmers' Alliances—the Colored

Farmers' Alliance and Co-operative Union, which formed in Texas in 1886 and advocated both labor organizing and co-operative development through chapters across the former Confederate States—experienced similar violence as did the Knights in Louisiana. In Leflore County, Mississippi, and Lee County, Arkansas, in 1889 and 1891, respectively, their Black labor organizing efforts resulted in the murder of 25 and 15 workers (Hild 2007, 143–44; Hild 2006, 287; Gordon Nembhard 2014, 57). The Leflore incident was sparked when a Colored Farmers' Alliance leader attempted to urge members to support a neighboring (White) Farmers' Alliance co-operative store rather than contract with local White merchants (Hild 2006, 287). The Farmers' Alliance co-operative was then ordered by local planters to desist in selling to the Colored Alliance or its members, most of whom by then had either been murdered or fled the area (Gordon Nembhard 2014, 57). The Colored Alliance collapsed in 1892, establishing what would become a long-standing pattern of "sabotage" by Whites against African American co-operatives (Gordon Nembhard 2018; see next chapter).

The Farmers' Alliances, which remained politically active via the populist movement and associated third-party campaigns through the 1890s (Goodwyn 1976), and some of whose co-operative stores and exchanges outlived the Knights (Cross, 1906; Sanders, 1999), remained fragmented racially and regionally and never organized nationally via a single entity. They were therefore unable to act nationally as an overarching political champion for the co-operative model in the way the Knights had, a problem that would persist for co-operatives through the Progressive Era of the early 20th century. As Hild (2007, 216) concludes, "[A] biracial southern farmer-labor movement did not participate in Progressive Era reform efforts. For that matter, the failure of farmer labor insurgency in the late nineteenth century occurred at the national level as well. Such movements failed even to materialize outside the South and some Western or Midwestern states. Reformers who tried to build farmer-labor coalitions in those regions faced some of the same problems as in the South."

Efforts to include some of the Knights' co-operative aims failed in the 1890s conventions of its successor, the all-White AFL (Grob 1961). For many decades after this transition, the AFL accordingly focused almost entirely on collective bargaining. With this transition from the Knights to the AFL, the rhetorical fight against "wage slavery" also changed. Not only would this framing term then shift in meaning (Hallgrimsdottir and Benoit 2007); it would substantively fall to the margins in the AFL-led national labor movement (Leikin 2004). Specifically, between 1880 and 1900 references to the framing term "wage slavery" in labor organizations' news publications began to change. Initially used to refer to *all wage work* and to make explicit contrasts with producer co-operative ownership, toward the end of the 19th century it referred to a *specific type* of wage work. There was "an increasing tendency to use the term wage slavery as a way to identify and denigrate particular segments of workers, especially immigrant workers, the unskilled, and black workers," signifying "an erosion of producerist meanings of wage slavery" (Hallgrimsdottir and Benoit 2007, 1400, 1399). This rhetorical framing shift maps onto the decline of the co-operative's standing in the labor movement, which directly corresponds to the movement's organizational leadership change from the Knights to the AFL. With this organizational shift, wage slavery no longer meant all IOF-based employment, to which the solution was a producer-owned co-operative system. It meant degraded wage work, performed by Black people, who were not then included in the AFL. Co-operatives, and with them, critiques of employment as wage slavery, would thereafter be relegated politically and economically to more marginal organizations on the national stage.[20]

With the death of the Knights, the idea of interlocking producer and consumer co-operatives, which had been included alongside other strategies in the early labor movement by the first comprehensive, national U.S. labor organization, would fade. The AFL would ultimately succeed in passing a national legal framework for unions, albeit a comparatively weaker one than in other nations. But it made little effort to advance co-operatives. Lacking such a national advocate, the co-operative movement thus had to operate without such a comprehensive legal or organizing framework, in contrast to most other rich democracies. After the Knights, an overarching, national approach to co-operative development would be replaced with a much more targeted, splintered set of initiatives, which would characterize the subsequent wave of activity, as the next chapter will show.

American Cooperation in the 19th Century: A Field Denied

Why did a new comprehensive, national co-operative field organizer not immediately emerge to replace the Knights of Labor, just as the Knights had emerged to advance the efforts of their predecessors, such as the

---

[20] After the Knights, even socialist and labor political third parties and organizations were less focused on co-operatives compared with other initiatives. If and when non-IOF ownership was featured, it typically involved public ownership.

communitarians? Why did the White AFL effectively drop the co-operative model? What had the AFL's leader, Samuel Gompers, learned from those who had come before him?

Perhaps Gompers realized that when the communitarians and the Knights promoted the co-operative strategy to end "wage slavery," particularly in the South, such framing inescapably evoked the race-based slavery system, which had only recently ended. Given this framing, co-operatives threatened not only proponents of the IOF but also those who supported slavery's successor system, the Jim Crow set of White supremacist institutional arrangements in the South. This interaction is one reason why the Knights' co-operative development plans had met with such racial animus and hostility in the South, culminating in the violence in Louisiana, and why related co-operative efforts in the Carolinas, Mississippi, and Arkansas similarly faced such marked White violence. Indeed, one need not speculate that this played a role in the broader political realignment whereby the AFL abandoned both co-operatives and the Populist movement in favor of working through and with the Democratic Party. As Alter (2022, 184) summarizes in tracing the demise of the farmer-labor bloc in Texas and the role of co-operatives in it, "Democrats learned their lessons from the interracial black-white unity that propelled Populists to the brink of power. In 1903 Democrats crafted a primary for whites only." Such state-level dynamics no doubt played out elsewhere as well.

Ultimately, through the nationally organized efforts of the Knights, the "wage slavery" framing and labor republicanist philosophy of co-operatives had threatened not just Southern plantation owners:

> The Knights wrote the co-operative program into their official constitution, the Declaration of Principles of the Knights of Labor, and, at their peak, organized thousands of co-operatives across the country. The co-operative ideal threatened Southern planters, Northern industrialists and Western railroad owners alike because it struck at the dominant industrial relations between employer and employee. Affording all workers shared ownership and management of an enterprise, whether a sugar plantation, newspaper press, or garment factory, was—according to the Knights—the only way to secure to everyone their social and economic independence. The abolition of slavery two decades earlier was but the first step in a broader project of eliminating all relations of mastery and subjection in economic life. Although these ideas had been around well before the Civil War, it was only the abolition of chattel slavery and the rise of industrial capitalism that allowed the republican critique of wage-labor to come forward as a unifying, national cause. (Gourevitch 2015, 7)

Due in part to the race question, the "tensions arising from a national labor movement building worker 'solidarity' in the South" (Kann 1977, 69) proved too great, splintering the national labor movement while *also* galvanizing the gathering force of employers, that is, IOFs. The Knights' efforts had "suggested co-operation was possible between White dominated urban assemblies and rural Black laborers. The organization of the 1887 strike, under the jurisdiction of the New Orleans Knights, was further testimony to such co-operation. Even after the defeat, one Black laborer praised the New Orleans Knights for their generous support and insisted that 'co-operation and kindly feelings still exist between Louisiana's white and black Knights'" (Kann 1977, 68). The violent response to such co-operative possibilities was not animated by the profit motive alone. The more compelling explanation is that it reflected the interaction of the profit motive with fears over the potential loss of White supremacy—fears of a great replacement—that the end of wage slavery might entail.

In conjunction with the co-operative's reduced standing with the White labor movement's subsequent field organizer, and with it the lack of a meaningful place on the national political and economic stages, what took root in the United States was a particularly virulent strain of liberalism, economically dominated by the IOF ownership model, which in turn embodies an incomplete conceptualization of freedom and liberty. Building on the work of political philosophers Skinner (2003) and Pettit (1997, 2008, 2012), Gourevitch (2015) argues that pro-co-operative, labor republicanist notions against "wage slavery" embed a "lost" conception of negative liberty, not as freedom from interference but as freedom from nondomination or potential interference. Because of how these notions of liberty mapped onto the existing racial cleavage and the White supremacist legacy of slavery, this conceptual strand of liberty was effectively lost in practice in the United States with the demise of the Knights of Labor. Elsewhere in the industrializing world, this notion of liberty was not extinguished in the same way but persisted institutionally through the continued development of the co-operative, which served to act as a "countervailing force" against the IOF (Galbraith 1952), enabling a fuller choir of ideas about ownership as freedom.

As American co-operatives began their decline, the dominance of the American IOF continued to grow. The Supreme Court case *Santa Clara County v. Standard Pacific Railroad* (1886), which established that the postbellum constitutional amendments to protect the formerly enslaved also protected corporations as people, only further cemented the hegemony of a well-developed "wage slavery" system in national law. At the same time, the profit incentive sparked a "race to the bottom" in the liberalization of corporate state law (Greenwood 2005). To attract revenue to pay off its Civil War debt, New Jersey removed a host of incorporation restrictions on IOFs; Delaware followed its lead, and by the turn of the century other states followed suit (Grandy 1989). Co-operatives, in contrast, benefited from no such motive and still relied on movement-related field-building organizations to fight for enabling legislation (Parker 1956). Meanwhile, *Plessy v. Ferguson* (1896) enshrined the "separate but equal" institutional arrangements of Jim Crow, which succeeded slavery in maintaining a racialized labor market regime and continued to undermine cooperation (see next chapter).

By the end of the 19th century, durable and formally organized cooperation was thus virtually nonexistent at the national scale. Beyond the highly fractured, fledgling strands of agricultural cooperation and mutually owned financial institutions, there was not much for future cooperators to institutionally layer onto to advance their future efforts. There was little left to drift or be displaced as well, though this did happen to a degree, most notably with the remnants of the early experiments of the Grangers, as I will return to in the next chapter. Historical institutionalism, which uses these concepts of layering, drift, and displacement to analyze the evolution of institutions which have *already* been established, lacks a conceptual language to describe or explain the co-operative's failure to establish itself.

Field theory, as this chapter has shown, effectively enables the telling of this story of 19th-century American cooperation as a field denied, through identification of both the forces which denied it, as well as the mechanisms and processes involved. Co-operative ownership of enterprise failed to emerge with any substantial, lasting, well-organized scale as a field in this era, because it was positionally blocked in its development by two other competing models of ownership which served as field incumbents. These incumbents—the IOF and the race-based slavery ownership system and its Jim Crow successor— occupied and defended significant field space in the economy. Further, the particular way co-operative actors *framed* the logic for their field of action—as a struggle against wage slavery—made the conflict with these two competitors worse. It did so by activating racial animus as an explicitly economic force, and by directing it explicitly against cooperators. As we shall see in the next chapter, these challenges would continue to shape and constrain American co-operative field development in subsequent periods.

7
American Cooperation since 1900
An Incomplete and Partially Organized Field

> The problem is not the number of national [co-operative] organizations. Rather it is the lack of coordination among them, the absence of a keen sense of common purpose.
> —Hon. Jerry Voorhis (1961), executive director, Co-operative League of the USA

> What Voorhis said in the 1960s, about how poorly coordinated we are . . . that's still true today.
> —U.S. co-operative developer, San Francisco, 2020

> What's the opposite of synergy? . . . When the whole is less than the sum of its parts? That's what we have today.
> —U.S. co-operative activist-scholar, New York, 2023

In 1961, nearly a half-century after Ira Cross had bemoaned the poorly organized state of the American co-operative movement, former congressman Jerry Voorhis restated the problem as one of insufficient interorganizational *coordination*. Voorhis was not speaking as a co-operative critic or adversary. He was then the head of the apex body for American co-operatives, the Co-operative League of the USA (CLUSA).

His remarks reflected the path American co-operative development had taken after the demise of the Knights of Labor. The field had developed in piecemeal, fragmented fashion, largely through specialist organizations representing specific fronts of cooperation, such as farmers cooperation, with little to knit together or coordinate the pieces into a coherent whole, still constrained by the same forces that had felled the Knights. It was not until the New Deal era that CLUSA, then the organizing body for the White consumer co-operative movement, became the national apex meta-organization for the broader co-operative field. Even then, CLUSA assumed this role only reluctantly and in the face of political attack, as it defended co-operatives against Red Scares as well as a tax war waged against them by IOFs, as this chapter will review. Throughout Voorhis's tenure, CLUSA continued to have limited involvement with the Black co-operative movement, as two distinct, racially organized co-operative movements persisted through the mid-20th century, acting as a further constraint to comprehensive and coordinated field development.

In the absence of an effective lead actor to champion and coordinate a broader vision of interlocking co-operatives across the economy, partial field organizing efforts produced isolated national frameworks for the three most prominent and lasting strains of widespread American co-operative enterprise: farming/agriculture, rural utilities, and household credit. Together, these account for 85 of the 100 largest co-operatives by revenue in the United States today.[1] Other individual fronts of cooperation either never developed at scale or were unable to sustain initial gains. Consumer-owned retail goods co-operatives and mutually owned financial services enterprises, for example, experienced significant development in the early and mid-20th century. But in the absence of effective, broader interorganizational coordination to develop and defend their shared co-operative interests, they subsequently experienced dramatic decline in the face of myriad forces, including entrenched IOF competition, the IOF-led tax war, and liberalization policies which resulted in widespread demutualization, that is, conversion of firms to IOFs. Worker co-operative development has experienced multiple waves of interest, in which rounds of localized effort have attempted to scale toward a national framework. But these waves historically faded before creating a durable national framework like the one constructed by the farmers. Meanwhile, a more IOF-like field competitor through which to attain employee ownership emerged in the 1950s, the employee stock ownership plan (ESOP), further crowding the field environment for the worker co-operative. Though criticized by a number of worker co-operative informants in this study for offering employees "ownership without voice," ESOPs have nonetheless experienced greater sustained development at scale and are now an entrenched competitor to the worker co-operative model in the United States.

The result is that American cooperation today remains an unfinished and incomplete field, which has not been organizationally developed and co-ordinated at national scale in the same way as occurred in the comparative

---

[1] This is based on my analysis of the National Co-operative Business Association-CLUSA International's (commonly called NCBA-CLUSA, or simply NCBA; please read this chapter for more detail on the evolution of this name) top 100 co-operatives list published in 2021.

success cases. Below, I trace how American co-operative field development unfolded in fragmented fashion after the end of the Knights of Labor, beginning with those strands of cooperation which achieved the most durable, lasting presence. As with the comparative cases and the earlier history of the U.S. case, while historical institutionalism can help describe how the successful strands evolved once they were nationally established, it does not offer an effective way to understand the national emergence or the lack thereof (i.e., the negative case) of any of the strands. Field theory not only enables conceptualization of these dynamics of emergence and evolution; it also enables us to understand and identify the mechanisms of *how* and *why*: entrenched competition from the IOF and the enduring American racial divide.

Partial Field Successes: Populist Farmers, Progressive Credit Unions, New Deal Utilities

As noted in Chapter 3, after the decline of the Knights in the late 1880s and early 1890s, the co-operative movement lacked a national coordinating body to shepherd its overall development. Though the all-White AFL was nominally sympathetic to cooperation as labor's "twin sister" (as stated in their 1896 convention; Parker 1956, 325), it primarily promoted trade unionism as the focus of its organizing and legislative/policy goals. While it nominally supported consumer cooperation as a way for workers to obtain fairly priced goods, it rejected workers' productive co-operatives in favor of unions, leaving the "co-operative commonwealth" idea of an interlocking co-operative system to the Socialist Labor Party (SLP)/Socialist Party of America (SPA) and the International Workers of the World (IWW), as well as the CIO (Congress of Industrial Organizations) before its merger with the AFL. All of these organizations ultimately came to occupy a comparatively marginal field space in the American labor movement (Kipnis 1952).

Co-operative field development thus advanced via targeted sectoral and race-segregated efforts in the first two-thirds of the 20th century, producing three areas of lasting strength: farmers' cooperation, credit unions, and rural utilities. Consistent with research on how movement-like processes create fields (Fligstein and McAdam 2012), actors across two of these three fronts engaged in field organizing efforts which display the scalar dynamics seen in social movements (McAdam, Tarrow, and Tilly 2001; Soule 2013), They moved horizontally, via the diffusion of local organizing efforts, then vertically to state-level enabling legislation and federal policy goals, leveraging both economic and social bonds of solidarity rooted in specific shared interests to do so, creating durable, nationally scaled subfield bounds and rules. Such progress was largely advanced through co-operative subspecialist organizations, with roots drawn from Populist and Progressive Era movements. Once achieved, the national field frameworks evolved in ways consistent with the pathways described by institutionalism, but again institutionalism does not explain why they formed as they did, as we will see.

Farmers' cooperation: "Successful" coordination in the face of antitrust competition laws. As of 2008, some 30% of farmers' products in the United States were marketed through co-operatives (Donna 2008), making it likely the most co-operative-dense industry in the nation. Of the 100 largest American co-operatives by revenue, according to my analysis of NCBA-CLUSA's 2021 data, more than half (53) are in agricultural production or farm credit, of which seven are in former Confederate States; almost all are producer co-operatives, that is, co-operatives owned by other businesses, which may be IOFs. Farmers' co-operation in the United States benefits from a well-developed set of policy and organizational infrastructure supports, most of which can be traced to early 20th-century field-building developments by multiple White farmers' and agricultural co-operative development organizations. In addition to organizing locally before building to national scale, once these organizations had achieved national legislative legitimacy and support, they continued to modify and add to their national policy supports over time, consistent with processes of institutional or field layering.

These organizations, whose efforts reached a peak in the Progressive (1910s–1920s) and Depression/New Deal eras, had roots in the Populist movement, which had faded after a national electoral defeat in 1896 (Sanders 1999; Saloutos and Hicks 1951). The Populist movement, meanwhile, had direct ties to prior co-operative organizing efforts among White farmers. Recall that at the same time as the Knights' efforts, the Grange and the Farmers' Alliances had organized White farmers, both economically and politically, and that co-operative development was a central component of their efforts, as reviewed in Chapter 6. These organizations, particularly their co-operative efforts, were central in stoking the Populist movement of the 1890s: "To describe the origins of Populism in one sentence . . . the co-operative movement recruited American farmers, and their subsequent experience within the co-operatives radically altered their political consciousness. The agrarian revolt cannot be understood outside the framework of the economic crusade that not only was its source but also created the culture of the movement itself"

(Goodwyn 1976, xiii). Though the largely White Grange[2] had declined after its 1870s peak, and played a less direct role in the populism of the 1890s, its membership rolls partially recovered in the early 20th century (Schneiberg 2011; Knapp 1969; Wiest 1923, 395–96). By then, the organization was far less focused on co-operatives and elected not to pursue national co-operative initiatives; it nonetheless still did offer some state-specific support to local and state-level co-operative organizing in the early 20th century (cf. Knapp 1969, 194–200; Saloutos and Hicks 1951). With respect to this co-operative support, however, "there was no uniformity to their plan of operations" (Cowling 1938, 86), which had always varied by state and reflected the strong degree of local control and lack of national coordination across Granges. As summarized by Knapp (1969, 200), by the early 20th century, the Grange was playing a more indirect role in the broader co-operative movement's development:

> While the total extent of the co-operative business done through the Grange or its agencies was not impressive, the training in co-operative thinking and methods given by the Grange did much to provide leadership for the new co-operative forces. Of particular importance was the policy followed by the Grange in aligning itself with other groups to achieve co-operative objectives that could not be encompassed by the Grange alone. The Grange not only encouraged its members to participate in the formation and operation of strong co-operative organizations independent of the Grange, but even welcomed the coming of another general farm organization—the American Farm Bureau—as a necessary business organization for agriculture.

In contrast to the more decentralized and indirectly involved Grange, though the three distinct Farmers' Alliances were separated by regional and racial lines until the 1890s, they had a "co-operative philosophy ... radically different from that of the Grangers" (Knapp 1969, 65; Reynolds 2003, 5). The Alliances sought to develop more centralized, large-scale nonstock co-operatives, with a focus on state-level exchanges which might ultimately be intercoordinated

---

[2] In principle, the Grange admitted Black members, and there may have been a few in Louisiana and some other states. In practice, however, while the Grange purportedly left decisions up to each local Grange, most did not admit Black members. As Saloutos (1953, 477) notes, Grange leadership was "quoted as saying that 'Every Grange must exercise its own discretion as to the admission of its members. The Constitution is silent in regard to color, and only prescribes that applicants must be of good moral characters, and must be interested in agriculture. If a Grange chooses to admit Negroes it may do so, as there is nothing in the Constitution to prohibit it. At the present time there are Negroes in the Granges. The matter is purely a local one.' This position was challenged by another observer ... who stated categorically that 'no colored people are admitted into southern Granges.' Diligent enquiry was made, and not an instance was found in the Middle, New England or Northern States where colored members have been admitted."

as well. After the collapse of the Knights, the three Alliances[3] ultimately merged and folded into the People's Party of the Populist movement, though not without debates about a range of issues, such as the inclusion of Black members, further evidence of the looming role of race in inhibiting a unified co-operative movement in the U.S. context (Goodwyn 1976, ch. 10).

After the Farmers' Alliance disappeared with the Populists' electoral losses in 1896, its participants developed new farmer advocacy organizations, which scaled from local efforts to operate at the national level, again consistent with the movement-like processes which yield the creation of new fields. Beyond the National Farmers' Union (formally Farmers' Educational and Co-operative Union of America, which was effectively the successor to the defunct Farmers' Alliances; cf. Knapp 1969, 176; Tucker 1947, 207) and American Society for Equity, both founded in 1902, there was the Farmers' Equity Union, founded in 1910, and the American Farm Bureau, which began in New York State in 1911 (Knapp 1969). Both the National Farmers' Union and the Farm Bureau remain leading lobbying and advocacy organizations for farmers' cooperation today, joined by the National Council of Farmers' Co-operatives (NCFC), founded in 1929, and the American Institute of Co-operation, founded in 1925 and which later merged into the NCFC.

These organizations faced two interrelated challenges with respect to organizing farmers co-operatives: a lack of enabling legislation for co-operative marketing entities in most states and the legality of enabled co-operatives under emerging state and federal antitrust law. On the first of these issues, Knapp (1969, 226–27) writes:

> The first co-operative elevators were largely organized as stock companies under general corporation law since there were at that time no adequate statutes which provided specifically for the incorporation of co-operative enterprises. This condition imposed a severe handicap to co-operative development, since it was difficult to establish and maintain effective co-operative associations under the general corporation law.... As a result many of the farmers' elevators set-up under such laws could scarcely be considered true co-operative associations although various means were used to make them as co-operative in character as possible.... [T]his impediment to effective co-operative growth became increasingly apparent as farmers gained more and more co-operative experience. Obviously they could not build strong co-operative organizations under laws which encourage them to operate in a non-co-operative manner. As Powell, writing in 1913, said "under the

---

[3] There had been one Northern (White and Black, integrated) and two Southern organizations, one White and one Black, a sharp contrast to the Knights' multiracial and national organizing strategy.

corporation laws of most of the states, it is generally impossible to organize a business agricultural association on a non-profit co-operative basis." ... Recognizing this limitation to their efforts farmers and their leaders ... turned to the state legislatures for relief.

The problems associated with the lack of legislation was reiterated by Roy (1969, 265): "Many co-op leaders believe that co-operatives should never charter except under specific co-op statutes. They recalled the Grange co-operatives of the 1880s which deteriorated into profit type corporations in the absence of specific co-op statutes."

Though by the end of the 19th century, as noted in Chapter 6, a handful of states had passed limited enabling laws for co-operatives, many of these did not specify (and therefore did not enable) the types of organizational features with respect to democratic voting, capital holding, and dividend patronage rules/limits which co-operatives sought to enact (Knapp 1969, 491). Parker (1956, 360) observed, "[B]y the end of the (nineteenth) century ... only three laws were at all adequate, however—those of Massachusetts, New Jersey, and Pennsylvania. Wisconsin enacted a new law in 1911 which the Right Relationship League labeled the first 'genuinely co-operative law in the United States.'"

The Wisconsin law was passed just two years after President Theodore Roosevelt's Commission on Rural Life, which, "besides emphasizing the need for co-operatives, called attention to the obstacles which impeded their growth.... The Commission also urged upon the states the necessity of passing enabling legislation and upon Congress the desirability of promoting co-operatives in every way it could, particularly with respect to co-operative rural credits. Naturally the advocates of farmer's co-operatives made good use of the Commission's findings. Farm groups and agricultural leaders saw to it that those phases of the report which favored co-operatives received wide circulation" (Saloutos and Hicks 1951, 61–62). During the decade after Wisconsin's 1911 law, more than 20 states would pass standardized co-operative market act legislation, which made it possible for agricultural distribution and marketing co-operatives to operate across these states utilizing standard rules (Knapp 1969, 491). By 1916, the Federal Farm Loan Act was enacted, allowing for the creation of the first in what would become a national network of agricultural co-operative financial institutions. The Packers and Stockyards Act of 1921, the Grain Futures Act of 1922, the Co-operative Marketing Act of 1926 and associated creation of the federal Division of Co-operative Marketing, and the Agricultural Marketing Act of 1929, all provided additional national financial and legal supports to agricultural co-operatives (Saloutos and Hicks 1951; Knapp 1944).

Building on the 1916 Federal Farm Loan Act, the 1933 Farm Credit Act further expanded the national network of government-sponsored farm co-operative credit institutions, which today collectively own and control CoBank, effectively a central co-operative agricultural bank, created out of a series of mergers enabled by federal law in the 1980s, 1990s, and early 2000s. The formation and evolution of CoBank is consistent with institutionalist notions of layering, in which a nationally established institution continues to evolve through incrementalist updates and changes to its structure to enable its continued relevance. Today CoBank (n.d.) "provides [U.S.] production agriculture with more than 30 percent of its credit and financial needs."

Collectively, these various acts, passed over a decade and a half, also became the basis for "a national policy of encouraging and even aiding farmers to help themselves by engaging in co-operative action to solve their problems in a businesslike manner, a policy . . . referred to as 'assisted laissez faire'" (Erwin 1966, 404).

While these actions helped address the challenge of agricultural co-operatives' lack of enabling legislation, they were relatedly being sued under antitrust law (the Sherman Act of 1890) as unlawful combinations and conspiracies, on the basis of their interfirm coordination (Frederick 2005; Hanna 1952). The earlier emergence of such antitrust law in the United States as a challenge for co-operatives (as compared to the other cases) can be directly connected to the nation's IOF-led economic development:

> [T]he United States for very specific reasons . . . was the first country to understand the potential of the large corporation and developed its organizational characteristics between 1860 and the First World War. . . . The economic system that forms in the presence of these large stand-alone corporations (those that do not coordinate with others) is a mix of markets (typically oligopolistic, with strategic moves best studied by game theory) and corporate planning. Their enormous size encourage[s] these companies to disregard all limits for the purpose of continuing their growth. . . . [T]he tendency towards monopoly quickly becomes clear. To avoid this outcome, which is held not to be acceptable for either consumers or democracy, the United States quickly enacted anti-trust laws. . . . Europe was much slower to adopt antitrust legislation and indeed allowed cartels (because its companies were smaller) and frequently its natural monopolies . . . were placed under public control. (Zamagni 2017, 104–6)

Antitrust laws thus developed earlier in the United States than elsewhere, in part because IOFs developed earlier as part the "the corporate reconstruction of American capitalism" (Sklar 1988) in the late 1800s and early 1900s, which would reach a peak under the presidency of Woodrow Wilson, who sought to regulate and advance, rather than eliminate, the "corporate-liberal ascendancy" in the economy (Sklar 1988). Perversely, however, these laws, which were intended to limit the concentrated power and uncompetitive actions of IOFs and their associated trusts, and not necessarily to inhibit "collusion among powerless actors" which "can represent socially desirable cooperation" (Vaheesan 2020, 29), would be used to either sue or threaten the legal status and interfirm coordination methods of U.S. co-operatives (Hanna 1952; Schneiberg 2011).

To address such concerns at the federal level, the Clayton Act was passed in 1914 (Varney 2010). It attempted to provide some relief to agricultural co-operatives from antitrust suits and associated uncertainty, but lawsuits continued apace, necessitating the 1922 passage of the Capper-Volstead Act, often called the Magna Carta of agricultural co-operatives in the United States, as it exempted them from antitrust prosecution. As the first major national legislative success which centrally featured agricultural co-operatives, Capper-Volstead commenced a series of national co-operative acts, as reviewed above. But it also demonstrated the growing entrenchment of the liberal variety of capitalism in the United States, in which the default assumption for expected and preferred firm behavior was of IOFs acting in atomistic, uncoordinated fashion, with informal and co-operative coordination between them heavily restricted by antitrust law. Specifically, Capper-Volstead was a *defensive* response to antitrust legislation, the Sherman Act of 1890 (Hanna 1952), which merely affirmed that agricultural co-operatives had a right to exist by asserting they were *exempt, by exception*, from the Sherman Act. It was intended to secure the status of these co-operatives, which, along with labor unions, were being sued by corporations and rival entities (Hanna 1952) for violating antitrust and restraint of trade laws in state courts (Varney 2010). It did *not* affirm a broader right of co-operatives in other sectors or for other purposes to engage in such coordination efforts. Even with the passage of Capper-Volstead, co-operatives' legitimacy was litigated in the U.S. Supreme Court, and their right to exist required additional passage of national laws (e.g., Robinson-Pateman Act of 1936; cf. Knapp 1944).

While most of these efforts to address these two challenges (state and federal enabling laws and federal antitrust laws) saw multiple farmers co-operative organizations playing substantive field-building and organizing roles, their efforts were collectively galvanized and coordinated across both fronts of challenge by a key field-building "skilled social actor," attorney Aaron Sapiro (Larsen and Erdman 1962; cf. Knapp 1969; Saloutos and Hicks 1951, 288): "A sensational leader, Sapiro was . . . the peerless evangelist of co-operation, the father of co-operative marketing, and the instigator of what was probably the most widespread and intensive promotional program that ever urged collective action on American farmers" (Larsen and Erdman 1962, 242). A California-based lawyer, Sapiro enabled the spread of standard state-level agricultural co-operative marketing acts and aided in the widespread development across the United States of the type of centralized large-scale agricultural co-operatives that the Farmers' Alliance had originally envisioned. Originally working for a California state office on retainer to provide legal support for agricultural co-operatives, Sapiro came to champion the co-operative model as the best way to organize farmers in California and concluded that "successful co-operative organization required large-scale commodity organization" (Larsen and Erdman 1962, 255). After his success in California, he traveled the country, winning over both farmers and legislators to the co-operative movement's cause:

> [H]e was a genius in winning farmers' confidence and exciting enthusiasm for his plan. He drew big crowds because of his reputation and the farmers' plight, and he swayed them into signing contracts by his dynamic speeches. . . . Co-operative associations mushroomed under the spell of Sapiro's enthusiasm. By 1922 he had organized or represented at least fifty-five co-operative associations in nineteen states, including California. By the following year . . . he had organized or served as counsel [to] co-operative groups whose membership totaled over half a million persons. Also in 1923, he assisted the Canadian wheat farmers in launching their vast wheat pool movement. According to another tabulation, he had by 1923 organized in the United States sixty-six associations with an estimated annual volume of $400,000,000. (Larsen and Erdman 1962, 256–57)

Critically, he did not just organize co-operatives; he also played a role in securing passage of state and federal laws, working with Senator Capper and various farmers' organizations, including the NCFC and the Farm Bureau, on various pieces of national legislation and national co-operative conferences and organizing initiatives (Larsen and Erdman 1962) and in successfully arguing for co-operatives' protection at the U.S. Supreme Court:

> Sapiro not only organized co-operatives but overcame in the process a major stumbling block—the lack of adequate legal machinery in the states to enable farmers to form the type of association he promoted. More than any other person, he has

> received credit for the adoption by most of the states, between 1920 and 1928, of some version of the so-called standard co-operative marketing act. In addition to its importance as a definition of public policy, the act had the advantage of any uniform law, namely, that acceptance by the highest court of one state tended to assure approval by the others. Thinking of this aspect of his career, one scholar has said that Sapiro was one of the few men of his generation whose individual activities "genuinely altered the world in which he found himself." Sapiro ... publicized the need for the standard act before state legislatures, legislative committees, and farm groups, and he helped to prepare the model. Of all the examples of the standard act, Sapiro considered ... Kentucky the best representative. In addition to his own role in preparing this act, he argued in its behalf before the United States Supreme Court in 1927. The Court's decision has been described as a landmark, expressing approval of the right of states to provide specifically for the organization of co-operative associations. Justice James C. McReynolds, who delivered the decision, stated: "The opinion generally accepted—and upon reasonable grounds, we think—is that the co-operative marketing statutes promote the common interest. The provisions for protecting the fundamental contracts against interference by outsiders are essential to the plan. This court has recognized as permissible some discrimination intended to encourage agriculture." (Larsen and Erdman 1962, 258–59)

Though Sapiro ultimately fell into controversy due to the high legal fees he charged, the mixed financial record of some co-operatives he advised, and the antisemitic attacks upon him in the press by Henry Ford (Larsen and Erdman 1962), his efforts in organizing farmers to lasting national legal and policy gains are clear, and by the 1930s and the Great Depression the various key policy and legal supports for farmers were already in place and largely remain so today.

Seemingly unencumbered by the racial divisions which had weighed on the Knights and the Farmers' Alliances, these various White-led farmers' organizations had constructed, finally, at national scale, a field and institutional framework, subsequently maintained in a manner consistent with institutional layering. To achieve their initial goals, however, they had to persistently organize to combat the limiting effects of liberalism in shaping the broader, emerging antitrust-based interfirm coordination legal environment, against which farmers co-operatives were allowed as an exception.

Could the farmers have won this battle had they attempted a more racially integrated strategy, as had the Knights and the Farmers' Alliances? While the standard accounts of farmers' cooperation in this era rarely reference race, a limited literature on Black farmers offers direct evidence of its role.

The Progressive Era programs which helped undergird and develop the financing, marketing, and distribution coordination system for agricultural co-operatives did little to help Black farmers, who largely remained sharecroppers and tenant farmers in the South and were often excluded from participation in these programs (Reynolds 2003).

The 1929 Agricultural Marketing Act's $500 million revolving loan fund, for example, which was primarily intended to benefit farmers co-operatives, was not open to Black farmers, as reported at the time in *Negro World* and as remarked upon by the National Negro Business League, which noted the lack of a national Black co-operative agricultural organization (Gordon Nembhard 2014, 13) to advocate for its inclusion. Such an organization would not come into existence until the late 1960s with the civil rights movement enabling the birth of the Federation of Southern Co-operatives (FSC), which persists today despite erratic access to U.S. government support and repeated harassment by government agencies, including FBI investigations of supposed fraud which could produce no evidence but nonetheless cost the FSC millions of dollars in defense costs (Gordon Nembhard 2018).

Meanwhile, there is little in the historical record to suggest any sustained effort by the White-led farmers' organizations to advocate for or include the substantial population of Black farmers in these programs. In particular, Southern Black farmers were no small constituency, with over 900,000 such farmers (three-fourths of whom were sharecroppers or tenant farmers) in 1920 (Reynolds 2003). A farming founder of FSC I interviewed stated that the racially disparate effect of Progressive Era farm co-operative assistance programs were amplified during the Great Depression by various agricultural subsidy programs, as the distribution of these resources was typically controlled at the "last mile" by local elites. This meant that their benefits were typically restricted, particularly in the South, by Whites. As a result, Black farmers did not often benefit from these specific programs, as confirmed by this Interviewee (cf. Reynolds 2003). This likely undermined some of the prior success of actors such as Booker T. Washington in advancing Black-owned farmer co-operatives (Reynolds 2003; Gordon Nembhard 2014), again particularly in the South, which included programs such as the short-lived co-operative efforts in the 1920s of the National Federation of Colored Farmers (Reynolds 2003; Gordon Nembhard 2014) and the Texas-based Farmers' Improvement Society of Texas (Zabawa and Warren 1998).

Indeed, political scientist Goldfield (2001, 2020) has argued more broadly that the racially exclusionary policies of the agrarian movements of this era, particularly in the South, help explain the inability of farmers and labor to cross-organize successfully in the United States. Specifically, he found that the polarizing effects of race undermined the development of an effective U.S. farmer-labor political alliance in the early 20th century. Such an alliance might have promoted a more comprehensive and racially inclusive co-operative framework nationwide. From this viewpoint, the narrow gains of the White farmers co-operative movement might be recast as a Faustian bargain, which won the battle at the expense of losing the broader war.

Credit unions: A Progressive Era legacy. Actors in the "credit union movement" (Moody and Fite 1971; Isbister 1994) used a similar, movement-like, field-building and organizing strategy as the farmers. They, too, built a national field framework by scaling up their efforts both horizontally—via local diffusion of the model—and vertically, moving from local efforts to achieve state and nationally scaled policy gains. The credit union model came to New England by way of Canada, where it was developed as something of a stand-alone organizational archetype, imported and modified from co-operative banking models developed in France and Germany, which had developed in response to various financial crises in the years immediately after the Rochdale success in England (Moody and Fite 1971; Isbister 1994). Mr. and Mrs. Alphonse and Doriméne Desjardins[4] of Québec cofounded Desjardins, a network of co-operative banks and credit unions, which collectively constitute the largest financial institution in Québec today. They spread the approach, which deployed a co-operative, democratic ownership model, to neighboring New England's population of French-speaking White Catholic and Québécois migrants, who were the early adopters of credit unions in the United States.

The same year the first U.S. credit union was founded in New Hampshire in 1909, Massachusetts became the first state to provide enabling legislation and a regulatory framework for the chartering of credit unions with a focus on their rural use, advanced by a state government actor who had studied the Desjardins' work. Subsequently, Edward Filene, a German American, Jewish department store founder and businessman, and a key agent of credit union development in New England (Moody and Fite 1971), became an organizational champion of their development nationwide. A skilled social actor, in the language of field theory, he played a similar role for credit unions as did Sapiro for the farmers. He founded a national credit union organization in 1921, the Credit Union National Extension Bureau, which promoted the passage of state-by-state legislation based on a modified version of the Massachusetts

---

[4] Many historical works reference Mr. Desjardins alone as the founder of the North American credit union movement. A Desjardins interviewee stated this reflects historical sexism in research coverage of credit unions, as Mrs. Desjardins was an equal partner in their efforts and should be credited as such.

law, which enabled their urban use, encouraged the formation and development of individual credit unions, and worked with multiple U.S. presidents to secure the passage of a federal chartering system and regulatory framework for credit unions. In 1934, the Bureau was replaced with the Credit Union National Association, which remains the organizing body for credit unions in the United States today. The same year, Congress passed the Federal Credit Union Act, exempting these nonprofit entities from income tax.

Based on Filene's leadership efforts, President Warren G. Harding sent letters to every governor urging them to enact credit union laws; then-State Senator Franklin Delano Roosevelt worked with Filene to pass a credit union law in New York and as president would pass similar laws for implementation at the national scale. Filene used his personal wealth and foundation, while also leveraging the funds of other interested foundations (e.g., Russell Sage), to fund the construction of these advocacy organizations because he recognized the model would not diffuse and achieve lasting scale without such organizations to coordinate their efforts (Moody and Fite 1971). By 1930, more than 38 states and more than 2,500 credit unions were in operation (Rosenthal 2018, 35).

With their stable performance throughout the Great Depression, credit unions grew rapidly, despite legal limits on their ability to offer the full range of banking services or to expand and achieve economies of scale comparable to those of a bank: typically, individual credit union members have been limited by a legal "common bond of association" requirement to a shared town or county or a shared employer and must focus most activity on meeting household credit needs (Spicer 2022). As a result, though these rules have recently been loosened by regulators to a limited degree to enable greater operational efficiencies, few reach significant size, and none compares in size to the largest 25 investor-owned banks in the United States (Spicer 2022). While credit unions can cross-collaborate to a limited degree to offer shared backend services, they do not have a full-service central lending bank to coordinate efforts and facilitate cross-lending, long a goal of Filene's, nor can they substantially engage in commercial lending, which eliminates them as a potential source of financing for other co-operative businesses.

They have also repeatedly had their tax-exempt status attacked by traditional investor-owned banks, in what has become one of the "long-running campaigns" (*American Banker* 2022) of traditional banking trade groups. These groups have argued that credit unions should be subject to income tax even though they are member-owned nonprofits whose surplus flows back to the members. The campaigns have been repeatedly waged, in 1951 and 1998 (Harper 2013), and again in the past decade (Young 2016; Credit Unions

Today 2022). Demands by investor-owned banks that Congress repeal or eliminate credit unions' tax-exempt status, however, have to date been unsuccessful, consistent with research on the persistence and stickiness of nationally scaled institutions and fields once formed.

While credit unions styled themselves as a "movement" intended to benefit working-class individuals, who often lacked sufficient resources to benefit from or participate in mutually owned savings banks (Moody and Fite 1971), and while they used movement-like organizational diffusion and scaling processes to build a field space, it is not clear that they can be characterized as necessarily resulting from truly movement-based, bottom-up organizing efforts to the same degree as other co-operative types in the United States.

The same cannot be said, however, of community development credit unions (CDCUs). As described by Isbister (1994, 63), "Three different groups emerged to promote these credit unions: [Credit Union National Association], a group of activists in the civil rights movement, and the federal government's Office of Economic Opportunity." While credit unions over the mid-20th century were increasingly criticized for mission drift and for primarily serving middle-income and upper-middle-income households (Rosenthal 2018), CDCUs are a different matter. These institutions, today certified by the U.S. Department of Treasury as a type of community development financial institution, must serve low-income areas, many of which are also majority-minority areas. Many CDCUs are accordingly majority-minority and/or Black-majority in terms of ownership (Gordon Nembhard 2013).

Though the early credit union movement included a small number of Black credit unions as early as 1918, including several in North Carolina (Parker 1956, 309; Rosenthal 2018, 37) and New York City[5] (Gordon Nembhard 2014, 128), it was not until the 1960s and 1970s that the CDCU organizational archetype formally emerged, through what were initially (and sometimes in an "uncomplimentary" way; Rosenthal 2018, 46) referred to as Office of Economic Opportunity credit unions. Some 400 were formed (Isbister 1994) as part of that era's War on Poverty government programs (Rosenthal 2018). While most of these credit unions failed—just 10% survived to the 1990s, many unable to survive the removal of government subsidy that began in the 1970s (Isbister 1994, 65)—next generation CDCUs have been comparatively more self-sustaining, in part due to their organizing to change various funding mechanisms and legislative restrictions, including on the types of households and areas they may serve (Rosenthal 2018). For example, in

---

[5] Baker, Ella. 1941. *"Consumers' Co-operation Among Negroes." Ella Baker* Papers, Box 2 Folder 2: Schomburg Center for Research in Black Culture, New York Public Library

the 1970s, as federal subsidy was removed, a group of Office of Economic Opportunity and other low-income-serving credit unions formed an informal Federation of Limited Income Credit Unions, before formally organizing as the National Federation of Community Development Credit Unions in 1974 (Rosenthal 201882), when they also developed the name CDCU to refer to a specific subtype of credit union (Inclusiv, n.d.). They succeeded by the end of the 1970s in obtaining congressional appropriations to support a small revolving loan fund for CDCUs (Rosenthal 2018, 87), with subsequent organizing in the 1980s and 1990s, alongside other non-co-operative community financial institutions (which created the term "community development financial institution") to achieve other forms of federal financial support. Though the organization was subsequently renamed Inclusiv in 2018, today it represents the interests of more than 400 CDCUs with over $242 billion in assets serving 17 million residents of low-income communities who are disproportionately Black and from other racial minority groups (Gordon Nembhard 2013). While ostensibly successful, their separate and delayed development nonetheless demonstrates, again, the role of race in fragmenting field development of American cooperation. To effectively improve access to financial services for low-income and non-White customers, a specialized, separate, and tightly restricted form of credit union was created. Their development and restricted nature are consistent with the "residual" logic of a liberal capitalist welfare state, where co-operatives and other alternatives are enabled only at the margins, where and if the IOF market is unable or unwilling to produce a viable "solution."

Rural utility/electric co-operatives: The New Deal's lasting legacy. The third successful front of American cooperation was a product of the New Deal era, and can arguably be cast as an appendage of the farmers co-operative movement (Knapp 1973, ch. 17). President Franklin Roosevelt created the Rural Electrification Administration (REA) by Executive Order in 1935, followed by Congress's passage of the Rural Electrification Act of 1936. These two actions created the funding and legal framework to allow the development of electricity distribution companies in rural areas, which at the time remained largely unelectrified. As noted by the University of Wisconsin Center for Co-operatives (2010), "[B]y the 1930s nearly 90% of U.S. urban dwellers had electricity, but 90% of rural homes were without power. Investor-owned utilities often denied service to rural areas, citing high development costs and low profit margins. Consequently, even when they could purchase electricity, rural consumers paid far higher prices than urban consumers." At the time the REA programs were established, there were already 45 electric co-operatives in existence, most having formed between 1914 and 1930 (Parker 1956, 134).

The new REA programs were not initially focused explicitly on co-operatives, but "within months, it became evident to REA officials that established investor-owned utilities were not interested in using federal loan funds to serve sparsely populated rural areas. But loan applications from farmer-based co-operatives poured in, and REA soon realized electric co-operatives would be the entities to make rural electrification a reality. In 1937, the REA drafted the Electric Co-operative Corporation Act, a model law that states could adopt to enable the formation and operation of not-for-profit, consumer-owned electric co-operatives" (National Rural Electric Co-operatives Association n.d.).

As private generation and transmission (G&T) utility companies sometimes refused to service these new electric distribution co-operatives (Spinak 2014, 107), the REA program also included funding for development of G&T companies, also co-operatives, which were owned by the new REA distribution co-operatives. Co-operative service would later be extended to include telephone and internet connections as well, through legislative updates in the 1960s and 1970s, consistent with processes of institutional layering. Today 864 distribution co-operatives and 66 G&T co-operatives provide electricity service to approximately 12% of U.S. households in rural areas, which the 1937 model legislation defined as unincorporated areas, or municipalities/incorporated areas with fewer than 1,500 persons.

As with credit unions, which are limited in geographic reach and product offers, such co-operatives are defined by restriction: they may not offer such services in urban areas where IOFs and public utilities were largely already willing and able to offer service. Like CDCUs, this is consistent with the "residual" logic of a liberal capitalist welfare state, where co-operatives are enabled only at the margins, where an IOF market does not seem viable.

Accordingly, the first urban electricity co-operatives were not created until the 1990s, when entities such as the 1st Rochdale Co-operative Group in the Bronx (Yaker, Thompson, and Goidner 2000) were formed, which a founder confirmed existed only briefly at the beginning of a period of energy deregulation, and Energy Co-operative of America, a western New York–based supplier of energy to businesses, which now serves a two-state area. A small number of new co-operative community solar-generation companies cover urban areas (sometimes as part of state enabling frameworks which cover both rural and urban areas): Co-operative Energy Futures in Minneapolis, the Sustainable Economies Law Center–Incubated People Power Solar Co-op in Northern California, Oregon Clean Power Co-op, and Co-op Power in New England. Such efforts however, appear to be comparatively rare and relatively smaller-scale.

Unsurprisingly, though many REA co-operatives were formed in Southern states to serve majority-Black areas, many were primarily or exclusively all-White in their governance and leadership, blunting their democratic effect, showing evidence of the same problems as other federal aid programs, where "last mile" local control allowed White elites to exclude Black Americans (Spinak 2014; Leifermann and Wehner 1996). Though this was an issue from the electric co-operatives' formation (Spinak 2014), high-profile community-organizing campaigns to mitigate and address the issue were undertaken in the 1980s (Schmidt 1984) and again in the 2010s, through the Southern Regional Council's Co-op Democracy Project in the 1980s–1990s and through ACORN/The Labor Neighbor Research & Training Center's Rural Power Project in the 2010s and 2020s. The first campaign occurred as the very viability of rural electrical co-operatives was being threatened by neoliberal policy changes of the Reagan administration, which wanted to end federal loan programs to the co-operatives (Schmidt 1984). Despite some success through community organizing and lawsuits to wrest control of all-White rural electric co-operatives to include more Black owners in governance, the problem has remained widespread, motivating the more recent campaign of the 2010s. This latter effort documented that Southern rural electrical co-operative boards, whose members receive five-figure annual honoraria, remain 95% White, far greater than their expected share based on the racial makeup of the local population. These dynamics have also been found in rural electric co-operatives beyond the South (Rural Power Project 2016a, 2016b, 2021, 2022).

In some ways, this third successful front of American cooperation appears not to follow the typical field-building process of the other two: it was not the product of local diffusion and experimentation with the model, followed by vertical scale shift to organize nationally for enabling frameworks. Conversely, it appears to have been created from the top down, by the federal government, which enabled state and local take-up of the model through the rapid development of model legislation (Knapp 1973).

However, rural electrical co-operatives likely would not have been developed were it not for the preceding widespread development of farmers co-operatives, which, as noted earlier, were not only the initial applicants to the REA programs when IOFs had failed to show interest in serving the rural market, but had advocated for the program (Knapp 1973). The financial co-operatives created by the 1933 Farm Credit Act, meanwhile, provided supplemental financing for electrical co-operatives beginning in the 1960s, and by 1971 had advocated for national legislation which expanded their mandate to formally finance rural electric and telephone co-operatives (CoBank, n.d.).

While their genesis may reflect efforts of individual farmers co-operatives, beyond these limited financial ties there is little evidence of systematic, ongoing coordination efforts between the REA electrical co-operatives and other strands of the co-operative movement.

Cooperation Lost: Consumers' Retail Goods and Mutually Owned Financial Enterprises

Two strands of consumer cooperation achieved some sustained level of development in the 20th century, only to experience subsequent, pronounced declines. In the case of consumer co-operatives for retail goods and groceries, which remained organizationally segregated by race through the first half of the century, increased competition from traditional IOFs coupled with a tax war waged on their behalf was followed by marked decline in the 1950s and 1960s. CLUSA, their apex organization, survived and became the overarching meta-organizing entity for all types of U.S. co-operatives (Voorhis 1961), today known as NCBA-CLUSA, or simply, NCBA. Mutually owned financial enterprises, meanwhile, which arguably had developed to a greater degree than all but farmers co-operatives, experienced a series of operational and liberalization-related policy crises which resulted in either wholesale bankruptcy and sale of their assets to IOFs or wide demutualization and conversion to IOFs by the 1980s and 1990s, consistent with institutionalist notions of conversion and displacement.

Mutually owned financial enterprises: Demutualization as co-operative destruction. Mutually owned financial and insurance firms are considered "co-operative adjacent" but not technically co-operatives, though in some countries (including the other case countries) they are formally included in the co-operative field's apex organization and are formally a part of the movement, as noted in Chapter 2. Such firms in the United States had developed to a significant degree in the early and mid-19th century, as noted in the previous chapter, and seemingly without the same degree of affiliation and aid of the formal co-operative movement, with the exception of those firms developed in association with the various farmers' movements reviewed above. Mutual life insurers, for example, are thus often omitted or given limited consideration in ostensibly exhaustive accounts of co-operatives (Parker 1956; Heflebower 1980; Roy 1969; Curl 2009).

In general, however, "by 1920 the logic of the mutual form of . . . insurance was accepted throughout industry and commerce, and by people in general" (Knapp 1969, 423), and historically by the mid- to late 20th century, "stock and mutual life insurers were equally represented" (Erhemjamts and Leverty 2010, 1011) within the industry. This was in part due to state laws which not only enabled but encouraged mutuals' formation, typically in response to fraud and ethics scandals in the industry; detailing one such period in New York in the early 1900s, Knapp (1969, 425) writes, "The state law was amended to facilitate mutualization of stock companies.... Significantly, three of the largest stock companies immediately reorganized on the mutual plan, and several more adopted the mutual form of organization by 1920." Similar dynamics appear to characterize the historical record of other types of mutual insurance (such as fire and casualty; cf. Knapp 1969).

Mutual savings and loans associations, which had evolved from building societies (Haveman and Rao 1997), also benefited from significant government intervention. As late as the mid-1970s, mutual savings and loan associations and mutual savings banks accounted for more than 40% of fixed-dollar contract institutions' savings, while traditional commercial banks and stock savings and loans accounted for just over 50% of the market (Heflebower 1980, 138–40). Notably, the mutual savings and loan associations had experienced a 20-fold increase in deposits after World War II (Heflebower 1980) due to a confluence of factors, including the benefits of the New Deal–era financial regulatory apparatus, which increased public faith in their soundness; the postwar boom in housing, which fueled demand for one of their main loan products (mortgages); and federal restrictions which limited the ability of traditional financial institutions to offer such loans on comparable terms (Heflebower 1980).

As part of broader neoliberal deregulatory developments in the 1980s, however, both mutual insurers and savings and loan institutions saw various supportive regulatory provisions removed. Related policy changes also made it easier and provided financial incentive to demutualize and convert, often via a two-step process, to IOF status (Heflebower 1980; Chaddad and Cook 2004; Schneiberg, Goldstein, Kraatz 2022; Erhemjamts and Leverty 2010; Spicer 2022). The net result of these "liberalized" policies (Chaddad and Cook 2004, 579) was a dramatic loss of both classes of institutions via demutualization. Such decline continues, as continued policy developments make the first of the two-step conversion process more attractive to firms (Clark and Haslett 2018).

As a result, mutuals are increasingly less common in the U.S. insurance industry and have all but disappeared in banking; similar neoliberal demutualization dynamics have occurred in the United Kingdom to similar effect (Spicer 2022). There seems to be little historical evidence that the co-operative movement or related movements substantively fought against these changes which enabled and incentivized demutualization (such fights did occur in the other case countries), perhaps reflecting the fact that these mutual institutions largely did not form in close relationship to the co-operative movement or allied movements, nor did they substantively co-organize thereafter. Having never been integrated into the co-operative field, it is therefore not surprising that there was little move to defend their status as neoliberal policy took hold in the 1980s and enabled their wholesale loss.

From consumer goods to CLUSA: An organizer to defend co-operatives' interests emerges . . . too late? Consumer-owned retail/goods co-operatives have never achieved the same lasting national success as did the partial field organizing efforts on the other fronts reviewed above. Today, just one of the 100 largest co-operatives in the United States is a consumer-owned retail/goods co-operative (REI). As chronicled by American economist Heflebower (1980, 124) in his monograph on U.S. cooperation, "No phase of (American) co-operative enterprise has a more ragged history than that of retail stores owned by consumers." Over the course of the early and mid-20th century, there was a sustained effort to develop and organize such co-operatives, led by what Carreiro (2015) refers to as the "White consumer's co-operative movement," which in the short term achieved some substantive scale and scope before falling into disarray by the 1960s.

Indeed, in 1936 President Franklin Roosevelt had commissioned a major study of the potential of consumer co-operatives, with a particular focus on their use in Sweden and other Nordic nations (Hilson 2013), and the role of such organizations and movements as offering a "middle way" between capitalism and communism. In referring to them as offering a "middle way," Roosevelt was referencing the title of Childs's (1936) recently released book on the topic, which had become a U.S. bestseller (Hilson 2013) and which would later inspire Galbraith (1952) to highlight co-operatives alongside unions as a means by which to build a "countervailing power" against capital. Despite this interest, by the early 1960s consumer-owned retail/goods co-operatives were all but spent as a significant force: "Of total volume of retail co-operatives as reported in the *Census of Business 1963* . . . when the farm supply volume is subtracted, the residual amounts to only one quarter of one percent of total retail volume of consumer goods. . . . Co-operative food stores volume in 1963 was only four tenths of one percent of total food store sales . . . probably the lowest percentage in any industrial country" (Heflebower 1980, 124, 130).

Separate from the main early/mid-20th century organizing thrust of these White-led consumer co-operatives were two largely separate consumer movements: the Black consumer activism and co-operative movement of the same era and the post-1960s wave of natural and organic food co-operatives, many organized as hybrid worker-consumer co-operatives (Upright 2020; Knupfer 2013), which today appear to be experiencing a modest revival after a period of decline (Spicer 2020). Given that many of the latter were functionally organized as what today would be called multi-stakeholder co-operatives (where the consumer-owners also staff the stores, as in high-profile examples such as the Park Slope Food Co-op in Brooklyn, or where full-time workers own a partial share), while some were and remain worker-owned co-operatives (e.g., Rainbow Grocery in San Francisco), this later movement is treated in the worker and multi-stakeholder co-operative section, which comes later in this chapter.

What went wrong for U.S. consumer co-operatives? As reviewed in the previous chapter, consumer co-operatives were comparatively late to emerge in the United States (with respect to other early industrializers like the United Kingdom), and were also late to develop a nationally scaled organizational, field-building champion. By the time they had developed a national apex organization (CLUSA), other ownership models, including the IOF, had already established themselves as formidable and entrenched field competitors in retail industries (Heflebower 1980). Consumer co-operatives accordingly could not sustain competition against them, particularly as IOF firms organized to attack the tax status of these co-operatives, which were simultaneously facing Red Scare accusations that they were communistic. Compounding these organizing challenges, the Black consumer co-operative movement continued to operate separately and impeded by Jim Crow restrictions and discrimination throughout the period of consumer co-operatives' brief strength.

Studies in the 1880s had found only between 70 and 80 consumer co-operatives in existence in the United States, with little to coordinate them, in contrast to movements in other countries (Bemis 1888). As noted by Parker (1956, 33), further highlighting the comparative lateness of their development in the United States, "Bemis told the First International Co-operative Congress, in 1895, that there were then no National or State co-operative federations, no central source of information (governmental or co-operative), and no co-operative papers." Bemis (1888), however, did report that consumer co-operative activity in New England had doubled in recent years (Bemis 1888), and by 1900 a U.S. Bureau of Labor Statistics (BLS) study documented at least 96 consumer co-operatives, with 100 more "semi-co-operatives" in operation among the Mormons in the Western states (Bemis 1888).

Within five years, in an updated study conducted on behalf of the BLS (Cross 1906), nearly 350 co-operative stores were documented in the United States. Approximately half of these offered detailed reports of their activity, with sales which totaled $10M, many of the stores reporting affiliations with social movement and/or labor-affiliated organizations. Such consumer co-operatives were comparatively more common in California, the Upper Midwest, and the Northeast, which each contained nearly 70 co-operative stores, as documented in the 1906 study. There were other significant clusters in Kansas, Texas, and Utah. Cross (1906) and Parker (1956) documented the emergence of some new state-level efforts to coordinate activity within these clusters through the formation of co-operative purchasing and advocacy associations, despite the lack of appropriate enabling legislation. Notably, many had ties to the farmers cooperation movement.

Reflecting the importance of economies of scale in driving overall activity volumes, in the 1905–6 study Utah housed just five co-operative stores, but they accounted for 40% of the total reported national revenue for consumer co-operatives.[6] Further demonstrating the history of co-operatives among those with a shared bond and those excluded or marginalized, these stores reflected the efforts of the Mormons; having been unable to acquire goods at a fair price from non-Mormons, they founded the Zion's Co-operative Mercantile Institution (Gardner 1917), arguably the first modern department store in the United States, in the 1860s, which, following the example of the Rochdale co-operative commonwealth model, would come to manufacture its own goods (Cross 1906).

By the end of the 1910s in the Upper Midwest, the Right Relationship League and the Northwestern Co-operative League had organized more than 300 consumer co-operatives (Parker 1956). Nationally by 1920, nearly 700 individual consumer co-operative societies (excluding agricultural co-operatives which engaged in consumer purchasing) responded to a BLS survey (Parker 1922, 11). Though these societies could be found in 45 states, by far the lowest rates per capita were again in the South, where the consumer co-operative density per capita was one-tenth the levels in the Northeast, Midwest, and Pacific Coast regions (Parker 1922, 10). These societies in turn were coordinated by an array of emergent state, regional, and national federations, again with varying degrees of formal or informal association with different labor and social reform groups as well as distinct ethnic groups. (Beyond the Right Relationship League, there were CIO-sponsored consumer co-operatives, and co-operatives centered in the Jewish and Finnish communities, among other social groups; Parker 1956; Chambers 1962; Congress of Industrial Organizations 1947.)

---

[6] As Parker (1956) notes, the "semi-co-operative" structure of the Mormon enterprises hastened their demise as co-operatives; with voting in proportion to shares owned, many effectively drifted to become joint-stock companies and eventually were unable to compete against traditional IOFs.

Nordic immigrants primarily from Finland, for example, created the nation's strongest consumer co-operative retailer and wholesale society for the North Central states, with additional supply chain and production operations, which became the "nexus of an essentially all-Finnish 'nation' built in the shadow of American democracy: a material, social, and political universe, in which working Finns ran their own affairs" (Finlandia University 2007, 2). A leading retailer in Minnesota and Wisconsin through the 1950s (Fowler 1936; Alanen 1975), by the early 1940s the Co-operative Central Exchange[7] had more than 100 local co-operative member societies, which collectively maintained more than a 5% retail market share in the North Central region and as part of a regional North Central States Co-operatives League (Canoyer 1945; Kercher, Kebker, and Leland 1941; Turner 1941; Dyson 1982). Some societies accounted for 15% of total retail sales in some local areas (Canoyer 1945; Kercher, Kebker, and Leland 1941; Turner 1941; Dyson 1982), higher than in most any other U.S. region. Finnish Americans created similar efforts in other areas where they were concentrated, including high-profile consumer co-operatives in New York, Virginia, and, most notably, the Consumers' Co-operative of Berkeley, which would become a major area retail chain and was briefly the largest U.S. consumer co-operative (Knupfer 2013; Patmore 2020). It ultimately faded, as did these other early and midcentury grocery and consumer goods consumer co-operatives and federations, in the wake of increased competition and the tax war of the 1950s and 1960s.

Splintered among all these affiliations, these stores lacked any effective, national central or unifying advocacy meta-organization until the late 1910s, when James Peter Warbasse, a wealthy New York–based medical doctor who had become a co-operative promoter, financially invested in the struggling New York–based Consumers' Co-operative Union and built it into a nationwide apex organization for consumers' cooperation. This was CLUSA, which he founded in 1916, initially as the Co-operative League of America (Warbasse 1923; Chambers 1962). By 1919, what would become National Co-operatives, Inc., had been founded as a national wholesale society (Parker 1937) for consumer co-operatives. Efforts in the 1930s to merge this entity into CLUSA were a failure, reflecting the organizing and coordinating challenges the movement faced, as "the abortive effort (to merge) had all but destroyed both National Co-operatives and the League itself" (Chambers 1962, 77).

---

[7] Later it would be called Central Co-operatives, Inc. and the Central Co-operative Wholesale, then merged with Midland Co-operatives, the remnants of which would join Land O' Lakes, the large agricultural co-operative (Stewart-Bloch 2018).

Despite these organizational constraints faced by CLUSA, consumers' co-operation would grow significantly during the Great Depression and New Deal era. In 1920, as noted earlier, nearly 700 consumer co-operative societies in the United States had responded to Parker's (1922) first exhaustive surveys. By 1947, according to updated data by Parker (1949), the responding number had surpassed 2,500. The 1920 study, however, is telling in regard to the then still-limited central organizational capacity of the U.S. consumer co-operative movement. Parker (1922, 6) begins by noting that the BLS conducted the study because no comprehensive statistics were tracked by a central co-operative organization, as was the custom in most other countries, where the Rochdale-style, consumer-led model had played a critical role in co-operatives' broader development.

By 1921, CLUSA had nonetheless become the official U.S. apex meta-organization and a member of the global apex body for co-operatives, the ICA, which was founded in 1895 and was one of the first such worldwide organizations. Formal U.S. participation in the ICA had come later than for other rich democracies. Also in contrast to many apex bodies elsewhere, CLUSA explicitly resisted including other types of co-operatives in their organizing efforts until the late 1930s, when Warbasse was replaced by a new leader, Eugene Bowen, who pushed to include them (Carreiro 2015). This change was considered controversial within the organization at the time, because some farmers co-operatives were not necessarily run according to the ICA or Rochdale principles (Carreiro 2015), nor did they subscribe to the "co-operative commonwealth" goal of building a broader economy-wide interlocking set of consumer and worker-owned co-operatives. With the decision to include farmer members, CLUSA would slowly evolve into the central apex organization for the co-operative sector in the United States.

CLUSA had been late to emerge as a field organizer for consumer co-operatives, and late in including other co-operatives as a general apex body. But under Warbasse's early leadership, in contrast to the American organizational bodies leading the far more successful farmers co-operatives and credit union organizing efforts, and again in contrast to co-operative movements elsewhere, CLUSA had also interpreted the co-operative movement's "political neutrality" to mean they should avoid interaction with the state at all, with Warbasse resisting and rebuking official support from President Harding:

> In a June 28th, 1923 speech in Idaho, President Harding spoke in favor of co-operation (Warbasse 1923b). Harding encouraged "government [to] give the largest encouragement, consistent with sound economic and sound government functions, to every effort of the people to help themselves in dealing with the high

cost of living and the relationship of incomes to our household budgets." CLUSA, rather than celebrate the President's support, took the opportunity to criticize government involvement in the consumers' co-operative movement and reaffirm its anti-state position: "The government or the state cannot promote the Co-operative Movement. Politically promoted Co-operation is built on sand. The only sort of Co-operation that will endure is that which the people themselves build independent of politics or government." (Warbasse 1923, 2; Carreiro 2015, 71)

Given this hands-off approach, consumer co-operatives never were able to effectively harmonize state co-operative enabling (and securities) law, which remains an impediment to a degree for some co-operative types today, according to multiple interviewed consumer co-operative developers. This was despite efforts to diffuse model general incorporation laws for co-operatives, as noted by Czachorska-Jones, Finkelstein, and Samsami (2013, 776): "The first draft of a uniform law was approved by the National Conference of Commissioners on Uniform Laws in 1936, and was approved by the American Bar Association. However, the uniform law was only adopted in three states and was withdrawn in 1943 for lack of acceptance by the states. The National Conference of Commissioners on Uniform State Laws has proposed a series of draft uniform co-operative law statutes for state considerations, the latest dated 2007. None of the drafts have been finalized or adopted by any states."

Beyond the issue of advocating for enabling legislation, the apolitical nature of CLUSA became more pronounced under the subsequent tenure of former congressman Voorhis of California, as the "co-operative commonwealth" language and goals, which CLUSA had previously centered in its materials and organizational discussions, was systematically removed (Chambers 1962). Critiques of capitalism were also newly discouraged, to avoid hostility to co-operatives:

> One of the more striking examples of the changes to CLUSA was the creation of a "terminology manual" in 1946 to regulate Consumers' Co-operation articles and any other League publications. Of note, the manual recommended that authors refrain from "indiscriminate criticism of capitalism," which contributed to misunderstanding and hostility toward the League. The manual also advised authors to refrain from "indiscriminate attacks on capitalism," which "may cause the speaker to be classified as a communist or fascist" (quoted in Chambers 1962, 77). Instead of criticizing capitalism, authors were encouraged to criticize monopolies, something the general public was more likely to oppose. Also of significance, the manual urged authors to cease writing about a co-operative commonwealth, which might lead people to believe that the League advocated replacing all enterprises with

co-operatives (which the League did advocate until the late-1930s). (Carreiro 2015, 78–79)

What motivated this apolitical approach? What type of hostility did they wish to avoid? The answer is likely the same kind of communist attacks which had ended Voorhis's political career. Immediately prior to leading CLUSA, he had spent a decade in Congress as a Roosevelt Democrat, coming to prominence through his association with the Depression-era California co-operative-promoting campaign End Poverty in California. Then he was falsely accused of being endorsed by a CIO political action committee and accordingly framed as a radical and communist by his opponent (Bullock 1973). That opponent, Richard Nixon, would go on to become a senator, vice president, and president. Though the CIO PAC had in fact not endorsed Voorhis, the charges stuck, and the explicit links between the CIO, communism, and racial integration, then a prominent issue in Southern California (Bullock 1973), all played a role in enabling Nixon's 1946 Senate victory (Bullock 1973).

The links between fears of anticommunism and co-operatives were not unfounded: the CIO, which had supported a number of consumer co-operatives and also became the first significant White labor organization in decades to attempt to include Black workers in its organizing, would purge communists in 1949–50 (Congress of Industrial Organizations 1954). Many New Deal Democrats, including those like Voorhis who had promoted co-operatives, had to recast themselves as liberals (rather than social democrats), as the Second Red Scare sought to chase out of government and business New Deal progressives, failing to distinguish between such approaches and communism (Storrs 2012). One was either a capitalist—and, by extension, an advocate for the IOF model of the firm—or one was not. Such challenges during the Second Red Scare that broke after World War II were not new for U.S. co-operatives: during the First Red Scare of the 1910s–1920s, Warbasse had ejected and banned Communist Party members from CLUSA for similar reasons (Chambers 1962), part of a split between the center left and far left. This split, as in Finland, and occurring also among Finnish American Midwestern agricultural and consumer co-operatives, had also manifested via competing co-operatives and associated inter-co-operative federations at the regional scale (Dyson 1982).

By the McCarthy era and the Second Red Scare, however, through CLUSA's directives and leadership, co-operative organizational leadership had stripped the movement of much of its political content in order to defend against mounting concerns that those who did not support capitalism (i.e., were not proponents of the IOF) were communist (Curl 2009; Voorhis 1961). The window of the Roosevelt/New Deal era, in which co-operatives had enjoyed a brief period of national support, had also closed, as had interest in pursuit of a "middle way."

At the same time, co-operatives faced other serious legislative "attacks" (Knapp 1973, 536), specifically regarding their tax status, culminating in an IOF-led, anti-co-operative "tax war," as it was termed in congressional committee hearings in 1947 (U.S. Congress, House Committee on Ways and Means 1947, 2315; see Figure 7.1). These hearings, which lasted for 17 days, generated some 1,400 pages of testimony on proposals to revise the tax status of co-operatives (U.S. Congress, House Committee on Ways and Means 1947) and included extensive debates about how co-operatives should be taxed. Various proposals made different arguments regarding the appropriateness of "equal and neutral" tax regimes, given the different purpose and nature of co-operatives as compared with IOFs.

At this time, nonprofit and for-profit distinctions in the U.S. tax code were emergent (Hall 2006). Comparable to today's tax treatment of limited liability

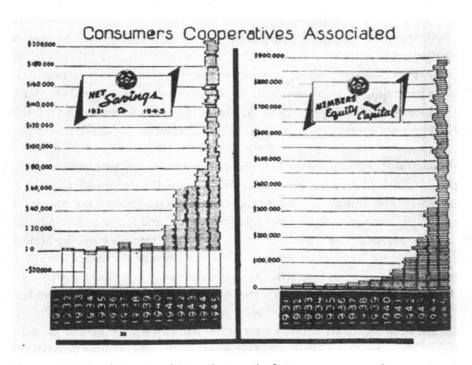

Figure 7.1 During the tax war, data on the growth of consumer co-operatives was introduced to argue they unfairly benefited from unequal tax treatment.
Source: U.S. Congress, House Committee on Ways and Means (1947, 2296).

companies (LLCs), some co-operative enterprises acted as "pass-through" entities with respect to some forms of revenue, which were exempt from tax at the entity level, that is, not subject to double taxation (explicitly discussed in U.S. Congress, House Committee on Ways and Means 1947, 2309–10). The National Tax Equality Association (NTEA), funded by IOFs in agribusiness and various other trades (Lauck 2000; Parker 1956, 354–58), launched an aggressive postwar campaign to require co-operatives to pay federal taxes on all income not distributed to members (McCabe 1945):

> Because of certain small tax advantages formerly accorded to farmers' (not urban) co-operatives under the Federal income tax law, agitation on this subject has for some years been one of the favorite anti-co-operative weapons. This began in 1943 with the formation of the organization now known as the National Tax Equality Association by retailers in the feed, hardware, coal, lumber, and grain business, under the leadership of Ben McCabe, Minneapolis grain dealer.... Each year since then the businessmen's association has widened its appeal, to reach additional groups, has carried on fund drives, hired high-powered lobbyists, and trained its guns on Congress to obtain heavier taxes on co-operatives. (Parker 1956, 354)

Co-operative enterprise had grown significantly during the Depression and World War II (Ford 1946), and IOFs were threatened by their success (Ford 1946; Parker 1956, 357). Co-operatives' various advocacy organizations (including CLUSA) were able to defend co-operatives from being subject to all of the NTEA's proposals via the creation of Subchapter T of the IRS Code, for tax-exempt co-operatives: "The exclusion of patronage refunds by co-operatives was the subject of vigorous attack in the late 1940's," and as a result of these attacks, "[t]he Revenue Act of 1951 made several changes in the existing statutory law on co-operative income tax treatment" (Frederick 2005, 44). Accordingly, as Frederick goes on to detail, "[a] new tax system for previously exempt co-operatives was introduced, and longstanding administrative practice related to treatment of patronage refunds made by nonexempt co-operatives was recognized" (44). The law also confirmed, however, that many forms of co-operatives were not exempt, and it placed restrictions on what costs, revenues, and expenses they could deduct or shield from tax. Challenges involving these rules were pursued against co-operatives by the IRS for several decades before a clear settlement of the law emerged, particularly with regard to the treatment of tax losses, with cases ongoing through the 1990s (Frederick 2005). Further, these rules, which were phased in between 1951 and 1962 (Frederick 2005), were contested legislatively, reflecting that co-operatives' tax status involved "decades of controversy" (Heflebower 1980,

185). The Tax Reform Act of 1969, for example, initially proposed to do away with most of the remaining tax exemptions for co-operatives (Zivan 1970), but this was struck from the final bill.

Meanwhile, separately and apart from the CLUSA-led White consumer co-operative movement, a fledgling Black consumer co-operative movement linked to a broader Black consumer activism movement had risen—and fallen—in parallel, with significant activity in the South, long a challenging area for consumer cooperation. In Cross's 1906 study, there had been virtually no consumer-owned co-operative stores in the old "cotton belt" states: there was one store in North Carolina, one in Tennessee, and none in Maryland, Virginia, Georgia, South Carolina, Alabama, Mississippi, or Florida. Cross glossed over these data in his study, which did not discuss the Black co-operative movement and is consistent with other accounts which note that formation of consumer co-operatives in the early 20th century was largely in areas "outside the South" (Heflebower 1980, 125). Accounts during the 1930s peak of consumer co-operatives further affirmed "the South was almost barren of (consumer) societies" (Parker 1937, 102), and Knupfer (2013, 38) found that "few food co-operatives were started by African Americans in the South" from the 1930s to the 1950s.

The year after Cross's study, however, Black scholar W. E. B. Du Bois (1907, 165–70; full list of stores 157–58), posthumously credited today as a founder of modern sociology (Morris 2015), had conducted a comprehensive study of Black cooperation, in which he documented the existence of 103 co-operative stores, an outright majority of which were in the Southern states. Most of these Black-owned and -controlled stores, however, were probably not formally structured as co-operatives at all, likely due to the aforementioned legal limitations of free assembly and association which Black Americans continued to face under the Jim Crow system, which also likely impeded their ability to make use of emerging state co-operative enabling laws (see Chapter 6). This may be why Cross failed to include them in his list. Regarding Du Bois's list, Parker (1956, 308) found that of his "103 Negro distributive 'co-operatives' in the United States, most were probably joint stock companies. Only 6 of the total had the word 'co-operative' in their names."

> A study made in 1917, covering "economic co-operation" among the colored people in Georgia, included few organizations of the Rochdale type. Of 1,907 businesses covered in the statistics, only 39 had members or stockholders (such as real co-operatives would have) and there was no indication how many of the 39 were actually co-operative. There are records now for only 77 organizations known to be co-operative and of Negro membership. The largest groups were in the Midwest

(31). . . . Of 61 for which year of organization is known, 26 were formed in the latter thirties, and 24 between 1940 and the end of the war. None formed prior to 1935 remains. Nine (organized between 1935 and 1945) were still alive at last reports. (308)

In fact, many of these organizations in Georgia were part of a fledgling Black consumer co-operative movement, which was in turn part of a larger Black consumer activism movement (Carreiro 2015; Glickman 2009) to overcome racial discrimination both by mainstream IOF-based retailers and by White co-operative stores alike, by supporting Black-owned and -controlled businesses (e.g., the Garveyite movement; Gordon Nembhard 2008). As Carreiro (2015, 18, 166) notes, however, "there was no black equivalent to CLUSA," that is, "no umbrella organization emerged to formally bring together the disparate groups working toward the development of black consumers' co-operatives. Nonetheless, a black consumers' co-operative movement can be identified" in this era.

It was not uncommon for Black communities to establish consumers' co-operatives in response to exploitative white-owned businesses that often charged higher prices for inferior goods. Others were established to fulfill the needs of those living in "food deserts"—areas characterized by a lack of access to nutritional needs. In response to the lack of a grocery store within a two-mile radius, several families residing in the segregated Frederick Douglass housing development in Washington, DC formed a buying club in January, 1941, just one year after the housing development opened. Within a two-and-a-half year period the buying club, operated out of a member's apartment, expanded to a 1,000 dollar per week operation. In September, 1944 the Frederick Douglass Co-operative opened adjacent to the housing project. (174)

This is not to say that there was no *attempt* to organize Black consumer co-operatives through an apex organization. Du Bois, who founded the Negro Co-operative Guild in 1918 (just two years after CLUSA), "maintained his commitment to a separate, black co-operative system, concerned that the wider consumers' co-operative movement was plagued by racial discrimination and that integration with the movement would guarantee black subordination" (Carreiro 2015, 109). His efforts were succeeded by George Schuyler's Young Negro Co-operative League (YNCL). Founded in 1930 by Schuyler, the YNCL resolved to remain independent of CLUSA (Carreiro 2015, 155) and undertook an ambitious five-year plan to organize thousands of Black Americans into a national network of consumer co-operatives, with the ultimate goals of adding a wholesale society, bank, and producers' associations/worker co-operatives (Carreiro 2015), that is, a Black co-operative commonwealth. Though their implementation effort fell far short of their goals, they did create a number of consumer co-operatives, in part through the efforts of YNCL participants like Ella Baker, later a civil rights leader, who also organized Black food co-operatives (Baker 1970; Gordon Nembhard 2014). Nonetheless, the YNCL lasted only four years, lacking substantive resources from CLUSA and unable to coordinate with the Colored Merchants' Association (CMA), a producer co-operative of independent, non-co-operatively owned Black grocery stores. The CMA too disbanded shortly thereafter, in 1936 (Gordon Nembhard 2014; Carreiro 2015).

Early CLUSA leadership, including Warbasse himself, expressed support in writing for Black self-determined, segregated co-operative efforts (Carreiro 2015, 156), but there was little formal or substantive integration or sharing of resources between the Black and White consumer co-operative movements, which continued to operate as "two separate movements" (Carreiro 2015, 13). This separation in part reflected serious concerns by Black cooperators about discrimination from the White co-operative movement specifically, and from White business in general, as noted above. Gordon Nembhard (2018) details the history of "sabotage" of Black co-operatives by White business interests and U.S. government agencies, which she finds persisted through the 1980s and in her view warrants payment of reparations.

Schuyler eventually viewed the separate strategy as a long-term challenge for Black cooperators and "held that any form of self-segregation would only encourage the continuation of belief in white superiority and invite negative and coordinated responses from white business aimed at undermining black-owned businesses" (Carreiro 2015, 159, 161), in part because "many successful black consumers' co-operatives relied on financially stable and educated black members to offset the uncertainty of the continued patronage of poorer members. This was a setback for the black consumers' co-operatives that was less significant for the white, CLUSA-led movement." The first-order point, however, is not to debate the merits of creating a separate Black economy. Rather, with respect to the construction of a comprehensive coordinated and organized co-operative movement at scale, this issue presents as a comparatively unique, constraining feature of the U.S. case.

Notably, as CLUSA navigated these various challenges through the postwar period into the 1950s, it began work in international development. By 1951 it was working in India to develop co-operatives, and by the 1960s it had begun formally conducting work with the U.S. Agency for International Development. Today, while NCBA-CLUSA (the name was changed in 1985) does advocate at the national scale for co-operatives for appropriate legislation and boasts annual revenues which can exceed $30 million, more than 90% of this figure is accounted for by international development contract work, often involving agricultural co-operatives in the Global South; domestic development activity, including for consumer co-operatives, is far more limited. This focus is not without its detractors. As one regional consumer co-operative developer in Minnesota stated in an interview, expressing frustration with NCBA-CLUSA, "I'm not saying do not do international development work, but get your own house in order first. . . . They were helping co-ops everywhere else for decades while we couldn't even get access to SBA [Small Business Administration] lending programs." But as a longtime former NCBA executive interviewed stated in response to a question about coordinating and managing competing priorities, "What choice did we have, actually? What were we going to do, turn down these resources? . . . We had to take what we could get."

Worker and Multi-Stakeholder Co-operatives: A Dream Deferred?

In the 2020s, worker and multi-stakeholder co-operatives[8] (e.g., tech-related platform co-operatives) are attracting outsized interest in the American co-operative movement, as affirmed by multiple interviewees, despite their comparatively small size and scale in the United States. A national co-operative organizer told me, "Worker co-ops, multi-stakeholder co-ops, platform co-ops . . . these are the smallest part of the overall co-op movement in the U.S., but it's where all the energy is . . . it's where the future of the movement is . . . and the organizational leaders at NCBA don't quite know what to do with us. . . . Besides ninety percent or more of NCBA's work is contract international development work in ag for federal . . . and international agencies. . . . We're not the big old White ag co-ops, we're not rural electric co-ops. . . . It's honestly like oil and water sometimes." To that end, the worker co-operative movement did not have its own national apex meta-organization until 2004, when the U.S. Federation of Worker Co-operatives (USFWC), today a member of NCBA, was founded; its sibling organization, the Democracy at Work Institute (DaWI), was founded in 2013.

What happened over the century between the collapse of the Knights of Labor and the emergence of USFWC? There have been at least three significant

---

[8] These include workers, consumers, and other stakeholders, such as mission-driven investors and community members.

waves of worker and multi-stakeholder co-operative formation and development over that period, again in a manner consistent with the movement-like field-building efforts which characterized the more successful strains. None of these waves of activity has ever achieved the same nationally scaled field-building gains as these other strains, making worker and multi-stakeholder cooperation a dream long deferred in the U.S. context.

The first wave, which stretched from the Progressive Era through to the self-help co-operative movement (SHCM) of the New Deal era, yielded virtually no long-lasting individual firms or field-level gains. It disappeared quickly with the postwar boom of the late 1940s and rise of McCarthyism; by the early 1960s, just 12 worker co-operatives were believed to be in existence (Roy 1969, 120–21, 190, citing 1962 data from the U.S. Department of Labor and the AFL-CIO on "workers' productive associations/co-operatives"). As with consumer co-operatives, these entities also faced tax "controversy" (Frederick 2013, 15; Seto and Chasin 2002) and were subject to ongoing litigation and IRS challenges in this era. After achieving some durable local and limited national organizing gains, the second wave, linked to the countercultural movements which peaked in the 1970s, also faded; a number of its national legislative goals were left unachievable after the 1980 election and subsequent rise of Reagan and neoliberalism. But regional pockets of activity remained, where larger-scale surviving entities seeded the current, third, revived wave of national efforts. These efforts resulted in significant new co-operative formation, legislative gains, and organizing, including the development of the national apex body for worker co-operatives, and have also witnessed a substantive effort to engage with and promote multiracial and Black-led worker co-operatives and to center Black leadership in the movement.

It is unclear, however, whether these gains will be sustained, because a competing ownership model through which to achieve worker ownership took root in the U.S. field environment during the second wave: the ESOP, which was explicitly created as a more capitalist worker ownership alternative to the co-operative model, and which has reached its comparatively greatest degree of institutional development in the U.S. context.

The socialists' fights against wage slavery and the New Deal self-help movement, 1910s–1940s. After the demise of the Knights, the formation of productive, worker-owned co-operative associations plummeted, dropping by roughly 75% over the two decades from 1895 to 1914 compared to levels from 1885–94 (Aldrich and Stern 1983). Reiterating this finding, Jones (1984) documented just one such firm that was founded in the first decade of the 20th century. This decline is not surprising given that the AFL, at its 1894 general meetings, had successfully fought to remove language calling for collective ownership of the means of production from its political program (which the SLP had fought to include in the prior year's convention (Aldrich and Stern 1983, 389; Quint 1953). The AFL instead focused on trade unionism in the subsequent decades, for which the "major alternative discredited ... was the producer's co-operative" (Aldrich and Stern 1983, 399).

There were accordingly two strands of worker ownership development in the first half of the century. First, the various socialist parties (SLP and SPA) of Eugene Debs, along with the IWW, had attempted to advance the idea of a co-operative commonwealth as a way to achieve ownership of the means of production, which they sometimes promoted through calls for creation of a large co-operative state in the West (Kipnis 1952, 50–51). Overall, Jones (1984) documents the creation of 44 productive co-operatives founded in the 1910s and 1920s. Larger such entities founded in this era include the Sunset Scavenger Company and the Golden Gate Disposal Company, two of a number of waste-related worker-owned San Francisco–area businesses which persisted for decades (Russell and Perry 1978). Often they specifically precluded Black workers, however, as well as members of other racial minority groups, from becoming member-owners, a practice which persisted through the 1970s (Pinto 2023, 301; Rothschild and Witt 1986, 96; Perry 1978, 142–44).

Reflecting Gourevitch's thesis regarding liberty, reviewed in the preceding chapter, the legacy of race-based slavery continued to play a limiting role in other ways, as the socialists persisted in deploying comparisons between wage slavery and race-based slavery, even after the mainstream labor movement had generally dropped such framing. In 1914 congressional testimony, as part of the "great debate" (*Le Monde Diplomatique* 2011) between Samuel Gompers, head of the AFL, and Hillquit, head of the socialists, Hillquit analogized the establishment of a co-operative commonwealth to the ending of race-based slavery, reflecting the persistence of the wage-slavery link (Figure 7.2). Other marginalized national political groups, such as the IWW, had also supported productive co-operatives in the United States as a means by which to overthrow the employer-based system to achieve a co-operative commonwealth (Brissenden 1920), but to little lasting significance or avail, as the AFL and, later, the CIO instead largely focused on the debate between trade/craft unionism and broader industrial unionism and whether or not to "cooperate" with employers through employer-sponsored unions to achieve workplace representation and "industrial democracy" through works councils, as they had in Europe (Rogers and Streeck 1994).

Certain regions, however, persisted in attempts to construct all or part of such co-operative commonwealth systems during and after the First Red

A. F. OF L., SOCIALISTS, AND INDUSTRIAL WORKERS. 1489

Mr. GOMPERS. What do you mean by legislation—the enactment of law?

Mr. HILLQUIT. The enactment of a law, a decree, an ordinance, or any other mandate which can be executed.

Mr. GOMPERS. Expropriating property of all who may hold it to the Government or the cooperative commonwealth.

Mr. HILLQUIT. I have not said, "Expropriate." It may be a question of purchase.

Mr. GOMPERS. Well, say—take hold——

Mr. HILLQUIT (interrupting). Take hold—take control and possession of.

Mr. GOMPERS. Well, by revolution?

Mr. HILLQUIT. Oh, I suppose it would probably be called a revolution anyhow, but it may be a very peaceful one, I don't know.

Mr. GOMPERS. By confiscation?

Mr. HILLQUIT. Not as we are inclined at present. At present we are in the market for buying out the capitalists.

Mr. GOMPERS. By compensation?

Mr. HILLQUIT. By compensation. However, again, Mr. Gompers, I do not guarantee the acts of the next generation. The capitalists may become very naughty and the people may become very displeased with them, and may take things, just as we took the negro slaves from the owners.

Mr. GOMPERS. You have an idea that the taking might be for compensation?

Mr. HILLQUIT. Might be; yes.

Mr. GOMPERS. Have you an idea how such a proposition could be financed?

Mr. HILLQUIT. How it could be financed? We haven't reached that point yet, Mr. Gompers——

Mr. GOMPERS (interrupting). No.

Mr. HILLQUIT (continuing). I suppose that if paid, it will be paid by some Government securities.

Mr. GOMPERS. I think—I take it that you are not in favor of what is generally known by the capitalists as State socialism—State socialism?

Mr. HILLQUIT. Yes; I am not.

Mr. GOMPERS. Not even as a step toward a democratic socialism?

Mr. HILLQUIT. Why, if it were State sollalism, it would not be a step toward democratic socialism?

Mr. GOMPERS. Under socialism, are not the present differences within the socialist parties in the United States significant of fatal differences in the management of a revolutionized society?

Mr. HILLQUIT. No; not fatal differences, Mr. Gompers. We have some differences of opinion within the Socialist Party, sometimes lively ones. I hope you have them in the American Federation of Labor. But we, nevertheless, manage to keep our organization to work for a common purpose. I presume there will be strong differences of opinion, and some fights, even under socialism. There have been in the American Federation of Labor. I should not want it to be otherwise.

Mr. GOMPERS. I mean as to liberty. Under socialism will there be liberty of individual action, and liberty of choice of occupation and liberty of refusal to work?

Mr. HILLQUIT. Plenty of it, Mr. Gompers.

Mr. GOMPERS. I take it that you have no apprehension that under the democratic management of socialism, the administrators could or would attempt to exploit the workers under them, and one set of laborers would exploit another set: the lazy office holders, the industrious artisans; the strong and bolder, the weaker and more modest ones; and the failures, the economically successful.

Mr. HILLQUIT. Why, I think there will be some abuses of some kind appear. Even under socialism men will still remain human, no doubt. But I think, Mr. Gompers, we have every reason to believe that they will be very small and slight, as compared to present abuses, for the system is based on a greater democracy and self-government, and provides for means of remedy; and furthermore, there is no great incentive to corruption such as we have under capitalism and private gain.

Mr. GOMPERS. In the event that the cooperative commonwealth should be established, taking it for granted for the sake of the question, that it is possible, it would mean or have for its present purpose, the highest material and social and moral improvement of the condition of the workers attainable at that time, would it not?

Mr. HILLQUIT. I think so.

Figure 7.2 Gompers vs. Hillquit, congressional testimony on co-operatives, labor, and socialism, 1916.

Source: Walsh and Manly (1916).

Scare, with varying degrees of success. Substantial efforts were made in California, the Upper Midwest, and the Northeast, which would pave the way for the second strain of development in this era, the SHCM. Centered in California, it developed from a direct predecessor effort, the End Poverty in California (EPIC) campaign. Upton Sinclair, in his unsuccessful 1930s bid for California governor on the Democratic ticket and as part of the EPIC movement, included plans for the state to support widespread worker and consumer co-operatives (Rothschild 2009). The state had a long history of attracting utopians (Fogarty 1990) and developing such co-operatives (Horner 1978), leading Cross (1905–1906, cf. 1911) to conclude, "In no place is the co-operative movement so strong or so successful." (33) ." Sinclair, though achieving the strongest performance by a Democratic candidate for state governor, lost the 1934 election after failing to gain Roosevelt's support and with conservative business elements alarmed by the implications of EPIC (Pasha 2014; Bullock 1973; Mitchell 1992). Notably, while EPIC included Black Americans, in many areas of the state they were explicitly segregated (Mitchell 1992, 193) in separate EPIC divisions.

Nonetheless, during Roosevelt's New Deal, the federal government effectively implemented the co-operative component of EPIC by investing in worker and hybrid consumer-worker co-operatives through the SHCM. Having emerged out of Southern California, where it had received support from the state government, it spread to other states before briefly being incorporated into New Deal programs (Piven and Cloward 1972; Pasha 2014). Jones (1984, 39) estimates that the 251 productive co-operatives/worker co-operatives created during the 1930s, mostly formed as part of the SHCM, made it the second-highest decade in U.S. history with respect to the number of worker co-operatives founded, surpassed only by the 1880s. As Jones and Schneider (1984, 57) noted, the SHCM "represent[s] the only major historical attempt by the U.S. legislature to incorporate workers' participation in management into government programs. Not only were state and federal funds provided to support self-help programs but also an array of rules were made to govern self-help activities."

The SHCM was detailed in a 1,200-page economic doctoral dissertation by Clark Kerr (1939), who would become the first chancellor of UC Berkeley. The work, supervised in part by Cross, documented how, working with both local and state agencies and partners, and with funding and support from the Federal Emergency Relief Administration and then the Works Progress Administration, more than 500,000 people in 600 local self-help co-operatives and associations in 37 states (with, again, particular weakness in the South) had been put to work over the course of the 1930s. These co-operatives were a mix of worker and consumer co-operatives and sometimes were not formally incorporated or structured as co-operatives per se. They were also typically racially segregated; in Southern California, for example, as documented by Kerr, while by 1933 there were 88 White self-help co-operative units in the region and a small number of Black or Black with other non-White racial group co-operatives, there was just one co-operative unit which included "Negroes" and Whites (241–42; cf. Pasha 2014). Nonetheless, as economic conditions improved and as the political climate changed with the rise of McCarthyism, these federal programs were terminated, reflecting the general tension between co-operatives and anticommunist McCarthyism (Cotterill 1979, 39; Pratt 1996), and the SHCM entities quickly disappeared. By 1961, as noted earlier, there were just 12 worker co-operatives in existence in the United States (Roy 1969).

Again reflecting how co-operatives emerge as a response to crisis, the New Deal era became one of the only periods when worker co-operatives appeared to enjoy broad and explicit U.S. federal government support. And yet these efforts quickly faded; by the time government support disappeared, participants had not organized nationally as a field to create a self-sustaining field infrastructure. Unsurprisingly, Jones (1984) finds that virtually no new worker-owned co-operatives were founded in either the 1950s or the 1960s, with the exception of a cluster of plywood co-operatives in the Pacific Northwest. These were subject to a tax "controversy" through the 1950s and 1960s (Frederick 2013), in part stemming from whether or not their worker-owners' patronage qualified for tax exemptions as 501(c)12 co-operatives by the IRS, which "has never distinguished the terms 'mutual' or 'co-operative' for purposes of I.R.C. 501(c)(12)" (Seto and Chasin 2002, 1). Lawsuits and adverse IRS rulings continued through the 1960s (Seto and Chasin 2002; Frederick 2013).

When the next movement-based wave of development came, in the 1970s, there was little that had survived in terms of field or organizational infrastructure from which to build from. Development would suffer, accordingly, from "a peculiar historical amnesia. Few . . . . . . co-op enthusiasts in the sixties learned anything from their predecessors in previous decades because they had never heard of them. The lessons of the recent past are just as obscure to the scattered activists of the present. New arrangements for living and working persist, but often in a vacuum. Without the support of a movement behind them, many soldier on in ignorance of the victories or mistakes of similar efforts" (Case and Taylor 1979, 4).

The countercultural wave: Limited lasting organizational gains and the development of a field competitor. The broader counterculture and communal movements of the 1960s and 1970s stoked interest in what Rothschild (1979) termed "collectivistic-democratic" organizations, with estimates running as high as 5,000 to 10,000 such organizations being formed and operated during this era (Rothschild 1979; Rothschild and Whitt 1986; Zwerdling, 1978; Case and Taylor, 1979). As a subset, this wave of alternative organizational founding included a number hybrid worker-consumer food co-operatives[9] and a significant number of small, artisanal production and worker co-operatives, all as a way to exit the capitalist system (Curl 2009; Spicer 2020). While the wave of development would achieve a small number of nationally scaled institutional gains, ultimately the selection effects with respect to the type of participants appeared to prove a limitation on the durability and field-building efforts of this wave. As noted by Jackall and Levin (1984, 87):

> One of the striking results of the tumultuous social upheavals of the 1960s and early 1970s was the development of the small worker co-operative or collective movement. In urban areas all across the country, but particularly in the San Francisco Bay Area, the Boston/Cambridge area, the Washington D.C. area, Minneapolis, Austin, Ann Arbor, Seattle and Eugene, hundreds of small, democratically organized businesses grew up. In the early days of the movement, many of the young men and women who staffed collectives were self-termed "refugees" from the 1960s movements. Even those who had not been deeply involved were aware that their lives had been significantly touched by one or another of the great issues from that period.

Mansbridge (1979, 194–95) is more specific: "Anarchists, adolescents, and other 'idealists' have insisted that complete equality was possible if only enough effort[s] were made to achieve it. Leninists, adults, and other 'realists' have usually abandoned the idea entirely. The collectives of the last ten years have generally fallen into the former camp" with a "general collapse of similar organizations in the mid-1970s." Indeed, the well-documented "co-op wars" over ideology in the Twin Cities (Cox 1994) and the Bay Area would destroy many of the organic food co-operatives in particular. (Again, these stores were largely unrelated to prior waves of general consumer-owned grocery co-operatives; Upright 2020.) Despite this, several food co-operatives from this era remain active in both regions today. The Black Panthers also developed

---

[9] Jones (1984) gives varying estimates of how many of these democratic collectives were actually co-operatives: it may have been as high as several hundred, though this has never been adequately documented, and the detailed time-series records produced by Jones and, relatedly, by Aldrich and Stern (1983) have been lost, per personal communication with the surviving authors. All sources agree, however, that most were quite small in scale.

some food co-operatives as part of their broader Black empowerment and economic self-determination work in this era (Gordon Nembhard 2014).

Beyond these efforts, various individual state governments in the Northeast and Midwest attempted to use worker co-operative and employee ownership business structures to save jobs in struggling enterprises in struggling de-industrializing regions (Zwerdling 1978). These were often brokered with the help of the federal government, states, and the labor movement (Dickstein 1991). Efforts sometimes involved the emergent ESOP trust. Having been created in the 1950s and granted favorable federal tax treatment in the 1970s, ESOPs allowed employees a way to participate in profits and ownership of their firm, though not necessarily with the democratic governance and workplace participation rights of a co-operative. The law also created a tax-advantaged, favorable way for small businesses to sell ownership to their employees through the ESOP trust.

In the wake of the height of McCarthyism in the mid-1950s, the ESOP had emerged to promote worker inclusion and as an explicit alternative to the co-operative commonwealth strategy; it was an economically liberal model. Developed by a "skilled social actor," attorney and businessman Louis Kelso, in 1956 as a way a retiring owner could sell a business to employees, he explicitly positioned the ESOP as the linchpin of a broader "capitalist manifesto," the title of a book he coauthored (Kelso and Adler 1958) as he spread and developed the ESOP model. Intentionally titled as a foil to Marx and Engels's (1848) *Communist Manifesto*, Kelso's book was explicitly ideological in its framing, positioning the ESOP as a means by which to "save" late-stage capitalism from its flaws, and as an alternative to the replacement of capitalism with "socialism, a co-operative system, a corporative order, or something else," and as a way to "make capitalists of their employees" (Kelso and Adler 1958, 6, 210). In effect, it turned the employees not into co-operative owners but into individual, profit-oriented investors of the firm, effectively an IOF with the potential for 100% profit sharing and lacking democratic governance. While 1970s activists attempted to codify the development of ESOPs with democratic bylaws (called the democratic ESOP or "DESOP" during the 1980s, today called an esoperative; Rothschild 1985; Spicer 2020), such firms are believed to be extremely rare. Accordingly, most ESOPs today lack employee representation on their boards (Dubb 2016, 150). Overall, however, majority-ESOP-owned companies in the United States have become far more common than worker co-operatives, particularly at scale, in part as a result of efforts which culminated in this era. The 100 largest majority-ESOP-owned companies today, for example, employ over 600,000 Americans, according to the National Center for Employee Ownership. This appears to be more than 75 times the number of individuals employed by all worker co-operatives in the United States today. (Roughly 7,000 employees were counted in the USFWC 2021 census, which is believed to capture 80% to 90% of the total worker co-operative universe of 8,000 to 10,000 employees). Despite its comparative success in the United States, the use of the ESOP as a means to achieve majority, broad-based employee ownership of firms has not spread widely beyond the United States: I have found limited evidence documenting uptake of the ESOP model for this purpose elsewhere.

Nonetheless, efforts to pass a national act—the 1978 Voluntary Job Preservation and Community Stabilization Act—to provide technical assistance and loans to financially support employee ownership conversions to ESOP and worker co-operative status in the late 1970s ultimately failed and was not revisited after Reagan's 1980 victory. This election, which also saw significant shifts in congressional representation, saw the departure of some longtime congressional staff with institutional knowledge of these issues (Whyte 1986). This loss of field knowledge and capability was affirmed by two such staff from this era who were interviewed for this study.

A national co-operative bank, however, was started, seeded with an initial federal investment, and a handful of states set up employee ownership centers to assist in conversion. With an initial loan from Congress, the National Consumer Co-operative Bank Act of 1978 authorized the creation of a bank to lend to consumer and worker co-operatives. Initially capitalized and owned by the federal government, it was fully cooperatized by the early 1980s, with the government's role removed. Natural food co-operatives, which again included a mix of worker-consumer- and consumer-owned stores, also declined rapidly starting in the 1980s, replaced by competition from traditional investor-owned corporations (St. Peter 2008). Most notably, John Mackey came out of the natural foods co-operative sector and founded Whole Foods with the express intent to "destroy them" (the food co-ops), one interviewee noted, only to lose control of his IOF to Amazon, to the bemusement of several food co-operative organizers interviewed. Beyond competition from IOFs like Whole Foods, many of the food co-operatives in this era also continued to struggle, despite their progressive political orientation, to address racial divides in their communities and serve a multiracial base of members, as detailed by Zitcer (2021) in his examination of how such issues manifested in Philadelphia and nationally.

While most of the era's worker co-operatives and food co-operatives disappeared (Jackall and Levin 1984; Mansbridge 1979; Dickstein 1991), a small number have survived to the current era, as documented by the recent census of such firms by the USFWC, playing a pivotal role in enabling both the current wave of worker co-operative development as well as today's modest revival in food co-operative development.[10] As noted in the 2019 USFWC directory of such entities, "Most of today's largest worker co-ops were founded during the 1970s and 1980s, as part of an explosion in alternative economic forms. The co-ops that survived have thrived, and have helped seed new growth through investment of capital and expertise in a second wave of worker co-op development starting in the late 1990s" (5).

The current wave. Elsewhere (Spicer 2020), I have analyzed the major developments of the current wave of U.S. action and contrasted it with the prior wave. To summarize that work, today American worker and community/multi-stakeholder co-operative organizers have been explicitly and self-reflectively engaging in strategic efforts to build a national field, from the local to the national scale, and are also explicitly attempting to rectify shortcomings of the preceding wave. Since the 2010s, they have engaged with municipal, regional, and state governments. Across more than 20 city-regions, national organizations such as USFWC, DaWI, Project Equity, and the Sustainable Economies Law Center, along with wide-ranging local and regional groups such as the Black-led Cooperation Jackson project in Mississippi, have worked to codify and diffuse model legislation at multiple scales. They have produced and diffused templates for engaging municipal governments to procure fee reductions, favorable consideration in city procurement contracts, enhanced loan fund eligibility, and education and technical assistance around business conversion to co-operative ownership, among other actions. They have also advocated updates of state enabling laws, including work to develop model statutes, to explicitly codify the organizational archetype for the worker co-operative in statutes, including in California and Illinois. At the federal level, they have achieved a range of policy improvements, such as changes to include worker and food co-operatives in small business lending, stemming from acts such as the successful Main Streets Employee Ownership Act of 2018 and the Worker Ownership, Readiness and Knowledge Act of 2022.

Obstacles remain, however; food co-operative and worker co-operative developers, for example, continue to find it challenging for co-operatives to organize across state lines given different enabling laws and different in-state securities laws. Though co-operative lawyers, including several interviewed for this study, often have ways to skirt such challenges, co-operative developers repeatedly pushed back on this as unacceptable. One

---

[10] Like worker co-operatives, the natural food co-operatives would also lack a national apex body at the end of this wave. The National Co+op grocers, a central co-operative which handles some marketing functions for food co-operatives, was not founded until 1999.

Minnesota-based informant who works nationally to develop co-operatives stated, "If you tell founders or organizers they can't have employees or members in multiple states unless they file all kinds of extra paperwork and extra legal work, that's a problem. . . . Then they wind up starting as an LLC perhaps with some co-operative bylaws, which winds up at risk of getting jettisoned when any type of challenge with democratic governance or fundraising arises."

Participants and field-building organizers are taking a more strategic approach to economic success. Instead of starting businesses in random industries selected for personal or political reasons, they are strategically incubating start-ups to maximize probability of success, focused on scalable industries and sectors. Rather than converting struggling businesses in legacy industries being destroyed by technological change, they are converting successful businesses in growing industries from retiring baby-boomer owners. Instead of fighting or resisting information and communication technologies and associated industry change, they develop high-tech "Y-combinator"-style business incubators and entrepreneurial support organizations, as well as platform co-operatives, which offer an alternative to corporate-sharing economy models. Participants are also markedly more diverse than in the prior wave: women and people of color now constitute a majority of worker co-operative member-owners, according to data from USFWC. Worker co-operative developers and funders are also explicitly highlighting the importance of Black-led co-operatives and the importance of addressing racial inclusion and justice to the success of the co-operative movement (Freilla 2022). Both the USFWC and DaWI, as well as Project Equity, are now Black-led organizations, and 2022 and 2023 witnessed the first and second National Conference on the Black Co-operative Agenda, which included all co-operative types but had an explicit focus on worker co-operatives. Black-led fund managers like Apis & Heritage, meanwhile, are focusing on transitioning Black- and people of color–led firms to employee ownership, including worker co-operatives.

Nonetheless, the South remains a weak region; according to the 2021 USFWC census, which documented the existence of over 600 enterprises, just four Southern metropolitan areas—Asheville, Durham, Atlanta, and Jackson—have at least five worker or multi-stakeholder co-operatives. Similarly, the USFWC 2019 directory, which detailed 465 such firms, counted just 36 in former Confederate States, making it one of the weakest regions in the country for worker co-operative density. Similarly, of the 148 food co-operatives (which include consumer, worker, and multi-stakeholder co-operatives) who are members of National Co+op Grocers, fewer than 20 are in the South, making it, as it was a century ago in Parker's 1920 study, the weakest region on this front as well.

As a result of these sustained efforts in the current wave, today's 600+ documented worker and/or multi-stakeholder co-operatives in operation are arguably the most that have ever existed at any single point in U.S. history. The two largest worker co-operatives are indicative of the changes outlined above: Co-operative Home Care Associates, based in the Bronx, has over 2,000 healthcare aides as member-owners, the majority being women of color. Their model has expanded to include a spinoff in Philadelphia. They were overtaken as the largest U.S. worker co-operative in 2021, when a cab-driver-owned platform co-operative competitor to Uber, The Drivers Co-operative, formed in New York. The Drivers Co-operative's leadership team, as of 2023, is entirely people of color (Abello 2023).

Worker co-operative developers and organizers are quick to contrast these types of firms and organizing efforts with the ESOP approach. They point to the fact that most ESOP participants are White and male and that ESOP account balances are far higher for White men (Weissbourd et al. 2021).[11] They also point to ESOP cases like New Belgium Brewing, which was bought out by a foreign IOF in 2019. Stated one informant, "That doesn't or frankly shouldn't be able to happen with a worker co-operative, especially if you have statutes in place which specify indivisible reserves and limit the ability of the firm to be sold, and if you have large co-operative and social business lending institutions ... as is the case in some countries." This sentiment was echoed by several others across the country, who detailed the persistence of tension between ESOP and worker co-operative advocates. "This model [worker co-ops] is not about marking the equity value to market and reselling it to make you rich. . . . [Instead] you preserve the equity at low cost so that future generations can have good work, too. Eventually, someone has to pay for that share value of ESOP. . . . Yes it's the company [paying for it], but what happens when that becomes too much?"

Despite emergent efforts to co-organize across ESOP and worker co-op advocacy organizations for national enabling policy and funding mechanisms, this tension between them can sometimes become pronounced, as occurred with a worker co-operative proponent who became disenchanted with the model. Now an advocate for other employee ownership models like the ESOP and the employee ownership trust (an emerging employee ownership model

---

[11] It should be noted that such analyses do not attempt to control for confounding factors which might explain the disproportionate presence of White men among high-balance ESOP participants, such as industry, location, education, or other factors.

from the United Kingdom which has spread to the United States; Nuttall 2022), interviewees stated that this person had actively sought to discourage use of the worker co-operative in their local context, resulting in tensions among local technical assistance providers for broader "shared ownership" models in the economy. As one worker co-operative developer stated, "There are many employee ownership people like [name redacted] who initially got into this through worker co-operatives, and basically turned on us . . . basically treat us like [we] shouldn't be taken seriously . . . because they concluded the co-op model can't work at scale here. . . . My response is . . . this model works all around the world. . . . Let's fix all the policy and [other] barriers we face here with it, before passing judgment."

Similar instances of tension were detailed as occurring at the national scale, by participants in both university-based consortia and federal government advisory committees that include both ESOP and worker co-operative advocates. Advocates of ESOPs allegedly accuse worker cooperators of being too focused on "dirty hippies," according to one informant, and worker cooperators accuse ESOP advocates of "extracting wealth without voice or democratic control." This is not to say that the ESOP model does not have benefit or value. Rather, the point is that such internecine clashes demonstrate the challenges stemming from the lack of coordinated, comprehensive field organizing within the U.S. co-operative movement over time, which allowed for a worker co-operative field competitor like the ESOP to take root and scale beyond the co-operative field itself. While there are, as mentioned, efforts to co-organize both ESOPs and worker co-ops for mutual policy benefit, such efforts are not necessarily well-integrated as part of a co-operative-led, coherent social and solidarity economy field-level organizing strategy, as occurs in contexts like the French case, where worker co-operatives have longer had their own specific advocacy organization, in turn federated into broader organizational structures encompassing the broader social economy.

American Cooperation: An Incomplete Field

To state that American co-operatives today remain constrained by incomplete and partial field organizing at national scale is hardly controversial, given the comparative lack of interfirm coordination and shortage of appropriate laws and policy to affirm the field's bounds, logic, and rules. The NCBA website today openly acknowledges "the challenge of [an] inconsistent legal framework for co-operative development in the U.S. . . . [B]oth incorporation legislation and enabling legislation are needed to create a legal environment conducive to co-operative growth" (NCBA, n.d.).

Why and how did this state of affairs come to develop and persist in the United States? Since the 19th-century demise of the Knights of Labor, actors associated with various countercultural and reform movements have attempted to organize to redress these structural field challenges. But they have never been able to comprehensively join their efforts in search of a broader, common purpose, as occurred in the comparative cases. Field theory helps us explain why. Even where partial field-building efforts in the United States were successful in the 20th century, they continued to be fragmented and limited by the force of competing ownership systems—by the Jim Crow successor arrangements to the race-based ownership system of slavery, and by the liberal, IOF-centric variety of capitalism—which had constrained co-operative field development and organization from the very start.

Today American co-operative actors are not only attempting to be far more comprehensive and strategic in their efforts to organize new co-operatives and amend policy to enable lasting field-level gains; they are also still seeking to address these underlying challenges. As noted above, there have been increased efforts to address, develop, and promote Black-led and multiracial worker and multi-stakeholder co-operatives, including in the model's Achilles's heel region, the South (Spicer 2020). But challenges on this front remain. As one worker co-operative organizer responded when asked about major stumbling blocks for their efforts, "It's one thing to co-own a business with a Black person if you are a consumer.... Even if it's a store, how often will you be interacting with that person? It's another thing entirely to talk about co-owning your place of work with a Black person.... This is where White supremacy and White discomfort with Black people will be the last to go.... This is where solidarity will be the hardest to achieve." Given this, the fact that worker co-operatives remain the most limited strain of American cooperation is no surprise. Meanwhile, American co-operatives more broadly still operate in a field environment marked by restrictions and limits upon their scale and scope of action, in a world where the economy and the rule-making power of the state remain dominated by the IOF firm and coordination model and by a racial economic divide. Lacking a major field rupture to dislodge IOFs' field incumbency and to redress slavery's ongoing socioeconomic legacies, U.S. co-operatives are likely to remain constrained in the scale of their gains.

8
Conclusions of a Chrononaut

> White man, hear me! History, as nearly no one seems to know, is not merely something to be read. And it does not refer merely, or even principally, to the past. On the contrary, the great force of history comes from the fact that we carry it within us, are unconsciously controlled by it in many ways, and history is literally present in all we do.... [T]o history... we owe our frames of reference, our identities, and our aspirations.
>
> —James Baldwin, *White Man's Guilt* (1965)

A number of years ago, I was introduced to a card game called Chrononauts (Figure 8.1). The multiplayer game, which comes in different versions and can also be played as solitaire, presents real historical timelines. Players variably travel through time and attempt to alter key linchpin or "ripple point" moments in these timelines so as to change the future. They can, for example, stop the *Titanic*'s sinking, prevent World War II, or fend off the assassination of a world leader. In so doing, they may markedly change the events which followed these "ripple point" moments.

The game thus teaches players how different historical moments collectively reflect those that have come before, calling to mind the words of James Baldwin, whose words opened this concluding chapter.[1] They also recall the well-worn proclamation of Marx's (1852, 15) *Eighteenth Brumaire of Louis Bonaparte*: "Men make their own history, but they do not make it just as they please; they do not make it under circumstances chosen by themselves, but under circumstances directly encountered, given and transmitted from the past. The tradition of all the dead generations weighs like a nightmare on the brain of the living."

Of course, many social scientists since Marx have wrestled more broadly with this issue of history-as-explanation. Weber (1905) famously did so to understand the rise of capitalism. But so, too, did Braudel (1949, 1982a, 1982b),

---

[1] Baldwin is quoted with permission from Ebony.

Figure 8.1 Cards from the classic version of Chrononauts, which enables players to reset historical timelines by changing critical moments or "ripple points," one of several ways to alter the past.

Stinchombe (1968), Moore (1966), Wallerstein (1974), Tilly (1975), Skocpol (1979), and Arrighi (1994). Their efforts all inform those of today's historical institutionalists and field theorists, whose frameworks have been at the explanatory center of this book. Their thinking collectively reminds us: we never start in a vacuum, but build, as opportunistic and entrepreneurial bricoleurs, from our surrounding environments as we seek to accomplish our goals. Cooperators in the United States and around the world are no exception: they have always started from an embedded historical context, working with the resources and constraints around them.

To this end, if the creators of Chrononauts decided to create a co-operative-themed version of their game, what historical insights might they glean from this book to help them? What went wrong in the American co-operative case? What events and conditions stand out as key to understanding the difference in outcomes for cooperators in different countries? Beyond the cases themselves, what generalizable conclusions can be drawn about the comparative potential of the two frameworks deployed in this book (HI and field theory) to ask and answer other comparative-historical social science questions? To what broader consequence? And last, beyond these academic concerns, what do the answers to these questions collectively imply for those interested in implementing and deploying models like the co-operative today?

Co-operatives as Exceptionally Un-American

On the first question: What went wrong in the American case? How did co-operatives become exceptionally un-American? As the preceding chapters showed, it is not as if co-operative enterprise lacked for interest or advocacy in the United States. Indeed, American history was marked by early and extensive experimentation with co-operative models. But outside of agriculture and, to a lesser extent, consumer credit, such efforts never produced lasting prevalence at substantial scale; even across the more "successful" fronts of American cooperation, their history has generally been marked by policy restrictions on their interfirm coordination, as well as on their scope and scale. This reflects the fact that advocates of the co-operative model were never able to effectively coordinate and organize into a complete and well-bounded field, hampering its ability to stand against formidable external competitors.

Indeed, two field competitors acted to undermine the American co-operative movement: one based on the IOF, which embodied the logic of economic liberalism, and another rooted in race-based chattel slavery and its successor systems, which embodied the logic of structural racism. The organized force of economic liberalism and racism damaged co-operative development into a field in two ways: both internally, within the co-operative field itself, and in its external relationship to competing fields. The forces of racism and liberalism repeatedly damaged the co-operative field's internal cohesion and organization, splintering its strength and undermining its generative substitute for profit maximization, the solidarity mechanism which is at the model's heart. These same two forces also directly bolstered, through the ecology of interfield competition, the economic resources and political effectiveness of external competitors; ingrained racism and liberalism only served to strengthen interest in the models most closely associated with them.

In contrast, the co-operative movement was unencumbered by these challenges in the success cases, where it was also aided by other tailwinds, such as particular geographic features and factor endowments/industry mix. Accordingly, in these other cases, national co-operative movements did not face the same degree of internal challenges or such well-developed external competitors. They were thus able to better activate and leverage co-operatives' solidarity mechanism to internally coordinate and organize to greater scale, channeling and framing national solidarities in ways which distinctly reflect the causal factors at work in each particular case. In so doing, they often benefited from the early, sustained, and effective leadership of coordinating meta-organizing apex bodies as well, to procure state sanction, legitimation, and support, which formally affirmed their logic and mode of operation in law and policy and enabled them to endure.

If one thinks like a Chrononaut and changes any one of the major conditioning factors identified as relevant in these various cases, the outcomes likely would have been quite different. What if the U.S. Congress, for example, had not merely outlawed the African slave trade in 1808 but had prohibited slavery itself well before the First Industrial Revolution in the United States was in full swing? I suspect a very different—and much stronger—American co-operative movement could have subsequently emerged. Conversely, had Metropolitan France legally allowed race-based slavery to continue through its own period of industrialization later in the 19th century, it is difficult to imagine a French socialism which so centrally featured the solidarity of worker co-operatives. It, too, might have been far more splintered by racial divides.[2] Had Finland's or New Zealand's geographic traits been somewhat different—if New Zealand, for example, lay just a few miles off the coast of Australia and was reachable by bridge, as Mark Twain quipped, or if Finland were not located next to Russia—far weaker and qualitatively different co-operative movements might have developed and persisted in these cases as well. This is not to suggest that history is mechanistically, physical, or environmentally determined (Diamond 1997), but rather that the factors interrogated in this book appear to have collectively played a causal role in explaining variations in the outcome of interest over time.

From Factors to Fields: The Value of a Field Theory Approach

Hopefully, if you have read this far, the evidence presented in the book has convinced you of the proposition restated above: certain factors have indeed causally shaped the comparative-historical trajectories of co-operative development at scale. In operationalizing and applying these causal factors to historical data, however, the book has attempted to accomplish a second

---

[2] This is not to say that France has no racial cleavages or that it lacks racism; rather, its institutional history with race, and specifically with slavery, are markedly different from the U.S. context in ways which shaped co-operatives.

task: to see how or if field theory might enable a more comprehensive explanation than HI with respect to how and why these factors shaped the outcome over time. After reviewing three such limits, I will summarize how field theory is more useful than HI in understanding the American and comparative cases, before considering broader academic implications beyond the co-operative case.

The limits of institutionalism. As introduced in Chapter 2, proponents of SAFs and field theory have suggested their framework offers a more comprehensive model of institutional development and change than HI. The comparative co-operative institutional development cases have affirmed three limits of HI vis-à-vis field theory: its more descriptive rather than explanatory orientation, its singular focus on the state, and its "negative case" problem, that is, its inability to address fields or institutions which fail to emerge at the national scale. These three limits can arguably be consolidated into two dimensions, pertaining to (a) description versus explanation in outcomes (with HI's limits related to politics and the state cast as a subordinate aspect of this dimension) and (b) emergence versus evolution of fields and institutions, as summarized in Table 8.1.

First, HI is more descriptive than explanatory in nature: it neither incorporates nor enables identification of the underlying forces which yield the institutional voids that challengers (like the co-operative) leverage to unseat incumbents. Nor does it help us understand how or why challengers are—or are not—variably able to leverage these voids. For example, HI does not enable explanation of why the Knights of Labor failed in their attempt to build a co-operative commonwealth in the United States as part of their broader labor organizing and political strategy, while the self-same Knights succeeded in New Zealand. It also does not enable explanation of why co-operatives in Finland were clearly, directly, and immediately propelled to economic prominence as part of a political revolution, while in France, revolution's effects were more evolutionary, playing out over the longue durée. It merely enables us to trace *how* these evolutions unfolded (e.g., through a process of policy layering).

Second, HI's focus on the state and politics means that it does not handle well or explain relevant exogenous causal forces outside of the state, that is, those extrastate forces beyond narrowly defined electoral or producer group politics as mediated through political parties and the bureaucratic apparatus of the state (Scoville and Fligstein 2020). For example, it does not explain how or why extrastate motivations—like those advanced by social movements, including the co-operative movement itself—might manifest in government policy or the business environment in ways which affect co-operatives.

Table 8.1 Comparing and Evaluating the Utility of Historical Institutionalism and Field Theory to Co-operative Development

	Emergence	Evolution
Describe	HI does not well handle U.S. case of comparative failure to emerge as a coherent national field, nor does it provide language for understanding the role of framing, the development of (legal) bounds, and the development of field champions in the success or failure cases. SAF accomplishes both.	HI and SAF both well describe pathways of evolution in success cases, but HI does not accommodate the repeated scale-shift dynamics in the evolution of the U.S. case. SAF does.
Explain	HI does not explain how or why voids were variably leveraged for institutional construction. SAF, with its grammar for field architecture and overlap, enables identification of incumbents'/competitors' relational position and bases for overlap and occupation of these voids.	HI treats causes of field ruptures/critical junctures as exogenous, whereas field theory internalizes these causes, enabling explanation of their effect on the framing, resources, and position of neighboring fields.

Plainly stated, HI does not allow us to internalize these underlying, extrastate motivations for field-building actions into its model of change, or to identify and understand the motives of institutional actors who engage in such actions to variably undermine or enable co-operatives. In the U.S. case, such motivations include racial animus, as shown in Chapters 6 and 7, which was initially activated against the co-operative movement through the frame of "wage slavery." Such factors are treated as exogenous or beyond scope in HI. This limitation can, as suggested above, be treated as a subdimension of the descriptive versus explanatory problem: HI does not well handle extrastate forces as an explanation for stability or change. Nonetheless, because HI was born of political science and has such an intensive focus on political institutions, I have separated this out as a distinct second limitation. It is constrained by its generating discipline, seemingly by design.

In a third limitation, HI has generally been deployed to consider variation in nationally scaled success cases and does not seem particularly well equipped to handle "negative cases" (Ragin 1987).[3] By this I mean that HI

---

[3] Though scholars have recently begun applying HI to understand urban-scaled institutions (Sorensen 2015, 2018), this work suffers from the same shortcoming: it does not address negative cases at the urban scale. It also does not address how institutions shift across scales in their formation and evolution. Relatedly, regional economic scholars have attempted to apply HI's concepts to understand regional economic variation (e.g., Benner 2021, and others deploying "evolutionary economic geography"), but this work has done little to address the limitations of HI reviewed here.

analyses typically cover only cases where a certain degree of national coherence in institutional formation, emergence, and development has occurred, that is, positive or "success" cases. It does not offer a way to understand cases of incomplete national formation or of outright national failure, that is, negative or counterfactual cases. This means that while HI enables partial explanations of how co-operative movements in the comparative success cases evolved, it does not handle the U.S. case well, where the co-operative framework never fully formed at national scale (e.g., a case of incomplete national formation), with segments of the U.S. co-operative movement long "trapped" at the subnational scale.

Indeed, these scalar dynamics explain why worker co-operatives, for example, have long been present as an urban policy and planning issue in the United States, in "locally" scaled organizing and policy advocacy efforts (Spicer 2020; Sutton 2019).[4] Having failed to create a nationally scaled field framework over long crisis-induced waves (i.e., during the interregnum periods of institutional/field evolution which occur between crises which stoke renewed interest in the model), American worker co-operative actors have repeatedly found themselves back at "square one" when the field environment shifts again and interest in the model declines, as occurred in the early 1980s (see Chapter 7). Having failed to finish creating a nationally scaled field in the years following a crisis-induced uptick in interest, they revert to organizing at the local scale again, in a form of what social movement scholars might call a downward "scale shift." They then must build again, locally, from pockets of strength, from the remnants of the field elements constructed in the prior cycle, until they can leverage the next opportunity to shift upward in scale again, to try anew to build a national field framework. HI lacks a developed grammar to account for and explain these scale-shifting dynamics of the "negative case."

How field theory better explains the U.S. and comparative cases. In contrast, field theory's taxonomy of field elements, which identifies cultural frames, logics, specific social practices, and practice/field bounds (all of which HI leaves unarticulated, apparently as part of its amorphously delineated "shared script"), coupled with field theory's syntax conceptualizing how these elements fit together, emerge, and evolve through the overlapping and nested structure of fields and their environments, allows for isolation and identification of

---

[4] This also helps explain why federalism per se fades as a compelling cause in explaining American co-operatives' rarity: skilled social actors across a host of fronts—from unions to civil rights in the United States—have repeatedly successfully navigated the federal environment to move from local to national organizing efforts via a movement-like process of scale shift and created a coherent national field of action, with nationally codified rules and bounds.

the underlying problem for American cooperators. But beyond the American case, it also allows us to explain the comparative success cases. That is because field theory enables us to induce a generalizable model of how co-operatives successfully achieve and sustain scale.

In the United States, the co-operative model's struggles have primarily stemmed from the combined historical effects of economic liberalism and systemic racism. These two forces directly manifested through the comparatively advanced development of third-party investor ownership and chattel slavery ownership as incumbent economic systems at the time of the co-operative's initial development. These two factors (see Table 8.2 for a "logic table"-style summary review of the role of major factors across cases), best explain the U.S. outcome in comparison. Field theory, however, allows us to more fully understand *how and why* these two factors manifested, and why they undermined cooperation at scale. To restate the book's findings a final time in the language of field theory: in the United States, the organizational models of ownership which most directly embodied the field logics of economic liberalism and racism—the IOF/joint stock corporation and the chattel slavery economic system of ownership, respectively—were far more developed in the United States at the time of industrialization and the rise of the co-operative model than were comparable field incumbents in the other case countries.

In the emergent world of privately owned, industrial-scaled enterprise in the broader field of "the economy," which is one of three first-order fields in the world today containing all others (Spicer, Kay, and Ganz 2019; Fligstein and McAdam 2012), these incumbent ownership models served as fierce and formidable field competitors to the co-operative ownership model in the U.S. context. With the initial failure of the co-operative model in its first round of comprehensive organizing, the IOF continued to consolidate its field incumbency in the United States. In the process, it also established its complementary set of institutional arrangements, so well described by the comparative capitalist LME model today, as the dominant interfirm coordination approach in the American economy.

The relative positional location of the field further explains how and why efforts to expand civil society's reach into the economy through the construction of the co-operative as a field (to embed markets into society, in Polanyian language) were less successful in the United States than elsewhere across the rich democracies. With its syntax and grammar for parsing interfield relations, field theory allows us to identify sources of conflict and overlap between fields, acting as a form of social positioning system (like GIS does for maps, as it were). This feature of field theory is of great value in explaining

Table 8.2 Factors Shaping Development of the Co-operative Field (and Its Field Environment), by Case

Factor	Case				Cross-Case Evidence by Factor: Summary
	Finland	France	New Zealand	United States	
Social Homogeneity	+	+	Unclear/Limited Evidence	-	Strong
	Co-operative field emerges and scales whole cloth as part of national political and economic independence strategy, rooted in part in national identity as a basis for solidarity, which also supports field/institutional layering over the longue durée.	National identity centers workers' solidarity, shaped by a concept of liberty, central in various national revolutions, directly tied to repeated experiments with co-operative field-building during formative moments of crisis. Co-operatives and IOFs alike slowly evolve, consistent with field and institutional evolutionary processes, in the long interregna.	Limited evidence: co-operatives appeal as a part of national identity and the "No. 8 wire" mentality, as a sensible way to keep wealth rooted domestically, thereby perhaps providing an impetus for continued evolution of the field and state support, but this seems to largely reflect/appear rooted in geographical dynamics related to size and remoteness.	Interaction between race-based slavery and wage slavery fragments and undermines social solidarity to support the field/institutional emergence and evolution of the co-operative, while directly supporting its well-entrenched field competitors. Lack of multiracial solidarity directly contributes to decline of early comprehensive organizational champion and delay of emergence of a subsequent one.	Social solidarity based on a common shared identity bond clearly supports the field framing and movement mechanisms that motivate the emergence of cooperation at scale, and provide a basis for civil society and state support for its continued evolution to remain economically relevant; the field implications of cleavages such as race are also significant in explaining the negative outcome in the U.S. case.

	+	+	+	-	-	Strong
Economic Liberalism						
Arrangements: Liberal Market Economy model	Co-operative models congruent with the Finns' "middle way," balancing logic of Finnish economic policy and coordinated market economy arrangements, which evolve and emerge together as both an offensive and a defensive strategy in relation to neighbors' adoption of state enterprise and IOF-centric models.	Co-operative models congruent with French state-led dirigisme and coordinated market economy arrangements, which evolve and emerge together slowly in the long shadow of the French Revolution, which abolished so many corporate forms.	Co-operative coordination congruent with state-led economic development model that prevailed from initial IOF failures through its revival in the 1980s, when it clashes with nascent LME dynamics, but a backlash enabled co-operatives to reorganize and recover.	Co-operative model does not achieve widespread scale or enabling framework in advance of the IOF. Antitrust legislation, which constrains co-operative-style interfirm coordination for IOFs, emerges earlier here and is used as a basis to sue and undermine the development of co-operatives through the early and mid-20th century.		In all four cases, the timing and relational development of the IOF and its native institutional arrangements play a significant role in shaping the field environment for co-operatives. In environments where the IOF faces obstacles in achieving early, sustained incumbency, cooperators had better opportunity to develop as a field and advocate for appropriate policy-enabling frameworks.
Form: IOF	Finland's economy and IOFs develop fairly late, constrained by colonization dynamics. IOF does not have first-mover field incumbency advantage over the co-operative.	French IOF emerges comparatively later than in U.S, UK, constrained by the long-lasting revolutionary abolishment of corporations.		IOF is the first mover, but fails due to distance, loses its initially incumbency, creates field opening for state and co-operative enterprise.	IOF model dominates early due to earlier industrialization and development of American concept of liberty; profit logic of IOF enables rapid spread of enabling framework across states without need for a field champion.	

(*continued*)

Table 8.2 Continued

Factor	Case Finland	France	New Zealand	United States	Cross-Case Evidence by Factor: Summary
Economic Homogeneity/ Industry Mix	+	+	+	Mixed	Substantial
	Economic development and industrialization in key industries where factor endowments readily lend themselves to the co-operative model, e.g., forestry, agriculture. Model widely used at sustained scale in expected industries: banking, insurance, agriculture, wholesale/retail.	Co-operatives sustain "success" across many highly homogeneous industries like agriculture, banking, insurance, wholesaling (+). But economy came to be comparatively dominated by more advanced, heterogeneous industries (−).	Economic development/ industrialization in key industries where factor endowments readily lend themselves to the co-operative model; model widely used at sustained scale in expected industries: banking, insurance, agriculture, wholesale/retail.	Co-operatives sustain "success" in some highly homogeneous industries like agriculture, but fail/decline long term at scale via field conversion/ displacement in others for which there is no clear industry-specific explanation (e.g., insurance, finance); economy comparatively dominated by more advanced, heterogeneous industries.	Appears across all four cases in varying degrees of strength; difficult to isolate as driving the outcome in any single case; helps provide a limited basis for field development, but other factors appear to play a more central role in explaining outcomes.

	+	Unclear/Limited Evidence	+	Mixed	Substantial
Geography	Remoteness and positioning at border of West and Eastern Bloc contributes to appeal of co-operative model as a geopolitical management strategy, forms repeated basis to justify field/institutional layering to mitigate displacement.	Little evidence that geographical dynamics play a significant role in shaping the field or its environment. Co-operative model widely used in both rural and urban development alike, does not appear as a significant national geopolitical strategy.	Remoteness and size contribute to failure of IOF; leaving an underpopulated field environment and creating an opening for the shift to state and co-operative economic models. Geography a repeated basis used to justify state enabling action on co-operatives' behalf, yielding field/institutional layering.	Co-operatives, especially electrical, agricultural, credit, "succeed" in remote/rural areas but appear less successful in highly urbanized areas; geography does not well explain why these forms are often statutorily limited from expanding across geographies. The Southern question of slavery and Jim Crow undermined cooperation regionally and nationally, but much of this manifests as an issue through social homogeneity.	Appears as a significant factor in three of four cases, and as a clear, direct factor to sustaining success outcome in two cases.

Table guide: + = clear positive factor in co-operative field development; − = clearly negative factor, undermined co-operative field development; mixed = mixed/weak evidence; unclear/limited evidence = does not appear as a significant factor in the case co-operative development in the United States. Co-operatives are, as introduced in Chapter 2, a hybrid field, one which blends social and commercial logics, and is therefore located at the overlap of civil society and the economy. Field-building efforts in the United States were positionally blocked in the field environment by powerful, *positionally adjacent* incumbents in the economy: the IOF and the slavery system (which, beyond being an economic institution, was directly and explicitly rooted in distinct civil society institutions and practices). Both were explicitly targeted by the co-operative movement through its field framing, which sought to fight the logic of "wage slavery." This choice of frame was not happenstance, as reviewed in Chapter 6, but again reflected the co-operative's relative and adjacent field position next to both the slavery system and the emergent wage system of IOFs. (Recall that most Americans were effectively self-employed at this time, and not wage workers, as reviewed in Chapter 2.)

Each of these two competitors presented field-level organizing problems for the co-operative. The co-operative model's interfirm coordination mechanism quickly ran afoul of the emerging logic of an IOF-based system, with its atomistic approach to interfirm coordination, producing an institutional incongruency between the co-operative and the emergent institutional arrangements of an IOF-dominated field environment, as manifest through the comparatively earlier and stronger antitrust challenges the co-operative faced in the United States. Meanwhile, the slavery-based ownership system and its successor, Jim Crow, not only occupied and blocked the potential field space for co-operative actors to claim and use as a base to form; they also directly deprived it of adherents. The racial animus advanced through these racialized economic systems also undermined the effectiveness of one of the key civil society–based solidarity mechanisms co-operatives deploy to scale. In so doing, the resources available for pro-co-operative actors to leverage and organize were reduced and fragmented, with especially detrimental effects in the American South but which reverberated nationally, leaving the co-operative movement unable to secure a long-term position in the national political agenda.

Furthermore, co-operative field development was particularly affected by how its efforts ran headlong into the *interaction* of both liberalism and race, in what is a striking early example of the violent power of American racial capitalism. Specifically, the co-operative movement's effort to fight a two-front war—or two-field war, as it were—against both the IOF and slavery was met with particularly strong resistance, which it ultimately could not overcome. This was not necessarily a tactical mistake but an inescapable reality given its relative field position. As co-operative models are generally deployed by workers to meet their needs, the constraint on participation of an entire class of workers—Black people who were enslaved—was an undeniable problem that American cooperators needed to solve, as reviewed in Chapter 6. Early co-operative field-building champions representing the emerging labor movement (the communitarian movement and the Knights of Labor) had accordingly selected a central rhetorical field-framing device ("abolishing the wage slavery" of the IOF) and a field-building strategy (marching into the unsettled field environment of the post-Reconstruction South to reorganize its former plantations) to address this problem but which also directly elicited *simultaneous* assaults from both of these adjacent field incumbents. Later, as we saw in Chapter 7, partial successes came, but via isolated and fragmented field-building efforts, which attempted to avoid further activating existing racial animus and/or avoid conflicts with the IOF, and without the backing of a major political party. Sometimes, however, interfield conflict was inescapable as a particularly virulent strain of American racial capitalism took hold, one which lacked a well-developed co-operative field to animate a lost strain of liberty, as reviewed in Chapter 6, and which could act as a Galbraithian "countervailing force" to attenuate and soften its deleterious effects.

Regardless, as compared with the success cases, American co-operative field-building efforts were never as well coordinated into a coherent whole, in direct response to how these conditioning factors manifested through interfield dynamics. These incumbent systems thus both occupied and defended field spaces in the American economy which co-operatives in the other cases were able to claim because they faced less well-entrenched or -developed competitors. In the comparative cases, the opportunities to claim field openings or voids were not only more readily available due to the absence of such well-entrenched incumbents, but co-operative actors were also able to successfully leverage other pro-co-operative factors as a base of national solidarity (e.g., remoteness in the Finnish and New Zealand case; national identity rooted in a definition of liberty consonant with the co-operative model in France) to support development at scale. Accordingly, the success cases reveal how different factors can be leveraged by skilled social actors to overcome obstacles in the field environment to create and sustain development over time. The bases for success vary from case to case, resulting in differences in their historical trajectories. But a common thread ran across them: the ability to animate and activate solidarity to cooperate, both within and across enterprises, and to organize to achieve accommodative policy as needed to secure their comparative legitimacy.

The degree to which these causal factors appear in the historical record varies in each case, of course. In Finland, supportive traits across all four causal dimensions systematically examined (see Table 8.2) aided and abetted the process of field development. Unsurprisingly, among all the rich democracies, co-operative prevalence at scale is greatest there today. As we move to cases with a mix of supportive and inhibiting characteristics across the four causal dimensions (France and New Zealand), the prevalence of co-operatives at scale relatively declines. In these cases, though not all the posited factors necessarily or clearly manifest as critical to co-operative field development over time, those that do appear as germane do so in a manner consistent with the theory advanced here. In the U.S. case, marked by inhibiting characteristics across all four dimensions, the historical evidence on the negative role played by two of these factors—race and liberalism—is particularly strong, and is again consistent with the theory advanced. Co-operatives could not animate a multiracial solidarity to compete against the IOF or its preferred coordination model, which came to dominate the country.

It is possible, of course, that in analyzing just four cases, there are other paths to success which display further meaningful variation. Denmark, as one longtime international co-operative leader and former ICA executive observed upon reading draft sections of this book, long lacked formal or robust co-operative-specific laws, and yet for many decades was host to a highly successful co-operative movement (Lampe and Sharp 2019). And yet Danish co-operatives are now seeking to enact such laws in the face of significant decline, as noted by other informants, including in nearby Finland, which some argued could serve as a legislative model for the Danes. Such other paths, as the Danish example suggests, may ultimately serve only to reinforce the general dynamics we can glean from the strategically selected cases of this book.

Field theory would thus appear to help us explain not only the U.S. case but the comparative ones as well, in so doing enabling generalizable insights into how co-operative enterprise movements do or do not become entrenched to achieve scale in different contexts vis-à-vis these competing ownership approaches. That is, it enables us to construct a generalizable theory of co-operation at scale to inform and support co-operatives' development. Co-operatives, animated by the social and economic solidarity of bonds between co-operative members, as well as bonds across co-operatives generated and sustained by the co-operative movement itself, emanate in part from the first-order field of civil society. As noted earlier, this is one of three such primary fields in the field environment, along with economy/market and the state, which each contain all other nested subfields (Fligstein and McAdam 2012; Spicer, Kay, and Ganz 2019). Deploying civil-society-based movement and/or movement-like processes, skilled social actors build a co-operative field by laying claim to a field opening/void located at the intersection of economy and civil society. They do so by leveraging solidarity, which can be rooted in different underlying types of bonds which may variably reflect macro-level forces, not only as a basis for cooperation within individually co-owned enterprises but to support development across them as well. By creating national meta-organizational apex bodies to coordinate within and across co-operatives, they can also act to make political demands legible to parties, coalitions, and directly to the government itself to achieve enabling legislative support which affirms their logic and practices, including their mode of coordination, thereby achieving formal state legitimation to enable maintenance of their field bounds long term. When the proximate field environment experiences shocks and shifts, co-operative leaders can then act to shore up and reaffirm their claims to resources and legitimacy by deploying these processes anew. Short-term success may be achieved without necessarily following every step of this script or playbook, but the more deviations there are from this model, the less likely the effort is to achieve and maintain success.

HI enables us to describe some of these processes, such as organizing to achieve incremental policy change, and some these elements, such as institutional voids. But it lacks the relational grammar to handle many of the dynamics and moving parts in this theory. The co-operative case thus affirms that field theory can handle the parts of the story that HI does, while going beyond it to explain more of that story, to help us understand how and why macro-level causal factors manifest at the meso scale in conditioning the construction and development of institutions and fields. This suggests that, as field theorists have suggested, HI can be understood as a partial application of field theory.

Implications beyond the co-operative case. Applying field theory to more fully tell the story of comparative co-operative development has implications which go far beyond the cases themselves.

First, for social scientists interested in comparative explanations of institutional variation in the economy, the case generates broader lessons about the value of field theory vis-à-vis other existing frameworks. A field theory lens allows us to move beyond static and mechanistic typologies, like those of political scientists' various comparative capitalism frameworks, in ways historical institutionalism alone cannot. As I reviewed in Chapter 2 and in other work (Spicer 2022), such comparative capitalist frameworks are directly relevant to our understanding of cooperation at scale. But their static ideal types (e.g., the LME), as mere snapshots of institutional arrangements at a moment in time, cannot explain how these arrangements evolved, which is where the work of historical institutionalists comes into play. And yet historical institutionalism merely gives us a descriptive vocabulary to think about how specific institutions changed internally over time once established. It does not enable us to conceptualize how different institutions fit together as a coherent whole, nor does it enable us to understand the external impetus for not just their evolution but also their origins, nor does it enable us to understand cases of comparative failure. Field theory, as outlined in Chapter 2 and as demonstrated across the various cases, does all these things.

Field theory *also* enables us to both reconcile and go beyond these other existing institutionalist approaches by articulating a more comprehensive theory of comparative institutional change. How? As applied to the co-operative case, it allows us to incorporate insights on *both* the ideal-type arrangements described by various comparative capitalism archetypes *and* the historical institutionalist evolutionary pathways which unfolded across the countries and which variably embody comparative capitalist archetypes today. It also allows us to understand how, when, and why these arrangements emerged to begin with, and subsequently evolved, as shown across the various cases.

In the case of the co-operative, field theory does this by considering how different ownership forms give life to competing challenger and incumbent fields. It enables us to cast both the broader institutional arrangements and evolutionary pathways across which they unfold as manifestations of the degree to which one of these ownership-oriented fields, the IOF, came to dominate all others. Co-operatives emerged in relation to other forms of ownership, including not only other alternative enterprise forms but the race-based slavery ownership system, the modern IOF, and state-owned enterprise, among others. While IOFs dominate co-operatives most everywhere, certain contexts were nonetheless more favorable for co-operatives and the solidarity-based mechanisms they deploy, while other settings were more congruent with the IOF.

In enabling us to tell this story, a field theory treatment of the co-operative case reveals the importance of an underconsidered variable—firm-type mix—in explaining the very types of institutional variations that both comparative capitalisms and historical institutionalism arose to explain. In centering this new variable, broader analytical possibilities are opened. This is not a particularly new idea; Schneiberg (2010) has referred to the existence of "diverse organizational ecologies of firms" in the economy, as of course have other scholars on alternative, social, and hybrid enterprise, as reviewed in Chapter 2. But what field theory does is allow us to take these ideas and operationalize them into a holistic model of the economic world. Inasmuch as different firm types are "organizational archetypes" (Greenwood and Hinings 1988, 1993) embodying different logics, with differential practices, frames, actors, and modes of coordination and policy needs, they may be said to exist as different fields, which persist in parallel and in relation to one another. We might begin to model economic variation in the world as reflecting differences in the ecological competition and mix of these firm types over time in different contexts, with incumbent firm types likely playing an outsized role in shaping the field environment for all other firm types operating in their shadow. This might lead us to conceive of three possible ideal types of economies which might plausibly exist today, after centuries of modern economic institutional development and change: one led by state ownership and control, one led by arm's-length markets through the IOF, and one in which ownership forms embedded in civil society, which might include not only co-operatives and related alternatives but also family- and kinship-based enterprises playing a leading role.

The frank reality is that most developed countries today are dominated by the IOF ideal-type firm. Even the United Kingdom, which begat the co-operative movement, ultimately developed into an IOF-dominated economy, eventually becoming an LME. But there is a difference between dominance and totality, between pure ideal types and mixtures. Just as we mix three primary colors to create all other hues, so too are distinct, ideal-type ownership forms (and their generated fields of action) mixed to form the basis of modern economies. These mixes, even if ultimately dominated by one model (the IOF), emerged through a contested process, as this book has shown, between incumbents and challengers, such as co-operatives. The LME label might thus merely be a shorthand for those countries now seemingly most dominated by the IOF. In reality, it may merely describe those countries where IOFs were able, in key critical moments and across sustained and specific interregnum evolutions, to assert dominance in shaping overarching policy and business environments.

Theorizing in this way helps us understand other structural economic phenomena beyond co-operatives. The early 20th-century rise of socialist states, for example, might be cast as a period in which the state-ownership model came to dominate in certain countries, and to more broadly challenge the IOF model. The demise of the Soviet Union and Eastern Bloc might be conceived of as a field rupture and critical juncture which closed that era, leaving voids and creating ripple effects in the field environment, with implications for IOFs and co-operatives, as the cases analyzed variably show. Operating with such a lens, as suggested above, might also help us reinterpret the historical development of capitalism (e.g., Braudel 1949, 1982a, 1982b), to center around the ecological competition between the IOF and other forms, which were each variably constrained and advanced by the presence or absence of structural traits in certain places and times. Such an approach might offer a considerable improvement over other efforts to extend the Varieties of Capitalism approach to address more contexts (i.e., those beyond the high-income democracies) and times, which remain fundamentally limited by their focus on differences in institutional arrangements rather than on understanding the underlying causes of such differences, which may reflect the formation and mix of different ownership models.

In a second broader implication, as part of this recentering, field theory can accommodate systematic incorporation of important "external" factors, like geography and race, in explaining the broader institutional structure of the economy. Obviously, extensive multidisciplinary literature chronicles the roles of race and geography in shaping the economy; as noted earlier, scholars of racial capitalism have made formidable contributions to the former, while economic geographers and geographical economists have advanced our understanding of the latter. But these literatures to date have not been well incorporated into institutionalist and field-based explanatory frameworks of the economy. They often result in treatments which are either merely descriptive or solely analyze these factors in isolation; they rarely consider these factors alongside other causal variables to holistically examine institutional economic stasis and change. Conversely, neither race nor geographic factors (like size and distance to either markets or states) have been well considered by either field theorists or institutionalists. But this book has shown that it is possible to incorporate factors such as geography and race to explain the comparative institutional development of economies, using structural, social science–based explanatory frameworks like field theory to do so. It is also impossible to understand the outcomes in any of the cases examined in this book without incorporating considerations of these two factors, as exemplified by the experiment of thinking like a Chrononaut to consider how an altered history of race and slavery in the United States and France might have affected co-operative development.

From Theory to Practice: Conclusions for the American Co-operative Movement

I have not written this book solely to advance a generalizable, social science–based understanding of co-operative development at scale, or to improve our ability to more generally analyze the emergence of economic fields and institutions.

I had a third goal: to produce something of use to co-operative field-builders themselves, particularly those operating in the American context, which is my own country of origin and was the central case in this book. In a way, I view these field-builders as real-life co-operative Chrononauts, for as they play a very real "game," they are bound by the past in various ways and must surely wonder how the weight of history limits and shapes their choices. For this audience, the historical cases collectively suggest it is difficult to achieve lasting cooperation at scale in a hostile external environment, that is, one full of well-entrenched competitors and lacking a widespread basis for internal solidarity between cooperators. Under such conditions, the ability to achieve co-operative agreements among members, to attract resources and more members from competing models, and to convince policymakers of the model's worthiness will be reduced.

To this end, American cooperators who read earlier drafts of the material for this book told me it left them depressed and discouraged. It seemed, in my estimation, to leave them feeling like Mr. Stevens, the character in Nobel laureate Kazuo Ishiguro's (1989, 179) novel *The Remains of the Day*:

> But what is the sense in forever speculating what might have happened had such and such a moment turned out differently? . . . [W]hile it is all very well to talk of "turning points," one can surely only recognize such moments in retrospect. Naturally, when one looks back to such instances today, they may indeed take the appearance of being crucial, precious moments . . . but of course, at the time, this was not the impression one had. Rather, it was as though one had available a never-ending number of days, months, years in which to sort out the vagaries . . . an infinite number of further opportunities in which to remedy the effect of this or that misunderstanding. There was surely nothing to indicate at the time that such evidently small incidents would render whole dreams forever irredeemable.

Mr. Stevens articulated how a dream he once held slowly slipped away and became an impossibility. As one cooperator put it to me, it sometimes feels as if the dream of a more co-operative America is permanently lost and unachievable. Why? Even if such a vision was not doomed from the start, due to the legacy of slavery and the particular notion of American liberalism which relationally developed with it, the subsequent actions which reinforced these legacies have rendered the dream unachievable. I do not, however, necessarily agree such pessimism is warranted based on the cases. French cooperators, for example, overcame serious obstacles to co-operative development, achieving slow and steady gains which took not just decades but centuries. In New Zealand, a dramatic field rupture which might have destroyed co-operatives was instead leveraged for reinvention.

But there is another key difference between the real situation of American cooperators and a novel like *The Remains of the Day* in which the cumulative impact of lost opportunities over a single lifetime eventually cannot be overcome by a character in order to pursue a different path. The difference is that one character, or one skilled social actor, gets only one lifetime, which is finite and ends in their death. Institutions and fields, however, offer the potential of immortality. The initial creators of the stable co-operative model in the United Kingdom, for example, have been dead for well over a century. And yet their legacy lives on, reclaimed, reshaped, repurposed, through those who have come since. Just as I doubt they could have dreamed of the path that not just co-operatives but world history itself subsequently took, so, too, we cannot realistically imagine future fields from the vantage point of today. We do not know what ruptures or junctures lie in wait or what new possibilities might emerge.

What we do know is that the current, IOF-led model of the world is not working for many people, and has not been working for some time and may be exhausting itself, leading many today to ask the age-old question anew: How might capitalism end? In considering this question, we already know that the state ownership–dominated and IOF-dominated ideal-type economies have been tried in practice in different countries. But the civil society–dominated model, at least as implemented through modern institutional forms like the co-operative, does not, in fact, appear to have been attempted with widespread scope and scale in any nation. And thus, to return to Naomi Klein's quote from the beginning of this book, which argued the co-operative model has never been tried: she has a point. Her statement contains a degree of truth. While the co-operative model has been extensively tried, there has never been a modern national economy outright entirely dominated by it or its allied forms, at scale. This is, perhaps, why so many students of cooperation flock to Mondragon in Spain's Basque Country. In Mondragon's eponymous hometown and host region, we start to get a glimpse of what a co-operative world could look like.

So, what can the real-life co-operative entrepreneurs take from this book to inform a strategy on how to create such a world? As the structure of fields shift as new circumstances unfold, opportunities to change the world are renewed. Yes, new organizational archetypes, with new skilled social actors and field champions, are constantly emerging. But existing models, like the co-operative, can be reinvigorated or reimagined as well. The key is that skilled social actors must creatively redevelop frames, practices, and coordinating actions to fit their contextual circumstances and meet the moment. In fact, cooperators have consistently done just that, through incubating and innovating new models and practices as warranted in new circumstances, as today's multi-stakeholder and platform co-operative models attest. Not all such experiments will succeed, but in engaging in such organizational and field-building trials, a new core may be constructed from the margins. The forces which have limited the ability of U.S. co-operative developers to succeed are daunting, to be sure, but they are always contingent, through carefully timed and coordinated action, both in critical moments in which worlds are rearranged and also via sustained efforts to achieve incremental changes, or what Gorz (1975) called "non-reformist reforms." As this book has shown, such small evolutionary reforms, undertaken as part of a Gramscian war of position, can collectively add up to significant differences in outcomes for cooperators over time. Another economy is still possible.

Thus, for American cooperators today, who operate in a context of both record socioeconomic inequality and a reckoning with systematic racism, the question becomes: How can co-operatives change to meet the moment and leverage the opportunities being generated in the current field environment? As noted in Chapter 7, for much of its history, and despite the best efforts of the multiracial Knights of Labor, the American co-operative movement was White-dominated and White-led. Today that is slowly changing. The USFWC is led by an executive director who is Black and also sits on the board of NCBA-CLUSA, where he was recently named board president. A majority of the senior executive team at Inclusiv, the organizing body for CDCUs, is Black. Project Equity, a nonprofit organization which helps traditional businesses convert to worker ownership, including worker co-operatives, is now Black-led. The Bronx Co-operative Development Initiative and Boston's Ujima Fund are also Black-led efforts, as are efforts like Co-operation Jackson in the state of Mississippi and Green Worker Co-operative Academy in the Bronx (Freilla 2022). These and other entities have incubated a number of Black-led co-operatives (Freilla 2022). The current strategic plan of the Co-operative Fund of the Northeast explicitly prioritizes racial justice, and the National Conference on the Black Co-operative Agenda, as noted in Chapter 7, seeks to further develop Black co-operative leadership in the United States, even as interest in cross-border Black alliances and the global Black social economy rises (Hossein 2013; Hossein, Wright Austin, and Edmonds 2023).

Many co-operative entrepreneurs and organizers are thus seeking to actively frame, message, and organize around co-operative development and policy change in a way which directly speaks to the underlying structural problems as identified and traced in this book—the historically divisive role of race and racism and its links to America's individualist, liberal economic institutions—that have long limited American co-operatives' success. But this is not to imply that the American co-operative movement more broadly has succeeded in transforming itself into a Black- and people-of-color-led movement. The largest U.S. co-operatives today are agricultural or producer-oriented in nature and are almost entirely White-led. NCBA-CLUSA remains a White-led organization, with, as of 2022, a White supermajority board and chief executive. Even on the worker co-operative front there is more work to be done. As I finished writing this book, a prominent Black American co-operative practitioner-scholar cited throughout this work was sued by a White man active among worker co-operatives; the case featured race-related allegations. Though ultimately settled—and I donated to a fundraising campaign to defray legal costs for the scholar—the case demonstrates these issues remain at the fore.

Given the history told in this book, it may very well be that until the entire American co-operative movement centers Black voices and remedies its past wrongs against Black Americans, perhaps through policies such as formal financial reparations from White-led co-operatives, it may fail to achieve its broader goals. Academics and scholars who study co-operatives must play a part too; that is why I am donating any royalties, meager though they might be, from this book to the Federation of Southern Co-operatives. But more broadly, the American co-operative movement's success may require that it play an even greater role in the much larger fight against racism. We know that co-operative enterprises will struggle to generate and sustain solidarity in the face of social cleavages between members. Yes, other factors matter to success, too, as this book has shown, but given the mix of factors which prevail in the U.S. context, it is difficult to imagine broader American co-operative success if systemic racism persists. And while racism, as this book has shown, has indubitably permeated the American co-operative movement since its inception, racism itself emanates from *beyond* the co-operative movement. This means that actions such as co-operative reparations, the centering of Black voices in co-operative leadership positions, or funding and developing Black-led co-operatives—these efforts alone will not be enough.

To realize a greater potential, the co-operative movement may need to become, to borrow from Ibram Kendi, antiracist. It may need to do so in ways which reach beyond co-operatives' internal bounds, through systematic engagement with the broader coalitions for racial justice. What such a multiracial, immigrant-inclusive strategy might look like is not for me to say, but, rather, one for the co-operative movement itself to determine, in consultation with its members and led by Black voices. Whatever form it takes, however, cannot be limited to Black participation in a White movement, or a Black co-operative movement in isolation, as in the past. Nor can it simply involve

White participation as mere allies in a Black-led multiracial coalition. As Ta-Nehisi Coates said in a conversation with Roxane Gay (2015, n.p.), "I think one has to even abandon the phrase 'ally' and understand that you are not helping someone in a particular struggle; the fight is yours."

To say "the fight is yours" may seem a tall order, a fight of David against Goliath. But as the American community, political, and labor organizer Marshall Ganz (2009) stated in his book title, sometimes David wins. Indeed, it is only through the sustained organizing efforts of David-like movements, to turn ideas and practices into fields, that other worlds have ever been made possible, and that Goliaths have been unmade.[5] Based on the evidence presented in this book, there is no reason to believe that the construction of another economy, one where co-operative models play a greater role, could occur any other way.

---

[5] Special thanks to James DeFilippis (2003), from whose book title, *Unmaking Goliath*, this idea is borrowed.

Appendix

Table A.1 Libraries, Special Collections, Archives, and Museums Consulted

Maison Alphonse-Desjardins	Levis, QC	Canada
Édifice Desjardins	Levis, QC	Canada
University of Helsinki Library	Helsinki	Finland
National Library of Finland	Helsinki	Finland
Workers' Library/Library of the Labor Movement	Helsinki	Finland
Työväenmuseo Werstas	Tampere	Finland
Le Centre Charles Gide/Centre de documentation sur l'économie sociale et solidaire, Centre de ressources du Crédit Coopératif	Nanterre	France
Musée Social	Paris	France
Bibliothèque Nationale de France	Paris	France
Sciences Po Bibliothèque	Paris	France
Cité des Sciences et de l'Industrie Bibliothèque	Paris	France
Les Champs Libres (Bibliothèque des Champs Libres/Musée de Bretagne)	Rennes	France
Maison Europe des Coopératives	Brussels	Belgium
University of Auckland Library	Auckland	New Zealand
Auckland Central City Library	Auckland	New Zealand
Co-operative Business New Zealand Archives	Auckland	New Zealand
Christchurch Public Library	Christchurch	New Zealand
Canterbury University Library	Christchurch	New Zealand
National Library of New Zealand	Wellington	New Zealand
Victoria University Library	Wellington	New Zealand
Wellington Public Library	Wellington	New Zealand
The British Library	London	England
London School of Economics Library	London	England
National Co-operative Archives	Manchester	England
The People's History Museum	Manchester	England

(*continued*)

Table A.1 Continued

Rochdale Pioneers Museum	Rochdale	England
Manchester University Library	Manchester	England
University of California, Berkeley, Doe Library	Berkeley, CA	United States
Oakland Public Library	Oakland, CA	United States
Daniel E. Koshland San Francisco History Center, San Francisco Public Library	San Francisco, CA	United States
U.S. Library of Congress	Washington, D.C.	United States
America's Credit Union Museum	Manchester, NH	United States
Minneapolis Public Library	Minneapolis, MN	United States
University of Minnesota Library	Minneapolis, MN	United States
Minnesota Historical Society	St. Paul, MN	United States
Wisconsin Historical Society	Madison, WI	United States
University of Wisconsin Library	Madison, WI	United States

Table A.2 Select/ Representative List of Organizations Interviewed.

United States		
Airbnb (CA)	Occupy–Alt Banking Group (NY)	**France**
Arizmendi (CA)	Organic Valley	Agr2mondiale
Association of Co-operative Educators (MN)	Park Slope Food Co-operative (NY)	Biocoop
	Project Equity (CA)	CN-CRESS
Bay Area Co-operative Association (CA)	Prospera (CA)	Clarabis
Bronx Co-operative Development Initiative (NY)	Rainbow Grocery (CA)	Coop de Comun
	RSF Social Finance (CA)	Coop de France
Business Alliance for Local Living Economies	SF Community Power Co-op	Coopname
	Self-Help Credit Union (CA)	CoopFr
Co-operative Economics Alliance of NYC	Seward Collective Café (MN)	Crédit Coopératif
	Shared Capital Co-operative (MN)	Enercoop
Cheeseboard Collective (CA)	SPUR/CarShare (CA)	Esfin Gestion
City of Berkeley (CA)	Stoel Rives (MN)	Finacoop
City of Boston (MA)	Sustainable Economies Law Center (CA)	FranceBarter
City of Madison (WI)	The ICA Group (MA/CA)	Groupe PBCE
City of Minneapolis (MN)	The Movement for Black Lives	Groupe SOS
City of New York	The Workers Lab (CA)	Groupe Up
City of Oakland (CA)	University of Minnesota	InVivo
City of Richmond (VA)	UC Berkeley Labor Center	La Confédération générale des SCOP (CG SCOP)
CoBank	Union Cab	
Co-opera (MN)	University of Wisconsin Center for Co-operation (WI)	Les grands voisins
Co-operative Development Services/Co-operative Network of Wisconsin and Minnesota		Les Rencontres du Mont Blanc/ESS Forum
	Uptima Bootcamp	Musée Social
	U.S. Department of Agriculture (USDA)	Solidarité Étudiante
Co-operative Home Care Association (NY)	U.S. Federation of Worker Co-operatives	SOCODEN
CUNA Mutual Group (WI)	We Own It	
CUNY (NY)	Willie Street Co-op	**New Zealand**
Cutting Edge Capital (CA)		Akina Foundation
Democracy at Work Institute (DAWI)	**Finland**	Auckland City Council
Design Action Collective (CA/MA)	City of Helsinki	CBNZ/NZ Co-op
Dorsey Whitney (MN)	CNS–University of Helsinki Ruralia Institute	Cognitius/AUT
Ehta Raha	Demos	Co-op Money NZ
Federation of Southern Co-ops (US)	Ehta Raha	Energyshare Co-operative
Filene's Research Institute (WI)	Finland Environmental Ministry	Enspiral
Food Co-op Initiative (MN)	Finnish Co-operative Council/Pellervo	Farmlands
Heartwood Co-operative (CA)	Finnish Water Co-operative Association/SVOSK	FMG
Institute for Local Self-Reliance		Fonterra Group
International Co-operative Alliance	HKScan	Foodstuffs (South Island)
Isthmus Engineering (WI)	Lahitapiola	Interflora
Land O' Lakes (MN)	Lilith	Loomio
LECD- Mercado Central (MN)	Luottamuksen löyly osk	Massey University
Loconomics (CA)	Metsä Group	Ministry of Business Industry and Economic Development
Madworc (WWI)	Nordic Climate Fund	
National Center for Employee Ownership	OP Group	
National Co-operative Bank (DC)	Osuustoiminnan Kehittäjät- Co-op Finland	Ministry of Social Development
NCBA/CLUSA (DC)	POP Pankkiliitto	
New Economy Coalition (MA)	Robin Hood Co-op	Rabobank NZ
Network of Bay Area Worker Co-operatives	S Group	The Co-operative Bank
	SOK Corporation	The FROOB
North Country Co-op Foundation	Tampere Co-operative Center–University of Tampere	United Forestry
NursesCan (CA)		University of Auckland
New York City Network of Worker Co-operatives	Tampere University of Technology	University of Otago
	Tradeka	Wellington City Council
	Valio	

References

Abello, Oscar Perry. 2023. "New York's Driver-Owned Ride-Hailing App Is Putting Its Foot on the Accelerator." *Next City*, June 13. https://nextcity.org/urbanist-news/new-yorks-driver-owned-ride-hailing-app-is-putting-its-foot-on-the-accelera.

Acemoglu, Daron, and James Robinson. 2012. *Why Nations Fail: The Origins of Power, Prosperity, and Poverty*. New York: Crown Business.

Adams, Herbert, ed. 1888. *History of Coöperation in the United States*. Baltimore: Publication agency of the Johns Hopkins University.

Ahdar, Rex. 2020. *The Evolution of Competition Law in New Zealand*. Oxford University Press.

Alanen, Arnold. 1975. "The Development and Distribution of Finnish Consumers' Co-operatives in Michigan, Minnesota and Wisconsin, 1903–1973." In Karni, Michael; Kaups, Matti; Ollila, Douglas (editors), *The Finnish Experience in the Western Great Lakes Region: New Perspectives* 112: 117. Institute for Migration, Turku, Finland, and Immigration History Research Center, University of Minnesota, Duluth.

Aldrich, Howard, and Robert N. Stern. 1983. "Resource Mobilization and the Creation of US Producer's Co-operatives, 1835–1935." *Economic and Industrial Democracy* 4(3): 371–406.

Alesina, Alberto, Edward Glaeser, and Bruce Sacerdote. 2001. "Why Doesn't the US Have a European-Style Welfare System?" Working Paper 8524. Cambridge, MA: National Bureau of Economic Research.

Allen, Mike. 2017. *The Sage Encyclopedia of Communication Research Methods*. Thousand Oaks, CA: Sage.

Alley, Geoffrey Thomas, and David Oswald William Hall. 1941. *The Farmer in New Zealand*. Wellington: NZ Department of Internal Affairs.

Alter, Thomas. 2022. *Toward a Co-operative Commonwealth: The Transplanted Roots of Farmer-Labor Radicalism in Texas*. Champaign: University of Illinois Press.

American Banker. 2022. "New ICBA Chair's Plan to Fight Regulation, Credit Union Tax Exemption." February 25.

Andrews, Naomi J. 2013. "Breaking the Ties: French Romantic Socialism and the Critique of Liberal Slave Emancipation." *Journal of Modern History* 85(3): 489–527.

Antoni, Antoine. 1980. *La coopération ouvrière de production*. Confédération générale des sociétés coopératives ouvriéres de production.

Archambault, Edith. 2001. "Historical Roots of the Nonprofit Sector in France." *Nonprofit and Voluntary Sector Quarterly* 30(2): 204–20.

Archer, Robin. 2007. *Why Is There No Labor Party in the United States?* Princeton, NJ: Princeton University Press.

Ahrne, Göran, and Nils Brunsson. 2005. "Organizations and Meta-Organizations." *Scandinavian Journal of Management* 21(4): 429–49.

Arrighi, Giovanni, 1994. *The Long Twentieth Century: Money, Power, and the Origins of Our Times*. Verso.

Arthur, W. Brian. 1989. "Competing Technologies, Increasing Returns, and Lock-In by Historical Events." *Economic Journal* 99(394): 116–31.

Autor, David, David Dorn, Lawrence F. Katz, Christina Patterson, and John Van Reenen. 2020. "The fall of the labor share and the rise of superstar firms." *The Quarterly Journal of Economics* 135(2): 645–709.

References

Bairoch, Paul. 1989. "L'économie Française Dans Le Contexte Européen à La Fin Du XVIIIe Siècle." *Revue Économique* 40(6): 939–64.
Baldwin, James. 1965. "White Man's Guilt." In "The White Problem in America." *Ebony*, August.
Baker, Bruce E. 1999. "The 'Hoover Scare' in South Carolina, 1887: An Attempt to Organize Black Farm Labor." *Labor History* 40(3): 261–82.
Baker, Ella. 1970. "Developing Community Leadership." 4.
Baldwin, James. 1965. "White Man's Guilt." In "The White Problem in America." *Ebony*, August.
Balnave, Nikola, and Greg Patmore. 2008. "'Practical Utopians': Rochdale Consumer Co-operatives in Australia and New Zealand." *Labour History* 2008(95): 97–110.
Balnave, Nikola, and Greg Patmore. 2017. "Managing Consumer Co-operatives: A Historical Perspective." In *A Global History of Consumer Co-operation since 1850: Movements and Businesses*, pp. 413 – 430. edited by Mary Hilson. Leiden: Brill.
Balsiger, Philip. 2021. "The Dynamics of 'Moralized Markets': A Field Perspective." *Socio-Economic Review* 19(1): 59–82.
Barber, William J., II, and Jonathan Wilson-Hartgrove. 2016. *The Third Reconstruction: Moral Mondays, Fusion Politics, and the Rise of a New Justice Movement*. Beacon Press.
Barkey, Karen. 2008. *Empire of Difference: The Ottomans in Comparative Perspective*. Cambridge: Cambridge University Press.
Barman, Emily. 2016. "Varieties of Field Theory and the Sociology of the Non-profit Sector." *Sociology Compass* 10(6): 442–58.
Barnard, Charles. 1881. *Co-operation as a Business*. New York: Putnam.
Battilana, Julie, and Silvia Dorado. 2010. "Building Sustainable Hybrid Organizations: The Case of Commercial Microfinance Organizations." *Academy of Management Journal* 53(6): 1419–40.
Battilani, Patrizia, and Harm G. Schröter. 2011. "Demutualization and Its Problems." SSRN Scholarly Paper ID 1866263. Rochester, NY: Social Science Research Network.
Battilani, Patrizia, and Harm G. Schröter. 2012. *The Co-operative Business Movement, 1950 to the Present*. Cambridge: Cambridge University Press.
Beach, Derek. 2017. "Process-Tracing Methods in Social Science." *Oxford Research Encyclopedia of Politics*, January 25. https://oxfordre.com/politics.
Béland, Daniel. 2007. "Ideas and Institutional Change in Social Security: Conversion, Layering, and Policy Drift." *Social Science Quarterly* 88(1): 20–38.
Belich, James. 2001. *Paradise Reforged: A History of the New Zealanders from the 1880s to the Year 2000*. Honolulu: University of Hawai'i Press.
Bell, Daniel. 1996. *Marxian Socialism in the United States*. Ithaca, NY: Cornell University Press.
Bell, Finn McLafferty. 2021. "Amplified Injustices and Mutual Aid in the COVID-19 Pandemic." *Qualitative Social Work* 20(1–2): 410–15.
Bemis, Edward Webster. 1888. "Sections I–X." In *History of Coöperation in the United States*, edited by Herbert Adams. Baltimore: Publication agency of the Johns Hopkins University.
Benford, Robert D., and David A. Snow. 2000. "Framing Processes and Social Movements: An Overview and Assessment." *Annual Review of Sociology* 26(1): 611–39.
Benner, Maximilian. 2021. "Retheorizing Industrial-Institutional Coevolution: A Multi-dimensional Perspective." *Regional Studies* (): 1–14.
Bennet, Jean. 1975. *La Mutualité française à travers sept siècles d'histoire*. CIEM.
Bennett, Andrew, and Jeffrey T. Checkel. 2014. *Process Tracing*. Cambridge: Cambridge University Press.
Berger, Suzanne. 2003. *Notre Première Mondialisation : Leçons d'un Échec Oublié*. Paris: Seuil.
Berger, Suzanne. 2017. "How the First Globalization Survived Populism." Unpublished ms.
Berk, Louis, and Rachel Kolsky. 2016. *Whitechapel in 50 Buildings*. Amberley.
Berkowitz, Héloïse, and Hervé Dumez. 2016. "The concept of meta-organization: Issues for management studies." *European Management Review* 13(2): 149–156.

Bernstein, Paul. 1976. *Workplace Democratization—Its Internal Dynamics.* Comparative Administration Research Institute.
Berrey, Ellen. 2018. "Social Enterprise Law in Action: Organizational Characteristics of U.S. Benefit Corporations." *Transactions: The Tennessee Journal of Business Law* 20: 21–114.
Berry, Mary Frances. 2005. *My Face Is Black Is True: Callie House and the Struggle for Ex-Slave Reparations.* New York: Alfred A. Knopf.
Bestor, Arthur. (1950) 1970. *Backwoods Utopias.* Philadelphia: University of Pennsylvania Press.
Bestor, Arthur E. 1953. "Patent-Office Models of the Good Society: Some Relationships between Social Reform and Westward Expansion." *American Historical Review* 58(3): 505–26.
Birchall, Matthew. 2022. "Mobilizing Stadial Theory: Edward Gibbon Wakefield's Colonial Vision." *Global Intellectual History*, 1–21.
Black, Paul V. 1963. "The Knights of Labor and the South: 1876–1893." *Southern Quarterly* 1(3): 201–12.
Board of Governors of the Federal Reserve System. (1943) 2021. "Total Consumer Credit Owned by Credit Unions." FRED, Federal Reserve Bank of St. Louis. January 1, 1943.
Borzaga, Carlo, and Leonardo Becchetti. 2010. *The Economics of Social Responsibility: The World of Social Enterprises.* London: Routledge.
Boston, Jonathan. 1991. *Reshaping the State: New Zealand's Bureaucratic Revolution.* Oxford: Oxford University Press.
Bouchard, Marie J. 2013. *Innovations and the Social Economy: The Québec Experience.* Toronto: University of Toronto Press.
Bourdieu, Pierre. 1990. *The Logic of Practice.* Stanford, CA: Stanford University Press.
Brash, Don. 1996. "New Zealand's Remarkable Reforms—Reserve Bank of New Zealand."
Braudel, Fernand. 1949. *La M'editerran'ee et le monde M'editerran'een 'a l'epoque de Philippe II.* Colin.
Braudel, Fernand. 1982a. *Civilization and Capitalism, 15th–18th Century: The Perspective of the World.* Vol. 3. Berkeley: University of California Press.
Braudel, Fernand. 1982b. *On History.* Chicago: University of Chicago Press.
Braudel, Fernand, and Ernest Labrousse. 1976. *Histoire Économique et Sociale de La France: 1789–1880.* Vol. 3. Paris: Presses universitaires de France.
Brazda, Johann, and Robert Schediwy. 1989. "Consumer Co-operatives in a Changing World." Geneva: ICA.
Brickell, Chris. 2006. "The Politics of Post-war Consumer Culture." *New Zealand Journal of History* 40(2): 133–55
Brissenden, Paul Frederick. 1920. *The I.W.W.: A Study of American Syndicalism.* New York: Columbia University Press.
Buchez, Philippe, and Pierre-Célestin Roux-Lavergne. 1836. *Histoire Parlementaire de la Révolution française, ou Journal des Assemblées Nationales, depuis 1789 jusqu'en 1815: Tome trente-deuxième.* Paris: Paulin, Librairie.
Bullock, Paul. 1973. "'Rabbits and Radicals': Richard Nixon's 1946 Campaign against Jerry Voorhis." *Southern California Quarterly* 55(3): 319–59.
Bunker, Raymond. 1988. "Systematic Colonization and Town Planning in Australia and New Zealand." *Planning Perspectives* 3(1): 59–80.
Burke, Edmund. 1790. *Reflections on the Revolution in France.*
Cameron, Rondo E. 1961. *France and the Economic Development of Europe, 1800–1914.* Princeton, NJ: Princeton University Press.
Canoyer, Helen G. 1945. "A Study of Consumer Co-operative Associations in the North Central States." *Journal of Marketing* 9(4): 373–80.
Carberry, E. J. 2011. "Employee Ownership and Shared Capitalism: Assessing the Experience, Research, and Policy Implications." In *Employee Ownership and Shared Capitalism: New Directions in Research*, edited by E. J. Carberry. 1–26. Ithaca, NY: Cornell University Press.

Carreiro, Joshua. 2015. "Consumers' Co-operation in the Early Twentieth Century: An Analysis of Race, Class and Consumption." PhD diss., University of Massachusetts.

Carroll, Glenn R. 1985. "Concentration and Specialization: Dynamics of Niche Width in Populations of Organizations." *American Journal of Sociology* 90(6): 1262–83.

Case, John, and Rosemary C. R. Taylor. 1979. *Co-ops, Communes and Collectives; Experiments in Social Change in the 1960s and 1970s*. New York: Pantheon.

Cavaignac, Éléonore L. 1832. *Opinion de G. Cavaignac sur le droit d'association*. Courlet.

Cazzola, Matilde. 2021. "Edward Gibbon Wakefield and the Political Economy of Emancipation." *Intellectual History Review* 31(4): 651–69.

CECOP. 2012. "A French Law for Worker Buyouts" CECOP Web Publication.

CECOP/CICOPA Europe. 2013. "Business Transfers to Employees under the Form of a Co-operative in Europe: Opportunities and Challenges." Bruxelles.

Chaddad, Fabio R., and Michael L. Cook. 2004. "The Economics of Organization Structure Changes: A US Perspective on Demutualization." *Annals of Public and Co-operative Economics* 75(4): 575–94.

Chaddad, Fabio R., and Michael L. Cook. 2007. "Conversions and Other Forms of Exit in US Agricultural Co-operatives." In *Vertical Markets and Co-operative Hierarchies*, edited by Kostas Karantininis and Jerker Nilsson, 61–72. Dordrecht, NED: Springer.

Chambers, Clarke A. 1962. "The Co-operative League of the United States of America, 1916–1961: A Study of Social Theory and Social Action." *Agricultural History* 36(2): 59–81.

Chandler, Alfred Dupont, and Takashi Hikino. 1990. *Scale and Scope: The Dynamics of Industrial Capitalism*. Cambridge, MA: Belknap Press.

Chanial, Philippe, and Jean-Louis Laville. 2005. "L'économie sociale et solidaire en France." In *Action publique et économie solidaire*, edited by Jean-Louis Laville, Genauto Carvalho da França, Jean-Louis Laville, Jean-Philippe Magnen, Alzira Medeiro et al., 47–74. Érès.

Chen, Katherine K. 2009. *Enabling Creative Chaos: The Organization behind the Burning Man Event*. Chicago: University of Chicago Press.

Chen, Katherine K., and Victor Tan Chen. 2021. *Organizational Imaginaries: Tempering Capitalism and Tending to Communities through Co-operatives and Collectivist Democracy*. Emerald.

Childs, Marquis W. 1936. *Sweden: The Middle Way*. New Haven, CT: Yale University Press.

Chile, Love M. 2006. "The Historical Context of Community Development in Aotearoa New Zealand." *Community Development Journal* 41(4): 407–25.

Clamp, Christina, Eklou R. Amendah, and Carole Coren. 2019. *Shared Service Co-operatives: A Qualitative Study Exploring, Applications, Benefits and Potentials*. Oak Tree Press.

Clark, Robert, and Kia Haslett. 2018. "Momentum, Interest Building in Mutual Holding Company Conversions." Report. S&P Global Market Intelligence.

Cleary, Mark C. 1989. *Peasants, Politicians and Producers: The Organisation of Agriculture in France since 1918*. Cambridge: Cambridge University Press.

Clemens, Elisabeth S. 1993. "Organizational Repertoires and Institutional Change: Women's Groups and the Transformation of US Politics, 1890–1920." *American Journal of Sociology* 98(4): 755–98.

Clough, Shepard Bancroft. 1946. *A Century of American Life Insurance: A History of the Mutual Life Insurance Company of New York, 1843–1943*. New York: Columbia University Press.

Coates, Ta-Nehisi. 2014. "The Case for Reparations." *The Atlantic*, June.

CoBank. n.d. "History of CoBank." Accessed July 25, 2022. https://www.cobank.com/web/cobank/corporate/history.

Coleman, Peter J. 1987. *Progressivism and the World of Reform: New Zealand and the Origins of the American Welfare State*. Lawrence: University Press of Kansas.

Collier, Paul. 2018. *The Future of Capitalism: Facing the New Anxieties*. New York: Harper.

Collier, Ruth Berins, and David Collier. 1991. *Shaping the Political Arena*. Princeton, NJ: Princeton University Press.

Combes, Pierre-Philippe, Thierry Mayer, and Jacques-François Thisse. 2008. *Economic Geography: The Integration of Regions and Nations*. Princeton, NJ: Princeton University Press.
Commons, John R. 1910. *A Documentary History of American Industrial Society*. Vol. 8: *Labor Movement*. Arthur H. Clark.
Commons, John Rogers, John Bertram Andrews, Selig Perlman, David Saposs, Helen Sumner, E. B. Mittleman, and H. E. Hoagland. 1918. *History of Labour in the United States*. New York: Macmillan.
Congress of Industrial Organizations. 1947. "Unions and Co-Ops." Report No. 152.
Congress of Industrial Organizations. 1954. *Official Reports on the Expulsion of Communist Dominated Organizations from the CIO*. Publicity Department.
Co-operative Workers Trust. 1985. *Nga Rongo Korero: Ten Years of Work Co-operatives and Trusts*. Auckland: Co-operative Workers Trust.
Cornforth, Chris. 1995. "Patterns of Co-operative Management: Beyond the Degeneration Thesis." *Economic and Industrial Democracy* 16(4): 487–523.
Cotterill, Ronald. 1979. "The Social Economics of Participatory Consumer Co-operatives." Agricultural Economic Report Series. No. 201254. Michigan State University, Department of Agricultural, Food, and Resource Economics.
Cowling, Ellis. 1938. *Co-operatives in America: Their Past, Present and Future*. New York: Coward-McCann.
Cox, Craig. 1994. *Storefront Revolution: Food Co-ops and the Counterculture*. New Brunswick, NJ: Rutgers University Press.
Coy, David V, Lay Wee Ng, and Massey University Department of Accountancy. 1989. "The Collapse of the Manawatu Consumers' Co-op: A Case Study."
Credit Unions Today. 2022. "Bankers Group Releases Policy Objectives for 2022 and, Yes, Targeting CU Tax Exemption Made the List." February 27. www.cutoday.info/Fresh-Today/Bankers-Group-Releases-Policy-Objectives-for-2022-And-Yes-Targeting-CU-Tax-Exemption-Made-the-List.
Cross, Ira B. 1906. *The Co-operative Store in the United States*. Wisconsin. Bureau of Labor and Industrial Statistics. Biennial Report. 12th., Pt. 1. Madison, WI: Democrat Print. Co., State printer.
Cross, Ira B . 1911. "Co-Operation in California." *American Economic Review* 1(3): 535–44.
Curl, John. 2009. *For All the People: Uncovering the Hidden History of Co-operation, Co-operative Movements, and Communalism in America*. Oakland, CA: PM Press.
Czachorska-Jones, Barbara, Jay Gary Finkelstein, and Bahareh Samsami. 2013. "United States." In *International Handbook of Co-operative Law*, edited by Dante Cracogna, Antonio Fici, and Hagen Henrÿ, 759–78. Berlin: Springer.
Dahl, Robert Alan. 1985. *A Preface to Economic Democracy*. Berkeley: University of California Press.
Dalziel, Raewyn. 1975. *The Origins of New Zealand Diplomacy: The Agent-General in London, 1870–1905*. Wellington: Victoria University Press.
Dattel, Gene. 2010. "Cotton, the Oil of the Nineteenth Century." *International Economy* 24(1): 60.
Dave Grace and Associates. 2014. "Measuring the Size and Scope of the Co-operative Economy: Results of the 2014 Global Census on Co-operatives." Report for the United Nations Department of Economic and Social Affairs.
Davis, Gerald F. 2016a. "Can an Economy Survive without Corporations? Technology and Robust Organizational Alternatives." *Academy of Management Perspectives* 30(2): 129–40.
Davis, Gerald F. 2016b. *The Vanishing American Corporation: Navigating the Hazards of a New Economy*. Berrett-Koehler.
Davis, Gerald F., and Eun W. Kim. 2021. "Social Movements and Organizational Change." In *The Oxford Handbook of Organizational Change and Innovation*, edited by Marshall Scott Poole and Andrew Van de Ven, 209–29. Oxford: Oxford University Press.

References

Davis, Kevin. 2007. "Australian Credit Unions and the Demutualization Agenda." *Annals of Public and Co-operative Economics* 78(2): 277–300.
DeFilippis, James. 2003. *Unmaking Goliath*. New York: Routledge.
Derrick, Ewen J. 1993. *Community Development and Social Change: Learning from Experience*. Auckland: Auckland District Council of Social Services.
DeSantis, John. 2016. *The Thibodaux Massacre: Racial Violence and the 1887 Sugar Cane Labor Strike*. History Press.
Desigauz, Charles. 1940. "Mutual Agricultural Credit in France." *Annals of Public and Co-operative Economics* 16(1): 31–42.
Deyle, Steven. 2006. *Carry Me Back: The Domestic Slave Trade in American Life*. Oxford: Oxford University Press.
Diamond, Jared. 1997. Guns, Germs, and Steel: The Fates of Human Societies. W. W. Norton: New York.
Dickstein, Carla. 1991. "The Promise and Problems of Worker Co-operatives." *Journal of Planning Literature* 6(1): 16–33.
DiMaggio, Paul J., and Walter W. Powell. 1983. "The Iron Cage Revisited: Institutional Isomorphism and Collective Rationality in Organizational Fields." *American Sociological Review* (2): 147.
Donna, Foster Abernathy. 2008. "A Day in the Life of Co-operative America." NCBA. https://community-wealth.org/content/day-life-co-operative-america.
Dreyfus, Michel. 2013. *Financer Les Utopies: Une Histoire Du Crédit Coopératif (1893–2013)*. Paris: Actes sud.
Dreyfus, Michel. 2016. "Mutualité et coopération: Une histoire par trop méconnue." *Cahiers d'histoire : Revue d'histoire critique* 133(October): 169–80.
Du Bois, W. E. B. 1907. *Economic Co-operation among Negro Americans: Report of a Social Study Made by Atlanta University under the Patronage of the Carnegie Institution of Washington, D.C.; Together with the Proceedings of the 12th Conference for the Study of the Negro Problems, Held at Atlanta University, on Tuesday, May the 28th, 1907*. Slavery, Abolition & Social Justice, no. 12. Atlanta, GA: Atlanta University Press.
Dubb, Steve. 2016. "Community Wealth Building Forms: What They Are and How to Use Them at the Local Level." *Academy of Management Perspectives* 30(2): 141–52.
Duverger, Timothée. 2014. "La réinvention de l'économie sociale: Une histoire du Cnlamca." *Revue internationale de l'économie sociale* (334): 30–43.
Duverger, Timothée . 2016a. *L'économie sociale et solidaire: Une histoire de la société civile en France et en Europe de 1968 à nos jours*. Lormont: Editions Le Bord de l'eau.
Duverger, Timothée 2016b. "Michel Rocard 'est le père de la reconnaissance de l'économie sociale.'" *Le Monde*, July 7.
Dyson, Lowell K. 1982. *Red Harvest: The Communist Party and American Farmers*. Lincoln: University of Nebraska Press.
Early, Frances H. 1980. "A Reappraisal of the New England Labour-Reform Movement of the 1840s: The Lowell Female Labor Reform Association and the New England Workingmen's Association." *Histoire Sociale/Social History* 13(25): 33–54.
Ellis, Oliver. 2013. "'The Much Wished-For Shore': Nationalism and Utopianism in New Zealand Literature: 1817–1973." University of Canterbury.
Emerson, O. B. 1947. "Frances Wright and Her Nashoba Experiment." *Tennessee Historical Quarterly* 6(4): 291–314.
Emmenegger, Patrick. 2015. "The Politics of Job Security Regulations in Western Europe: From Drift to Layering." *Politics & Society* 43(1): 89–118.
Emmenegger, Patrick. 2021. "Agency in Historical Institutionalism: Coalitional Work in the Creation, Maintenance, and Change of Institutions." *Theory and Society* 50(4): 607–26.
Engels, Friedrich. 1880. *Socialism: Utopian and Scientific*. C. H. Kerr.

Engels, Friedrich, and Florence Kelley Wischnewetzky. 1887. *The Condition of the Working Class in England in 1844: With Appendix Written 1886, and Preface 1887*. Lovell.

Erhemjamts, Otgontsetseg, and J. Tyler Leverty. 2010. "The Demise of the Mutual Organizational Form: An Investigation of the Life Insurance Industry." *Journal of Money, Credit and Banking* 42(6): 1011–36.

Erwin, Carl C. 1966. "The Dark Tobacco Growers Co-operative Association, 1922–1926." *Business History Review* 40(4): 403–31.

Escalona, Fabien. 2016. "France: Who Wants to Be a Social Democrat?" In *The Three Worlds of Social Democracy*, edited by Ingo Schmidt, 29–45. Pluto Press.

Esping-Andersen, Gosta. 1990. *The Three Worlds of Welfare Capitalism*. John Wiley & Sons.

Esping-Andersen, Gøsta. 1999. *Social Foundations of Postindustrial Economies*. Oxford: Oxford University Press.

Esteve-Pérez, Silviano, and Juan A. Mañez-Castillejo. 2008. "The Resource-Based Theory of the Firm and Firm Survival." *Small Business Economics* 30(3): 231–49.

Evans, David S., Andrei Hagiu, and Richard Schmalensee. 2008. *Invisible Engines: How Software Platforms Drive Innovation and Transform Industries*. Cambridge, MA: MIT Press.

Evans, David S., and Richard Schmalensee. 2016. *Matchmakers: The New Economics of Multisided Platforms*. Cambridge, MA: Harvard Business Review Press.

Evans, Lewis, and Richard Meade. 2005. "The Role and Significance of Co-operatives in New Zealand Agriculture, A Comparative Institutional Analysis."

Evans, P. 2019. "Ikea Apologises after Leaving New Zealand Off a Map." BBC News. https://www.bbc.com/news/blogs-trending-47171599.

Evans, Rhonda, and Tamara Kay. 2008. "How Environmentalists 'Greened' Trade Policy: Strategic Action and the Architecture of Field Overlap." *American Sociological Review* 73(6): 970–91.

Fairweather, John R. 1985. "Land Policy and Land Settlement In New Zealand: An Analysis of Land Policy Goals and an Evaluation of Their Effect."

Finlandia University. 2007. *The Finnish-American Co-operative Movement: Finding Aid*. Finnish American Heritage Center: Hancock, MI.

Fink, Leon. 1983. *Workingmen's Democracy: The Knights of Labor and American Politics*. Champaign: University of Illinois Press.

Fischer, David Hackett. 2012. *Fairness and Freedom: A History of Two Open Societies: New Zealand and the United States*. Oxford: Oxford University Press.

Fitzsimmons, Michael P. 1996. "The National Assembly and the Abolition of Guilds in France." *Historical Journal* 39(1): 133–54.

Fitzsimons, Bevin. 1982. "Work Co-Operatives: A Manual." Occasional Paper on Community Development, No. 1. Wellington: NZ Department of Internal Affairs.

Fligstein, Neil. 2001. "Social Skill and the Theory of Fields." *Sociological Theory* 19(2): 105–25.

Fligstein, Neil, and Doug McAdam. 2011. "Toward a General Theory of Strategic Action Fields." *Sociological Theory* 29(1): 1–26.

Fligstein, Neil, and Doug McAdam. 2012. *Toward a Theory of Strategic Action Fields*. Oxford: Oxford University Press.

Fligstein, Neil, and Doug McAdam. 2019. "States, Social Movements and Markets." *Socio-Economic Review* 17(1): 1–6.

Fogarty, Robert S. 1990. *All Things New: American Communes and Utopian Movements, 1860–1914*. Lexington Books.

Foner, Philip S. 1947–94. *History of the Labor Movement in the United States*. 10 vols. New York: International Publishers.

Foner, Philip Sheldon. 1974. *Organized Labor and the Black Worker, 1619–1981*. Westport, CT: Praeger.

Ford, James. 1913. *Co-operation in New England: Urban and Rural*. Survey Associates.

Ford, T. 1946. "Taxation of Co-operatives." Washington, D.C.: CQ Researcher by CQ Press.
Fourcade, Marion. 2012. "On Erik Olin Wright, Envisioning Real Utopias, London and New York, NY, Verso, 2010." *Socio-Economic Review* 10 (2): 369–402.
Fourier, Charles. 1808. *Théorie Des Quatre Mouvements et Des Destinées Générales: Prospectus et Annonce de La Découverte*. Vol. 4. Librairie sociétaire.
Fourier, Charles. 1822. *Oeuvres Complètes: Le Nouveau Monde Industriel et Sociétaire*. Vol. 6. Lib. Sociétaire.
Fourier, Charles. 1829. *Plan d'un Phalanstère: Le nouveau monde industriel*.
Fowler, Bertram Baynes. 1936. *Consumer Co-operation in America: Democracy's Way Out*. New York: Vanguard Press.
Fraser, Nancy. 1997. *Justice Interruptus: Critical Reflections on the "Postsocialist" Condition*. Psychology Press.
Frederick, Donald A. 2005. "Co-operatives: Handling of Losses." Co-operative Information Report 44, Part 5. Washington, D.C.: IRS.
Frederick, Donald A. 2013. "Income Tax Treatment of Cooperatives: Background." Co-operative Information Report 44, Part 1. Washington, D.C.: IRS.
Freeman, Richard B., ed. 1994. *Working under Different Rules*. National Bureau of Economic Research Project Report. New York: Russell Sage Foundation.
Freilla, Omar. 2022. "Sustaining the Rising Tide of Black Co-ops: An Ecosystem Approach." *Non Profit News/Nonprofit Quarterly*.
Friedland, Roger, and Robert Alford. 1991. *Bringing Society Back In: Symbols, Practices, and Institutional Contradictions*. Edited by Walter W. Powell and Paul J. DiMaggio. Chicago: University of Chicago Press.
Friedman, Gerald. 1988a. "The State and the Making of the Working Class: France and the United States, 1880–1914." *Theory and Society* 17(3): 403–30.
Friedman, Gerald. 1988b. "Strike Success and Union Ideology: The United States and France, 1880–1914." *Journal of Economic History* 48(1): 1–25.
Frobert, Ludovic, and Marie Lauricella. 2015. "Naissance de l'association de production: L'Européen de Buchez." In *Quand les socialistes inventaient l'avenir*, edited by Thomas Bouchet Vincent Bourdeau, Edward Castleton, Ludovic Frobert, François Jarrige, 75–83. La Découverte.
Frost, N. 2018. "Why Is New Zealand So Often Left Off World Maps?" Atlas Obscura. https://www.atlasobscura.com/articles/new-zealand-left-off-world-map.
Fukuyama, Francis. 1989. "The End of History?" *National Interest* 16: 3–18.
Furlough, Ellen. 1991. *Consumer Co-operation in France: The Politics of Consumption, 1834–1930*. Ithaca, NY: Cornell University Press.
Gabaix, Xavier. 2016. "Power Laws in Economics: An Introduction." *Journal of Economic Perspectives* 30(1): 185–206.
Gagneur, Wladimir. 1839. "Des fruitières ou associations domestiques pour la fabrication du fromage de gruyère." Bureau de la Phalange.
Galbraith, John Kenneth. 1952. *American Capitalism: The Concept of Countervailing Power*. New York: Houghton Mifflin.
Galloway, Scott. 2017. *The Four: The Hidden DNA of Amazon, Apple, Facebook, and Google*. New York: Random House.
Ganz, Marshall. 2009. *Why David sometimes wins: Leadership, organization, and strategy in the California farm worker movement*. Oxford University Press.
Gardner, Hamilton. 1917. "Coöperation among the Mormons." *Quarterly Journal of Economics* 31(3): 461–99.
Garicano, Luis, Claire Lelarge, and John Van Reenen. 2016. "Firm Size Distortions and the Productivity Distribution: Evidence from France." *American Economic Review* 106(11): 3439–79.

Garnevska, E., L. Callagher, M. Apparao, N. Shadbolt, and F. Siedlok. 2017. "The New Zealand Co-operative Economy." Massey University Palmerston North, New Zealand. Unpublished ms.

Garrioch, David. 2011. "Mutual Aid Societies in Eighteenth-Century Paris." *French History and Civilization: Papers from the George Rude Seminar* 4: 22–33.

Gaumont, Jean. 1924. *Histoire générale de la coopération en France: Les idées et les faits, les hommes et les oeuvres*. Fédération nationale des coopératives de consommation.

Gay, Roxane. 2015. "The Charge to Be Fair: Ta-Nehisi Coates and Roxane Gay in Conversation." B&N Reads.

Gebhard, Hannes. 1916. *Co-operation in Finland*. Williams and Norgate.

Geddes, Barbara. 1990. "How the Cases You Choose Affect the Answers You Get: Selection Bias in Comparative Politics." *Political Analysis* 2: 131–50.

George, Alexander. 1979. "Case Studies and Theory Development: The Method of Structured, Focused Comparison." In *Diplomacy: New Approaches in History, Theory, and Policy*, edited by P. G. Lauren, 43–68. New York: Free Press.

George, Alexander L., and Andrew Bennett. 2005. *Case Studies and Theory Development in the Social Sciences*. Cambridge, MA: MIT Press.

Gerring, John. 2016. *Case Study Research: Principles and Practices*. Cambridge: Cambridge University Press.

Gerring, John, and Lee Cojocaru. 2016. "Selecting Cases for Intensive Analysis A Diversity of Goals and Methods." *Sociological Methods & Research* 45(3): 392–423.

Gibaud, Bernard. 1986. *De la mutualité à la sécurité sociale: Conflits et convergences*. Paris: Editions de l'Atelier.

Gibaud, Bernard. 1998. *Mutualité, assurances (1850–1914): Les enjeux*. Economica.

Gide, Charles. 1904. *Les sociétés coopératives de consommation*. Paris: A. Colin.

Gide, Charles. 1905a. *Coopération économique et sociale 1886–1904*. Paris: Editions L'Harmattan.

Gide, Charles. 1905b. *Économie Sociale: Les Institutions Du Progrès Social Au Début Du XXe Siècle*. Paris: L. Larose et L. Tenin.

Gide, Charles. 1922. *Consumers' Co-operative Societies*. Vol. 21922. New York: Alfred A. Knopf.

Gilbert, Jarrod. 2010. "The Rise and Development of Gangs in New Zealand." PhD diss., Canterbury University.

Gilbert, Jarrod. 2013. *Patched: The History of Gangs in New Zealand*. Auckland: Auckland University Press.

Glickman, Lawrence B. 2009. *Buying Power: A History of Consumer Activism in America*. Chicago: University of Chicago Press.

Goldfield, Michael. 2001. "Roots of Reform: Farmers, Workers, and the American State, 1877–1917. By Elizabeth Sanders. Chicago: University of Chicago Press, 1999. 528p. 16.00 Paper." *American Political Science Review* 95(3): 739–40.

Goldfield, Michael. 2020. *The Southern Key: Class, Race, and Radicalism in the 1930s and 1940s*. Oxford: Oxford University Press.

Goldstein, Robert Justin. 1983. *Political Repression in 19th Century Europe*. New York: Routledge.

Gomory, Ralph, and Richard Sylla. 2013. "The American Corporation." *Daedalus* 142(2): 102–18.

Goodwyn, Lawrence. 1976. *Democratic Promise: The Populist Moment in America*. New York: Oxford University Press.

Gordon Nembhard, Jessica. 2008. "Alternative Economics—A Missing Component in the African American Studies Curriculum: Teaching Public Policy and Democratic Community Economics to Black Undergraduate Students." *Journal of Black Studies* 38(5): 758–82.

Gordon Nembhard, Jessica. 2013. "Community Development Credit Unions: Securing and Protecting Assets in Black Communities." *Review of Black Political Economy* 40(4): 459–90.

Gordon Nembhard, Jessica. 2014. *Collective Courage: A History of African American Co-operative Economic Thought and Practice*. State College, PA: Penn State Press.
Gordon Nembhard, Jessica. 2018. "African American Co-operatives and Sabotage: The Case for Reparations." *Journal of African American History* 103(12): 65–90.
Gorz, André. 1975. *Socialism and Revolution*. Allen Lane.
Gourevitch, Alex. 2015. *From Slavery to the Co-operative Commonwealth: Labor and Republican Liberty in the Nineteenth Century*. Cambridge: Cambridge University Press.
Gourlay, H. W. 1942. *Odd Fellowship in New Zealand: A Century of Progress*. Wellington: Published by the Grand Master and Board of Directors of the Order in New Zealand.
Grabher, Gernot, and David Stark. 1997. *Restructuring Networks in Post-Socialism: Legacies, Linkages, and Localities*. Oxford: Clarendon Press.
Gramsci, Antonio. 1926. *Selections from the Prison Notebooks*. Edited by Quintin Hoare and Geoffrey Nowell Smith. New York: International Publishers.
Grandy, Christopher. 1989. "New Jersey Corporate Chartermongering, 1875–1929." *Journal of Economic History* 49(3): 677–92.
Greenwood, Daniel J. H. 2005. "Democracy and Delaware: The Mysterious Race to the Bottom/Top." *Yale Law & Policy Review* 23: 381.
Greenwood, Royston, and Christopher R. Hinings. 1988. "Organizational Design Types, Tracks and the Dynamics of Strategic Change." *Organization Studies* 9(3): 293–316.
Greenwood, Royston, and Christopher R. Hinings. 1993. "Understanding Strategic Change: The Contribution of Archetypes." *Academy of Management Journal* 36(5): 1052–1081.
Griffin, Sean. 2018. "Antislavery Utopias: Communitarian Labor Reform and the Abolitionist Movement." *Journal of the Civil War Era* 8(2): 243–68.
Griffith, Barbara S. 1988. *The Crisis of American Labor: Operation Dixie and the Defeat of the CIO*. Philadelphia: Temple University Press.
Grob, Gerald N. 1961. *Workers and Utopia*. Quadrangle Books.
Guarneri, Carl J. 1983. "Two Utopian Socialist Plans for Emancipation in Antebellum Louisiana." *Louisiana History: The Journal of the Louisiana Historical Association* 24(1): 5–24.
Guarneri, Carl. 1991. *The Utopian Alternative: Fourierism in Nineteenth-Century America*. Ithaca, NY: Cornell University Press.
Guentzel, Ralph P. 2022. *The Quest for a Feasible Utopia: Historical Variants of Democratic Socialism and Their Contemporary Implications*. Tectum Wissenschaftsverlag.
Gueslin, André. 1998. *L'invention de l'économie sociale: Idées, pratiques et imaginaires coopératifs et mutualistes dans la France du XIXè siècle*. Economica.
Guinnane, Timothy W., Ron Harris, Naomi R. Lamoreaux, and Jean-Laurent Rosenthal. 2008. "Pouvoir et Propriété Dans l'entreprise: Pour Une Histoire Internationale Des Sociétés à Responsabilité Limitée." *Annales. Histoire, Sciences Sociales* 63(1): 73–110.
Guzman, Carmen, Francisco J. Santos, and Maria de la O. Barroso. 2020. "Co-operative Essence and Entrepreneurial Quality: A Comparative Contextual Analysis." *Annals of Public and Co-operative Economics* 91(1): 95–118.
Habermas, Jürgen. 1973. *Legitimation Crisis*. Boston: Beacon Press.
Hacker, Jacob S. 2004. "Privatizing Risk without Privatizing the Welfare State: The Hidden Politics of Social Policy Retrenchment in the United States." *American Political Science Review* 98(2): 243–60.
Hacker, Jacob S., Paul Pierson, and Kathleen Thelen. 2015. "Drift and Conversion: Hidden Faces of Institutional Change." In *Advances in Comparative-Historical Analysis*, edited by James Mahoney and Kathleen Thelen, 180–209. Cambridge University Press.
Hall, Peter A. 1983. "Policy Innovation and the Structure of the State: The Politics-Administration Nexus in France and Britain." *Annals of the American Academy of Political and Social Science* 466(1): 43–59.

Hall, Peter A. 1993. "Policy Paradigms, Social Learning, and the State: The Case of Economic Policymaking in Britain." *Comparative Politics* 5(I): 275–96.

Hall, Peter A. 2016. "Politics as a Process Structured in Space and Time," In *The Oxford Handbook of Historical Institutionalism*, edited by Orfeo Fioretos, Tulia G. Falleti, and Adam Sheingate (2016; online edn, Oxford Academic, 2 May 2016)

Hall, Peter A., and David Soskice. 2001. *Varieties of Capitalism: The Institutional Foundations of Comparative Advantage*. Oxford: Oxford University Press.

Hall, Peter A., and Rosemary C. R. Taylor. 1996. "Political Science and the Three New Institutionalisms." *Political Studies* 44(5): 936–57.

Hall, Peter A. and Kathleen Thelen. 2008 "Institutional Change in Varieties of Capitalism." *Debating Varieties of Capitalism* 7: 251–72.

Hall, Peter Dobkin. 2006. "A Historical Overview of Philanthropy, Voluntary Associations, and Nonprofit Organizations in the United States, 1600–2000." *Nonprofit Sector: A Research Handbook* 2: 32–65.

Hallgrimsdottir, Helga Kristin, and Cecilia Benoit. 2007. "From Wage Slaves to Wage Workers: Cultural Opportunity Structures and the Evolution of the Wage Demands of the Knights of Labor and the American Federation of Labor, 1880–1900." *Social Forces* 85(3): 1393–411.

Hallsten, Ilmi, and Hedvig Gebhard. 1933. *L'activité politique et sociale des femmes en Finlande*. Vol. 1: *Avant l'égalité civique et politique*. Helsinki: Impr. de l'état.

Halpern, Rick, and Jonathan Morris. 1997. *American Exceptionalism? US Working-Class Formation in an International Context*. Springer.

Hanna, John. 1952. "Co-operatives and the Antitrust Laws." *Indiana Law Journal* 27(3): 430–466

Hannah, Les. 2014. "Corporations in the US and Europe 1790–1860." *Business History* 56(6): 865–99.

Hannah-Jones, Nikole. 2021. *The 1619 Project: A New Origin Story*. New York: Random House.

Hansmann, Henry. 1990. "When Does Worker Ownership Work? ESOPs, Law Firms, Codetermination, and Economic Democracy." Faculty Scholarship Series, January. http://digitalcommons.law.yale.edu/fss_papers/5037.

Hansmann, Henry. 1996. *The Ownership of Enterprise*. Cambridge, MA: Belknap Press.

Hansmann, Henry, and Steen Thomsen. 2013. "Managerial Distance and Virtual Ownership: The Governance of Industrial Foundations."

Hansmann, Henry, and Steen Thomsen. 2021. "The Governance of Foundation-Owned Firms." *Journal of Legal Analysis* 13(1): 172–230.

Hanson-Schlachter, Laura. 2017. "Stronger Together? The USW-Mondragon Union Co-op Model." *Labor Studies Journal* 42(2): 124–47.

Harcourt, Bernard E. 2023. *Cooperation: A Political, Economic, and Social Theory*. New York: Columbia University Press.

Hare, Anthony E. C. 1945. "Co-operative Contracting in New Zealand." *International Labour Review* 51(2): 167–90.

Harper, Christina. 2013. "Credit Unions Campaign to Preserve Tax-Exempt Status." *BBJ Today*, September 29.

Hartz, Louis. 1955. *The Liberal Tradition in America: An Interpretation of American Political Thought since the Revolution*. New York: Harcourt Brace.

Hartz, Louis. 1969. *The Founding of New Societies: Studies in the History of the United States, Latin America, South Africa, Canada, and Australia*. New York: Houghton Mifflin Harcourt.

Harvey, Rebecca. 2018. "What Has Caused the Number of US Worker Co-ops to Nearly Double?" *Co-operative News*, August 7.

Haveman, Heather A. 2022. *The Power of Organizations*. Princeton, NJ: Princeton University Press.

Haveman, Heather A., and Hayagreeva Rao. 1997. "Structuring a Theory of Moral Sentiments: Institutional and Organizational Coevolution in the Early Thrift Industry." *American Journal of Sociology* 102(6): 1606–51.

Hawke, G. R. 1985. *The Making of New Zealand: An Economic History*. New York: Cambridge University Press.

Hayward, Margaret. 1981. *Diary of the Kirk Years*. Wellington, NZ: Reed.

Heflebower, Richard Brooks. 1980. *Co-operatives and Mutuals in the Market System*. Madison: University of Wisconsin Press.

Heggie, Ian, and Piers Vickers. 1998. *Commercial Management and Financing of Roads*. World Bank Publications.

Henderson, Rebecca. 2021. *Reimagining Capitalism in a World on Fire*. London: Penguin UK.

Henretta, James A., Rebecca Edwards, and Robert O. Self. 2012. *America: A Concise History, Volume One: To 1877*. Vol. 1. Macmillan: New York.

Henry, Hagen. 2005. *Guidelines for Co-operative Legislation*. Geneva: International Labour Office.

Henrÿ, Hagen. 2013. "Public International Co-operative Law." In *International Handbook of Co-operative Law*, edited by Dante Cracogna, Antonio Fici, and Hagen Henrÿ, 65–88. Berlin: Springer.

Hiez, David. 2017. "National Reports: France." In *Principles of European Co-operative Law: Principles, Commentaries and National Reports*, edited by Antonio Fici, David Hiez, Deolinda A. Meira, Gemma Fajardo-García, Hagen Henrÿ, Hans-H. Muenker, and Ian Snaith, 163–252. Intersentia.

Hild, Matthew. 2006. "Colored Farmers Alliance." In *Encyclopedia of US Labor and Working-Class History*, edited by Eric Arnesen, 286–88. New York: Routledge.

Hild, Matthew. 2007. *Greenbackers, Knights of Labor, and Populists: Farmer-Labor Insurgency in the Late-Nineteenth-Century South*. Athens: University of Georgia Press.

Hillquit, Morris. 1903. *History of Socialism in the United States*. New York: Funk & Wagnalls.

Hilson, Mary. 2013. "Consumer Co-operation and Economic Crisis: The 1936 Roosevelt Inquiry on Co-operative Enterprise and the Emergence of the Nordic 'Middle Way.'" *Contemporary European History* 22(2): 181–98.

Hilson, Mary, ed. 2017. *A Global History of Consumer Co-operation since 1850: Movements and Businesses*. Leiden: Brill.

Hilson, Mary. 2018. *The International Co-operative Alliance and the Consumer Co-operative Movement in Northern Europe, c. 1860–1939*. Manchester: Manchester University Press.

Hilt, Eric. 2015. "Corporation Law and the Shift toward Open Access in the Antebellum United States." NBER Working Paper No. 21195. National Bureau of Economic Research.

Hilt, Eric. 2017. "Early American Corporations and the State." In *Corporations and American Democracy*, edited by William J. Novak and Naomi R. Lamoreaux, 37–73. Cambridge, MA: Harvard University Press.

Hjerppe, Riitta, and Erkki Pihkala. 1977. "The Gross Domestic Product of Finland in 1860–1913: A Preliminary Estimate." *Economy and History* 20(2): 59–68.

Hobsbawm, Eric J. 1968. *Industry and Empire: An Economic History of Britain since 1750*. London: Weidenfeld & Nicolson.

Hoicka, Christina E., and Julie L. MacArthur. 2018. "From Tip to Toes: Mapping Community Energy Models in Canada and New Zealand." *Energy Policy* 121(October): 162–74.

Holler, Jean. 1992. "Les coopératives de commerçants: Une force d'avenir pour les commerçants indépendants associés." Culture technique, ISSN 0223-4386, 1993, No. 27. Neuilly-sur-Seine: Centre de recherche sur la culture technique.

Holmstrom, Bengt. 1999. "Future of Co-operatives: A Corporate Perspective." *Liiketaloudellinen Aikakauskirja* (5):404–17.

Hooks, Gregory, and Brian McQueen. 2010. "American Exceptionalism Revisited: The Military-Industrial Complex, Racial Tension, and the Underdeveloped Welfare State." *American Sociological Review* 75(2): 185–204.

Hoover, Melissa, and Hilary Abell. 2016. "Co-operative Growth Ecosystems."

Horner, Clare Anna Dahlberg. 1978. "Producers' Co-operatives in the United States, 1865–1890." PhD diss.

Hossein, Caroline Shenaz. 2013. "The Black Social Economy: Perseverance of Banker Ladies in the Slums." *Annals of Public and Cooperative Economics* 84(4): 423–42.

Hossein, Caroline Shenaz, Sharon D. Wright Austin, and Kevin Edmonds. 2023. *Beyond Racial Capitalism: Co-operatives in the African Diaspora*. Oxford: Oxford University Press.

Howard, Ebenezer. 1898. *Garden Cities of To-Morrow*. Vol. 23. London UK: Swan Sonnenschein & Co.

Howard, Ellie. 2020. "Victory Gardens: A War-Time Hobby That's Back in Fashion." BBC, May 25

Hubert-Valleroux, P. 1884. *Les associations coopératives en France et à l'étranger*. Guillaumin.

Hutt, Jennifer. 1978. *Work Co-operatives*. Wellington: NZ Ministry of Recreation and Sport.

Inclusiv. n.d. https://www.inclusiv.org/about-us/what-is-a-cdcu/

Institut français de la coopération (1978). .« Manifestes Coopératifs », , *Revue des études coopératives* #193. https://gallica.bnf.fr/ark:/12148/bpt6k62001928

International Co-operative Alliance. 1995. "Statement on the Co-operative Identity." https://www.ica.coop/en/cooperatives/cooperative-identity.

International Co-operative Alliance. 2021. "World Co-operative Monitor 2021.".

Ip, Manying, ed. 2003. *Unfolding History Evolving Identity: The Chinese in New Zealand*. Auckland: Auckland University Press.

Isotalo, Jukka. 1995. "Development of Good Governance in the Road Sector in Finland." SSATP Working Paper No. 21. Geneva: World Bank.

Isbister, John. 1994. *Thin Cats: The Community Development Credit Union Movement in the United States*. Berkeley: Center for Co-operatives, University of California.

Ishiguro, Kazuo. 1989. *The Remains of the Day*. New York: Knopf/Random House.

Jackall, Robert, and Henry M. Levin. 1984. *Worker Co-operatives in America*. Berkeley: University of California Press.

Jalkanen, Ralph J. 1969. *The Finns in North America: A Social Symposium*. Ann Arbor: Michigan State University Press & Suomi College.

Jeantet, Thierry. 2016. *Économie Sociale: La Solidarité Au Défi de l'efficacité*. La Documentation française.

Jensen, Nathan M., and Edmund J. Malesky. 2018. *Incentives to Pander: How Politicians Use Corporate Welfare for Political Gain*. Cambridge: Cambridge University Press.

Johnson, Chalmers. 1982. *Miti and the Japanese Miracle: The Growth of Industrial Policy: 1925–1975*. Stanford, CA: Stanford University Press.

Jones, Derek. 1977. "The Economics and Industrial Relations of Producer Co-operatives in the United States, 1791–1939." *Economic Analysis and Workers' Management* 12(3–4): 295–317.

Jones, Derek. 1979. "US Producer Co-operatives: The Record to Date." *Industrial Relations: A Journal of Economy and Society* 18(3): 342–57.

Jones, Derek. 1980. "Producer Co-operatives in Industrialised Western Economies." *British Journal of Industrial Relations* 18(2): 141–54.

Jones, Derek. 1984. "American Producer Co-operatives and Employee-Owned Firms: A Historical Perspective." In *Worker Co-operatives in America*, edited by Robert Jackall and Henry M. Levin, 37–56. Berkeley: University of California Press.

Jones, Derek C., and Donald J. Schneider. 1984. "Self-Help Production Co-operatives: Government-Administered Co-operatives during the Depression." In *Worker Co-operatives in America,* edited by Robert Jackall and Henry M. Levin, 57–84. Berkeley: University of California Press.

Jones, Jacqueline. 1985. *Labor of Love, Labor of Sorrow: Black Women, Work, and the Family from Slavery to the Present.* New York: Basic Books.

Jussila, Osmo. 1984. "The Historical Background of the February Manifesto of 1899." *Journal of Baltic Studies* 15(2–3): 141–47.

Kagay, Donald J. 2010. "The Utopian Colony of La Réunion as Social Mirror of Frontier Texas and Icon of Modern Dallas." *International Social Science Review* 85(3–4): 87–106.

Kalberg, Stephen. 1980. "Max Weber's Types of Rationality: Cornerstones for the Analysis of Rationalization Processes in History." *American Journal of Sociology* 85(5): 1145–79.

Kalderimis, Daniel. 2000. "Pure Ideology: The 'Ownership Split' of Power Companies in the 1998 Electricity Reforms." *Victoria University of Wellington Law Review* 31: 255–316.

Kalmi, Panu. 2013. "Catching a Wave: The Formation of Co-operatives in Finnish Regions." *Small Business Economics* 41(1): 295–313.

Kann, Kenneth. 1977. "The Knights of Labor and the Southern Black Worker." *Labor History* 18(1): 49–70.

Kanter, Rosabeth Moss. 1972. *Commitment and Community: Communes and Utopias in Sociological Perspective.* Cambridge, MA: Harvard University Press.

Karafolas, Simeon. 2016. *Credit Co-operative Institutions in European Countries.* Springer.

Kaswan, Mark J. 2014. "Developing Democracy: Co-operatives and Democratic Theory." *International Journal of Urban Sustainable Development* 6(2): 190–205.

Katko, Tapio, 2016. *Finnish Water Services: Experiences in Global Perspective.* IWA.

Katznelson, Ira. 2013. *Fear Itself: The New Deal and the Origins of Our Time.* New York: W. W. Norton.

Katznelson, Ira, Theda Skocpol, and Paul Pierson. 2002. *Political Science: State of the Discipline.* New York: W. W. Norton.

Kaufman, Jason. 2001. "Rise and Fall of a Nation of Joiners: The Knights of Labor Revisited." *Journal of Interdisciplinary History* 31(4): 553–79.

Keillor, Steven James. 2000. *Co-operative Commonwealth: Co-ops in Rural Minnesota, 1859–1939.* Minnesota Historical Society Press.

Kelso, Louis O., and Mortimer J. Adler. 1958. *The Capitalist Manifesto.* New York: Random House.

Kercher, Leonard Clayton, Vant W. Kebker, and Wilfred C. Leland. 1941. *Consumers' Co-operatives in the North Central States.* JSTOR.

Kerr, Clark. 1939. "Productive Enterprises of the Unemployed: 1931–1938." PhD diss.

King, Gary, Robert O. Keohane, and Sidney Verba. 1994. *Designing Social Inquiry: Scientific Inference in Qualitative Research.* Princeton, NJ: Princeton University Press.

Kipnis, Ira. 1952. *The American Socialist Movement 1897–1912.* New York: Columbia University Press.

Kirby, David. 2006. *A Concise History of Finland.* Cambridge: Cambridge University Press.

Klinge, Matti. 2003. *Suomen kansallisbiografia.* Suomalaisen Kirjallisuuden Seura.

Kluttz, Daniel N., and Neil Fligstein. 2016. "Varieties of Sociological Field Theory." In *Handbook of Contemporary Sociological Theory,* edited by Seth Abrutyn, 185–204. Cham, Switzerland: Springer.

Knapp, Joseph Grant. 1944. "EM 23: Why Co-Ops? What Are They? How Do They Work?" G.I. Pamphlet Series. American Historical Association.

Knapp, Joseph Grant. 1969. *The Rise of American Co-operative Enterprise: 1620–1920.* Interstate Printers.

Knapp, Joseph Grant. 1973. *The Advance of American Co-operative Enterprise: 1920–1945.* Interstate Printers.

Knupfer, Anne Meis. 2013. *Food Co-ops in America: Communities, Consumption, and Economic Democracy.* Ithaca, NY: Cornell University Press.

Komulainen, Anitra, and Sakari Siltala. 2015. "Business, Politics, and Ideology in the Age of Extremes: A Case Study of the Finnish Consumer Co-op HOK-Elanto 1905-2014" Unpublished ms.
Komulainen, Anitra, and Sakari Siltala. 2018. "Resistance to Inequality as a Competitive Strategy?–The Cases of the Finnish consumer Co-ops Elanto and HOK 1905–2015." *Business History* 60 (7): 1082-1104.
Kornai, Janos. 1990. "The Affinity between Ownership Forms and Coordination Mechanisms: The Common Experience of Reform in Socialist Countries." *Journal of Economic Perspectives* 4(3): 131–47.
Kuisma, Markku, Michael Wynne-Ellis, and Pellervo-Seura. 1999. *The Pellervo Story: A Century of Finnish Co-operation, 1899–1999.* Helsinki: Kirjayhtymä: Pellervo Confederation of Finnish Co-operatives.
Kumar, Krishan. 1990. "Utopian Thought and Communal Practice: Robert Owen and the Owenite Communities." *Theory and Society* 19(1): 1–35.
Kuusterä, Antti, and Juha Tarkka. 2012. *Bank of Finland, 200 Years.* Translated by Pat Humphreys. Helsinki: Otava.
Lakey, George. 2016. *Viking Economics: How the Scandinavians Got It Right—and How We Can, Too.* Brooklyn: Melville House.
Lamartine, Alphonse de, Francis Alexander Durivage, and William S. Chase. 1851. *History of the French Revolution of 1848.* Boston: Phillips, Sampson.
Lambersens, Simon, Amélie Artis, Danièle Demoustier, and Alain Mélo. 2017. "History of Consumer Co-operatives in France: From the Conquest of Consumption by the Masses to the Challenge of Mass Consumption." In *A Global History of Consumer Co-operation since 1850*, edited by Mary Hilson, 99–120. Leiden: Brill.
Lampe, Markus, and Paul Sharp. 2019. *A Land of Milk and Butter: How Elites Created the Modern Danish Dairy Industry.* Markets and Governments in Economic History. Chicago: University of Chicago Press.
Larsen, Grace H., and Henry E. Erdman. 1962. "Aaron Sapiro: Genius of Farm Co-operative Promotion." *Mississippi Valley Historical Review* 49(2): 242–68.
Lasne, Laurent. 2001. *1900–2000: Un siècle de Coopération, De l'abolition du salariat à l'invention du salariat moderne.* Revue Particiiper No. 582.
Lauck, Jon. 2000. *American Agriculture and the Problem of Monopoly: The Political Economy of Grain Belt Farming, 1953–1980.* Lincoln: University of Nebraska Press.
Laville, Jean-Louis. 2010. *L'économie Sociale et Solidaire: Théories, Pratiques, Débats.* Paris: Seuil.
Lazonick, William. 2014. "Profits without Prosperity." *Harvard Business Review* 92(9): 46–55.
Lazonick, William, and Mary O'Sullivan. 2000. "Maximizing Shareholder Value: A New Ideology for Corporate Governance." *Economy and Society* 29(1): 13–35.
Le Galès, Patrick. 1993. *Politiques Urbaines et Développement Local.* Paris: L'Harmattan.
Leifermann, Henry, and Pat Wehner. 1996. "A Question of Power: Race and Democracy in Rural Electric Co-Ops." *Southern Changes* 18(3–4): 3–15.
Leikin, Steve. 2004. *The Practical Utopians: American Workers and the Co-operative Movement in the Gilded Age.* Detroit, MI: Wayne State University Press.
Leikin, Steve. 2006. "Co-operatives." In *Encyclopedia of US Labor and Working-Class History*, edited by Eric Arnesen, 321–24. New York: Routledge.
Lek, Monkol, Konrad J. Karczewski, Eric V. Minikel, Kaitlin E. Samocha, Eric Banks, Timothy Fennell, Anne H. O'Donnell-Luria, et al. 2016. "Analysis of Protein-Coding Genetic Variation in 60,706 Humans." *Nature* 536(7616): 285–91.
Le Monde Diplomatique. 2011. "The US Left's Great Debate." November, 2011.
Lenin, V. I. 1910. "The Question of Co-operative Societies at the International Socialist Congress in Copenhagen." *Sotsial-Demokrat*, October 25, No. 17 edition.

Le Rossignol, James Edward, and William Downie Stewart. 1910. *State Socialism in New Zealand*. New York: T. Y. Crowell.
Les Scop, dir. 2012. "Benoit Hamon Au Conseil National Des Scop 2012." YouTube. https://www.youtube.com/watch?v=0hQV7EC2tM4.
Lichtenstein, Alex. 1991. "Industrial Slavery and the Tragedy of Robert Starobin." Edited by Robert S. Starobin. *Reviews in American History* 19(4): 604–17.
Lichtenstein, Peter M. 1986. "The U.S. Experience with Worker Co-operation." *Social Science Journal* 23(1): 1–15.
Lind, Clive. 2014. *Till the Cows Came Home: Inside the Battles That Built Fonterra*. Overland.
Lingane, Alison. 2015. "Bay Area Blueprint: Worker Co-operatives as a Community Economic Development Strategy." *Carolina Planning Journal* 5(I): 19–28.
Lipset, Seymour Martin. 1996. *American Exceptionalism: A Double-Edged Sword*. New York: W. W. Norton.
Lipset, Seymour Martin, and Gary Marks. 2000. *It Didn't Happen Here: Why Socialism Failed in the United States*. New York: W. W. Norton.
Locke, Richard M., and Kathleen Thelen. 1995. "Apples and Oranges Revisited: Contextualized Comparisons and the Study of Comparative Labor Politics." *Politics & Society* 23(3): 337–67.
Lofton, Saria, Marjorie Kersten, Shannon D. Simonovich, and Akilah Martin. 2022. "Mutual Aid Organisations and Their Role in Reducing Food Insecurity in Chicago's Urban Communities during COVID-19." *Public Health Nutrition* 25(1): 119–22.
Loubère, Leo A. 1959. "The Intellectual Origins of French Jacobin Socialism." *International Review of Social History* 4(3): 415–31.
Lucas, Percy. 1966. "Land Settlement." In *An Encyclopedia of New Zealand*, edited by A. McLintock. New Zealand Ministry for Heritage and Culture. Wellington.
Mackinder, H. J. 1904. "The Geographical Pivot of History." *Geographical Journal* 23(4): 421–37.
Mahoney, James, and Kathleen Thelen, eds. 2010. "A Theory of Gradual Institutional Change." In *Explaining Institutional Change: Ambiguity, Agency, and Power*, 1–37. Cambridge University Press .
Mahoney, James, and Kathleen Thelen, eds. 2015. *Advances in Comparative-Historical Analysis*. New York: Cambridge University Press.
Mair, Johanna, and Ignasi Marti. 2009. "Entrepreneurship in and around Institutional Voids: A Case Study from Bangladesh." *Journal of Business Venturing, Special Issue Ethics and Entrepreneurship* 24(5): 419–35.
Mair, Johanna, and Nikolas Rathert. 2019. "Alternative Organizing with Social Purpose: Revisiting Institutional Analysis of Market-Based Activity." *Socio-Economic Review* 19(2): 817–36.
Mansbridge, Jane J. 1979. "The Agony of Inequality." In *Co-ops, Communes, and Collectives: Experiments in Social Change in the 1960s and 1970s*, edited by John Case and Rosemary C. R. Taylor, 194–214. New York: Pantheon Books.
Marable, Manning. 1983. *How Capitalism Underdeveloped Black America: Problems in Race, Political Economy and Society*. Boston: South End Press.
Marshall, F. Ray. 1958. "The Finnish Co-operative Movement." *Land Economics* 34(3): 227–35.
Marshall, F. Ray . 1967. *Labor in the South*. Cambridge, MA: Harvard University Press.
Martin, Cathie Jo, and Duane Swank. 2012. *The Political Construction of Business Interests: Coordination, Growth, and Equality*. Cambridge: Cambridge University Press.
Martin, N. 1947. "La Coopération Ouvrière de Production En France." *Revue Des Études Coopératives* 80(November): 82–7.
Martin, Ron, and David Turner. 2000. "Demutualization and the Remapping of Financial Landscapes." *Transactions of the Institute of British Geographers* 25(2): 221–41. https://doi.org/10.1111/j.0020-2754.2000.00221.x.
Marx, Karl. 1867. *Das Kapital: Kritik Der Politischen Ökonomie*. Vol. 1. Meissner.

Marx, Karl. 1868. "Letter to Schweitzer." Kenneth Lapides, Marx and Engels on the Trade Unions.
Marx, Karl. 1847. The Poverty of Philosophy.
Marx, Karl. 1852. *Eighteenth Brumaire of Louis Bonaparte*.
Marx, Karl, and Friedrich Engels. 1848. *The Communist Manifesto*. New edition. New York: International Publishers.
Massey, Claire. 2016. *The New Zealand Land and Food Annual: Why Are We Wasting a Good Crisis?* Palmerston North: Massey University Press.
Massey, Patrick. 1995. "Market Liberalization in a Developed Economy." New York.
McAdam, Doug. 1982. *Political Process and the Development of Black Insurgency, 1930–1970*. Chicago: University of Chicago Press.
McAdam, Doug, Sidney Tarrow, and Charles Tilly. 2001. *Dynamics of Contention*. Cambridge: Cambridge University Press.
Mcalevey, Lynn, Alexander Sibbald, and David Tripe. 2010. "New Zealand Credit Union Mergers." *Annals of Public and Co-operative Economics* 81(3): 423–44.
McAloon, Jim. 2008. "Land Ownership." In *Te Ara Encyclopedia of New Zealand*. Manatu Taonga: New Zealand Ministry for Heritage and Culture.
McCabe, Ben C. 1945. "Big Business without Taxes." In *Proceedings of the Annual Conference on Taxation under the Auspices of the National Tax Association* 38: 279–87. Washington, DC, National Tax Association.
McCalman, Janya, and Paul Evans. 1982. *Rural Co-operatives in New Zealand: Twelve Case Studies*. Wellington, NZ: Community Enterprise Loan Trust.
McDonnell, Erin Metz. 2020. *Patchwork Leviathan*. Princeton, NJ: Princeton University Press.
McKenna, Megan, Richard Le Heron, and Michael Roche. 2001. "Living Local, Growing Global: Renegotiating the Export Production Regime in New Zealand's Pipfruit Sector." *Geoforum* 32(2): 157–66.
McKenna, Megan K. L., and E. Warwick Murray. 2002. "Jungle Law in the Orchard: Comparing Globalization in the New Zealand and Chilean Apple Industries." *Economic Geography* 78(4): 495–514.
McLauchlan, Gordon. 2002. *New Zealand Credit Unions—The First Forty Years: People Helping People*. Four Star Books.
McLaurin, Melton Alonza. 1978. *The Knights of Labor in the South*. Greenwood Press.
Mélo, Alain. 2012. "Quelle histoire pour nos coopératives? L'exemple des coopératives de Savoie." *Revue internationale de l'économie sociale* (325): 94–102.
Mélo, Alain 2015. "'Fruitières Comtoises' (Franche-Comté, France)." *Journal of Alpine Research/ Revue de Géographie Alpine* 103-1 (May): 1–9.
Menz, Georg. 2005. "Making Thatcher Look Timid: The Rise and Fall of the New Zealand Model." In *Internalizing Globalization*, International Political Economy Series, edited by Susanne Soederberg, Georg Menz, and Philip G. Cerny, pp. 49–68. London: Palgrave Macmillan.
Meyers, Frederic. 1940. "The Knights of Labor in the South." *Southern Economic Journal* 6(4): 479–87.
Meyers, Joan. 2022. "Working Democracies: Managing Inequality in Worker Cooperatives." In *Working Democracies*. Ithaca, NY: Cornell University Press.
Michie, Jonathan. 2017. "The Importance of Ownership." In *The Oxford Handbook of Mutual, Co-operative, and Co-owned Business*, edited by Jonathan Michie, Joseph R. Blasi, and Carlo Borzaga . Oxford: Oxford University Press. https://doi.org/10.1093/oxfordhb/9780199684 977.013.1, accessed 12 May 2024.
Mitchell, Greg. 1992. *The Campaign of the Century: Upton Sinclair's Race for Governor of California and the Birth of Media Politics*. New York: Random House.
Moody, J. Carroll, and Gilbert C. Fite. 1971. *The Credit Union Movement*. Vol. 540. Lincoln: University of Nebraska Press.

Moore, Barrington. 1966. *Social Origins of Democracy and Dictatorship*. Boston: Beacon.
Moore, James F. 1993. "Predators and Prey: A New Ecology of Competition." *Harvard Business Review*, May 1.
Moore, James F . 1996. *The Death of Competition: Leadership and Strategy in the Age of Business Ecosystems*. New York: HarperCollins.
Morris, Aldon. 2015. *The Scholar Denied: W. E. B. Du Bois and the Birth of Modern Sociology*. Berkeley: University of California Press.
Moss, Bernard H. 1976a. *The Origins of the French Labor Movement, 1830–1914: The Socialism of Skilled Workers*. Berkeley: University of California Press.
Moss, Bernard H. 1976b. "Producers' Associations and the Origins of French Socialism: Ideology from Below." *Journal of Modern History* 48(1): 69–89.
Moss, Bernard H . 1994. "Radical Labor under the French Third Republic." *Science & Society* 58(3): 333–43.
Moysich, Alane. 1997. "The Mutual Savings Bank Crisis." In *History of the Eighties—Lessons for the Future: An Examination of the Banking Crises of the 1980s and Early 1990s* 211–34. Federal Deposit Insurance Corporation: Washington, D.C. https://www.fdic.gov/resources/publications/history-eighties/volume-1/index.html.
Murphy, Sharon Ann. 2005. "Securing Human Property: Slavery, Life Insurance, and Industrialization in the Upper South." *Journal of the Early Republic* 25(4): 615–52.
Murphy, Sharon Ann . 2010. *Investing in Life: Insurance in Antebellum America*. Baltimore: Johns Hopkins University Press+ORM.
Naett, Caroline. 2015. "L'élaboration de La Loi ESS Du Point de Vue Du Mouvement Coopératif." *Revue Internationale de l'économie Sociale* (335): 41–52.
Nagel, Jack H. 1998. "Social Choice in a Pluralitarian Democracy: The Politics of Market Liberalization in New Zealand." *British Journal of Political Science* 28(2): 223–67.
National Rural Electric Co-operatives Association. n.d. "History: The Story behind America's Electric Co-operatives and NRECA." America's Electric Co-operatives. Accessed July 19, 2022.
NCBA. n.d. https://ncbaclusa.coop/blog/ncba-clusa-usda-rural-development-preview-state-cooperative-statute-library-at-press-club-event/ /.
Neison, Francis G. P. 1877. "Some Statistics of the Affiliated Orders of Friendly Societies (Odd Fellows and Foresters)." *Journal of the Statistical Society of London* 40(1): 42–89.
Nixon, Chris, and John Yeabsley. 2010. "Overseas Trade Policy." In *Te Ara Encyclopedia of New Zealand*. Manatu Taonga: New Zealand Ministry for Heritage and Culture.
North, Douglass C. 1966. *The Economic Growth of the United States: 1790–1860*. New York: W. W. Norton.
North, Douglass C . 1990. *Institutions, Institutional Change and Economic Performance*. Cambridge: Cambridge University Press.
Noyes, John. 1870. *History of American Socialisms*. New York: Lippincott.
Nuttall, Graeme. 2022. "How the UK Is Encouraging Employee Ownership Internationally." Field Fisher.
Ojala, Jari, Jari Eloranta, and Jukka Jalava. 2006. *The Road to Prosperity: An Economic History of Finland*. Finnish Literature Society.
Ollus, S., and H. Simola. 2006. "Russia in the Finnish Economy." Sitra.
Olssen, Erik. 1996. "Friendly Societies in New Zealand, 1840–1990." In *Social Security Mutualism: The Comparative History of Mutual Benefit Societies*, edited by Marcel van der Linden and Michel Dreyfus, 177–208. Peter Lang.
Olssen, Erik . 1997. "Mr. Wakefield and New Zealand as an Experiment in Post-Enlightenment Experimental Practice." *New Zealand Journal of History* 31(2): 197–218.
Omi, Michael, and Howard Winant. 2014. *Racial Formation in the United States*. New York: Routledge.

O'Neill, Rob. 2010. "Call for Alternative Kiwibank Future—as a Co-Operative." *Sunday Star-Times*, May 30.
Orren, Karen, and Stephen Skowronek. 1996. "Institutions and Intercurrence: Theory Building in the Fullness of Time." *NOMOS:American Society for Political and Legal Philosophy* 38: 111.
Orren, Karen, and Stephen Skowronek. 2004. *The Search for American Political Development*. Cambridge: Cambridge University Press.
Paavonen, Tapani. 2001. "From Isolation to the Core: Finland's Position towards European Integration, 1960–95." *Journal of European Integration History* 5(1): 53–75. .
Paavonen, Tapani. 2004. "Finland and the Question of West European Economic Integration, 1947–1961." *Scandinavian Economic History Review* 52(2–3): 85–109.
Palier, Bruno, and Kathleen Thelen. 2010. "Institutionalizing Dualism: Complementarities and Change in France and Germany." *Politics & Society* 38(1): 119–48.
Palo, Matti, and Erkki Lehto. 2012. *Private or Socialistic Forestry? Forest Transition in Finland vs. Deforestation in the Tropics*. World Forests. Springer Netherlands.
Pareto, Vilfredo. 1896. *Course of Political Economy*.
Parker, Florence E. 1922. "Consumers' Co-operative Societies in the United States in 1920: Bulletin of the United States Bureau of Labor Statistics, No. 313." October. https://fraser.stlouisfed.org/title/consumers-co-operative-societies-united-states-1920-3977.
Parker, Florence E. 1937. "Consumers' Coöperation." *Annals of the American Academy of Political and Social Science* 191: 91–102.
Parker, Florence E. 1949. "Consumers' Co-operatives: Operations in 1947: Bulletin of the United States Bureau of Labor Statistics, No. 948." January.
Parker, Florence E. 1956. *The First 125 Years: A History of Distributive and Service Co-operation in the United States, 1829–1954*. Co-operative League of the USA.
Parker, Florence Evelyn, and Helen I. Cowan. 1944. "Co-operative Associations in Europe and Their Possibilities for Post-war Reconstruction." Vol. 770. Washington, D.C.: U.S. Government Printing Office.
Pérotin, Virginie. 2012. "The Performance of Workers' Cooperatives" pp. 195-221 in Battilani, Patrizia, and Harm G. Schröter (eds), *The Co-operative Business Movement, 1950 to the Present*. Cambridge: Cambridge University Press.
Parker, Geoffrey G., Marshall W. Van Alstyne, and Sangeet Paul Choudary. 2016. *Platform Revolution: How Networked Markets Are Transforming the Economy and How to Make Them Work for You*. New York: W. W. Norton.
Pasha, Abdurrahman. 2014. "The Self-Help Co-operative Movement in Los Angeles, 1931–1940." PhD diss.
Pasquier, Romain. 2003. *La capacité politique des régions*. PUR.
Pateman, Carole. 1970. *Participation and Democratic Theory*. Cambridge: Cambridge University Press.
Pateman, Carole. 2012. "Participatory Democracy Revisited." *Perspectives on Politics* 10(1): 7–19.
Patmore, Greg. 2020. *Innovative Consumer Co-operatives: The Rise and Fall of Berkeley*. New York: Routledge.
Patmore, Greg, Nikola Balnave, and Olivera Marjanovic. 2021. "Resistance Is Not Futile: Co-operatives, Demutualization, Agriculture, and Neoliberalism in Australia." *Business and Politics* 23(4): 510–28.
Pearson, David G., and David C. Thorns. 1983. *Eclipse of Equality: Social Stratification in New Zealand*. London: Allen & Unwin.
Pease, William Henry, and Jane H. Pease. 1963. *Black Utopia: Negro Communal Experiments in America*. State Historical Society of Wisconsin.
Peden, Robert. 2011. *Making Sheep Country: Mt. Peel Station and the Transformation of the Tussock Lands*. Auckland: Auckland University Press.

Peltola, Aarre. 2003. *Finnish Statistical Yearbook of Forestry*. Finnish Forest Research Institute.
Perry, Stuart. 1978. *San Francisco Scavengers: Dirty Work and the Pride of Ownership*. Berkeley: University of California Press.
Pessen, Edward. 1956. "The Workingmen's Movement of the Jacksonian Era." *Mississippi Valley Historical Review* 43(3): 428–43.
Pettit, Philip. 1997. *Republicanism: A Theory of Freedom and Government*. Oxford: Oxford University Press.
Pettit, Philip. 2008. *Republican Freedom: Three Axioms, Four Theorems*. Oxford: Blackwell.
Pettit, Philip. 2012. *On the People's Terms*. Cambridge: Cambridge University Press.
Phillips, Jock, and Terrence John Hearn. 2008. *Settlers: New Zealand Immigrants from England, Ireland and Scotland, 1800–1945*. Auckland: Auckland University Press.
Pierson, Paul. 2000. "Increasing Returns, Path Dependence, and the Study of Politics." *American Political Science Review* 94(2): 251–67.
Pierson, Paul. 2004. *Politics in Time: History, Institutions, and Social Analysis*. Princeton, NJ: Princeton University Press.
Pihkala, Erkki. 1999. "The Political Economy of Post-war Finland, 1945–1952." *Scandinavian Economic History Review* 47(3): 26–48.
Pinto, Sanjay, 2023. "Economic Democracy against Racial Capitalism: Seeding Freedom." *Politics & Society* 51(2): 293–313.
Piketty, Thomas. 2014. *Capital in the Twenty-First Century*. Translated by Arthur Goldhammer. Cambridge, MA: Belknap Press.
Piketty, Thomas. 2020. *Capital and Ideology*. Cambridge, MA: Harvard University Press.
Piore, Michael, and Charles Sabel. 1984. *The Second Industrial Divide: Possibilities for Prosperity*. New York: Basic Books.
Pitzer, Donald E. 1997. *America's Communal Utopias*. Chapel Hill: University of North Carolina Press.
Piven, Frances Fox, and Richard A. Cloward. 1972. *Poor People's Movements: Why They Succeed, How They Fail*. Vol. 697. New York: Vintage.
Plessis, Alain. 2003. "The History of Banks in France." In *Handbook on the History of European Banks*, edited by Manfred Pohl and Sabine Freitag, 184–94. Elgar.
Power, Richard Anderson. 1939. "The Co-operative Primer."
Pratt, William C. 1996. "The Farmers Union, McCarthyism, and the Demise of the Agrarian Left." *The Historian* 58(2): 329–42.
Price, Roger. 2006. *A Concise History of France*. Cambridge: Cambridge University Press.
Quint, Howard H. 1953. *The Forging of American Socialism: Origins of the Modern Movement*. Columbia: University of South Carolina Press.
Ragin, Charles C. 1987. *The Comparative Method: Moving beyond Qualitative and Quantitative Strategies*. Berkeley: University of California Press
Randall, Daniel. 1888. "Sectiona XI–XII." In *History of Coöperation in the United States*, edited by Herbert Adams. Baltimore: Publication agency of the Johns Hopkins University.
Rayback, Joseph G. 1959. *History of American Labor*. New York: Simon and Schuster.
The Register. 2018. "Amazon Australia Confirms It Doesn't Ship to New Zealand." February 22.
Reid, Donald. 2018. *Opening the Gates: The Lip Affair, 1968–1981*. Verso Books.
Revue des études cooperatives (1938), Vol. 67. Les Presses universitaires de France.
Reyes, Oscar. 2007. "After Shock." Red Pepper, October 3. https://www.redpepper.org.uk/Aftershock/.
Reynolds, Bradley. 2023. "Finland's Long Road West." The Wilson Center. April 6.
Reynolds, Bruce. 2003. "Black Farmers in America, 1865–2000." Rural Business—Co-operative Service. Washington, D.C.: U.S. Department of Agriculture.
Ricardo, David. 1817. *The Works and Correspondence of David Ricardo*. Vol. 1: *On the Principles of Political Economy and Taxation*.

Richardson, Ruth. 1995. *Making a Difference*. Shoal Bay Press.
Richardson, Ruth 2016. "Co-operatives Require a Farmers' Fixit." *National Business Review*, September 2.
Robinson, Cedric J. 1983. *Black Marxism*. Revised and updated 3rd edition. The Making of the Black Radical Tradition. Chapel Hill: University of North Carolina Press.
Rochat, Jean. 2009. "The Various Uses of Law: The Société Anonyme in France." Paper presented at Eighth Conference of the European Historical Economics Society, Geneva, September 3–6.
Rodgers, Diane M., Jessica Petersen, and Jill Sanderson. 2016. "Commemorating Alternative Organizations and Marginalized Spaces: The Case of Forgotten Finntowns." *Organization* 23(1): 90–113.
Rogers, Joel, and Wolfgang Streeck. 1994. "Workplace representation overseas: The works councils story." pp. 97-156 in Richard Freeman (ed.), *Working under different rules*. Russell Sage Foundation, New York.
Rodrigue, John. 2007. "Thibodaux Massacre." In *Encyclopedia of U.S. Labor and Working-Class History*, edited by Eric Arnesen, 827. Taylor & Francis.
Roediger, David R. 1991. *The Wages of Whiteness: Race and the Making of the American Working Class*. Verso Books.
Ros, Agustin J. 2001. *Profits for All? The Cost and Benefits of Employee Ownership*. Nova.
Rosenthal, Clifford N. 2018. *Democratizing Finance: Origins of the Community Development Financial Institutions Movement*. Friesen Press.
Rothschild, Joyce. 1979. "The Collectivist Organization: An Alternative to Rational-Bureaucratic Models." *American Sociological Review* 44(4): 509–27.
Rothschild, Joyce. 1985. "Who Will Benefit from ESOPs?" *Labor Research Review* 1(6): 71–80.
Rothschild, Joyce. 2009. "Workers' Co-operatives and Social Enterprise: A Forgotten Route to Social Equity and Democracy." *American Behavioral Scientist* 52(7): 1023–41.
Rothschild, Joyce, and Marjukka Ollilainen. 1999. "Obscuring but Not Reducing Managerial Control: Does TQM Measure up to Democracy Standards?" *Economic and Industrial Democracy* 20(4): 583–623.
Rothschild, Joyce, and J. Allen Whitt. 1986. *The Co-operative Workplace: Potentials and Dilemmas of Organisational Democracy and Participation*. Cambridge: Cambridge University Press.
Roy, Ewell Paul. 1969. *Co-operatives: Today and Tomorrow*. Danville, IL: Interstate Printers.
Rozwenc, Edwin C. 1941. *Co-operatives Come to America: The History of the Protective Union Store Movement, 1845–1867*. Mount Vernon, IA: Hawkeye-Record Press.
Runcie, Neil. 1969. *Credit Unions in the South Pacific: Australia, Fiji, New Zealand, Papua and New Guinea*,. Studies in Finance 2. London: University of London Press.
Rural Power Project. 2016a. "The Crisis in Rural Electric Co-operatives in the South."
Rural Power Project. 2016b. "Examining the Governance Crisis of Rural Electric Co-operatives: Following the Money!"
Rural Power Project. 2021. "Electric Cooperative Board Diversity Is a Failure in the South."
Rural Power Project. 2022. "Beyond Backward: Rural Electric Cooperative Leaderships' Exclusion of Women and Minorities."
Russell, James W. 2009. *Class and Race Formation in North America*. Toronto: University of Toronto Press.
Russell, Raymond, and Stewart E. Perry. 1978. *Collecting Garbage: Dirty Work, Clean Jobs, Proud People*. New York: Routledge.
Rydberg, C. 2009. "Changing Fonterra's Ownership Model? Changing Fonterra's Ownership Model." PhD diss., Swedish University of Agricultural Sciences.
Salmond, James David. 1950. *New Zealand Labour's Pioneering Days: The History of the Labour Movement in N.Z. from 1840 to 1894*. Auckland: Forward Press.

Saloutos, Theodore. 1953. "The Grange in the South, 1870–1877." *Journal of Southern History* 19(4): 473–87.
Saloutos, Theodore, and John D. Hicks. 1951. *Twentieth-Century Populism: Agricultural Discontent in the Middle West, 1900–1939*. Lincoln: University of Nebraska Press.
Salustri, Andrea, Michele Mosca, and Federica Viganò. 2015. "Overcoming Urban-Rural Imbalances: The Role of Co-operatives and Social Enterprises." University Library of Munich, Germany.
Sanders, Bernie. 2016. *Our Revolution: A Future to Believe In*. New York: Macmillan.
Sanders, Bernie, with John Nichols. 2023. *It's OK to Be Angry about Capitalism*. New York: Crown.
Sanders, Elizabeth. 1999. *Roots of Reform: Farmers, Workers, and the American State, 1877–1917*. Chicago: University of Chicago Press.
Sargisson, Lucy, and Lyman Tower Sargent. 2017. *Living in Utopia: New Zealand's Intentional Communities*. New York: Routledge.
Schickler, Eric. 2001. *Disjointed Pluralism: Institutional Innovation and the Development of the U.S. Congress*. Princeton, NJ: Princeton University Press.
Schimmelfennig, Frank. 2014. "Efficient Process Tracing: Analyzing the Causal Mechanisms of European Integration." In *Process Tracing: From Metaphor to Analytic Tool*, edited by Andrew Bennett and Jeffrey T. Checkel, 98–125. Strategies for Social Inquiry. Cambridge: Cambridge University Press.
Schmidt, William E. 1984. "Electric Co-ops Facing Challenges on Racial Makeup of Boards." *New York Times*, March 5.
Schneiberg, Marc. 2010. "Toward an Organizationally Diverse American Capitalism—Co-operative, Mutual, and Local, State-Owned Enterprise." *Seattle University Law Review* 34: 1409.
Schneiberg, Marc. 2011. "Movements as Political Conditions for Diffusion: Anti-Corporate Movements and the Spread of Co-operative Forms in American Capitalism." *Organization Studies* 34(5–6): 653–82.
Schneiberg, Marc. 2017. "Resisting and Regulating Corporations through Ecologies of Alternative Enterprise: Insurance and Electricity in the US Case." In *The Corporation*, edited by Andre Spicer and Grietje Baars, 512–26. Cambridge: Cambridge University Press.
Schneiberg, Marc, Adam Goldstein, Matthew Kraatz. 2022. "Embracing Market Liberalism? Community Structure, Embeddedness, and Mutual Savings and Loan Conversions to Stock Corporations." *American Sociological Review*.
Schneiberg, Marc, Marissa King, and Thomas Smith. 2008. "Social Movements and Organizational Form: Co-operative Alternatives to Corporations in the American Insurance, Dairy, and Grain Industries." *American Sociological Review* 73(4): 635–67.
Schneiberg, Marc, and Sarah A. Soule. 2005. "Institutionalization as a Contested, Multilevel Process." In *Social Movements and Organization Theory*, edited by Davis, Gerald F., Doug McAdam, W. Richard Scott, and Mayer N. Zald, 122–60. . Cambridge: Cambridge University Press.
Schneider, Nathan, and Trebor Scholz. 2016. *Ours to Hack and Own*. OR Books.
Schrader, Ben. 1996. "A Brave New World? Ideal versus Reality in Postwar Naenae." *New Zealand Journal of History* 30(1): 61–79.
Schweninger, Loren. 1989. "Black-Owned Businesses in the South, 1790–1880." *Business History Review* 63(1): 22–60.
Scotts, Margaret. 2011. "Beyond Aid: Sustainable Community-Owned Co-operative Business." Unpublished ms. Wellington, NZ: Victoria University.
Scoville, Caleb, and Neil Fligstein. 2020. "The Promise of Field Theory for the Study of Political Institutions." In *The New Handbook of Political Sociology*, edited by Thomas Janoski, Cedric de Leon, Joya Misra, and Isaac William Martin, 79–101. Cambridge: Cambridge University Press.

Seeberger, Loïc. 2014. "Historique de l'évolution Du Droit Des Coopératives, de Ses Origines à Nos Jours." *Revue Internationale de l'économie Sociale* (333): 60–76.
Seto, Michael, and Cheryl Chasin. 2002. "E. General Survey of Irc 501 (C)(12) Cooperatives and Examination of Current Issues." Report. Washington, D.C.: Internal Revenue Service.
Sewell, William Hamilton. 1980. *Work and Revolution in France: The Language of Labor from the Old Regime to 1848*. Cambridge: Cambridge University Press.
Shaffer, Jack. 1999. *Historical Dictionary of the Co-operative Movement*. Scarecrow Press.
Shirom, Arie. 1972. "The Industrial Relations Systems of Industrial Co-operatives in the United States, 1880–1935." *Labor History* 13(4): 533–51.
Sibalis, Michael David. 1988. "Corporatism after the Corporations: The Debate on Restoring the Guilds under Napoleon I and the Restoration." *French Historical Studies* 15(4): 718–30. https://doi.org/10.2307/286555.
Sibalis, Michael David. 1989. "The Mutual Aid Societies of Paris, 1789–1848." *French History* 3(1): 1–30.
Simonen, Seppo. 1949. *Pellervolaisen Osuustoiminnan Historia*. Pellervo-Seura.
Simpson, James. 2011. *Creating Wine: The Emergence of a World Industry, 1840–1914*. Princeton, NJ: Princeton University Press.
Skinner, Quentin. 2003. *A Third Concept of Liberty: Isaiah Berlin Lecture*. British Academy.
Sklar, Martin J. 1988. *The Corporate Reconstruction of American Capitalism*. New York: Cambridge University Press.
Skocpol, Theda. 1979. *States and Social Revolutions: A Comparative Analysis of France, Russia and China*. Cambridge: Cambridge University Press.
Skrubbeltrang, F. 1964. "The History of the Finnish Peasant." *Scandinavian Economic History Review* 12(2): 165–80.
Skurnik, Samuli. 2002. "The Role of Co-operative Entrepreneurship and Firms in Organising Economic Activities—Past, Present and Future." *Finnish Journal of Business Economics* 1(2): 103–24.
Skurnik, Samuli, and Lee Egerstrom. 2007. "The Evolving Finnish Economic Model: How Co-operatives Serve as 'Globalisation Insurance.'"
Smith, Peter A. 2000. *The Private Prescription: The Story of Southern Cross Healthcare*. Auckland, N.Z.: Southern Cross Healthcare.
Smith, Philippa Mein. 2005. *A Concise History of New Zealand*. Cambridge: Cambridge University Press.
Soederberg, Susanne, Philip G. Cerny, and Georg Menz. 2005. *Internalizing Globalization: The Rise of Neoliberalism and the Decline of National Varieties of Capitalism*. Houndmills: Palgrave Macmillan.
Soifer, Hillel. 2021. "Shadow Cases in Comparative Research." *Qualitative and Multi-Method Research* 18 (2): 9–18.
Sombart, Werner. 1906. "Why Is There No Socialism in the United States?"
Sorensen, Andre. 2015. "Taking Path Dependence Seriously: An Historical Institutionalist Research Agenda in Planning History." *Planning Perspectives* 30(1): 17–38.
Sorensen, Andre. 2018. "Multiscalar Governance and Institutional Change: Critical Junctures in European Spatial Planning." *Planning Perspectives* 33(4): 615–32.
Soule, Sarah A. 2012. "Social Movements and Markets, Industries, and Firms." *Organization Studies* 33(12): 1715–33.
Soule, Sarah A. 2013. "Diffusion and Scale Shift." In *The Wiley-Blackwell Encyclopedia of Social and Political Movements*. New York.
Spence, Alan. 1993. *Lenin on Co-operatives and Other Articles on Marxism, Philosophy and Society*. Socialist Platform.
Spicer, Jason. 2020. "Worker and Community Ownership as an Economic Development Strategy: Innovative Rebirth or Tired Retread of a Failed Idea?" *Economic Development Quarterly* 34(4): 325–42.

Spicer, Jason. 2022. "Co-operative Enterprise at Scale: Comparative Capitalisms and the Political Economy of Ownership." *Socio-Economic Review* 20(3): 1173–209.

Spicer, Jason and Tamara Kay. 2022. "Another Organization Is Possible: New Directions in Research on Alternative Enterprise." *Sociology Compass* 16(3): E12963.

Spicer, Jason S., Tamara Kay, and Marshall Ganz. 2019. "Social Entrepreneurship: A Neoliberal Movement to Construct a New Field." *Socio-Economic Review* 17(1): 195–227.

Spicer, Jason, and Christa R. Lee-Chuvala. 2021. "Ownership and Mission Drift in Alternative Enterprises: The Case of a Social Banking Network." In Research in the Sociology of Organizations, edited by Chen, Katherine and Chen, Victor, vol. 72, 257–91, also known as *Organizational Imaginaries: Tempering Capitalism and Tending to Communities through Co-operatives and Collectivist Democracy*. Emerald.

Spicer, Jason, and Michelle Zhong. 2022. "Multiple Entrepreneurial Ecosystems? Worker Co-operative Development in Toronto and Montréal." *Environment and Planning A: Economy and Space* 54(4): 611–33.

Spinak, Abby Elaine. 2014. "Infrastructure and Agency: Rural Electric Co-operatives and the Fight for Economic Democracy in the United States." PhD diss., Massachusetts Institute of Technology.

St. Peter, Bob. 2008. "Co-opted: The Fall of the Natural Foods Co-operative and What We Can Do about It." *Saving Seeds*, Summer/Fall.

Staber, Udo. 1989. "Age-Dependence and Historical Effects on the Failure Rates of Worker Co-operatives: An Event-History Analysis." *Economic and Industrial Democracy* 10(1): 59–80.

Stampp, Kenneth Milton. 1956. *The Peculiar Institution: Slavery in the Ante-Bellum South*. New York: Vintage Books.

Standing, Russell Archie John. 2005. *Pride, Passion and Parochialism: A History of FMG 1905–2005*. Dunmore Press.

Standish, Reid. 2016. "How Finland Became Europe's Bear Whisperer." *Foreign Policy* (blog).

Starobin, Robert S. 1970a. "The Economics of Industrial Slavery in the Old South." *Business History Review* 44(2): 131–74.

Starobin, Robert S. 1970b. *Industrial Slavery in the Old South*. Oxford: Oxford University Press.

State Services Commission. 1996. "The Spirit of Reform: Managing the New Zealand State Sector in a Time of Change." June 28.

Steinlin, Simon, and Christine Trampusch. 2012. "Institutional Shrinkage: The Deviant Case of Swiss Banking Secrecy." *Regulation & Governance* 6(2): 242–59.

Steinmetz, George. 2005. "Return to Empire: The New US Imperialism in Comparative Historical Perspective." *Sociological Theory* 23(4): 339–67.

Stepan, Alfred. 2001. "Toward a New Comparative Politics of Federalism, (Multi)Nationalism, and Democracy: Beyond Rikerian Federalism." In *Arguing Comparative Politics*, edited by Alfred Stepan, 315–61. Oxford: Oxford University Press.

Stevenson, Philippa. 2000. "Corporates Wage Battle for Slice of Apple Pie." *New Zealand Herald*, July 21. https://www.nzherald.co.nz/business/corporates-wage-battle-for-slice-of-apple-pie/TMI7HBZ3V3MTVSOKVSBBC7CM5I/.

Stewart-Bloch, Nick. 2018. "From Co-operative Commonwealth to Yardstick Capitalism: Midland's Evolving Vision of Co-operation in Mid-Century Minnesota." *Minnesota History* 66(1): 6–19.

Stinchcombe, Arthur L. 1968. *Constructing Social Theories*. Chicago: University of Chicago Press.

Stockton, Frank T. 1931. "Productive Co-operation in the Molders Union." *American Economic Review* 21(2): 260–74.

Storrs, Landon R. Y. 2012. *The Second Red Scare and the Unmaking of the New Deal Left*. Princeton, NJ: Princeton University Press. https://doi.org/10.1515/9781400845255.

Stout, Lynn A. 2012. *The Shareholder Value Myth: How Putting Shareholders First Harms Investors, Corporations, and the Public.* Berrett-Koehler.
Stout, Lynn A. 2015. "Corporations Don't Have to Maximize Profits." New York Times, April 16.
Streeck, Wolfgang. 2016. *How Will Capitalism End?* Verso Books.
Streeck, Wolfgang, Craig Calhoun, Polly Toynbee, and Amitai Etzioni. 2016. "Does Capitalism Have a Future?" *Socio-Economic Review* 14(1): 163–83. https://doi.org/10.1093/ser/mwv037.
Streeck, Wolfgang,. 1997. "Beneficial Constraints: On the Economic Limits of Rational Voluntarism." In *Contemporary Capitalism: The Embeddedness of Institutions*, edited by J. Rogers Hollingsworth and Robert Boyer, 197–219. Cambridge: Cambridge University Press.
Streeck, Wolfgang, and Kathleen Ann Thelen. 2005. *Beyond Continuity: Institutional Change in Advanced Political Economies.* Oxford: Oxford University Press.
Stringleman, Hugh, and Frank Scrimgeour. 2008. "Dairying and Dairy Product." In *Te Ara Encyclopedia of New Zealand.* Manatu Taonga: New Zealand Ministry for Heritage and Culture. /en/city-history-and-people.
Sutherland, Benjamin. 1947. "Self Help Silver Jubilee: 25 Years at Your Service for Savings: A Record of 25 Years Community Service."
Sutton, Stacey A. 2019. "Co-operative Cities: Municipal Support for Worker Co-operatives in the United States." *Journal of Urban Affairs*, 1–22.
Swidler, Ann. 1986. "Culture in Action: Symbols and Strategies." *American Sociological Review*, 51(2):273–86.
Sylla, Richard, and Robert E. Wright. 2013. "Corporation Formation in the Antebellum United States in Comparative Context." *Business History* 55(4): 653–69.
Systems, eZ. n.d. "Bankers' Group Launches National Ad Campaign Questioning of Credit Unions Have 'Lost Their Way.'" CUToday. Accessed July 20, 2022.
Tai Awatea. n.d. "The New Zealand Company." Museum of New Zealand Te Papa Tongarewa.
Tanner, Rachael A. 2013. "Worker Owned Co-operatives and the Ecosystems That Support Them." Massachusetts Institute of Technology. Thesis.
Telegraph—Press Association. 1902. "State Coal Mine." *New Zealand Herald*, February 24.
The New York Times. 1864. "The French Co-operative Societies" May 8th, 1864. https://timesmachine.nytimes.com/timesmachine/1864/05/08/78723799.pdf?pdf_redirect=true&ip=0
Thelen, Kathleen. 1999. "Historical Institutionalism in Comparative Politics." *Annual Review of Political Science* 2(1): 369–404.
Thelen, Kathleen. 2000. "Timing and Temporality in the Analysis of Institutional Evolution and Change." *Studies in American Political Development* 14(1): 101–8.
Thelen, Kathleen. 2004. *How Institutions Evolve.* Cambridge: Cambridge University Press.
Thelen, Kathleen. 2009. "Institutional Change in Advanced Political Economies." *British Journal of Industrial Relations* 47(3): 471–98.
Thelen, Kathleen. 2012. "Varieties of Capitalism: Trajectories of Liberalization and the New Politics of Social Solidarity." *Annual Review of Political Science* 15: 137–59.
Thelen, Kathleen. 2014. *Varieties of Liberalization and the New Politics of Social Solidarity.* Cambridge: Cambridge University Press.
Thorns, David, and Ben Schrader. 2010. "City History and People." In *Te Ara Encyclopedia of New Zealand.* Manatu Taonga: New Zealand Ministry for Heritage and Culture. /en/city-history-and-people.
Thompson, Edward Palmer. 1963. *The Making of the English Working Class.* IICA.
Thomsen, Steen, Thomas Poulsen, Christa Børsting, and Johan Kuhn. 2018. "Industrial Foundations as Long-Term Owners." *Corporate Governance: An International Review* 26(3): 180–96.
Thomson, Keith Westhead, and Andrew Trlin, eds. 1970. *Immigrants in New Zealand.* Palmerston North: Massey University Press.

References

Thornton, Patricia, William Ocasio, and Michael Lounsbury. 2012. *The Institutional Logics Perspective: A New Approach to Culture, Structure, and Process.* Oxford: Oxford University Press.

Tilly, Charles, ed. 1975. *The Formation of National States in Western Europe.* Princeton, NJ: Princeton University Press.

Tirole, Jean. 2017. *Economics for the Common Good.* Princeton, NJ: Princeton University Press.

Tocqueville, Alexis de. 1835. *La démocratie en Amérique.* Gosselin.

Tombs, Robert. 1984. "Harbinghers or Entrepreneurs? A Workers' Cooperarive during the Paris Commune." *Historical Journal* 27(4): 969–77.

Trampusch, Christine, and Dennis C. Spies. 2014. "Agricultural Interests and the Origins of Capitalism: A Parallel Comparative History of Germany, Denmark, New Zealand, and the USA." *New Political Economy* 19(6): 918–42.

Tregle, Joseph G. 1979. "Thomas J. Durant, Utopian Socialism, and the Failure of Presidential Reconstruction in Louisiana." *Journal of Southern History* 45(4): 485–512. https://doi.org/10.2307/2207711.

Tuchinsky, Adam-Max. 2005. "'The Bourgeoisie Will Fall and Fall Forever': The New-York Tribune, the 1848 French Revolution, and American Social Democratic Discourse." *Journal of American History* 92(2): 470–97.

Tucker, William P. 1947. "Populism Up-to-Date: The Story of the Farmers' Union." *Agricultural History* 21(4): 198–208.

Turner, Frederick Jackson. 1893. "The Significance of the Frontier in American History." Proceedings of the State Historical Society of Wisconsin. A.S.931.

Turner, Howard Haines. 1941. *Case Studies of Consumers' Co-operatives: Successful Co-operatives Stated by Finnish Groups in the United States Studied in Relation to Their Social and Economic Environment.* New York: Columbia University Press.

Twain, Mark. 1897. *Following the Equator: A Journey around the World.* Hartford, CT: American Pub. Co.

Tyrrell, Ian. 1991. "American Exceptionalism in an Age of International History." *American Historical Review*, 96(4):1031–55.

University of Wisconsin Center for Co-operatives. 2010. "Research on the Economic Impact of Co-operatives."

Upright, Craig B. 2020. *Grocery Activism: The Radical History of Food Co-operatives in Minnesota.* Minneapolis: University of Minnesota Press.

U.S. Census Bureau, 2006. Data set on U.S. Slave Population by County as of 1860 (Data in Author-Created Map). Obtained via University of Minnesota, Minnesota Population Center.

U.S. Congress, House Committee on Ways and Means. 1947. *Revenue Revisions, 1947–48: Hearings Before the Committee on Ways and Means, House of Representatives, Eightieth Congress, First Session, on Proposed Revision of the Internal Revenue Code.* Washington, D.C.: U.S. Government Printing Office.

U.S. Department of State, Office of the Historian. 1989. "The United States and Finland: An Enduring Relationship, 1919–1989."

U.S. Federation of Worker Co-operatives. 2019. "Worker Co-ops and Democratic Workplaces in the United States."

U.S. National Security Council. 1952. "Foreign Relations of the United States, 1952–1954, Western Europe and Canada, Volume VI, Part 2. Office of the Historian."

Vaheesan, Sandeep. 2020. "Privileging Consolidation and Proscribing Cooperation: The Perversity of Contemporary Antitrust Law." *Journal of Law and Political Economy* 1(1).

Valgren, V. N. 1924. *Farmer's Mutual Fire Insurance in the United States: Materials for the Study of Business.* Chicago: University of Chicago Press.

Van Der Heijden, Jeroen. 2010. "A Short History of Studying Incremental Institutional Change: Does Explaining Institutional Change Provide Any New Explanations?" *Regulation & Governance* 4(2): 230–43.

Van Der Heijden, Jeroen, and Johanna Kuhlmann. 2017. "Studying Incremental Institutional Change: A Systematic and Critical Meta-Review of the Literature from 2005 to 2015." *Policy Studies Journal* 45(3): 535–54.

Van der Linden, Marcel, ed.. 1996. *Social Security Mutualism: The Comparative History of Mutual Benefit Societies*. Peter Lang.

Varney, Christine A. 2010. "The Capper-Volstead Act, Agricultural Co-operatives, and Antitrust Immunity." *Anti-Trust Source*, December 9.

Vienney, Claude. 1986. "Les Organismes de l'économie Sociale r Enforcent-Ils Leur Identité Dans La Période Contemporaine?" In *Économie Sociale et Financements Publics*.

Vieta, Marcelo. 2019. *Workers' Self-Management in Argentina: Contesting Neo-Liberalism by Occupying Companies, Creating Co-operatives, and Recuperating Autogestión*. Leiden: Brill. https://brill.com/view/title/25183.

Voorhis, Jerry. 1961. "American Co-operatives: Where They Come from, What They Do, Where They Are Going."

Voss, Kim. 1993. *The Making of American Exceptionalism: The Knights of Labor and Class Formation in the Nineteenth Century*. Ithaca, NY: Cornell University Press.

Wainwright, Nicholas B. 1953. "Philadelphia's Eighteenth-Century Fire Insurance Companies." *Transactions of the American Philosophical Society* 43(1): 247–52.

Walker, Juliet E. K. 1986. "Racism, Slavery, and Free Enterprise: Black Entrepreneurship in the United States before the Civil War." *Business History Review* 60(3): 343–82.

Wallerstein, Immanuel Maurice. 1974. *The Modern World-System: Capitalist Agriculture and the Origins of the European World-Economy in the Sixteenth Century*. Studies in Social Discontinuity. New York: Academic Press.

Walsh, Francis, and Basil Manly. 1916. "Industrial Relations: Final Report and Testimony." Washington, D.C.: U.S. Government Printing Office.

Warbasse, James Peter. 1923. *Co-operative Democracy Attained through Voluntary Association of the People as Consumers: A Discussion of the Co-operative Movement, Its Philosophy, Methods, Accomplishments, and Possibilities, and Its Relation to the State, to Science, Art, and Commerce, and to Other Systems of Economic Organization*. New York: Macmillan.

Ware, Norman Joseph. 1929. *The Labor Movement in the United States 1860–1895: A Study in Democracy*. New York: Vintage Books.

Weare, Walter B. (1973) 1993. *Black Business in the New South: A Social History of the North Carolina Mutual Life Insurance Company*. Durham, NC: Duke University Press.

Weber, Max. 1905. *The Protestant Ethic and the Spirit of Capitalism*. Student's ed. New York: Scribner.

Webster, Anthony, Linda Shaw, Rachael Vorberg-Rugh, John F. Wilson, and Ian Snaith. 2016. "Learning to Swim against the Tide: Crises and Co-Operative Credibility—Some International and Historical Examples." In *Mainstreaming Co-operation*, 1–13. Manchester: Manchester University Press.

Weil, David. 2014. *The Fissured Workplace*. Cambridge, MA: Harvard University Press.

Weir, Robert E. 2009. *Knights Down Under: The Knights of Labour in New Zealand*. Cambridge, UK: Cambridge Scholars.

Weissbourd, Jenny, Maureen Conway, Joyce Klein, and Yoorie Chang, Joseph Blasi, Douglas Kruse, Melissa Hoover, Todd Leverette, Julian McKinley, and Zen Trenholm. 2021. "Race and Gender Wealth Equity and the Role of Employee Share Ownership." *Journal of Participation and Employee Ownership* 4(2): 116–35.

Wiest, Edward. 1923. *Agricultural organization in the United States* (Vol. 2). University of Kentucky.

Whyte, William Foote. 1986. "On the Uses of Social Science Research." *American Sociological Review* 51(4): 555–63.

Whyte, William Foote, and Kathleen King Whyte. 1991. *Making Mondragon: The Growth and Dynamics of the Worker Co-operative Complex.* Ithaca, NY: Cornell University Press.

Williams, Linda. 2003. *The Constraint of Race: Legacies of White Skin Privilege in America.* State College, PA: Penn State Press.

Wilson, John, Anthony Webster, and Rachael Vorberg-Rugh. 2013. "The Co-operative Movement in Britain: From Crisis to 'Renaissance,' 1950–2010." *Enterprise & Society* 14(2): 271–302.

Wilson, John F., Anthony Webster, and Rachael Vorberg-Rugh. 2014. *Building Co-operation: A Business History of the Co-operative Group, 1863–2013.* Oxford: Oxford University Press.

Wright, Erik Olin. 2010. *Envisioning Real Utopias.* London: Verso.

Wright, Erik Olin. 2013. "Transforming Capitalism through Real Utopias." *American Sociological Review* 78(1): 1–25.

Wright, Robert E., and Christopher Kingston. 2012. "Corporate Insurers in Antebellum America." *Business History Review* 86(3): 447–76.

Wright, Robert E., and Richard Sylla. 2011. "Corporate Governance and Stockholder/Stakeholder Activism in the United States, 1790–1860: New Data and Perspectives." In *Origins of Shareholder Advocacy*, edited by Jonathan G S Koppell, 231–51. New York: Springer.

Yaker, Ed, Thomas Thompson, and Fredric Goidner. 2000. "The Co-operative Alternative Case Study: The First Urban Electric Coop." ACEEE Buildings Conference Proceedings.

Yeoman, Ruth. 2017. "From Traditional to Innovative Multi-Stakeholder Mutuals: The Case of Rochdale Boroughwide Housing." In *The Oxford Handbook of Mutual, Co-operative, and Co-owned Business*, edited by Jonathan Michie, Joseph R. Blasi, and Carlo Borzaga, . Oxford: Oxford University Press.

Young, Daniel. 2016. "Bankers Attack Credit Unions' Tax Status." *Credit Union Times*. Accessed July 20, 2022.

Zabawa, Robert E., and Sarah T. Warren. 1998. "From Company to Community: Agricultural Community Development in Macon County, Alabama, 1881 to the New Deal." *Agricultural History* 72(2): 459–86.

Zald, M. N. 1988. "History, Sociology, and Theories of Organization." University of Michigan Working Paper Series.

Zamagni, Vera. 2017. *An Economic History of Europe since 1700.* Newcastle: Agenda.

Zeuli, Kimberly A., and Jamie Radel. 2005. "Co-operatives as a Community Development Strategy: Linking Theory and Practice." *Journal of Regional Analysis and Policy* 35 (1100-2016-89741): 43–54.

Zitcer, Andrew. 2021. *Practicing Co-operation: Mutual Aid beyond Capitalism.* Minneapolis: University of Minnesota Press.

Zivan, Jerome A. 1970. "Need for Reform in Taxation of Agricultural Co-operatives." *Georgia Law Review* 5(3): 529–39.

Zwerdling, Daniel. 1978. *Democracy at Work: A Guide to Workplace Ownership, Participation and Self-Management Experiments in the United State and Europe.* Association for Self-Management.

Index

For the benefit of digital users, indexed terms that span two pages (e.g., 52–53) may, on occasion, appear on only one of those pages.

Tables are indicated by an italic *t* following the page number.

ACORN/The Labor Neighbor Research & Training Center, 215
AFL (American Federation of Labor), 157–58, 167–68, 180, 186, 187–88, 193–95, 200, 231–32
　Whiteness, 157, 180, 193–95, 200
AFL-CIO, 231. *See also* AFL (American Federation of Labor)
aggressive seagulls, 50
Agricultural Marketing Act, 204–5, 209
Air New Zealand, 148–49
Alabama, 172–73, 187, 227
Allarde Decree, 90–91, 103–4
Alsace, 117–18, 121
American abolitionists, 160–61, 165–66, 176, 192, 195
American Communist Party, 174
American Exceptionalism, 1–16, 157, 187–88, 189, 246–47
American Farm Bureau, 202, 203
American Federation of Labor. *See* AFL
American Institute of Co-operation, 203
American labor movement, 157, 162–63, 165, 174, 180–81, 182, 183, 185–86, 187–89, 200
American New Left, 174
amorçage, 116
ancien régime, 89, 92
Ancient Order of Foresters, 137
André Malraux, 119–20
Antebellum South, 158, 160, 161–62, 171–72, 173, 175, 178. *See also* South, U.S
Antitrust (laws and regulations), 10, 33–34, 73, 148, 155, 203, 205–7, 251–56
apex organization (co-operative), 2, 11, 18, 20–22, 29–30, 37–38, 48, 60, 61, 65, 143, 145, 198–99, 216, 219, 221, 222, 228–29, 230, 231, 238–39
Apis & Heritage, 240

associationism (France), 85–86, 87–88, 90–92, 93–94, 97, 101, 103–4, 121, 126, 223
Associationists (U.S.), 159, 164, 167–68, 170–71, 172, 176, 186
associations, loan, 160–61, 162, 180, 217
Ateliers Nationaux, 98–99
Auckland, 48–49, 127, 135, 137, 139, 144–45, 149, 152, 154
Australia, 5–6, 13–14, 35–36, 127, 129, 133, 134, 141, 149, 154, 247

Baker, Ella, 212–13, 228–29
Baldwin, James, 244
Ballance Agri-Nutrients, 142–43
banking and banks (general), 22, 25, 29–30, 52–53, 56, 62–63, 64, 73, 78, 84–85, 94–96, 103, 107, 110, 114–15, 124, 127, 136, 137–38, 140, 142–43, 148–49, 150–51, 152–53, 160, 161–62, 163–64, 182, 211–12, 217–18, 228–29, 238, 251–56
Bank of Finland, 69–70
Banque du Peuple (Proudhon), 94–95, 98–99
Banque Publique d'Investissement (BPI), 116–17
B-corps, 23
Belle Époque (France), 101–2
Beluze, Jean-Pierre, 94–95
Benefit Corporations, 23
Bensançon, 114
Black Americans, 7, 10, 145, 157, 160, 161–62, 166, 168, 173, 174, 175, 177–78, 183–84, 185–87, 188–94, 195, 196, 201–3, 205, 208–9, 212–13, 215, 219, 224, 227, 228–29, 231, 232, 234–35, 236–37, 240, 243, 256–57, 265–67
Black co-operation, 10, 166, 187, 198–99, 209, 218–19, 227, 228–29, 231, 232–34, 240, 243, 265, 266–67
Black Panthers, 236–37

Blanc, Louis, 97, 98–100, 163–64
BLS (Bureau of Labor Statistics), 219–20, 222
Board of Industry and Trade in Finland, 60
Bonaparte, Louis, 244
Bonaparte, Napoleon, 85–86, 91–92, 95–96, 99
BPCE, 107, 110, 124
Brandeis, Louis (Justice), 180
Bronx Co-operative Development Initiative, 265
Buchez, Philippe, 97, 98, 99–100
Buffalo, NY, 163–64
Bureau of Labor Statistics. See BLS

Cabet, Etienne, 94–95, 168–69
CAE, 116–17, 119–20
CAE Clara, 120, 121
caisses d'épargnes, 95–96, 122–24
California, 48–49, 206–7, 214, 219–20, 223, 224, 232–35, 239
CAMIF, 117–18
canuts, 94
capitalism, 1, 2, 4, 8–9, 26–27, 32–33, 36–37, 39, 50, 70–71, 72, 75–76, 86–88, 92, 94, 99–100, 102, 109, 115, 116, 125, 126, 129–30, 134–35, 158–59, 164, 173, 186–87, 206, 218, 223–24, 235–36, 237–38, 243, 244–45, 261–62, 264
  comparative capitalist families, 32–33, 34, 35, 36–37, 47–48, 51, 55–56, 73, 75, 80–81, 259–61
  platform capitalism, 31–32
  rich capitalist democracies, 26, 147
  utopian capitalism, 134, 138–39
Capper-Volstead Act, 206
CASDEN, 110, 124
CDCUs (community development credit unions), 212
CECOP/CICOPA Europe, 83
Center for Socialist Studies, Research, and Education, 115
central case with comparisons approach, 35
centralized planning, 145–46
Chapelier Law, 90–91, 103–4
CHCA (Co-operative Home Care Associates), 24–25, 241
cheesemakers, rural, 89–90
Chevènement, Jean-Pierre, 115
Christchurch, 48–49, 135, 137, 139, 143–45, 151–52

CIO (Congress of Industrial Organizations), 192, 200, 220, 224, 232
Civil War (Finland), 64–65, 66–67
Civil War (United States), 14–15, 89, 158–59, 160–61, 162, 168, 172–73, 177–81, 186, 195, 196–97
Clark, Helen, 150–51
Clayton Act, 206
Clemenceau, Georges, 100
CLUSA (Co-operative League of the USA), 198–99, 216, 218, 219, 221–25, 226–27, 228–30
CMA (Colored Merchants' Association), 228–29
CME (Coordinated market economies), 33–34, 36–37, 51, 55–56, 75–76, 86–87
CoBank, 205, 215–16
Cold War, 55–56, 68–69, 71–72, 75–76, 78–79
Collective interest co-operatives, 23
Collèges Coopératifs, 110–11
Colored Farmers' Alliance and Co-operative Union, 192–93
Colored Merchants' Association (CMA), 228–29
Colored National Labor Union, 185–86
Combination Acts (U.K.), 90–91
commerce véridique et social, 94
communism, 1, 70–71, 72, 117, 218, 219, 223–25
Communist Manifesto, 237–38. See also communism
communitarians (American movement), 9–10, 14–15, 156–59, 164, 166–67, 168–72, 175–78, 179, 185, 194–95, 256–57
  role of race and slavery, 172, 175, 177–78
communities, co-operative, 175–76
community benefit societies, 23
community development credit unions. See CDCUs
compagnonnages, 84–85, 89–90, 91, 95–96, 97
companies
  community contribution, 23
  community interest, 23
  limited liability, 77, 225–26
competition laws, 73–74, 148, 150, 201. See also Antitrust (laws and regulations)
confréries, 84–85, 89–90, 91, 95–96
consumer co-operatives, 4–5, 22–24, 30–31, 64, 71, 76, 86, 93–94, 104–5, 107,

108–10, 111, 113, 117–19, 137, 144–45, 146–47, 152, 166, 167–68, 183, 185–86, 194, 199, 200, 216, 218, 219–21, 222, 223, 224, 225–26, 227, 228–30, 231, 232–35
Consumers' Co-operative of Berkeley, 221
Co-op Alsace, 117–18
Coopaname, 120, 122–24
Co-op Democracy Project (Southern Regional Council), 215
Co-operation Jackson, 239, 265
co-operative banks, 23, 51–52, 62–63, 66, 73–74, 77–78, 93–95, 124, 150–51, 210
Co-operative Business New Zealand, 150
Co-operative Central Board, 29–30
Co-operative Central Exchange, 221
co-operative commonwealth, 9–10, 29–30, 51–52, 62, 66, 73, 98–99, 143–44, 184, 185–86, 200, 220, 222, 223–24, 232–34, 237–38, 248
Co-operative Companies Act, 145–46, 149–50
Co-operative Home Care Associates (CHCA). *See* CHCA (Co-operative Home Care Associates)
Co-operative League of the USA. *See* CLUSA
Coopérative Pointcarré, 122–24
co-operative republic, 102–12
co-operative stores, 66, 155–56, 158, 164, 166, 167–68, 170–71, 183–84, 193, 219–20, 227
co-operative subtypes, 15, 32, 92, 102–3, 122–24, 145
Co-operative Union, 29–30, 192–93
Co-operative Wholesale Society (CWS), 20–22, 29–30, 66, 183–84, 192
CoopFR, 114
Co-op Money, 150–51
Co-op Power, 214
Coordinated market economies. *See* CME
corporations, 13, 84–85, 87–88, 89–92, 93, 97, 159–60, 164, 174, 178, 205, 206, 251–56
corps métiers, 89–90
cotton, 172–73, 180–81, 182, 227
Countdown, 144
countercultural movements, 4–5, 231, 235–36, 243
countervailing power (Galbraith, John Kenneth), 30–31, 157–58, 196, 218, 256–57

COVID-19 Pandemic, 1–2, 56, 73, 78
Crédit Coopératif, 107–8, 124
Crédit Foncier, 105–6
Crédit Maritime, 124
Credit Union National Association (CUNA), 210–11, 212
Credit Union National Extension Bureau, 210–11
credit unions, 3–4, 22, 23, 200–1, 210–13, 214, 222
   Black credit unions, 212–13
   CDCUs (community development credit unions), 212–13, 214, 265
   Credit Union and Friendly Societies Act, 145–46
   Credit Union and Friendly Societies Act (New Zealand), 145–46
   Credit Union National Association (CUNA), 210–11, 212
   Credit Union National Extension Bureau, 210–11
   low-income-serving, 212–13
Crimean War, 58
Cross, Ira, 155, 198

Dain, Charles, 99
Dairy Industry Restructuring Act, 150
Danish co-operatives, 258
DaWI (Democracy at Work Institute), 230, 239, 240
Debs, Eugene, 232
Delaware, 196–97
democracies, rich, 1, 4–5, 7, 8, 9–11, 17, 22, 23, 26, 30–31, 33–34, 35–37, 49, 53, 56, 57, 96, 112, 130, 194, 222, 251–56, 257–58
Democracy at Work Institute. *See* DaWI
Democratic Party, 177, 180, 195, 224, 232–34
demutualization, 77, 83, 122–24, 148, 150, 151–52, 199, 216, 217–18
Denmark, 5–6, 23, 51, 258
Department of State (U.S.), 69–70
Desjardins, Mr. and Mrs. Alphonse and Doriméne, 210–11
Desroche, Henri, 110–11
Detroit, 163–64
developmental state, 130–31, 139, 143
dividend rebate and patronage, co-operative, 24–25, 117–18, 149, 204, 226–27, 229, 235
Douglas, Roger, 147, 148

Drivers Co-operative, 1–2, 3–4, 241
Du Bois, W. E. B., 10, 25, 227, 228–29
Dunedin, 135, 137
Durant, Thomas Jefferson, 177

Ebony, 244
economic democracy, 5–6, 30, 46, 126
economic independence, 12–13, 54, 61, 66, 70, 149, 195, 251–56
economies of scale, 31–33, 211, 220
"effervescence of special provision" (France), 103–4
E-group, 76
Elanto, 65, 71–72
electrical co-operatives, 24–25, 140, 155, 213–14, 215–16, 230
Elisa, 77
Ely-Bemis Wisconsin School of Labor history, 167–68, 174
employee stock ownership plans. See ESOPs
Enercoop, 118–20
Energy Co-operative of America, 214
Engels, Friederich, 20–22, 94, 98, 182–83, 237–38
England, 135, 137, 141, 162–63, 188, 210. See also Great Britain, United Kingdom
English Laws Act, 141
entrepreneurship grants (France), 120
Entrust, 149
EPIC movement, 232–34
equity, 22, 27, 37–38, 83, 115–16, 149–50, 151–52, 203, 241
ESFIN Gestion, 115–16, 119–20
ESOPeratives/democratic ESOP (DESOPs), 22–24, 237–38
ESOPs (employee stock ownership plans), 22–24, 199, 231, 237–38, 241–42
ESS, 82–83, 84–85, 86, 87–88, 112–13, 115, 116–17, 120–21, 122–24. See also Social and Solidarity Economy
European Economic Community (EEC), 69–70, 146–47
European Research Institute on Co-operatives and Social Enterprises (EURICSE), 4–5
European Union (EU), 12–13, 73–79
exception culturelle française, 119–20

Farm Bureau (American Farm Bureau), 203, 207
Farm Credit Act, 205, 215–16

farmer-labor coalitions, 186–87, 191–92, 193, 195, 209–10
Farmers' Alliances, 183–85, 192–93, 201–3, 206–7, 208–9
farmers co-operatives, 64, 208, 215–16
Farmers' Equity Union, 203
Farmers' Improvement Society (TX), 209
Farmers Mutual Group, 142–43
Farmers' Union, 142–43
Farmlands, 142–43
Farmsource, 142–43
FBI investigations (of Southern Black co-operatives), 209
featherbedding system (Finland), 75–76
February Manifesto, 60–61
Federal Credit Union Act, 210–11
Federal Emergency Relief Administration, 234–35
Federal Farm Loan Act, 204–5
federalism, 8, 34, 36–37, 250
Fennoman movement, 54, 58–59, 61
fields, 12, 15, 26, 29, 39–49, 53–54, 55, 75, 78–81, 86–88, 101–12, 113, 117, 126, 130–31, 154–97, 198–201, 208, 210–12, 235, 243, 245–46, 247–48, 250–56, 258–61, 262, 264, 267
  architecture and overlap, 42–43, 84–85, 87–88, 156, 248
  field bounds, 41, 44, 45–46, 86–87, 155–56, 200–1, 242–43, 246, 248, 250–51, 258–59, 266–67
  field bricoleurs and bricolage, 44, 60, 125–26
  field challengers, 11, 42–43, 44, 54, 81, 248, 261
  field competitors, 199, 219, 235–36, 241, 242, 246–47, 251–56, 257, 262–63
  field environment(s), 9–10, 35, 40, 42–43, 44, 46, 47–48, 53–55, 60, 73, 75–76, 80–81, 89, 91, 102, 112–13, 124–25, 130–34, 136–37, 156, 180–81, 199, 231, 243, 244–45, 250, 251–57, 258–59, 260–63, 265
  field framing, 10, 14–15, 91, 156, 157–58, 193–94, 195, 232, 237–38, 246–47, 248, 251–57
  field logics, 41, 251
  field openings, 11, 42–43, 54, 85, 88, 130–31, 133–34, 147–48, 258–59
  field rupture, 39–40, 42, 44, 54, 81, 87–88, 89, 102, 126, 146–54, 179–81, 243, 248, 261–62, 263–64

Index

field settlement, 42, 44, 88–89, 132–33, 138, 147, 154, 180–81, 186, 187–88
field space, 54, 87–88, 103, 125–26, 131–33, 152, 154, 156, 175–76, 197, 200, 212, 256, 257
field tracing, 12, 46–49
hybrid fields, 44, 54, 251–56
incumbents, 9, 11, 42–43, 44, 54, 88–89, 93, 131, 132–33, 138, 141–42, 156, 160, 165–66, 178, 180, 197, 243, 248, 251–57, 260–61
partial fields, 199, 218, 242–43
skilled social actors, 11, 41, 42–43, 44t, 44, 54, 60, 97, 125–26, 155–56, 206–7, 210–11, 237–38, 257, 258–59, 264–65
Filene, Edward, 210–11
finance and financial enterprises, institutions, and processes (general), 1–2, 3–4, 13, 18–20, 27–28, 52–53, 65, 76–77, 82–83, 86–87, 95–96, 97, 103–4, 106–8, 111, 114–15, 116, 117, 119–20, 122–24, 136, 148, 150–51, 155, 158–59, 160–61, 162, 178–79, 180, 183–84, 189–90, 197, 199, 208–9, 210, 211, 212–13, 215–16, 217, 266
Finlandization, 12–13, 68–72
Finnish Americans, 25, 221
Finnish Diet, 58, 59, 62, 64–65
Finnish independence, 12–13, 54, 56, 60–61, 65, 148–49
Finnish Labor Museum, 66–67
First Industrial Revolution, 133, 181, 247
First International Co-operative Congress, 219
First Red Scare, 224, 232–34
Florange Law, 83
Florida's Natural Orange Juice, 24–25
Floyd, George, 7, 11
FNCC, 109–10, 117
fonds communs de placement d'entreprise solidaire (90/10 funds), 116–17
food and agriculture
agriculture and agricultural co-operatives, 4–5, 23, 25, 36–37, 51, 56, 60, 61, 64, 66–67, 77, 80–81, 84–85, 89–90, 93–94, 104–7, 109, 127, 135–36, 142–44, 150, 152, 155, 158, 172, 186–87, 197, 199, 201, 202–5, 206–9, 220, 225–26, 229–30, 246, 251–56
dairy and dairy co-operatives, 25, 34, 62–64, 127, 138–39, 141–43, 147, 150

food and food co-operatives, 1–2, 51–52, 78, 84–85, 91–92, 109–10, 118–19, 122–24, 218–19, 227, 228, 235–37, 238–41
Foodstuffs, 144
Ford, Henry, 208
forestry, 58, 66–67, 140, 251–56
four estates system, 59
Fourier, Charles, 99
Fourierian/Owenite, 171–72
Fourierian phalanxes and phalanstères, 94, 167–68, 169–70, 177, 179
Fourierism, 159, 165–66, 167–68, 170–71, 176, 179
Fourth Republic (France), 102–3, 105, 111–12
Fox, William, 137
Franche-Comté, 89–90
Franklin, Benjamin, 160–61
Frederick Douglass Co-operative, 228
French Revolution, 13, 84–85, 88, 89, 90–92, 102, 105, 113, 251–56
Second French Revolution (The July Revolution), 84–85, 94, 95–96, 97
Third French Revolution, 96
FTD/Interflora, 151–52

Galbraith, John Kenneth (countervailing power), 30–31, 157–58, 196, 218, 256–57
Garden Cities, 135
Garveyite movement, 228
Gebhard, Mr. and Mrs. Hannes and Hedvig, 59–60, 61–65, 66–67
geography (economic, including remoteness, scale, size/distance), 8, 13–14, 15, 35, 36–37, 46, 47–48, 55, 79–81, 128–29, 130–31, 132–33, 148–49, 155, 178–79, 246–47, 248, 251–56, 262
Georgia (U.S.), 172–73, 227–28
Germany, 5–6, 23, 36–37, 51, 57, 60–61, 66, 68, 79, 103, 160, 163–64, 210
Gide, Charles, 65, 94, 109, 113–14
Golden Gate Disposal Company, 232
Gompers, Samuel, 194–95, 232, 234
Grain Futures Act, 204–5
Grange, The (The National Grange of the Order of Patrons of Husbandry), 183–85, 191–92, 197, 201–3, 204
Granstrom, Axel, 60
Grant, Ulysses, 165–66
Great Britain, 53, 68, 79, 122–24, 129, 131–32, 133, 134–35, 139, 141–42, 146–48, 160, 180–81. *See also* England, United Kingdom

Great Depression, 4–5, 144–45, 201–2, 208, 209, 211, 222, 226–27
Greeley, Horace, 165–66, 170–71, 177, 185–86
Greenback Labor Party, 191–92
Greensboro Mutual Life, 160–61
Green Worker Co-operative Academy, 265
Groupama, 107
Guesde, Julian, 109
guild system, 84–85, 89–92, 95–96

Haiti, 169–70
Hamer, Fannie Lou, 15–16
Hankkija, 64, 75–76
Harding, President Warren G., 211, 222–23
Haymarket riots (Chicago), 187–88, 190
Helsinki, 48–49, 50, 52–53, 58, 59–60, 62–63, 66, 72
Hillquit, Morris, 168–69, 232, 234
HKScan, 75–76
HOK, 71–72
Homestead Acts, 136
homogeneity and homophily, 25–26, 36–37, 46, 134, 141–42, 251–56
  economic homogeneity, 36–37, 46, 47–48, 80, 141–42
Hoover Scare, 192–93
housing, co-operative, mutual, and other social models, 22, 56, 84–85, 104–5, 122–24, 135, 140, 145–46, 148, 217, 228
Howard, Ebenezer, 135
Hubert-Valleroux, 94–95, 97–99

ICA (International Co-operative Alliance), 2, 4–6, 18–20, 24–25, 29–30, 37–38, 65, 109–10, 222, 258
immigration and immigrants, 25, 134, 140, 163–64, 169–70, 174, 193–94, 221, 266–67
Inclusiv, 212–13, 265
incorporation, 28, 92, 94, 159–60, 174, 178–79, 180, 203–4
  requirements, 82–83
  restrictions, 196–97
  statutes, 22
India, 229–30
Industrial and Provident Societies Act, 140, 141
Industrial Brotherhood, 183
industrialization, 4, 10, 59–60, 99–100, 137–38, 143, 156, 172–73, 174–75, 180–81, 247, 251–56

institutions and institutionalism, 11, 13–14, 15, 25, 39–40, 41–42, 43, 44–46, 53, 70, 71, 87–88, 105–7, 114–15, 133–34, 161–62, 175–76, 181, 187–88, 197, 200–1, 212, 217, 244–45, 248, 259–60, 262, 264
  critical junctures, 1, 12–13, 39–40, 44–45, 53–54, 70, 87, 102, 130–31, 187–88, 248, 261–62, 264
  developmental pathways and path-dependency, 2, 10–11, 15–16, 35–36, 39–40, 85, 125–26, 130, 180, 187–88, 198–99, 200–1, 248, 258, 260, 264
  historical institutionalism, 12, 17–18, 39, 43–44, 197, 199–200, 248, 259–61
  conversion, 40, 44, 55–56, 130, 147–48, 199, 216, 238, 251–56
  displacement, 40, 42–43, 44, 55–56, 75–76, 80–81, 113, 130, 147–48, 197, 216, 251–56
  drift, 40, 44, 78–79, 81, 130, 149–50, 164, 197
  layering, 13, 40, 44, 55, 71, 80–81, 85–86, 102–3, 112–13, 130, 140, 145–46, 197, 201, 205, 208, 214, 248, 251–56
  institutional arrangements, 8, 10, 14–15, 39–41, 44, 46, 73, 86–87, 90–91, 128–29, 148, 195, 196–97, 251–56, 259–60, 261–62
  institutional bricolage, 40–41, 45, 86, 244–45
  institutional evolution, 12, 13–14, 39–41, 42, 53–54, 55–56, 75, 80, 81, 85–86, 87–104, 107–8, 112–13, 118–19, 125–26, 162, 197, 199–200, 205, 248, 250, 251–56, 259–60, 261, 264–65
  institutional incongruencies and discordance, 40, 125
  institutional recombination, 44, 85–86
  institutional voids, 10–11, 40–41, 42–43, 44–45, 53, 54, 60, 85, 88, 133–34, 136–37, 248, 257, 259, 261–62
interfirm coordination (and co-operatives), 9–10, 26, 29–30, 31–32, 33–34, 37–38, 43, 46, 51, 61, 64, 66, 73, 80–81, 93–94, 97, 98–99, 102, 103, 110–12, 124–25, 131, 136, 142–43, 145, 150–51, 152–53, 155–56, 163–64, 167–68, 180, 184, 198–99, 201–2, 205–6, 208–9, 211, 215–16, 219–20, 228–29, 242–43, 246–47, 251–56, 257–59, 260–61
Intermarché, 111

International Co-operative Alliance. *See* ICA
investor-owned firms. *See* IOFs
IOFs (investor-owned firms), 1, 2, 9, 14–15, 18, 22–24, 26, 27–30, 32, 33–34, 36–37, 43, 53–54, 55–56, 58, 70–71, 73–74, 75–76, 86, 87–88, 93–94, 112–14, 117–18, 124–25, 126, 128–29, 130–32, 134, 137–38, 139, 142, 143–44, 147–48, 150, 154, 156, 159, 160, 162, 164, 168, 174, 178, 180, 185, 188, 189–90, 195, 196–97, 198–200, 201, 206, 214, 215–16, 219, 224–27, 237–38, 243, 246, 251–58, 260–62
Iron Curtain, 55
Iron Molders' Union, 183–84
IRS, 226–27, 231, 235
IWW (International Workers of the World), 200, 232

Jacksonian Era, 166–67
Jacobin France, 86, 112, 115
Jean Royer Law, 117–18
Jim Crow, 9, 10, 14–15, 156, 189–90, 195, 196–97, 219, 227, 243, 251–56
Journal of United Labor, 139, 187, 192
Judaism and Jewish-related co-operation, 25, 210–11, 220

Kajak Games, 78
Kalevela (national epic poem of Finland), 61
Kelso, Louis, 237–38
Kerr, Clark, 234–35
King Jr, Martin Luther, 15–16
KK, 66, 76. *See also* Kulutusosuuskuntien Keskusliitto
Klein, Naomi, 1, 4–5, 51–52, 264
Knights of Labor, 9–10, 13–15, 59–60, 129–30, 138–40, 143–44, 156–58, 165, 175, 179–96, 198–200, 201–3, 208–9, 230–32, 243, 248, 256–57, 265
Knights of St. Crispin, 183–84
Kulutusosuuskuntien Keskusliitto, 66, 76

labor and wait, 192
labor republicanists, 14–15, 185–86, 192, 195
Labour Party, 130, 139–40, 145–46, 147, 148, 150
La Réunion (TX), 169–70
Laverdant, Désiré, 99
Lazarus, Emma, 15–16
Lechevalier, Jules, 99

Leclerc, 111, 117–18
Leflore incident, 192–93
legislation, 3–4, 22, 58, 61–62, 70–71, 77–78, 83, 102–4, 105, 107–8, 111–12, 115–17, 118–19, 122–24, 140, 151, 160, 178–79, 184–85, 200, 204–5, 206, 207–8, 210–11, 214, 229–30, 242–43, 258–59
legitimacy, 4, 13, 86–87, 88–89, 101–2, 103–5, 192, 201, 206, 246–47, 257, 258–59
Les Canaux, 122–24
L'ESPER (L'Économie Sociale Partenaire de l'École de la République), 84, 124
liberalism, 8, 12–14, 34, 55–56, 73, 94–95, 116, 117–18, 125, 127–54, 157–58, 178–79, 196, 206, 208, 212–13, 214, 231, 246, 251–58, 263, 265–66
  economic liberalism, 8–9, 10, 11, 13–14, 55–56, 80–81, 87–88, 93–94, 112, 124–25, 126, 127, 128–29, 130–31, 132–33, 134, 143–44, 145–46, 154, 156, 246, 251
  liberalization, 13–14, 55–56, 70–71, 73–79, 86, 112, 117–18, 120–21, 122–24, 125, 130, 131–33, 143–44, 147–54, 196–97, 199, 216
  relationship to race, 8, 10, 246, 256–58
Liberal-Labour alliance (Lib-Lab alliance), 139–40
liberal market economy. *See* LMEs
Lilith (co-operative), 78
Limited Co-operative Association, 23
limited liability companies (LLCs), 225–26, 239–40
LMEs (liberal market economy), 13–14, 32–34, 36–37, 73, 75–76, 86–87, 127, 129, 130, 133, 148, 259–60, 261
Loi Olivier, 91–92
London (England), 134, 136, 154, 192
Louisiana, 169, 174, 177, 186–87, 190–93, 195, 196, 201–2
Luxembourg Commission, 98–99

Mackinder, Sir Halford, 79–80
Madison, WI, 18–20, 48–49
Main Streets Employee Ownership act, 239
Manchester (England), 20–22, 25–26, 62–63, 180–81
Manchester Unity, 137
Maori, 133, 134, 136, 145
Marshall Plan, 68–69
Marx, Karl, 26–27, 98–99, 134, 165–66, 181, 182–83, 237–38, 244–45

Maryland, 165, 168, 227
Massachusetts, 168, 177–78, 184–85, 204, 210–11
McCarthyism (anticommunism), 224–25, 231, 234–35, 237–38
McReynolds, Justice James C., 207–8
meta-organizations, 2, 11, 12–13, 18, 20–22, 29–30, 41–42, 82–83, 84, 102–3, 107–8, 111–12, 114, 116–17, 122–24, 143, 145, 149–50, 216, 221, 222, 246–47, 258–59. *See also* apex organization
Metropolitan France, 85–86, 247
Metsä Group, 66–67, 73–74
Minneapolis, 7, 48–49, 184, 214, 226, 236
Minnesota, 23, 48–49, 171–72, 184–85, 221, 229–30, 239–40
Mitterand, François, 112, 115–16, 117
mix, firm-type, 15, 55–56, 260–61
mixed-member proportional system, 150–51
Monáe, Janelle, 15–16
Mondiale, 107
Mondragon, 57, 264
Mormons, 25, 219, 220
Muldoon, Robert, 146–47
multi-stakeholder co-operatives, 18–20, 23, 118–19, 122–24, 218–19, 230–31, 240–41, 243
mutual aid, 1–2, 89–90, 95–96
mutual aid societies, 84–85, 89–90, 95–96, 101–2, 160–62
mutual benefit societies, 22, 144, 161–62
mutual insurance, 77, 83, 103–5, 106–7, 124, 151–52, 160–62, 180, 216–17
mutualization, 149, 216–17

Napoleonic Code, 91, 92
Napoleonic Wars, 58
Nashoba, 169–70, 177–78
National Conference of Commissioners on Uniform State Laws, 223
National Consumer Co-operative Bank Act, 238
National Co-operative Parliament, 107–8
National Council of Farmers' Co-operatives, 203
National Farmers' Union, 203
National Federation of Colored Farmers, 209
National Industrial Congresses, 164, 166–67, 179
National Labor Union, 183, 185–87
National Negro Business League, 209
National Party, 144–47, 148
National Rural Electric Co-operatives Association, 214
National Tax Equality Association (NTEA), 225–27
National Workshops (France), 98–100
NATO, 68–69, 79
NCBA, 216, 229–30, 242–43
NCBA-CLUSA, 199, 201, 216, 229–30, 265–66
NCFC, 203, 207
Negro Co-operative Guild, 228–29
New Bedford, 168
New Belgium Brewing, 241
New Deal (Great Depression Programs), 198–99, 200–16, 217, 222, 224, 231–32, 234, 235
New England, 160–61, 162, 164, 166, 167–68, 184–85, 202–3, 210–11, 214, 219
New England Association of Farmers, 166–67
New England Protective Union, 167–68
New Hampshire, 184–85, 210–11
New Jersey, 184–85, 188–89, 196–97, 204
New Orleans, 161–62, 174, 191–92, 196
New York, including New York City, 1–2, 7, 24–25, 48–49, 59, 154, 155, 163–64, 165–66, 168, 198, 203, 211, 212–13, 214, 216–17, 221, 241
New Zealand and Australian Land Company, 142
New Zealand Companies Act, 149–50
New Zealand Company, 134–37, 138–39, 142
New Zealand Co-operative Alliance, 145
New Zealand Federation of Co-operatives, 145
New Zealand Honey Producers' Co-operative, 151–52
New Zealandize, 137–38
Nixon, Richard, 224
NLU, 183, 185–87. *See also* National Labor Union
Normandie-Picardie, 117–18
North American Students of Co-operation, 84–85
Northampton, 177–78
North Carolina, 169, 177, 212–13, 227
North Carolina Mutual Life, 160–61
Northwestern Co-operative League, 220
NTEA. *See* National Tax Equality Association
Number 8 Wire, 57–58, 252*t*

Occupy Wall Street, 5–6
Ohio, 168, 177–78, 183–85
OKO Bank, 62–63, 64
Operation Dixie, 192
Oregon Clean Power Co-op, 214
Organic Valley, 24–25
organizational archetypes, 20–22, 41–42, 43, 45–46, 210, 212–13, 239, 260–61
organizational forms, 32–33, 35, 36–37, 54, 84, 88–89, 90–91, 94–95, 113–14, 154
organizational models, 11, 88, 135, 251
Osuuskassojen Keskuslainarahasto Osakeyhtiö, 62–63. *See also* OKO Bank
Osuuskauppojen, 64
Osuustukkukauppa, 66. *See also* OTK
Otago, 135, 141–42
OTK, 66–67, 71, 72, 76
Owenites (Owen, Robert), 20–22, 159, 160, 163–64, 166, 168–70, 172, 186

Paasikivi, Juho, 62
Palmerston North, 143–44
Pareto (power law), 31–32
Paris, 48–49, 82, 91–92, 94–96, 97–100, 107–8, 110–11, 120, 121, 122–25
  chambres syndicales, 100
  commune(s), 99, 100–1, 103–4, 107–8, 122–24
Park Slope Food Co-op, 218–19
Pellervo (Pellervo-Seura or Pellervo Society), 12–13, 50, 60, 61–64, 65, 66–67, 70–71, 73–74, 75–76, 78
Pennsylvania, 168, 184–85, 204
People Power Solar Co-op, 214
Philadelphia Contributionship, 160–61
policies, 12, 13, 15–16, 17, 18–20, 23, 29–30, 32–34, 35, 36–37, 39–40, 41–42, 44–45, 48, 53, 61, 68–69, 70, 73–74, 80–81, 82–83, 85–86, 87–88, 103–4, 115–16, 122, 126, 130, 133, 138–39, 142, 145, 146–48, 149–50, 178–79, 180, 187, 201, 202, 205, 207–8, 209–10, 217–18, 239, 241–43, 246–47, 250, 251–56, 257, 259, 260–61, 262–63, 265–66
politics, 1, 9, 10, 12, 13, 14–15, 20–22, 32–33, 35, 36–37, 39–40, 46, 53–54, 55–56, 57, 59, 60, 61, 65, 68–69, 70, 71, 80–81, 85–86, 89, 93, 97, 98–99, 103–4, 113–14, 125–26, 132–34, 139, 157–58, 166–67, 180, 185–87, 190–91, 193, 201–2,
209–10, 222–23, 224–25, 238, 248, 256–57, 258–60
  geopolitics, 12–14, 55, 68–69, 73, 78, 79–81, 132, 251–56
POPPankki Bank, 78
Populist movement (U.S. historical), 180, 193, 195, 200–16
Powderly, Terence, 190
process tracing, 12, 46–47
producer co-operatives, 23, 78, 86, 117–18, 127, 132, 142–44, 145, 151–52, 162, 164, 184, 201
producers' associations and productive associations (forerunner of worker co-operatives), 84–86, 89–90, 93–95, 96–97, 107, 108–9, 112–13, 158, 162, 163–64, 165–67, 170–71, 172, 185–86
profits, 24–25, 52–53, 77, 150–51, 152–53, 166, 183–84, 237–38
Progressive Era, 193, 200–1, 209, 210, 231
Project Equity, 239, 240, 265
Protective Union, 166, 167–68, 184–85
Proudhon, Pierre-Joseph, 93–95, 99–100
PSIS, 150–51

Québec, 210

Rabobank New Zealand, 142–43
race and racism, 1–2, 7–9, 10, 11, 13–16, 20–22, 34, 39, 47–48, 56, 84, 88, 93–94, 99, 110, 130–31, 132–33, 156, 157–58, 169–70, 172, 177–78, 183, 188, 189–91, 192, 196, 199–201, 202–3, 208–10, 212–13, 216, 243, 246, 247, 248, 251–58, 262, 265–66
racial capitalism, 9, 256–57, 262
Radical Republicans (France and U.S.), 104, 179
Raiffeisen banking co-operatives (Germany), 60
Rainbow Grocery, 218–19
Ravensdown Fertiliser, 142–43
REA (Rural Electrification Administration), 213–14, 215–16
Reagan, Ronald (President), and Reaganism/Reaganomics, 130, 147, 215, 231, 238
Reconstruction (postbellum, U.S.), 180–81, 190–92
red co-operatives (In Finland and France), 66, 72, 75–76, 109
"red diaper baby," 174

Red Guard, 66
Red Scares, 10, 70, 198–99, 219
Reeves, William Pember, 140
REI, 24–25, 218
Rémoise (French co-op), 111
remoteness, 13–14, 36–37, 46, 128–29, 135–36, 152, 154, 251–56, 257
Rencontres Mont Blanc, 84–85
Rennes, 48–49, 120–21
revolution, 12–13, 39–40, 53–54, 81, 84–85, 88, 89–90, 91, 94–95, 96–100, 103, 125–26
Richardson, Ruth, 147
Richmond (VA), 161–62, 173, 187, 190–91
Right Relationship League, 204, 220
Riksdag of Finland, 58
Robinson-Pateman Act, 206
Rocard, Michel, 115–16
Rochdale, co-operative model and principles, 20–22, 25–26, 29–30, 59–60, 62–63, 94, 137, 143–44, 158, 159, 166, 167–68, 183–84, 210, 214, 220, 222, 227–28
Rogernomics, 130, 147, 150–51, 152
Roosevelt
    Franklin Delano (State Senator, Governor, and President), 211, 213, 218, 224–25, 232–34
    Theodore (Governor and President), 204–5
Russia, 12–13, 53–54, 56–59, 60–61, 62, 64, 65, 68–70, 73–80, 154, 160, 247. *See also* Soviet Union
Russian Revolution, 53–54, 65, 66
Russification measures, 60–61, 64
Ruthanasia, 147

Sanders, Bernie (Rep. and Sen.), 1, 2
San Francisco, 48–49, 198, 218–19, 236
Sanitarium, 152–53
Santa Clara County v. Standard Pacific Railroad, 196–97
Sapiro, Aaron, 206–8, 210–11
Say, Leon, 94–95, 100
SBA (Small Business Administration), 116–17, 229–30
Scarabée Biocoop, 119–20
School of Nîmes approach, 109. *See also* Gide, Charles
Scop (French worker co-operative), 83, 107–8
SDP, 72

Second Empire, 94–96, 98–99, 100, 101–2, 103–4
Second Industrial Revolution, 14–15, 102, 137–39, 154
Second Red Scare, 70, 224–25
Second Republic (France), 98–101
Self-Help Co-operative Grocery, 144
self-help co-operative movement. *See* SHCM
Service Employees International Union, 24–25
Seventh Day Adventists, 152–53
shadow cases, 36–37
Shaking Quakers (Shakers), 168–70
sharecroppers, 189–90, 208–9
SHCM (self-help co-operative movement), 231, 232–35
Sherman Act, 205, 206
Sinclair, Upton, 232–34
SKP/SKDL, 72
slavery, 9–10, 11, 14–15, 80–81, 85–86, 99, 135, 156–57, 159, 165–66, 171–73, 175–77, 178, 180–81, 182, 188, 195, 196, 243, 247, 251–57, 262, 263
    industrial slavery, 172–73, 177–78, 180–81
    race-based and chattel slavery, 9–10, 11, 14–15, 85–86, 99, 134, 139, 156, 157–58, 159, 161–62, 165–66, 170–74, 175–77, 178, 179, 180–81, 182, 185, 188, 189–90, 192, 195, 196–97, 232, 243, 246, 247, 251–57, 260, 262, 263
    "wage slavery," 10, 14–15, 85–86, 96, 99, 100, 135, 139, 156, 157–58, 175, 176–78, 179, 180, 182, 185, 189–90, 192, 193–94, 195, 196–97, 231–32, 248, 251–57
Smith, Adam, 135
Snellman, Johan Vilhelm, 58–59, 61, 64–65
Social and Solidarity Economy, 23, 82–126
social economy, 86, 104–5, 109, 112–14, 115–16. *See also* Social and Solidarity Economy
social enterprises, 4–5, 86, 116, 152–53
socialists and socialisms, 8, 66, 71, 79, 98–99, 100, 104, 106–7, 108–9, 112, 115, 180, 187–88, 193–94, 231–32, 234, 237–38
    American socialism, 94–95, 158–59, 163–64, 189–90
    Christian and Catholic, 97, 106–7, 109
    democratic socialism, 50
    Fabian, 140
    France's three pillars of socialism, 115
    French socialism, 85–86, 96, 99–101, 108–9, 113–14, 115, 117, 200, 247

SLP (Socialist Labor Party), 200, 231–32
state-led, 13–14, 129–30, 138–39, 261–62
trade socialism, 101
utopian socialists (including temporary villages and communities), 14–15, 85–86, 93–95, 122–24, 129–30, 134–35, 165–66, 167–69, 170–72, 179, 232–34
société anonyme (SA), 84–85, 92, 93
société coopérative, 92, 101–2, 107–8, 111, 116–17
societies
fraternal, 98–99
friendly, 89–90, 140, 144, 160–61
SOCRAM, 111
SOK Group, 52–53, 64, 66–67, 71, 73–74, 76–77
Solidarité Étudiante, 122–24
solidarity economy, 13, 22, 82–83, 84, 110, 112–25. *See also* Social and Solidarity Economy
South, U.S., 9, 10, 14–15, 139, 156–57, 158–59, 160, 161–62, 164, 165, 168, 169, 170–73, 174–75, 176, 178–79, 180–81, 184, 187, 188–92, 193, 195, 196, 208–10, 215, 220, 227, 234–35, 240–41, 243, 256–57
South Carolina, 160–61, 186–87, 190–91, 192–93, 227
Southern Cross, 144
Southern plantation owners (and co-operatives), 173, 190–91, 192, 195, 256–57
Southern rural electrical co-operative boards, 215
Sovereigns of Industry, 183–85
Soviet Union, 12–13, 55, 56, 68–71, 73, 75–76, 79–80, 261–62. *See also* Russia
State Coal Mines Act, 140
state-owned enterprises, 1, 131–32, 148, 152–53, 260
Suomen Ammattiliittojen Keskusjärjestö (SAK), 65
Suomen Osuuskauppojen Keskuskunnan. *See* SOK Group
Sustainable Economies Law Center, 214, 239
Sweden, 5–6, 30–31, 51, 53, 54, 57–58, 59, 69–70, 79, 218
Systeme U, 111, 117–18

Tampere, 48–49, 62–64, 65, 66–67
taxes, issues pertaining to co-operative development, 22, 23, 57–58, 77, 102–3, 116, 140, 142, 152–53, 210–12, 219, 225–27, 231, 235, 237
Tax Reform Act, 226–27
tax war, 10, 152–53, 198–99, 216, 221, 225–26
Thatcherism, 130, 147
Third Reconstruction, 7
Third Republic (France), 85–86, 88, 94, 99, 101–2, 103–5, 108–9
titre participative, 115–16
TLK, 73–74, 75–76
tobacco factories, southern, 173
Tocqueville, 8
Tradeka, 76
Trente Glorieuses, 88, 102–12, 122
trusts, 22, 131–32, 145, 149, 152–53
charitable trusts, 132–33, 144, 152–53
community/consumer trusts, 23, 132–33, 148–49, 150–51, 152–53
employee ownership trusts (EOTs), 23, 241–42
perpetual purpose trusts (PPTs), 23
work and co-operative trusts, 144–45, 152
Truth, Sojourner, 177–78
Tsar Nicholas II, 60–61
TSB, 150–51
Tui Bee Balms, 152
Turku, 48–49
Twain, Mark, 127, 154, 247

Ujima Fund (Boston), 265
unions, 6–7, 65, 68, 88–89, 100–1, 103–4, 107–8, 109–10, 111–12, 115–16, 119–20, 124–25, 157–58, 162–63, 164, 166–67, 168, 185–86, 187–88, 189, 194, 200, 212–13, 218, 232, 250
industrial unionism, 187, 232
labor unions (general), 65, 68, 103–4, 106, 107, 186, 206
trade unionism, 91–92, 100, 101, 108–10, 124–25, 140, 158–59, 162–63, 166–68, 179, 200, 231–32
unionized co-operative, 24–25
United Kingdom, 4, 13, 18–22, 23, 35–37, 47–48, 55, 64, 69–70, 90–91, 92–93, 96, 103, 109–10, 133, 134–35, 136–38, 141, 145–47, 158, 160–61, 166, 170–71, 178–79, 217–18, 219, 241–42, 261, 264. *See also* England, Great Britain
United Nations, 127
use value, 2, 27–29
U.S. Federation of Worker Co-operatives. *See* USFWC

USFWC (U.S. Federation of Worker Co-operatives), 83, 230–31, 237–39, 240–41, 265
Utah, 219–20

Vaino Tanner, 65
Valio, 64, 73–74
Vantaa, 48–49
Varma, 76
Vichy France, 103–4
Vogel, Julius, 136
Voluntary Job Preservation and Community Stabilization Act, 238
Voorhis, Jerry (Congressman), 198–99, 216, 223, 224–25

Wakefield, Edward Gibbon, 134–36
Waldeck-Rousseau, René, 106
Walras, Leon, 94–95
Warbasse, James Peter, 221, 222–23, 224, 229
Warren, Josiah, 166
Warsaw Pact, 68–69
Washington, Booker T., 209
welfare regimes, 33, 36–37, 50, 138–40
Wellington, 48–49, 135, 137, 149, 152–53
wertrational, 26–27
West Germany, 69–70
West Virginia, 165
Whitechapel, 192
White Guard, 66
Wilberforce, 177–78
Willy Street Co-op, 18–20
worker co-operatives, 1–2, 3–5, 23–25, 28–29, 30, 32, 52–53, 78, 83, 93–95, 97–98, 99, 104–5, 107–9, 112–13, 114, 116, 130–31, 134, 143–45, 146–47, 152–53, 162, 164, 218–19, 230, 231, 234–36, 237–39, 240, 241–42, 243, 247, 250, 265–66
  relationship to ESOPs, 241–42
  worker and hybrid consumer-worker co-operatives, 234
workers' corporations, 84–85, 91, 94, 96, 98–99
Workers Dwelling Act, 140
Works Progress Administration, 234–35
World War I, 65, 66–67, 100–1, 104, 107–8, 205
World War II, 56, 65, 66, 68, 70, 103–4, 107–8, 145–46, 217, 224, 226–27, 244
Wright, Frances, 169–70

YNCL (Young Negro Co-operative League), 228–29

Zion's Co-operative Mercantile Institution, 220
Zuccotti Park, 5–6
zweckrational, 26–27